Race and Ethnicity

To all instructors and students who put sociology into action.

Sara Miller McCune founded SAGE Publishing in 1965 to support the dissemination of usable knowledge and educate a global community. SAGE publishes more than 1,000 journals and over 600 new books each year, spanning a wide range of subject areas. Our growing selection of library products includes archives, data, case studies and video. SAGE remains majority owned by our founder and after her lifetime will become owned by a charitable trust that secures the company's continued independence.

Los Angeles | London | New Delhi | Singapore | Washington DC | Melbourne

Race and Ethnicity

Sociology in Action

Kathleen Odell Korgen
William Paterson University

Maxine P. Atkinson
North Carolina State University

Los Angeles | London | New Delhi
Singapore | Washington DC | Melbourne

FOR INFORMATION:

SAGE Publications, Inc.
2455 Teller Road
Thousand Oaks, California 91320
E-mail: order@sagepub.com

SAGE Publications Ltd.
1 Oliver's Yard
55 City Road
London, EC1Y 1SP
United Kingdom

SAGE Publications India Pvt. Ltd.
B 1/I 1 Mohan Cooperative Industrial Area
Mathura Road, New Delhi 110 044
India

SAGE Publications Asia-Pacific Pte. Ltd.
18 Cross Street #10-10/11/12
China Square Central
Singapore 048423

Library of Congress Cataloging-in-Publication Data

Names: Korgen, Kathleen Odell, 1967- editor. | Atkinson, Maxine P., editor.

Title: Race and ethnicity : sociology in action / [edited by] Kathleen Odell Korgen, William Paterson University, Maxine P. Atkinson, North Carolina State University.

Description: Los Angeles : SAGE, [2021] | Includes bibliographical references and index.

Identifiers: LCCN 2021009833 | ISBN 978-1-5443-9471-8 (paperback) | ISBN 978-1-5443-9472-5 (epub)

Subjects: LCSH: Racism—United States. | Ethnicity—United States. | Minorities—United States. | United States—Race relations. | United States—Ethnic relations.

Classification: LCC E184.A1 R243 2021 | DDC 305.800973—dc23

LC record available at https://lccn.loc.gov/2021009833

This book is printed on acid-free paper.

21 22 23 24 25 10 9 8 7 6 5 4 3 2 1

Acquisitions Editor: Jeff Lasser

Editorial Assistant: Tiara Beatty

Content Development Editor: Tara Slagle

Production Editor: Rebecca Lee

Copy Editor: Mark Bast

Typesetter: diacriTech

Indexer: Integra

Cover Designer: Gail Buschman

Marketing Manager: Jennifer Jones

BRIEF CONTENTS

DETAILED CONTENTS

LEARNING ACTIVITIES

PREFACE

If you, like us, have found yourself searching for activities to bring into your classroom and engage your sociology students, you know why we wrote this book and the others in the *Sociology in Action* series. We knew we couldn't be alone in our quest to get students to do more than read the text—we want them to *do* sociology, to understand and apply the terms and concepts they read about and realize them in the real world. Over the course of writing and refining the manuscript, as well as reading the reviews of instructors excited to see activities many of us have been cobbling together over the years now residing within a textbook, we became even more convinced that our approach is one that offers instructors material for how they want to teach and offers students the foundational content they need in sociology, as well as engaging activities that will help them *do* sociology. The overwhelmingly enthusiastic response to *Sociology in Action: Introduction to Sociology* and *Social Problems: Sociology in Action* provided further evidence that this book can help all race and ethnicity instructors get their students excited about sociology and what they can do with it.

Race and Ethnicity: Sociology in Action puts all the tools instructors need to create an active learning course into one student-friendly text. Active learning teaching techniques increase student learning, retention, and engagement with course material, but they also require more creative effort than traditional lectures. No other textbook works to ease this load by providing full coverage of race and ethnicity content *and* active learning exercises fully integrated into the text (with clear instructions on how to use and assess them available through the instructor resources). *Race and Ethnicity: Sociology in Action* provides instructors of small, medium, large, and online courses with the material they need to create learning experiences for their students, including creative, hands-on, data-analytic, and community learning activities.

A group of gifted instructors who use active learning techniques in their own classrooms has written the book's chapters. The contributors, focusing on their respective areas of expertise, expertly weave together content material, active learning exercises, discussion questions, real-world examples of sociologists in action, and information on careers that use sociology. Together, we have created a book that requires students to *do* sociology as they learn it and creates a bridge between the classroom and the larger social world.

ORGANIZATION AND FEATURES

The clear organizational style of each chapter helps students follow the logic of the text and concentrate on the main ideas presented. Each chapter opens with focal learning questions, and each major section ends with review questions to remind students of the emphasis in the presented material. Chapters close with conclusions, and end-of-chapter resources include lists of key terms and summaries that address the focal learning questions. The active learning activities and *Consider This* questions throughout each chapter help create a student-centered class that engages student interest.

The book's rich pedagogy supports active learning and engagement throughout each chapter.

Learning Questions start off every chapter, introducing students to the focus of the chapter and preparing them for the material it covers. These questions are tied to the learning objectives provided in the instructor resources. Each main section of the chapter addresses a learning question.

Check Your Understanding questions appear at the end of every major section in a chapter, providing students with an opportunity to pause in their reading and ensure that they comprehend and retain what they've just read.

Doing Sociology activities appear multiple times in each chapter. These active learning exercises enable students to apply the sociological concepts, theories, methods, and so on covered in the text. Each chapter contains a variety of exercises so that instructors can use them in class, online, or as assignments conducted outside of class. Reference the Doing Sociology activities and the clear instructions on how to carry them out—and on how they relate to the chapter objectives—in the Activity Guide available through the book's instructor resources. Additional exercises can be found in the digital resources accompanying the text.

Consider This questions are designed to spark deep thinking as well as classroom discussions.

Sociologist in Action boxes feature a student or professional "sociologist in action" doing public sociology related to the material covered in the chapter. This feature provides examples of how sociology can be used to make a positive impact on society.

Key Terms appear in boldface type where they are substantially discussed for the first time and are compiled in a list with page numbers at the end of their respective chapters. Corresponding definitions can be found in the glossary.

Every chapter concludes with a ***Chapter Review*** that restates the learning questions presented at the start of the chapter and gives answers to them. This provides an important way for students to refresh their understanding of the material and retain what they've learned.

In addition, we include chapters not found in other race and ethnicity books but crucial for students eager to understand race and ethnic relations today. For example, *Race and Ethnicity: Sociology in Action* includes chapters on Whiteness, ethnocentrism, how to address racism, and why antiracism benefits everyone in society. This book gives students the content to understand and the skills to address racial and ethnic inequality.

ACKNOWLEDGMENTS

We would like to acknowledge the many people who worked with us on *Race and Ethnicity: Sociology in Action*. Our thanks, first and foremost, go to the contributors who wrote the chapters and helped us create an active-learning race and ethnicity course in one text. Their exceptional ability to use active learning in the classroom has impressed and inspired us. We appreciate their willingness to share what they do so well and to collaborate with us on *Race and Ethnicity: Sociology in Action*.

The two of us would also like to extend our gratitude to the wonderful people at SAGE for their tremendous work on this project. Acquisitions Editor Jeff Lasser believed in the need for this text, brought us together, and is the chief reason this book (and the entire *Sociology in Action* series) became a reality. Tara Slagle, our content development editor, provided her great expertise in helping us shape this book. Mark Bast made sure the book was copy edited beautifully, while production editor Rebecca Lee engineered the transformation of the manuscript into real book pages. Editorial assistant Tiara Beatty managed to keep everything on track and moving forward throughout this long process.

We are also deeply indebted to the following reviewers who offered their keen insights and suggestions:

- Dr. Guia Calicdan-Apostle, Stockton University

- Kim L. Dulaney, Chicago State University

- Nora Fellag, Rowan University

- Jairo R. Ledesma, Miami Dade College

- Cliff Leek, University of Northern Colorado

- Peter Loebach, Elizabeth City State University

- Joylin Namie, Truckee Meadows Community College

- Tricia Noone, Georgia Southern University

- Yvonne Vissing, Rivier University

- Lisa Lamb Weber, Texas State University

Finally, we offer our great thanks to our families for their support and patience as we devoted so much of our time to *Race and Ethnicity: Sociology in Action*.

—Kathleen Odell Korgen and Maxine P. Atkinson

ABOUT THE AUTHORS

Kathleen Odell Korgen, PhD, is a professor of sociology at William Paterson University in Wayne, New Jersey. Her primary areas of specialization are teaching sociology, racial identity, and race relations. She has received William Paterson University's awards for Excellence in Scholarship/Creative Expression and for Excellence in Teaching.

Maxine P. Atkinson, PhD, is a professor of sociology at North Carolina State University in Raleigh. Her primary area of specialization is the scholarship of teaching and learning. She has received the American Sociological Association's Distinguished Contributions to Teaching Award and the University of North Carolina Board of Governors' Award for Excellence in Teaching.

ABOUT THE CONTRIBUTORS

María Isabel Ayala is an associate professor in the Department of Sociology and the Chicano/Latino Studies Program at Michigan State University. Her research agenda calls attention to the intragroup diversity and capital of the Latinx population by examining the relationship between their unique and complex racialization and sociodemographic experiences and behaviors. Moreover, Ayala explores the role of Latinx identities in reconstructing structures, centering and highlighting agentive and resilient behaviors and cultures in the navigation of physical, symbolic, and social White spaces.

Sarah Becker is director of the Center for Community Engagement, Learning, and Leadership (CCELL) and an associate professor of sociology and women's, gender, and sexuality studies and affiliate faculty member in African and African American Studies at Louisiana State University. She teaches courses in the fields of criminology, gender studies, race relations, and methods classes such as ethnography, using community-engaged approaches. Her primary research agenda examines the collective processes through which people come to define and address local crime problems.

Stacye A. Blount is an associate professor of sociology at Fayetteville State University. Her teaching interests focus on medical sociology, mental health, career and professional development, and race. Her research interests include mental health, race, teaching and learning in sociology, and debutante cotillions. Prior to returning to graduate school, Blount was employed as a clinical laboratory scientist for 13 years.

Ifeyinwa F. Davis is a Louisiana BOR/SREB doctoral fellow and doctoral candidate in the Sociology Department at Louisiana State University. She holds minors in African and African American studies and women's, gender, and sexuality studies. Her research centers Black woman and girlhood, exclusively concerning the healing of Black women. Her dissertation examines the impacts of the presence or absence of birth workers on the care Black birthing people and their children receive during pregnancy, labor and delivery, and postpartum.

Daniel Herda is an associate professor of sociology at Merrimack College in North Andover, Massachusetts. He received his doctoral degree in 2013 from the University of California–Davis. At Merrimack, he regularly teaches courses on the sociological imagination, research methods, immigration, and social inequality. In addition, Dr. Herda is an award-winning survey researcher who analyzes immigration, race relations, crime, and public opinion. His work on population innumeracy reveals just how poorly informed Americans and Europeans are about various groups in their societies. His research on race relations reveals the many ways that interpersonal discrimination can be consequential for adolescents.

Naliyah Kaya is an associate professor of sociology at Montgomery College in Takoma Park, Maryland. She previously served as the coordinator for multiracial and Native American/Indigenous student involvement at the University of Maryland, where she also created a multiracial leadership course and continues to facilitate TOTUS spoken word experience. As a poet, artist, and public sociologist, Dr. Kaya centers her energy on the intersections of art and activism. She has participated in social justice community art collaborations in Baltimore and College Park, Maryland, and organizes arts programming in her role on the Critical Mixed Race Studies Association Executive Committee.

Nikki Khanna is an associate professor of sociology at the University of Vermont. Her research looks at racial identity among multiracial Americans, transracial adoption, and most recently, colorism among Asian Americans. She is the author of *Biracial in America: Forming and Performing Racial Identity* and editor of *Whiter: Asian American Women on Skin Color and Colorism*. She also has a forthcoming coauthored book (with Noriko Matsumoto of the University of Vermont) titled *Race Relations in America*.

SunAh Laybourn is an assistant professor of sociology and an affiliate faculty member for the Center for Workplace Diversity & Inclusion at the University of Memphis. She earned her PhD in 2018 from the University of Maryland. Her work focuses on race, ethnicity, and social psychology with a particular emphasis on racial boundary-making.

David J. Luke earned bachelor's degrees in sociology and accounting from Grand Valley State University, in Allendale, Michigan, working for 2 years as a certified public accountant before returning to higher education and earning his master's and PhD in sociology at the University of Kentucky. He currently serves as chief diversity officer and director of the Intercultural Center at the University of Michigan–Flint.

Crystal Paul is the director of administration and research for the Department of Political Science and an adjunct lecturer for the Departments of Political Science and Sociology at the University of Massachusetts Amherst. She teaches courses in the fields of research methods and human rights. Her research considers the gendered experiences of clandestine border crossers.

Michael L. Rosino is an assistant professor of sociology at Molloy College in Rockville Centre, New York. His research and teaching focus on racial politics, media, social movements, crime, law and deviance, and human rights. His work emphasizes social change, policy, and community and civic engagement. He has published widely on the connections among racial oppression, struggles for racial equality, political conflicts, debates over public policy, and everyday social life in various scholarly and public outlets. His current research examines how activists within progressive grassroots political organizations engage with racial and political inequality through their identities, habits, and political strategies. The project illuminates the possibilities and barriers for building a racially just and inclusive grassroots democracy and advances new understandings of racial politics grounded in everyday social life.

Katya Salmi is an assistant professor at Montgomery College, Maryland, where equity and public sociology inform her teaching and service. Her research and teaching focus on race, gender, and racialization, as well as structural issues relating to inequality, discrimination, and social justice. Prior to joining Montgomery College, she was a fellow at Human Rights Watch leading research on migration in North Africa, maternal mortality in Nigeria, and equity policies in international financial institutions. She also works with community nonprofit organizations in Montgomery County. Much of Dr. Salmi's work in and out of the classroom is centered around questions of antiracism and equity.

Richard Maurice Smith is an associate professor of sociology, the special advisor to the provost on diversity initiatives, and the 2020 recipient of the Ira G. Zepp Distinguished Teaching Award at McDaniel College, Westminster Maryland. His research and teaching focuses on African American communities and culture, race and racism, and criminal justice. He is the cofounder of the Racial Healing Clinic and a sought-after speaker and consultant. Smith works with religious, cultural, and health care organizations to meet diversity, equity, and inclusion goals. He earned his PhD in sociology from Temple University.

Bradley J. Zopf is an assistant professor of sociology at Carthage College, Kenosha, Wisconsin. He earned his PhD in 2017 from the University of Illinois at Chicago. He teaches courses on race and racism, sex and gender, and sociological theory. His current research focuses on the racialization of the Arab and Muslim American communities in the United States. In addition, he is a licensed intercultural development inventory qualified administrator.

1 LOOKING AT RACE AND ETHNICITY—AND POWER

Sarah Becker, Ifeyinwa Davis, and Crystal Paul

LEARNING QUESTIONS

1.1 What is the connection between racial slavery in America and the social construction of race?

1.2 How are racial categories tied to power, and how have they changed in meaning over time?

1.3 What is intersectionality? How does intersectionality help us understand the ways people experience racial inequality?

1.4 What are the sociological definitions of race, ethnicity, prejudice, discrimination, ethnocentrism, and racism?

1.5 How might you best handle the challenges that come with a course about race and ethnicity?

Has anyone ever advised you to steer clear of certain topics at a dinner party? If so, what did they tell you not to talk about? Politics? Religion? How much money someone has? Their embarrassing family secrets?

If you search "topics to avoid in polite conversation" on the Internet, race is not likely to come up in your results. Why is that? Race is among topics people avoid in "polite conversation," especially in interracial (i.e., cross-race) settings. Why is talk about race so taboo we can't even be honest about the fact that many people avoid talking about it?

In this chapter, you take a first step toward unpacking the complex history of race that helps explain why so many people don't talk about it—particularly with people who do not share their race or ethnicity. We explore how race as a concept is rooted in the development of racial slavery in America, myths about its biological origins, and its ties to power. We examine its socially constructed nature and the importance of thinking about it intersectionally. Finally, we discuss how you can best prepare yourself to engage fully in a course on race and ethnicity.

WHAT ARE RACE AND ETHNICITY? WHY DO THEY MATTER?

We all know what "race" refers to, right? Ask most people, and they will probably refer to skin color or a handful of labeled human groups: White, Black, Asian, or Latinx[1], for example. The belief that humans can be sorted into separate groups based on visible markers such as skin color, hair type, and facial features illustrates one basic assumption about race: that it is biological. After all, we classify people based on what we see. But have you ever heard someone accuse a White person of "acting Black"? Or thought someone was White, only to learn later they identify as Latinx, Asian, Black, Pacific Islander, American Indian, or mixed race? These kinds of experiences reveal race is socially constructed or created by human beings in their interactions with one another.

---

[1] Latinx is a gender-neutral and nonbinary term we use in place of Latino/Latina or Hispanic.

Race is a system of organizing people into groups *perceived* to be distinct because of physical appearance (not genetic makeup). We tend to categorize people into racial groups based on their skin tone, facial features, and other physical cues. Our categorizations may not match how people racially identify themselves.

Ethnicity is not the same as race, though the two are often conflated. **Ethnicity** is shared cultural heritage including, but not limited to, a person's birthplace or country of origin, familial ties and lineage, religion, language, and other social practices. People of different ethnicities can fall in the same racial category. For example, a Nigerian person who recently immigrated to the United States and an African American person whose family has been in the United States for generations are ethnically distinct but share the racial classification of Black in America.

Race as a Concept Rooted in North American Racial Slavery and Colonialism

Race is so central to the American experience that people easily assume humans have always viewed one another as belonging to different racial groups. However, race as a concept is relatively recent in human history. It emerged alongside the birth of science as a means of knowing the world and solidified in connection with the development of a system of racial slavery in the United States. **Racial slavery** was a unique form of enslavement forcing lifelong servitude onto one group of people based on new ideas about race and racial categories. In other words, race and racism's emergence was not just about people (later labeled as White) coming into contact with foreign "others." Power, economics, ideology, and a constellation of other social and historical factors fed the development of race. Most importantly, race-based worldviews solidified because of colonizers' desire to control a captive labor force.

Colonialism is a tactic of expanding one nation into another geographic area through violent social control practices. Control generally takes one of two forms: co-option of a segment of the colonized space's preexisting social hierarchy (i.e., getting some people in the colonized country to go along with the takeover because they can profit from it) and/or slaughter and expulsion of Indigenous populations coupled with repopulation by immigration from the colonizing country (i.e., killing or relocating residents and moving your own people in) (Allen 2012). Colonialist practices often work to weaken or destabilize a target population's culture (social practices, languages, traditions, customs) and identities in order to maintain power and erode their social status.

CONSIDER THIS

How do you identify ethnically? Do you engage in practices tied to your ethnicity? If yes, what are they? If no, why do you think that is? Can you link your ethnic practices to the history of race in the United States?

Biological/Social Data on Race

A popular misconception about race is that it is biological. Scholars across multiple fields, however, have carefully documented how race is *not* a biological reality. For example, genes that produce skin color and other attributes we associate with race are just a small fraction of the genes in our bodies. We know there are more biological differences between people in the *same* racial category than there are differences across racial categories. Powerful groups constructed the concept of race and racial superiority to justify racist practices, such as racial slavery.

Even today, the repercussions of this creation are very real. For example, we know race impacts health outcomes, stress levels, access to health care, maternal and fetal mortality rates, criminal justice system experiences, education, employment opportunities, and income and wealth disparities. Race affects identity and our social networks and relationships. Race influences these aspects of human life in ways that accumulate disadvantages for people in marginalized racial status positions and advantages to those in dominant racial status positions.

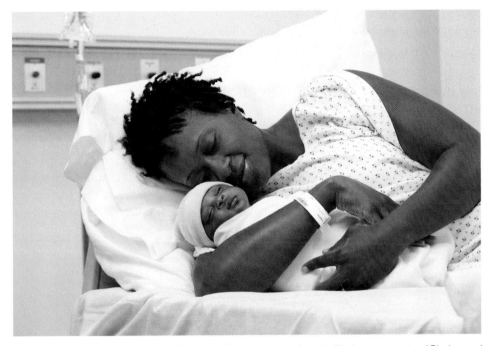

PHOTO 1.1 Combating high maternal and fetal mortality rates is a complex task. Black-woman-centered Black-owned businesses work to address the social problem through education, advocacy, and personalized birth services.

Ariel Skelley/Getty Images

The effects of race, however, are not uniform. How you experience it depends on your social class, country of origin, residence, ethnicity, embodiment, sexuality, and many other aspects of social identity and status. For example, as Chapter 3 explores, race is not understood the same way in different global settings. Also, its meaning and systems of categorization (i.e., who counts as White, Black, and more) have shifted over time.

DOING SOCIOLOGY 1.1

Letter to Your Race(s)*

In this exercise, you will think about the impact race has on your life and experiences.

Write a one-page letter to your race(s) as if it were a person. If you could talk to it, what would you tell it? If it were a person, what would you ask it? How would you let it know how it has affected your life? How does the history of slavery in the United States affect what you would say to your race? Note that you are not writing a letter to all the people in your racial category (e.g., "Dear White people"). Instead, you are writing to your racial category, with all its social constructions, as if it were a single person (e.g., "Dear Whiteness"; "Dear Latinx-ness"; "Dear Blackness").

Your instructor may ask you to write your letter as homework and then share it with other students in class. If your class is online, your instructor may ask you to read it aloud in online video discussion forums or share with others in written format.

---

*This assignment is modeled after Dr. Dana Berkowitz's "Dear Gender Letter" activity at Louisiana State University. Her assignment and our recrafted version of it were inspired by the 2017 "Dear Masculinity" campaign undergraduate student Eneale Pickett started at University of Wisconsin-Madison, represented in KC Councilor's art in *Male Femininities* (Berkowitz, Windsor, and Han, forthcoming).

Check Your Understanding

1. What is the difference between race and ethnicity?

2. What are the two primary means of maintaining colonial social control?

3. What is the relationship between biology and racial categories?

4. What are two ways race impacts people's lives today?

5. What does it mean to say race is socially constructed?

HOW IS POWER RELATED TO RACE? DOMINANT AND SUBORDINATE GROUPS

One of the primary reasons race plays such an important role in society is its connection to power relations. **Power** is the possession of authority over individuals, groups, or systems. To have power over someone or something suggests garnering and maintaining influence. The way we see race today emerged from a context where one group (later seen as "White") was conquering and extracting resources from other groups of people across the globe (Allen 2012; Smedley 2011). Those with power used race as a tool to dominate vulnerable populations.

NICOLAVS   V   PAPA   SERGIANENSIS

PHOTO 1.2 The Catholic Church helped set moral foundations for slavery. Pope Nicholas V (pictured here) issued a Papal Bull in 1455 giving the Portuguese king permission to "invade, search out, capture, vanquish, and subdue" all "enemies of Christ" in colonial territories, to seize their property and possessions, and to "reduce their persons to perpetual slavery" (Davenport 1917).

Chris Hellier / Alamy Stock Photo

Power, Dominance, and the Construction of Race

As early as the 1500s, European men were writing in the new tradition of a "scientific method." They typically used secondhand data sources such as missionary, colonizer, or traders' diaries—all of which were tainted by European cultural biases and judgments. Nonetheless, authors used that data to sort humans into ranked groups. At first, and for nearly 200 years, they did so in ways that acknowledged a common human ancestry. If and when they used the term *race*, it typically referred to familial or generational lines or to types of people belonging to the same species (Smedley 2011). It was not until westward expansion intensified the slaughter of Indigenous populations and a system of racial slavery emerged in European colonies that the idea of multiple human origins and distinct races fully crystallized into a dominant worldview. This was no accident. Seeing some people as less human than others was critical to preserving White Americans' claims to moral authority while enslaving, stealing from, murdering, and brutalizing other people.

Racial classification systems in this pseudo-scientific literature grouped humans into categories based broadly on phenotypic markers such as skin color, hair texture, and skull shape. Europeans maintained influence over science as a discipline, which began associating physical differences with assumed behavioral and psychological differences such as group ethics (or lack thereof). Methods and data used by writers on the subject were flawed, and in some cases *made up*, but still justified the enslavement of African people for more than 400 years and the near elimination of American Indian populations.

Europeans further sustained their power over ways of understanding human groups by writing the history of their colonization efforts in ways that erased dominated populations' narratives or framed them as morally depraved and developmentally stunted. These efforts are a good example of Karl Marx's classic argument: people who control the means of production also control the ruling ideas (Marx and Engels 1932).

PHOTO 1.3 The "Indian Mounds" at Louisiana State University, dating back 9,200 years, are the oldest human-made structures still in existence in the Americas (and older than the Great Wall of China, Stonehenge, and the Egyptian Pyramids). LSU sits on traditional territories of the Bayogoula and Chahta Yakni peoples.

CONSIDER THIS

How many classes in high school taught you about Indigenous, Black, Asian, or Latinx American history? Do you know how many of the texts you read were written by authors from those backgrounds? How many were written by White people? What difference might this make for how you understand "American history"?

The Relationship of Other Racial Categories to Whiteness

One way power manifests in racial categorizations is largely invisible. Whiteness is often seen as a neutral reference category: the basis for what counts as generically "human." For example, it is easier for White people to see themselves as humans or Americans without qualifiers. People of color do not have this luxury. Their race is so visible in daily experiences that they are more likely to have a strongly defined racial identity. Whiteness also occupies a position of centrality when it comes to mainstream cultural images. When someone mentions Santa Claus, for example, most people immediately picture a White man with a large belly and snow-white beard. If a particular Santa is phenotypically different than that, you often hear people refer to him as "Black Santa" or "Asian Santa," while White Santa is just "Santa."

Whiteness is slippery in this way; it is often difficult to describe what exactly counts as Whiteness because it operates invisibly. The invisibility of Whiteness teaches us about the power it holds; oftentimes, we can only define Whiteness by characterizing what it is *not*. Whiteness, then, becomes a reference category for other racial groups, further contributing to its exertion of power.

DOING SOCIOLOGY 1.2

Making Whiteness Visible

This exercise helps make visible how Whiteness and other racial categories relate to power.

1. Pick a cultural symbol of your choice. For example, you might choose Santa, Jesus, God, doctor, mom, or professor. First, consider the term on its own. Write down a description of the image as it is typically portrayed in popular media. Second, reconsider the term with different racial-ethnic descriptors (e.g., Asian doctor, Black doctor, Latinx doctor). How do the racial-ethnic versions of the term relate to what you originally described?

2. Explain what this exercise teaches us about the relationship between race and power.

3. Then write a paragraph on how you think this impacts people's lives. Be prepared to share your thoughts with your peers.

Beyond the White/Black Dichotomy

Many people think about race in terms of White and Black while other people of color, such as Asians and Latinxs, experience race by occupying something called the "racial middle" (O'Brien 2008). This term challenges us to think about race beyond a Black/White dichotomy. It gets us to think about how groups like Asians, Latinxs, and Native Americans are sometimes viewed in comparison to White or Black people. For example, as Chapter 9 discusses, Asian Americans are often viewed as a "model minority" or "honorary Whites." Indigenous persons, American Indians, or Native populations, on the other hand, are frequently left out of sociological research altogether—an alarming fact, considering how they also face racism in the United States. Moreover, when researchers do include them, they often do so in ways that homogenize the group rather than acknowledging how categories like "Native American" are made up of a tremendous variety of nations and cultural traditions, such as Sisseton-Wahpeton Dakota, Diné/Navajo, and Houma.

Examples of How Racial Categorizations Have Changed Over Time

The United States Census provides a good illustration of how racial categories have changed over time. From 1790 to 1950 census workers called enumerators recorded people's race for them, according to bureau directions. From 1960 onward, people could self-select one racial identification. Beginning in the year 2000, people could check multiple racial categories. This means a person could be racially classified very differently, depending on census year.

Here are some examples to illustrate how census racial categories have historically shifted (Parker et al. 2015):

- First, Black people were only counted as enslaved peoples, but in 1820, the census added a "free colored persons" category.

- "Mulatto" was a category from 1850 to 1890 and 1910 to 1920.

- Native American populations were not in the census until 1860—and then enumerators only counted those assimilated into White society.

- Asian categories did not appear until 1860, when the census added "Chinese."

- In 1970, the census instructed mixed-race people to choose one race or be automatically counted as their father's race.

- In 1980 and 1990, if those same people chose multiple categories, the census typically assigned them to their mother's race.

- Before 1970, census workers filled out census forms for people. In doing so, they categorized people who were White and another race as members of the non-White race

As the last example illustrates, one theme in racial categorization is competition over who is counted and treated as White—because the social context is one where White people have historically had more rights and privileges than other people. Census rules therefore limited who counted as White (Parker et al. 2015). You may already be familiar with the "one drop rule," a law mandating people with any amount of non-White blood in their lineage be legally classified and treated as a person of color. The last example in the list provides an example of how the census once followed that rule.

Whiteness carrying social and legal benefits is a powerful force that has influenced race relations since colonial times. It is one of the reasons Irish people, for example, who came to the United States with a long history of being colonized and oppressed by the British, quickly "came to insist on their own Whiteness and on White supremacy" (Roediger 2007, 137) rather than fighting for racial equality alongside Black people. You will learn more about this in Chapter 7.

Resistance to Race-Based Systems of Inequality

From the beginning, people disadvantaged by a racial classification system doling out unequal life chances have resisted. The threat of violent resistance to institutionalized racial inequality has always loomed large for those benefitting from that inequality. White slaveholders, for example, intensely feared insurrections by enslaved peoples. Revolts by enslaved peoples took place throughout the South, with some of the most significant occurring in Louisiana, South Carolina, and Virginia.

In the largest rebellion by enslaved peoples ever to occur in the South, more than 500 enslaved people from three Louisiana parishes came together to march toward New Orleans in January 1811. Armed and formidable in numbers, the rebels caused substantial damage to plantations they crossed. Just days after the revolt began, however, resisters were met by federal troops, and many of their leaders were put to death. Some were beheaded. White authorities placed their heads on stakes along the river around the property of plantations resisters came from, to serve as a constant reminder of rebellion's consequences. This uprising is recognized today in artwork by Woodrow Nash at the Whitney Plantation Museum in Wallace, Louisiana, as part of an optional extended tour for visitors, because it is so graphic in nature.

The civil rights movement of the 1960s and 1970s is probably the most widely known example of Black people's efforts to challenge racism in the United States. Many people are familiar with leaders such as Dr. Martin Luther King Jr. and Rosa Parks. A long list of lesser-known moments and activists, however, remain largely invisible to the public. Sociologist in Action Dr. Lori Latrice Martin works to address this in her scholarship and activism.

PHOTO 1.4 Activists and scholars in Baton Rouge, Louisiana, worked hard to recognize the 1953 Baton Rouge Bus Boycott. Pictured here are committee members who got a bench installed in memory of the 1953 protesters. Dr. Lori Latrice Martin is fifth from the left.

Courtesy of Dr. Lori Latrice Martin. Photo by Tat Yau.

SOCIOLOGISTS IN ACTION

Dr. Lori Latrice Martin

Memorializing Local Black History

I am proud to follow in the tradition of Black intellectual thinkers committed to using their time and talents to improve the quality of life of historically marginalized groups. This tradition is very strong among sociologists. W. E. B. Du Bois and E. Franklin Frazier are two well-known sociologists who exemplify this commitment. I firmly believe I have a responsibility both as a sociologist and resident of Baton Rouge, Louisiana, to contribute to efforts addressing community-identified needs. It is also important to me that my employer, Louisiana State University (LSU), is not only *in* the community but an integral part *of* the community.

Raising awareness about historic and contemporary contributions of neighborhoods is vital to revitalization efforts and to the accumulation of community cultural wealth. I was afforded the opportunity to work on such a project with the predominately Black community of South Baton Rouge, also known as Old South Baton Rouge and the Bottoms, situated near LSU. South Baton Rouge was a thriving community prior to the 1960s, before highways and other public policies literally divided the area. The Bottoms included a host of historic houses of worship, Black-owned businesses, and the only school in the area where Black people could earn a high school diploma. South Baton Rouge was also the site of one of the first successful bus boycotts.

I assembled and cochaired a committee of local community leaders to work on an effort to honor the men, women, children, and organizations that made the 1953 Baton Rouge Bus Boycott possible. The boycott was organized in response to a number of racial injustices. First, a law was passed in the early 1950s eliminating Black-owned buses. A few years later, bus fares increased. Black riders were forced to sit in the back of the bus. At times, Black riders were forced to stand, even though seats were available in the front section reserved for White riders.

The city council soon passed an ordinance allowing Black riders to sit anywhere on the bus. However, the bus drivers—all White men—protested and resisted the ordinance and the council revoked it. In response, the Black community organized and refused to ride city buses. They created a car ride share, which Dr. Martin Luther King, Jr. used as a model during the 1955 Montgomery Bus Boycott. The Baton Rouge boycott ended with a compromise that allowed Black riders to sit anywhere on the bus with the exception of the first few seats, which were reserved for White riders.

Thanks to the committee's efforts, the Toni Morrison Society Bench by the Road Project supported our efforts and allowed us to recognize the bravery and commitment of those who participated in this important—but little remembered—bus boycott. They donated one of their memorial benches—one of fewer than 30 such benches in the world. I am proud to have played a critical role in publicly marking and ensuring people will remember this important moment in history.

Lori Latrice Martin is a professor in African and African American studies and in the Department of Sociology at Louisiana State University.

Discussion Question

How might the preservation of local history serve as a catalyst for social and economic development in underresourced communities?

Check Your Understanding

1. What were two fundamental flaws of early "scientific" publications on race?

2. What does it mean to say people who control the means of production also control the ruling ideas? How does this apply to race?

3. What is one way Whiteness operates as an invisible norm or standard?

4. What does the U.S. census reveal about how racial categories have shifted over time?

MORE THAN A MEMBER OF A RACIAL GROUP: INTERSECTIONALITY

Recognizing intersectionality is a key tool of modern resistance to racial and other forms of oppression. Coined in 1991 by lawyer and civil rights advocate Kimberlé Crenshaw, intersectionality refers to how the social categories we belong to—such as social class, gender, and race—are interconnected and work together to reinforce our advantages or disadvantages in society. This helps us see, for example, that all women's experiences are not the same and vary according to their other social positions such as race, citizenship status, or class.

PHOTO 1.5 Maretta McDonald (left) and Heeya Datta (right), two LSU PhD women students with varying experiences during the COVID-19 pandemic.

left, Sadie O'Keefe; right, ©Jishnu Datta

Contrasting the experiences of two LSU graduate students during the COVID-19 crisis reveals how women's experiences vary by race, citizenship, and other status positions. Maretta McDonald, a Black working-class doctoral candidate and U.S. citizen, worried about COVID exposure for herself and her loved ones, due to the disproportionate infection and death rates among Black Americans (Russell and Carlin 2020). Heeya Datta, an Indian doctoral student on a student visa, did not have family members at higher comparative risk, but she feared deportation when the Trump administration announced it would force international students whose degree programs were entirely online in fall 2020 to leave the United States (a decision that was later revoked) (Anderson and Svrluga 2020).

Intersectional Approaches to Activism

History provides examples of activists who approached their work with an intersectional perspective even before the term was coined. Journalist Ida B. Wells took an intersectional approach when documenting cases of thousands of Black men lynched in her time. Wells advocated for Black people's lives by writing about how race, gender, and power worked to create this horrific reality. As she wrote in *Lynch Law*, "[Rape] is only punished when White women accuse Black men, which accusation is never proven. The same crime committed by Negroes against Negroes, or by White men against Black women is ignored even in the law courts" (1893, 2). Gender and racial stereotypes worked together to portray White (but not Black) women as helpless victims and Black (but not White) men as violent sexual predators. Her brave and tireless journalistic work helped people understand these patterns.

PHOTO 1.6 Ida B. Wells risked her life to write about lynching in America. She did so in a way many claim was sociological in its approach to data and analysis. (Photo from University of Chicago Illinois Special Collections Research Center.)

CONSIDER THIS

In Germany, many museums and historical sites document the Holocaust's horrifying atrocities. How might people's understanding of racial slavery and terror, and modern race relations, in the United States be different if sites like these were common here?

A push for intersectional activism and scholarship moved feminism from the second wave into more inclusive third-wave approaches. The Combahee River Collective played an important role in this process. Combahee was a national Black lesbian feminist organization in Boston, Massachusetts, in the 1970s. Named after the Combahee River Raid led by Harriet Tubman during the Civil War, the Combahee River Collective (1979) is most known for its Combahee River Collective statement, which emphasizes the shortcomings of the White feminist movement's exclusion of Black women's realities. As the collective put it,

> As Black feminists we are made constantly and painfully aware of how little effort White women have made to understand and combat their racism, which requires among other things that they have a more than superficial comprehension of race, color, and Black history and culture. Eliminating racism in the White women's movement is by definition work for White women to do, but we will continue to speak to and demand accountability on this issue.

The collective explored multiple forms of oppression with an intersectional lens, criticizing how racism, sexism, heterosexism, and classism all work together to oppress people in a variety of ways. As the statement proclaims, "The inclusiveness of our politics makes us concerned with any situation that impinges upon the lives of women, Third World and working people." Women in Combahee have since become involved with many forms of activism, even transnationally. Member Margo Okazawa-Rey, for example, went on to earn her doctorate in education from Harvard, to hold scholarly positions across the nation, and to produce scholarship and engage in direct activism focusing on militarism, violence against women, and capitalism. She is a cofounder of PeaceWomen Across the Globe, which networks women peace activists transnationally and works to make women's contributions visible.

Another example of intersectional activism beyond American borders can be seen in rural Latin America. At the sixth congress of the Latin American Coordinating Committee of Rural Organisations, women activists came together to address global capitalism and its impacts on other forms of exploitation, such as gender oppression (Frayssinet 2015). In doing so, they made clear how a historical social class spilt between urban and rural women made alliances difficult. They clearly articulated how an intersectional approach, which acknowledges those class differences, could help infuse activism in Latin America by addressing issues such as the following:

- Women produce 50% of Latin America's food supply but hold only 30% of land titles

- The need to preserve seeds as rural women historically have and resist corporate efforts to make the practice illegal so farmers are forced to buy seeds

- Higher rates of violence against women in rural areas

- Pesticide spraying negatively impacting rural residents' health

As these examples make clear, when people look at multiple forms of oppression, their efforts to combat injustice can potentially impact a much larger number of lives. Ida B. Wells forced people to recognize gender- and race-based violence as it manifested in lynching. Pushing second-wave feminists to acknowledge their racial biases totally transformed feminism. And rural Latin American women gathering collectively helped bridge a class divide and bring urban and rural women together to address capitalism's negative impacts in the region.

DOING SOCIOLOGY 1.3

Intersectional Themes in the Arts

For this exercise, you will think of and explain an intersectional theme in the arts.

Think of a creative work (e.g., a song, a television show, a movie, a painting) with an intersectional theme or message that acknowledges how race, class, gender, ethnicity, sexual orientation, or other parts of social status are tied together.

Write a one- to two-paragraph essay explaining the theme and how the work reflects it. Be prepared to share your essay with your classmates.

Check Your Understanding

1. What is intersectionality?

2. Who is Ida B. Wells, and how was her work intersectional?

3. How does intersectionality help explain the tensions between second- and third-wave feminists?

4. How can using an intersectional approach help transform activist work?

DEFINING TERMS RELATED TO RACE AND ETHNICITY

You will need to understand sociological terms used in this class. For example, it is hard to have a good discussion of racism if not everyone knows the sociological definition of the concept.

Prejudice is believing one group is superior to another. Prejudice can occur without power or action. Anyone can be prejudiced. Ethnocentrism is believing one's own ethnic group is superior to others and therefore seeing other groups' language, cultural practices, and other ethnic distinctions as inferior in comparison to one's own. Discrimination occurs when somebody treats people differently based on prejudicial beliefs about their race, ethnicity, sex, class, age, sexual orientation, ability, religion, belief system, or other aspect of their status. Anyone can engage in discrimination. Not everyone has the power to make their prejudicial feelings or discriminatory actions impactful, however.

When prejudicial beliefs and/or discriminatory actions lead to widespread harm for a specific racial group, we are talking about racism. Racism *can* involve coupling (a) the belief that one racial group is superior to another and (b) the power to enforce consequences in favor of the preferred group and to the detriment of other groups. In an era of colorblindness, however, we can find many examples of racism without anyone involved ever saying they think White people are superior or that Black, Asian, Pacific Islander, Latinx, Native American, or multiracial people are of any less value or worth. In other words, racism today can exist without overt prejudice, as simply part of the normal operation of society.

The Emergence of Colorblind Racism

One of the ways racism today can exist without openly admitted prejudice is through colorblind ideology and practices. Colorblindness, or pretending one does not "see color" or treat people differently because of it, crept its way into the consciousness of many Americans after Jim Crow segregation and 1960s civil rights movement successes. Acting on racist feelings or publicly sharing racist thoughts was suddenly looked down on and mostly relegated to the confines of home and/or all-White private spaces. White people, aware overt racism was declining in social acceptability, learned not to commit openly racist acts, to fear being labeled a racist, and started insisting on their own colorblindness.

Explored more in Chapter 5, colorblind racism is a dominant racial ideology colloquially referred to as "racism lite" by sociologist Eduardo Bonilla-Silva (2018). It operates discreetly, with social actors who frequently make mention of "not seeing color" while advocating for the maintenance of White supremacist ideals in the form of structural inequalities such as mass incarceration, housing discrimination, and wealth inequality.

It is also reflected in ostensibly "colorblind" social policies that are supposed to apply to everyone but in practice disproportionately negatively affect people who are not White. The 2020 killing of Breonna Taylor is a good example. She was shot to death by police executing a no-knock warrant as they conducted a drug investigation. Startled and fearing for their lives, her boyfriend fired his (licensed) gun through the door as the intruders tried to enter and they returned fire, killing Breonna. The police did not find any drugs on the premises (Simko-Bednarski, Snyder, and Ly 2020).

No-knock warrants, allowable in specific legal circumstances, are not equally applied across race. Disproportionately applied to Black and brown citizens, they are part of the reason Black women have higher rates of violent victimization by police (Ritchie 2017). They also lead to higher rates of physical and psychological injury among populations of color (Lopez et al. 2018).

DOING SOCIOLOGY 1.4

Reflecting on Colorblind Language and Racism

In this exercise, you will analyze colorblind language.

Colorblind racism often manifests itself in specific language styles that generally allow White people to "talk nasty about minorities without sounding racist" (Bonilla-Silva 2010). Have you ever heard a person say or do any of the following?

- "I'm not prejudiced, but . . ." (followed by a prejudiced statement)

- "Some of my best friends are . . ." (after making a prejudiced statement about people in the group the person's "best friends" belong to)

- "I'm not [Black/Latinx], so I don't know" (followed by a prejudiced statement)

- "Yes, but couldn't that just be due to (social class, poverty, or any other factor that isn't race)?"

- Stutter, take awkward lengthy pauses, repeat themselves, say *um* or *ah* a lot, or simply be incoherent when talking about race

Reflect on one of the times you have heard (or heard of) someone saying or doing one of these things. Briefly write down the story and then answer the following questions.

1. Who was part of the interaction?

2. Why do you think the person said what they did?

3. How might these language choices affect the possibility of honest conversation about race?

Structural, Cultural, and Interpersonal Racism

Structural mechanisms that reproduce racism are often seen as racially neutral. **Structural mechanisms** are large-scale factors and practices typically constructed by White people in positions of power. No particular person has full control over them. Instead, they are built into institutions and legal systems. Housing segregation is a good example. Douglas S. Massey and Nancy A. Denton's (1993) groundbreaking work *American Apartheid* identifies racial residential segregation as a principal cause of racial inequality in American society. Racial segregation in housing leads to multiple types of racial disparities (e.g., in wealth, education, interactions with the criminal justice system, and exposure to pollution and other environmental problems).

People also experience racial oppression through culture. This can be seen in misrepresentation or misuse of cultural symbols, music, art, religious beliefs, legal systems, food, language, or other aspects of people of color's traditions and histories for more powerful (typically White) groups' entertainment or profit. A prominent example is school and sports teams' use of images of Native American peoples for mascots. Consider the Washington Redskins in American football or Cleveland Indians in baseball. Mascots for both teams use Native images adorned with sacred iconography—clothing, headdresses, jewelry, prayer sounds, acts of war—but stripped of their original meaning, promoting a corrupted, distorted, inauthentic, and damaging portrayal of Native American populations (Guiliano 2013). In 2020, after many years of protests by Native American and other social justice organizations and as widespread support for #BlackLivesMatter grew (Buchanan, Bui, and Patel 2020), Washington's football team announced it would finally change its name, and Cleveland's baseball team dropped "Indians" from its name (De la Fuente and Sterling 2020).

People also experience racism interpersonally, or in social actions, communications, or exchanges between two or more people in small or intimate groups. Often exhibited in the form of **racial microaggressions**, or harmful interpersonal statements or behaviors (usually by White people toward people of color), individuals who are not negatively impacted by such interactions typically do not notice them. For example, White people may be unaware of the pain associated with the following examples of microaggressions:

- A Muslim woman of color wearing a headscarf getting scowled at in the supermarket

- People touching a Black woman's hair without asking

- A coworker assuming his Mexican friend always wants to eat tacos

Other more obvious microaggressions you may have encountered include a friend or family member asking someone who looks racially ambiguous, "What are you?"; someone asking an Asian, Latinx, or other person of color, "Where are you *really* from?" when they first provide an answer like "Cleveland"; individuals assuming an Asian person is successful in school *because* they are Asian; or people speaking louder to a Latinx person because they assume they can't speak English well. These interactions may seem innocuous, but all function to identify the person as other or not belonging.

More serious forms of racism can be found in interpersonal relations, too. Widespread discrimination in employment, for example, can start at the interpersonal level. Research consistently demonstrates that even before entry into the workplace, people of color are screened by race, limiting their opportunities for success. Several formal and informal studies (see Bertrand and Mullainathan 2004, and Kang et al. 2016, among others) have shown people with White-sounding names are much more likely to be invited for an interview than those with Black, Latinx, Asian, or other names of (assumed) non-White racial or foreign origin. Later chapters cover this topic in more depth. At its base, however, practices like these position White people for higher levels of employment and economic success while disadvantaging people of color.

CONSIDER THIS

Researchers have found evidence of interpersonal discrimination benefiting White students and disadvantaging students of color at American universities. How could these informal practices affect people's chances for success in and after school?

Check Your Understanding

1. What are prejudice, ethnocentrism, and discrimination, and how are these concepts distinct from racism?

2. What are racial microaggressions?

3. What are some examples of racism at the structural, cultural, and interpersonal levels?

HOW YOU CAN PREPARE FOR THIS CLASS

If we look across research covered in this chapter, one thing should be clear: taking a class about race, racism, or race relations will not be the same experience for everyone. If you've gone through life "not seeing color" or were encouraged to believe people of color are poor, less educated, or locked up at higher rates because of character flaws such as laziness or their community's lack of morals or inability to raise children "the right way," you have a lot to unpack before you can accurately understand how race influences modern social life. If you've experienced or witnessed these manifestations of racial inequality directly, you might begin the class with a stronger understanding of racial inequality but could have to deal with listening to classmates go through the messy process of unlearning victim-blaming logics that situate causes of racial disadvantage in the people who disproportionately experience it (Becker and Paul 2015).

Things to Expect

Courses on race are also about *power*. This means you need to learn how race and racism benefit people in a dominant group while harming marginalized persons. In other words, it means studying both people of color and White people. It also means diving into what history and social science tell us about how power works. You will examine mechanisms and practices that create and sustain race-based uneven access to resources, opportunities, and positive life outcomes, while being mindful of how other aspects of a person's status (such as gender, class, or nationality) affect their experiences with race.

Studying race when people are often discouraged from talking about or acknowledging it for fear of being labeled racist or of being accused of "playing the race card" can be difficult. It is likely to be uncomfortable. Prepare yourself for this. Rather than fighting against the discomfort, you can anticipate and potentially accept it.

Studies show that White students unfamiliar with accurate historical accounts of racial slavery or of people's struggles to fight racial inequality might experience challenging emotions in a class on race: guilt, anger, resentment, or fear, for example (DiAngelo 2018; McIntosh 2009). Students of color might experience a different set of challenging emotions, such as anxiety, depression, or frustration (Mitchell and Donahue 2009; Tatum 2017). But there can also be emotional overlap and space for connection.

Picture a White student who grew up in a mostly Mexican working-class neighborhood. They might not share experiences with wealthy White peers who grew up in all-White spaces. Think of an upper-middle-class multiracial woman with a White dad and Black mother. She might just be coming to understand how social class and light skin (if she has it) gave her privileges her Black peers who grew up working poor didn't get. So, while you can anticipate discomfort associated with honestly addressing racial inequality and racism, you can also prepare for the liberation that comes from facing emotionally challenging subjects head-on with openness, bravery, and integrity.

Racial Terminology in This Book

As you read this book, you will notice that we use a variety of terms to indicate the different racial and ethnic groups in the United States. Depending on generation, region, context, and various other factors, people within the same racial or ethnic group often use different terminology (e.g., Native, Native American, Indigenous, American Indian, Indian, specific tribal affiliation and Hispanic, Latino, Latina, Latinx, specific nation). We also capitalize *Black* and *White* when referring to these two racial groups. This helps us relay that Black and White "are both historically created racial identities" (Appiah 2020). It is important to remember that racial and ethnic terms, like race and ethnicity themselves, are socially constructed and vary over time and place.

Be Aware That Race and Racism Affect Everyone—Even Toddlers

Many people believe young children "don't see race." Debra VanAusdale and Joe Feagin's (2001) *The First R: How Children Learn About Race and Racism* blows this assumption out of the water with data gathered in a daycare observing and carefully documenting kids' behavior. Their work shows how children as young as 2 or 3 quickly ascertain race-based meanings associating Whiteness with goodness and superiority. Consider a boy who is a member of an interracial family. By the age of 3, he had already picked up on White beauty standards, complimenting his White sisters' hair as "pretty" while insisting his thick, curly hair was not. In addition, little kids quickly learn adults are uncomfortable talking about race and do not want them talking about it either. As a result, preschoolers in VanAusdale and Feagin's study knew to keep their comments about racial difference, often issued in the midst of play, out of adults' earshot. This allowed adults to continue to believe little kids don't see race.

DOING SOCIOLOGY 1.5

When, Where, and How Have You Talked About Race?

In this exercise, you will think about why and how conversations about race differ among racial groups.

Write answers to the following questions and be prepared to share your thoughts on Question 3:

1. Did your parents talk to you frankly about race as a child? Did they give you "the talk" about "surviving interactions with police or other members of authority" (Whitaker 2016, 303) and/or facing racism in America?

2. Have you witnessed "two-faced" racism, where White people publicly claim not to see race but in all-White spaces openly express prejudice (Picca and Feagin 2007)?

3. How do you think your answers to these questions might compare to your peers'? Your classmates'? Why? What difference might that make for your ability to connect with or understand one another?

VanAusdale and Feagin's data underscore a theme in this chapter: many Americans, in particular White Americans, have been taught since a very young age that talking about race is taboo. For that reason, honest and respectful conversation about it can be incredibly challenging in a classroom setting. A few basic guidelines of engagement can help make your classroom experience less turbulent, though, if you adopt them.

First: Be radically self-honest. Being honest with yourself about what you have learned and experienced around race in your lifetime is a crucial starting point. For example, it's important to identify any racist ideas you've internalized. Without acknowledging them and understanding where they come from, you cannot change the ways they might impact your behavior. Interrogating your own beliefs and experiences is a crucial step on the path to developing a fuller and more accurate picture of how race and racism impact your life and society, broadly speaking.

Second: Choose to believe one another. If someone shares an experience or viewpoint, you and your classmates can analyze it, think about its connection to broader social patterns, explore its ramifications, and link it to course materials. Sharing personal stories can be scary in a classroom full of strangers, especially when learning about race and racism, which many of us have been taught to deny or not talk about—so give each other the benefit of the doubt. Believe what people say about their own lives, even when subjecting one another's experiences to critical analysis.

Third: Recognize the difference between personal opinions and research. No one has the authority to speak for *all* straight people, gay people, people of color, women, men, students at your university, or even for *one* other person without their consent. Say what *you* believe and feel when talking about a personal experience or viewpoint. If making an assertion beyond that, find research-based evidence to support it and cite the studies you reference. Always be clear about which of the two you are doing. Ask yourself *Am I talking about personal views or discussing research findings? How can I be clear, careful, and honest about the sources of my knowledge?*

CONCLUSION

As you can see, taking a course focused on race and ethnicity can be illuminating and challenging. It can also be empowering. The first step in understanding racial and ethnic issues today is learning how they affected society's past, as Chapter 2 will help you do.

CHAPTER REVIEW

1.1 What is the connection between racial slavery in America and the social construction of race?

How we think about race today emerged alongside racial slavery in colonial/early America. Thinking about races as groups with different biological origins—some less human than others—developed when English colonists needed a justification for (a) forcing lifetime hereditary enslavement on Africans brought to the colonies against their will and (b) slaughtering members of Native American nations. This reveals how race is tied to power and social relations, not science or biology.

1.2 How are racial categories tied to power, and how have they changed in meaning over time?

In addition to its rootedness in racial slavery and violence against Indigenous people, other aspects of race reveal its ties to power. One way power can be seen is in the invisibility of Whiteness. Whiteness is often seen as neutral or generically "human." No one calls traditional Santa images "White Santa," for example, in the way they call him "Black Santa" if he is Black. In addition, the U.S. census helps us see how racial categorizations have changed in law and social practice over time.

1.3 What is intersectionality? How does intersectionality help us understand the ways people experience racial inequality?

Intersectionality refers to seeing how social categories we belong to—such as class, gender, and race—are interconnected and work together to reinforce our advantages or disadvantages in society. It helps reveal things like (a) how women's experiences vary according to factors like race, citizenship status, and social class or (b) how men and women's experiences with race and ethnicity might be dissimilar.

1.4 What are the sociological definitions of race, ethnicity, prejudice, discrimination, ethnocentrism, and racism?

Prejudice is believing one group is superior to another. Ethnocentrism is believing one's own ethnic group is superior to others and the practice of negatively assessing other groups' languages, cultural practices, and other ethnic distinctions in comparison to one's own. Discrimination occurs when somebody treats a person differently based on prejudicial beliefs about their race, ethnicity, sex, class, age, sexual orientation, ability, religion, belief system, or other aspect of status. Racism is when prejudicial beliefs and/or discriminatory actions lead to widespread harm for a specific racial group because members of the prejudiced/discriminatory group are disproportionately in positions of power. In an era of colorblindness, racism can also exist without overt prejudice.

1.5 How might you best handle the challenges that come with a course about race and ethnicity?

Be honest with yourself about preexisting beliefs you carry into class. Unpacking them, thinking about where they come from, choosing to believe people who share experiences in class, and being clear about the difference between personal opinion and research can help make a challenging academic dive into race, ethnicity, ethnocentrism, and racism easier for yourself and your peers.

KEY TERMS

Colonialism (p. 4)

Colorblind racism (p. 14)

Colorblindness (p. 14)

Discrimination (p. 14)

Ethnicity (p. 4)

Ethnocentrism (p. 14)

Intersectionality (p. 11)

Power (p. 6)

Prejudice (p. 14)

Race (p. 4)

Racial microaggressions (p. 16)

Racial slavery (p. 4)

Racism (p. 14)

Socially constructed (p. 3)

Structural mechanisms (p. 15)

2 IDENTIFYING RACISM THROUGHOUT U.S. HISTORY

Stacye Blount

LEARNING QUESTIONS

2.1 Why is racism a fundamental part of U.S. history?

2.2 What are some examples of systemic racism in U.S. history?

2.3 How did racism in the field of sociology hurt Black sociologists—including W. E. B. Du Bois?

2.4 How can we use the sociological imagination to explain the effects of systemic racism on individual lives?

In his book *The Souls of Black Folk*, W. E. B. Du Bois (1903/1997, 3) stated that "the problem of the twentieth century is the problem of the color line." The term **color line** refers to segregation between White and Black people in the United States. Du Bois maintained that racial inequities related to wealth, education, housing, and safety are inextricably tied to this color line problem.

Du Bois used the term **double consciousness** to describe an individual whose identity is split into two parts—one around Black people and one around White people. When in the presence of White people, he sees himself through their eyes (as a Black person rather than an American). Du Bois writes,

> It is a peculiar sensation, this double-consciousness, this sense of always looking at one's self through the eyes of others, of measuring one's soul by the tape of a world that looks on in amused contempt and pity. One ever feels his two-ness, —an American, a Negro; two souls, two thoughts, two unreconciled strivings; two warring ideals in one dark body, whose dogged strength alone keeps it from being torn asunder. (1903/1997, 38)

Furthermore, African Americans were forced to reckon with the reality that their African American identity denied them the privileges and rights attached to their American identity.

The Souls of Black Folk was published in 1903, at the beginning of the twentieth century. Why was racism still a problem decades after the Civil War and the abolishment of slavery? Can you imagine the United States without a color line problem? By the end of this chapter, you will see how race and racism are inextricably linked to the history of the United States.

PHOTO 2.1 Sociologist W. E. B. Du Bois (1868–1963).

Sarin Images/GRANGER.

HOW I GOT ACTIVE IN SOCIOLOGY

Stacye Blount

I have to admit that my journey to becoming active in sociology was not a direct route. As a child, science and math courses were very interesting to me. My parents nurtured those interests, and I was on track to pursuing a STEM major in college. Armed with an undergraduate degree in clinical laboratory science, I spent 13 years in the clinical laboratory industry before returning to graduate school to pursue the doctoral degree.

One day, I decided to enroll in a master's-level sociology course just to "see how the other side of academic disciplines thought." I enjoyed the course, and my curiosity was peaked to learn more sociology. Of course, the rest is history. In fall 2010, I began my career as a sociology professor. I have taught medical sociology, sociology of mental health, social change, social movements, social stratification, professional and career development, and senior capstone. It is a joy to engage with students.

SEEING THE BIG PICTURE: THE UNITED STATES AND RACISM

Why did slavery persist even after Thomas Jefferson declared that "all men are created equal" in the Declaration of Independence? The short answer is money. Racism is a fundamental part of U.S. history because it provided justification for exploiting human beings (e.g., Africans, Native Americans) for financial success in a capitalist society. The institutions of race-based slavery and capitalism in the United States were interdependent.

No United States Without Racism

Racism developed alongside colonial America and what became the United States. Colonial America became inextricably tied to slavery in 1619, the year Jamestown colonists purchased a group of kidnapped Africans from English pirates. As noted in Chapter 1, the United States became a financial powerhouse at the expense of enslaved laborers. The site of abundant land, colonial America, particularly in the South, focused on agricultural production.

PHOTO 2.2 In 1619, Jamestown colonists purchased a group of enslaved Africans from English pirates.

GRANGER.

The South was ideal for farming due to its climate and fertile soil. However, farming, particularly with crops such as indigo, cotton, and tobacco, was tremendously labor intensive. Plantation owners realized that they needed a cheap labor source to make a profit. Enslaved Africans provided such a source.

Although slavery was concentrated more in southern than in northern states, all northern states had enslaved peoples up until the late 1700s. Moreover, in many ways, northerners benefited from enslaved laborers in the South. For example, northerners purchased many of the crops and material objects created on plantations. Northern manufacturers relied on southern plantations to supply the raw material they turned into clothing and other goods(Kendi 2016; Wilder 2013). Northern insurance companies aided the slave trade directly by underwriting it. For example, insurance companies in Rhode Island covered slave-trading voyages, and Aetna Insurance Company in Connecticut wrote policies on the lives of the enslaved (Groark 2002). Even after the abolishment of slavery in the North, members of both the southern and northern elite were able to pass wealth to their children from profits generated through their slave-related businesses.

DOING SOCIOLOGY 2.1

What Would You Do?

In this exercise, you will put yourself in the shoes of Thomas Jefferson.

One of the reasons Jefferson kept so many people enslaved, despite declaring that all men are created equal, was the fact that he was a big spender, constantly in debt, and the people he enslaved were worth a lot of money.

Imagine yourself in Jefferson's shoes in his Virginia society during the late 1700s and early 1800s. If you free the people you enslaved, you will be in even greater debt and never be able to pay back all you owe. You will have no money to hire people to work on your plantation. You will become financially ruined and lose much of your social status. Most people will think you have lost your mind.

Write your answers to the following questions:

1. What would you do? Why?

2. What acts of racial injustice being committed today might draw condemnation in the future? In what ways would society have to change to lead most people to view these acts as unjust?

3. How does this exercise help reveal how society influences the beliefs and actions of individuals?

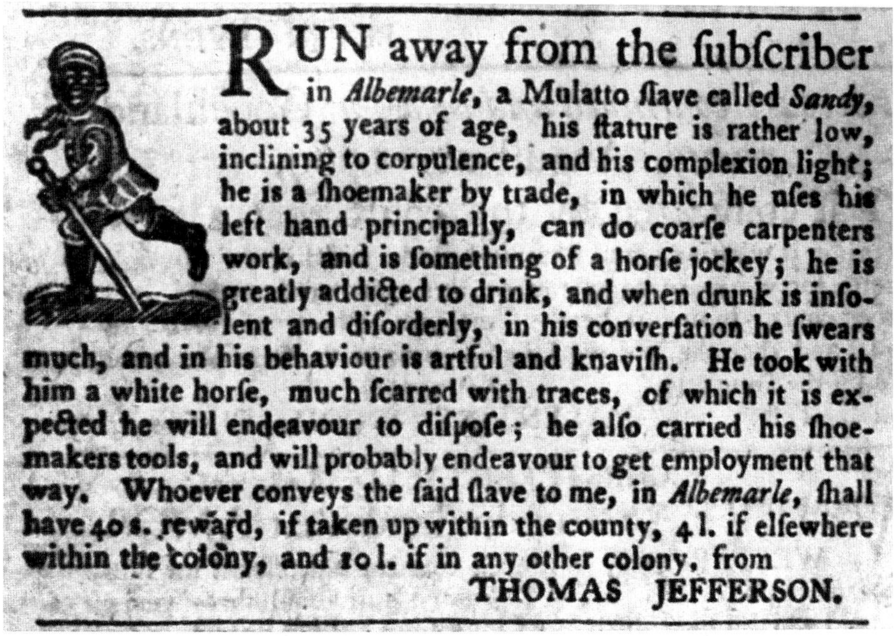

RUN away from the subscriber in *Albemarle*, a Mulatto slave called *Sandy*, about 35 years of age, his stature is rather low, inclining to corpulence, and his complexion light; he is a shoemaker by trade, in which he uses his left hand principally, can do coarse carpenters work, and is something of a horse jockey; he is greatly addicted to drink, and when drunk is insolent and disorderly, in his conversation he swears much, and in his behaviour is artful and knavish. He took with him a white horse, much scarred with traces, of which it is expected he will endeavour to dispose; he also carried his shoemakers tools, and will probably endeavour to get employment that way. Whoever conveys the said slave to me, in *Albemarle*, shall have 40 s. reward, if taken up within the county, 4 l. if elsewhere within the colony, and 10 l. if in any other colony, from

THOMAS JEFFERSON.

PHOTO 2.3 Thomas Jefferson, third president of the United States, professed to hate slavery but kept hundreds of enslaved people whom he forced to work for him.

The United States Constitution and Racism

The first constitution for the United States, the Articles of Confederation, did not mention slavery and left decisions about it to individual states. As it quickly became apparent that the new country would not survive without a stronger federal government, political leaders began work on a new constitution. They knew if the new constitution threatened slavery southern delegates would not sign it.

To appease southern members of the Constitutional Convention, the northern delegates agreed that Congress could not abolish the international slave trade before 1808, taxes on imported enslaved people would not exceed $10, and enslaved people who ran away must be returned to their enslavers (Applestein 2013). Delegates also agreed on a compromise that, for representation and tax purposes, enslaved peoples would count as three-fifths of a person. This allowed southern states to gain more representatives in the House of Representatives. So, to gain approval for the Constitution from all the colonies, slavery remained an integral part of the United States. The division it created between the North and the South, however, remained—the Constitution simply papered over it.

CONSIDER THIS

Imagine if the northern delegates did not compromise on the issue of slavery. In what kind of society might you be living now? How would it differ from the United States we know today?

Check Your Understanding

1. Why did slavery exist in the United States even after Jefferson declared that "all men are created equal" in the Declaration of Independence?

2. How did many northerners benefit from the institution of slavery in the South?

3. Why did northern delegates to the Constitutional Conventional compromise with southern delegates when they created the U.S. Constitution still used today?

RACISM AND SYSTEMIC RACISM

Sociologist Joe Feagin (2006) developed the term systemic racism to explain the significance of race and racism from a historical context. He states that the marriage between the history of the United States and slavery created systemic racism—racism present in the very fabric of society, its institutions. Feagin (2012) describes systemic racism as the deeply rooted, institutionalized racial oppression that gives the dominant group (White people in the United States) power over individuals of color. As noted in Chapter 1, in a society with racism, racial discrimination exists at the individual (one person discriminates against another person based on race and/or ethnicity), institutional (policies, laws, and institutions that produce and reproduce racial inequities), and structural (interactions across institutions that produce and reproduce racial inequities) levels.

Let's look at some examples of racism on the individual, institutional, and structural levels. Examples of individual-level racism include telling racist jokes, refusing to hire people of color because of their race, and racial microaggressions. Institutional racism is more difficult to notice than individual racism because it is embedded in institutions, laws, and policies. It is "just the way things work." Those who help run the institutions and carry out the laws and policies might not want to hurt people of color or even be aware that they are doing so. Some examples of institutional racism over the history of the United States include slavery, redlining (a government-endorsed policy that hindered individuals of color seeking to buying homes), Jim Crow laws (e.g., laws that legalized segregation in the United States), predatory lending practices, exclusion from unions and other organizations, underfunding schools in neighborhoods with a high percentage of people of color, and health disparities between dominant and subordinate racial groups.

Structural racism focuses on the accumulation of the effects of a racialized society over time and interactions among institutions that reinforce racial inequality. For example, past policies that produce racial inequality in housing affect where people of color can go to school, which can lead to fewer opportunities in the labor market. Likewise, racial inequality in housing can lead to health problems, such as asthma and lead poisoning.

Once you start looking, it is easy to see examples of systemic racism throughout U.S. history. We now look at how the social construction of race and racial inferiority led to a racist society that (mostly) benefits wealthy White people at the expense of people of color.

CONSIDER THIS

Why is it more important to focus on the institutional and structural effects of systemic racism than on the effects of individual racism?

Racism and Genocide Against American Indians

White colonists used ideas of racial inferiority to try to justify their treatment of Native American bodies, culture, and land. For example, Europeans concluded that American Indians did not make "good use" of land because they did not use it as Europeans did. While they made good use of the resources supplied by the land, they did not treat it as a commodity or clear huge swaths of it for farmland, like settlers from Europe tended to do. The European colonists used this ethnocentric observation as an excuse to take the land from American Indians. After killing or forcing the exodus of American Indians in the American colonies, White colonists seeking land pressed the government to let them push American Indians out of more fertile land to the west of the colonies. This removal of American Indians from their land occurred from the colonial era through the urbanization movement in the 1950s. You will read more about it in Chapter 6.

PHOTO 2.4 Building railroads was one of the dangerous jobs that Asian male immigrants undertook in the United States.

Asians and Racism in the United States

Asians first came to the United States in sizeable numbers in the 1850s. They were usually males who worked exhausting and dangerous low-skilled jobs such as farming, mining, and building railroads. They faced prejudice and discrimination by Whites who saw them as a "yellow peril" and a threat to their jobs. Indeed, negative attitudes toward Asian immigrants prompted the first racially discriminatory immigration laws. You will read much more about this in Chapter 9.

PHOTO 2.5 This image shows immigrants from Ukraine and Poland. These two countries are in eastern Europe. Eastern European immigrants were once considered "less than" White.

Rue des Archives/GRANGER.

European Ethnic Groups Who Eventually "Became" White

Did you know that at times in U.S. history, not all ethnic Europeans were considered White? For many years, Anglo-Saxon White people tended to view Europeans from eastern and southern Europe (e.g., Italians, Polish, and Russians) as racially inferior to Whites. The 1924 Immigration Act created a national origins quota that prohibited all but a small number of individuals from eastern and southern Europe to migrate to the United States. Most of the quota slots went to racially "superior" people from western and northern Europe from Anglo-Saxon backgrounds. You will read how and why the White racial category expanded in Chapter 7.

Latinx Experience With Racism in the United States

Latinxs did not escape the perils of racism. Their dealings with racism in the United States began in earnest in 1848—the year the United States won the Mexican-American War. The Treaty of Guadalupe marked the official end of the war and granted 55% of Mexican territory to the United

States (Blakemore 2018). Mexicans who decided to remain in United States territory were granted citizenship, causing the United States to gain a large population of Mexican Americans. Anti-Mexican sentiment quickly grew among Whites, particularly among those who coveted the land of Mexican Americans. Negative stereotypes and discrimination followed. You will read more about the Latinx experience in Chapter 10.

Scientific Racism and Justifications for Racial Inequalities

Perceptions of racial inferiority developed alongside racial discrimination. As Anglo-Saxon Americans convinced themselves that Africans were inferior to them, the process of dehumanization necessary to enslave and exploit them for financial gain became easier. Racial classifications for human beings gave rise to scientific racism, the use of pseudoscience to "prove" the innate racial inferiority of some and the superiority of other racial groups (Elshabazz-Palmer 2017). Pseudoscience supported widespread discrimination against African Americans and other non-White groups until World War II, when Adolf Hitler's barbaric use of scientific racism made most people recognize its folly.

While scientific racism held sway, the field of eugenics promoted selective breeding and involuntary sterilization of the "biologically and genetically unfit" as appropriate means to ensure that the U.S. population consisted of the most fit and superior human beings. During the first half of the 20th century and even into the second half, White doctors and scientists sterilized many American Indian, Black, and Puerto Rican women without their consent (Nittle 2019). Eugenicists were convinced it was important to implement measures that would keep "undesirables" from producing children and "polluting" the population in the United States.

Henrietta Lacks

Another example of scientific racism is the story of Henrietta Lacks, a poor African American woman whose cancer cells changed the course of medical research (Skloot 2011). In late January 1951, Mrs. Lacks visited the Johns Hopkins Hospital because she was experiencing health challenges. During segregation in the United States, the Johns Hopkins Hospital was one of the few hospitals to treat poor African American patients (Johns Hopkins Medicine 2019; Skloot 2011).

When the physician examined Lacks, he found a malignant tumor on her cervix and sent a sample of her cancer cells to a tissue laboratory. The physician in the tissue laboratory recognized that her cells were unique in that they multiplied exponentially in approximately 24 hours. Medical scientists started using these HeLa cells (*He* for her first name and *La* for her last name) on January 29, 1951, and still do. Seven decades after her death on October 4, 1951, scientists are still studying the effects of various entities on the growth of cancer cells and other medical ailments with Henrietta Lacks's cells (Johns Hopkins Medicine 2019, Skloot 2011). These scientists harvested her cells without her consent or the idea that they were doing anything wrong.

Because of the ability of Lacks's cells to remain alive after multiple cell divisions, the sale of HeLa cells became a multi-million-dollar industry. Today, her children do not benefit from profits generated from the sale of their mother's cells.

PHOTO 2.6 Henrietta Lacks was a poor African American woman from Virginia. Her cells, known as HeLa cells, revolutionized medical and scientific research. They were important in the development of the polio vaccine, cloning, gene mapping, and in vitro fertilization.

GL Archive/Alamy Stock Photo

Tuskegee Experiment

From 1932 to 1972, approximately 600 men living in Macon County, Alabama (Tuskegee, Alabama), were tapped to participate in a scientific experiment with syphilis. Tuskegee was chosen because at the beginning of the study it had the highest syphilis rate in the United States. The study was sponsored by the United States Public Health Service. This experiment involved blood tests, spinal taps, x-rays, and autopsies (Jones 1993). Medical professionals' desire to observe the natural course of untreated syphilis led to approximately 200 men never receiving treatment—even after penicillin became a safe and reliable cure for the disease. In 1997, President Clinton publicly apologized on behalf of the U.S. government for the experiment.

DOING SOCIOLOGY 2.2

What Do You Understand?

In this exercise, you will check your understanding of this section of the chapter.

Write down your answers to the Check Your Understanding questions. Then, share and compare your answers with a partner to make sure you each have correct and complete answers for each question.

Check Your Understanding

1. How did European colonists justify taking land from Native Americans?
2. What federal policies hindered Asian immigration to the United States?
3. Regarding European immigration to the United States, which ethnicities were most welcome?
4. What is scientific racism?

RACISM AND THE HISTORY OF SOCIOLOGY

People of color have faced racism in many, if not all, fields of work—including academia. For example, although W. E. B. Du Bois made robust contributions to the discipline of sociology, White leaders in sociology tended to ignore his work. Moreover, despite his Harvard education and cutting-edge sociological research, no White-run university would hire him for a permanent position. He spent much of his time as a professor at Atlanta University (Atlanta, Georgia), a historically Black college and university (HBCU).

DOING SOCIOLOGY 2.3

Discrimination Through the Years

This exercise requires you to step outside of the current culture in the United States and recognize discriminatory behavior you may have overlooked.

Answer the following questions in writing. Be prepared to share your answers with a partner.

1. In the late 1800s and early 1900s, Du Bois faced systemic racism in the field of sociology, and women sociologists had to deal with systemic sexism. What do you think the chances were for women of color to become successful sociologists during Du Bois's time in the field?
2. It's easy to disapprove of the blatant discrimination against women and people of color in the past. Such obviously sexist and racist behavior is outside the norms of today's culture. But what other marginalized groups of people faced systemic discrimination 100 years ago?

3. What current systemic discriminatory behavior would people of the future be appalled by?

4. Were any of these questions difficult to answer? Why or why not?

Du Bois's work contrasted sharply with the racist views held by most White social scientists during his life (Morris 2015; Romero 2019). Robert E. Park, a leading sociologist based at the University of Chicago, the home of the first department of sociology, knew of Du Bois's contributions to sociology. However, he and most other White sociologists did not give credit to his research in their writings nor did they expose their students to his findings. Most of his work involved studying and advocating for Black Americans—a subject many White sociologists deemed unimportant. The lack of inclusion in mainstream sociology affected Du Bois's access to funding for research and influence in the field during his lifetime.

CONSIDER THIS

Do you think your race will influence your professional opportunities? Why or why not?

A More Inclusive Sociology

Today, sociology is a much more inclusive discipline and one of the most racially diverse (National Science Foundation 2018). Many sociologists apply their research findings to help create and test social policies and to advocate for solutions to social challenges, as Du Bois did. Social policy refers to the implementation of a course of action through a formal program or law, and advocacy denotes the employment of resources to empower communities. Tnesha Shaw, the sociologist in action featured in this chapter, describes how she used her sociological tools to improve society and make important connections as an undergraduate sociology major.

SOCIOLOGISTS IN ACTION

Tnesha Shaw

Sociology: The Bridge to a Fulfilling Life

During my senior year in high school, I scheduled an appointment with the guidance counselor to discuss options for college. She told me that my best two options were to enroll in a community college or get a job. Her statements crushed my confidence level because I assumed that she had higher expectations for me, as I had for myself. With her statements and my lowered self-esteem in tow, I abandoned my interest in college and started working two minimum-wage jobs. After 5 years of minimum-wage work, I realized that my life was not fulfilling and I had to make a change. I enrolled at Fayetteville State University (FSU), a historically Black college and university (HBCU) founded in 1867 by seven African American men.

At FSU, I took advantage of extracurricular activities that allowed me to put my sociological tools into practice, influence society, gain leadership experiences, and attain social capital by getting to know and impress many people. For example, I served as president of the collegiate chapter of the National Association of the Advancement of Colored People (NAACP), a racial justice organization W. E. B. Du Bois helped establish. Under my leadership, the organization sponsored various panels and discussions about racial justice issues—a major part of the culture at FSU. We also participated in rallies off campus and mobilized our fellow students and people in the surrounding community to vote.

I also dove into curricular opportunities. For example, I was tapped to participate in a China study-abroad trip sponsored by Congressmen Butterfield and Clyburn. The experience was extraordinary—I couldn't believe I got to go to China! Fortunately, my sociological knowledge made it easy for me to interact in a different culture.

I was the only FSU student chosen to serve as an intern at the National Institute of Food and Agriculture (NIFA) in the United States Department of Agriculture (USDA). There I served on Feds Feed Families, a national campaign focused on food security. As part of my tasks, I conducted comparative sociological research on land grant colleges' agriculture-related curricular offerings in the late 1800s. I am proud to say that my internship supervisor said she selected me for the internship because of my civic engagement initiatives and activities.

As I delved into the discipline of sociology and engaged in curricular and cocurricular activities, it became easier for me to apply the sociological imagination to my life. I now realize that you must understand how society works to make it better. Working with others, we can gain power and make our society better. I also learned that a life spent doing so is empowering and fulfilling.

Tnesha Shaw is a graduate student working toward a master's degree in sociology at Fayetteville State University in Fayetteville, North Carolina.

Discussion Question

What extracurricular experiences have helped you make a positive impact on society and gain skills and contacts needed to succeed in the job market?

Check Your Understanding

1. How did racism affect W. E. B. Du Bois's career in sociology?

2. In what ways has the field of sociology changed from what it was like when Du Bois was looking for his first position as a sociology professor?

USING SOCIOLOGY TO RECOGNIZE AND ADDRESS INSTITUTIONAL AND STRUCTURAL RACISM

Sociology is unique in that it helps us to see how our personal experiences are influenced by larger social forces. Turn your attention now to one sociologist, C. Wright Mills, who developed a concept that helps us see the connection between individuals and larger social forces and how it is more effective to address social issues on a societal, rather than an individual, level.

Using the Sociological Imagination to Uncover and Address Systemic Racism

In *The Sociological Imagination*, C. Wright Mills (1959/2000) proposed that optimal critical thinking about the social world requires that individuals need to develop and use their sociological imagination, the ability to view our personal experiences and lives within a broader social context. Experiences unique to individuals or small groups (e.g., making yourself happy or sad by winning or losing a board game, stubbing your toe, getting first dibs on dessert) are best addressed within the confines of your personal sphere. They do not relate to larger social forces. Behavior and attitudes connected to social patterns that affect a lot of people (e.g., effects of the climate crisis, racial segregation in schools, voter suppression), on the other hand, are public issues and best addressed on the societal level.

Race-Based Policies and Schoolchildren's Access to Healthy Foods

Consider schoolchildren's access to healthy foods. In 2010, former first lady Michelle Obama launched the Let's Move! initiative, a campaign focused on eradicating obesity in children. The movement rested on five pillars, two of which focused on access to healthy foods for households and for children in schools. You may ask, Why don't all children have access to healthy foods in their schools and homes? Why was it necessary for Obama to establish the Let's Move! initiative?

Answers to both questions can be traced back to residential segregation and a lack of supermarkets in poor communities.

When middle-class Whites moved from cities to suburbs after WWII, businesses, including grocery stores, moved there as well. They wanted to continue to take advantage of the spending habits common among White people. Thus, many poor urban areas where many people of color lived were left without access to supermarkets that sell healthy foods. People without a sociological imagination will not notice the connection among these practices, the policies that permitted them, and what individuals eat. This allows many policymakers to ignore the constricted circumstances within which individuals in poor urban areas must make food choices. In other words, people tend to perceive choices made within constrained circumstances as being based on personal tastes rather than systemic racism.

This lack of attention to social issues has many negative social repercussions. People with access to only unhealthy food tend to gain weight—and weight-related health problems—from consistent consumption of foods laden with artificial ingredients and refined sugar and processed in a manner designed to increase rather than decrease feelings of hunger. Moreover, people living in neighborhoods void of healthy foods tend not to exercise much because their neighborhoods do not have gyms (which they likely could not afford anyway) or safe spaces to walk or jog. All these—and more—negative repercussions of a lack of healthy food increase the cost of health care for everyone.

The COVID-19 Pandemic and Racial Health Inequities

The coronavirus pandemic has magnified racial disparities in health outcomes. Compared to Whites, Black people in the United States—as a racial group—have suffered much more harm from the virus. For example, among people 45 to 54 years old, the death rate for Black people was *6 times* that of Whites (Ford, Reber, and Reeves 2020).

What are some reasons for this dramatic disparity? Blacks are more likely to live in densely populated neighborhoods rooted in the historical legacy of race-based housing policies. Black people tend to have less access to quality health care and health insurance. Many have preexisting conditions linked to poor diets and lack of exercise that are related to race-based inequities in income, employment, education, and housing. If they do have access to health care, they often experience racial bias in medical treatment. Finally, Blacks are much more likely than Whites to have "essential" jobs that require them to work amid the pandemic, increasing their chances of contracting the coronavirus.

Cumulative Disadvantage

These examples show us we need a sociological imagination to recognize institutional and structural racism. They also reveal what happens when we do not address racism. These cases show some of the cumulative disadvantages associated with racial segregation and other racist policies and laws. Cumulative disadvantage refers to inequities and negative consequences of those inequities throughout our lives. The Let's Move! initiative is helpful, but to end the root cause of the lack of healthy food in poor, racially segregated neighborhoods, we must change the policies that perpetuate racial segregation in housing and schools. Likewise, we must change policies that perpetuate health inequities. You will learn more about the policies and laws that helped create racial inequality—redlining in housing, local funding for schools, the creation of neighborhood schools—in later chapters.

Recognizing systemic racism will also help members of society, particularly White Americans, understand that racial inequities come from laws, policies, and practices—not individual triumphs of White people or the failures of people of color. According to Ibram Kendi (2019), the first step in this process is to help people understand that it is necessary to dispense with the notion that individual people are racist. He suggests that we should focus on defining actions, policies, and laws as racist—not people. Once people stop thinking they must deny they are racist, they can begin to recognize how they can act in antiracist ways by supporting ideas, actions, and policies that promote equity, inclusion, and belonging. In doing so, they can help dismantle systemic racism and stop its generational effects on individuals' lives.

PHOTO 2.7 Former first lady Michelle Obama launched Let's Move!, an initiative that focused on reducing child obesity with education, healthy eating habits, and exercise. The campaign was launched in 2010.

Larry Marano/WireImage

CONSIDER THIS

What are some of the negative consequences of calling people racist or denying that you are racist?

DOING SOCIOLOGY 2.4

Why Should Students Get Free Breakfasts and Lunches?

In this exercise you will use your sociological imagination to help create a policy (or policies) to ensure that all students at a predominantly low-income school district can have free, healthy lunches and breakfasts provided by their schools.

In late 2019, the Trump administration put forth a proposal to reduce the number of people on the Supplemental Nutrition Assistance Program (SNAP). If enacted, about 500,000 students would have no longer been eligible for free meals at school. It would have also made it harder for some schools to automatically enroll all their students for free meals (schools with at least 40% of students on SNAP can feed all students, without any paperwork required).

With this in mind, answer the following questions in writing:

1. What argument(s) would you have used to convince the Trump administration to cancel this proposal? If that effort failed, how might you convince your school board to enact and the state to fund free school lunches and breakfasts for all students in low-income schools? For example, you could point out that it is difficult for hungry students to concentrate on learning, show positive results from similar schools that already do this (and where they get their funding), or explain

how offering free and healthy lunches to everyone can diminish the hassle and paperwork costs for schools and the discomfort students face when they are one of a small number of students who get free meals at school.

2. How would you organize support for your efforts? Whose support would you want to make sure you had—and why?

3. If the Trump administration and the Board of Ed and/or the state refuses to provide lunches and breakfasts for all students in low-income schools, how would you have responded? Why?

Share and refine your answers with another student and then join another pair of students. As a group, create one plan and prepare to share it with the class.

Check Your Understanding

1. What is the sociological imagination?

2. How does the sociological imagination help us understand the effects of systemic racism on individual lives?

3. How is the need for the Let's Move! initiative tied to policies and practices that produce both residential segregation and racial inequality in health outcomes?

4. What is cumulative disadvantage?

5. Why should we focus less on calling individuals racist and more on policies and laws if we want to reduce racial inequality?

CONCLUSION

This chapter provided a sneak peek of what you will learn in later chapters and a brief look at the history of race and racism in the United States. Racism is also a global issue, however, and exists in nations throughout the world. In Chapter 3 we look at racism through a global perspective.

CHAPTER REVIEW

2.1 Why is racism a fundamental part of U.S. history?

Racism is a basic part of U.S. history because it provided a means of justifying stealing the land that is now the United States and the exploitation of human labor to grow wealth in a capitalist society. It also helped divide the nonelite members of society by creating a racial bond among wealthy and nonwealthy Whites.

2.2 What are some examples of systemic racism in U.S. history?

Systemic racism refers to racism present at institutional and structural levels in society. Examples include slavery, genocide, residential segregation, redlining, and Jim Crow laws.

2.3 How did racism in the field of sociology hurt Black sociologists—including W. E. B. Du Bois?

In the early years of the field of sociology, White sociologists tended to be as racist as their peers outside the discipline. They tended not to give non-White men and women sociologists the respect they gave to fellow White male sociologists. They were neither obliged nor accustomed to accepting people of color and women (of any race) as their peers. The treatment of W. E. B. Du Bois provides a powerful example of how racism trumped brilliant research in the field.

2.4 How can we use the sociological imagination to explain the effects of systemic racism on individual lives?

The sociological imagination is a concept coined by C. Wright Mills that encourages people to connect their individual lives to societal forces. People can use their sociological imaginations to explain the effects of systemic racism as they evaluate individual lives within social, political, historical, and economic contexts.

KEY TERMS

Advocacy (p. 29)

Articles of Confederation (p. 24)

Color line (p. 21)

Cumulative disadvantage (p. 31)

Double consciousness (p. 21)

Individual racism (p. 24)

Institutional racism (p. 24)

Scientific racism (p. 27)

Social policy (p. 29)

Sociological imagination (p. 30)

Structural racism (p. 24)

Systemic racism (p. 24)

Shukar
alen khere!
Berlin!
zu Rassism
Politik, Alltag und Insti
GENUG – gemordet, geschwiegen, gedul

3

RECOGNIZING SYSTEMIC RACISM AS A GLOBAL ISSUE

Katya Salmi

LEARNING OBJECTIVES

3.1 How is race socially constructed?

3.2 How did imperialism and colonialism enshrine racial hierarchies?

3.3 How are contemporary forms of racism rooted in historical forms of oppression?

3.4 What are examples of systemic racism in different parts of the world?

3.5 How do transnational relationships and migration issues reflect racial dynamics?

In September 2019, as two Italian soccer teams squared off in Cagliari, Italy, fans from one team greeted Inter Milan's newest player, Romelu Lukaku, with monkey chants. This is a common experience for non-White soccer players in Europe, but fans and sporting officials argued that the chants had nothing to do with racism. In fact, fans of Lukaku's own team claim that what happened was not racist. As they put it, in a letter to him, "We are really sorry you thought that what happened in Cagliari was racist. You have to understand that Italy is not like many other north European countries where racism is a REAL problem. We understand that it could have seemed racist to you, but it is not like that" (Mezzofiore 2019). During other games, referees punished players who complained about racist abuse from fans (Panja 2019).

The media, however, clearly noticed race—and pointed out Lukaku's race when the team was not performing well. As Lukaku puts it, "When things were going well, I was reading newspapers articles and they were calling me Romelu Lukaku, the Belgian striker. When things weren't going well, they were calling me Romelu Lukaku, the Belgian striker of Congolese descent" (Lukaku 2018).

This denial of racism is common in European countries. Issues around race and racism are perceived as external and contrary to European values of democracy and equality. This sense of exceptionalism stems from the assumption that to be European is to be antiracist. This is in large part due to post–World War II efforts to stop thinking about difference through the prism of race in response to the way the Nazis used racial hierarchies to justify killing millions of Jewish people during the Holocaust. These efforts to get rid of race, however, did not rid European countries of racism. Not only did racism persist, but as colonies gained independence and migration from former colonies toward Europe increased, racism took on new dimensions that we see today.

Born in Antwerp, Belgium, to Congolese parents, Lukaku has played on the Belgian national team in international games his entire professional life. Lukaku's firsthand account of his experiences highlights how, despite his contributions to the nation, he cannot escape racism. Lukaku's story also exemplifies how racism in Europe excludes those who do not fit into a generalized idea of what it means to be European—which includes being White. Even the children and grandchildren of migrants of color, especially those from former European colonies, experience racism daily. Consciously or not, many Europeans tend to look through the lens of a "fortress Europe" that must be protected from refugees and migrants with non-Christian religions (i.e., Muslims) and races (i.e., not White).

PHOTO 3.1 Romelu Lukaku, shown here scoring a goal for the Belgian national team in October 2019, has faced racism during his career.

Soccrates/Getty Images

This chapter provides the historical context that gave life to the racial hierarchy in Europe and other nations around the world, drawing on contemporary examples that reflect their lasting impact. In doing so, we do not attempt to explain every relevant historical event, nor could we provide an exhaustive accounting of systemic racism in our world. Instead, we lay out key historical moments and current examples that reflect general trends.

HOW I GOT ACTIVE IN SOCIOLOGY

Katya Salmi

As a Moroccan-French migrant to the United States, I have always navigated several worlds and identities at the same time. After high school, I moved to Canada and then to Europe for grad school, and each step of the way, I was amazed by the different experiences of race and ethnicity I encountered. I was especially confused by the French assertion that "race doesn't exist," as it conflicted with my own personal experiences as a racialized woman in France.

Sociology gave me the tools and the words to understand and discuss race in a more meaningful way. It provided an avenue for me to better understand how race could be so prominent in one country like the United States and then hidden and taboo in a country like France.

After graduate school, I worked in nonprofit and human rights organizations where I applied my sociological training and research skills to advocate for the rights of migrants, refugees, and racialized groups. Today, I teach sociology of race, gender, and global issues, while continuing to collaborate and consult with local nonprofit organizations who work with vulnerable groups and migrant populations around Washington, DC.

RACE IS NOT A UNIQUELY AMERICAN EXPERIENCE

Race impacts people's everyday lives in every corner of the globe. Systemic racism, the policies and practices embedded in a society that advantage White people and disadvantage people of color, exists in Europe, Africa, Asia, Oceania, and Latin America. Each nation and time period, however, has its own spin on race and racism.

At the turn of the 20th century, segregation was in full swing in the United States, with southern states enacting restrictive Jim Crow legislation, entrenching the second-class citizenship of African Americans. Across the Atlantic Ocean, however, African Americans could live their everyday lives without the restrictions experienced back home. For, example, African Americans from the South could go about their business—shopping, going out to eat, watching a movie—without showing deference to Whites, and unhindered by Jim Crow laws. Some African American soldiers serving in World War I chose to stay in France after the war ended rather than return to live in a country that treated them like second-class citizens. African American artists and intellectuals also sought refuge in Paris, France, where they were more respected.

At the same time, however, Europeans racialized colonial subjects—by ascribing racial characteristics to them—and discriminated against them. In the postwar period, for example, African soldiers who served for France during the war were met with hostility and renewed repression after the war both in France and in the colonies. Many had to fight for social benefits the government had promised them but not provided (Berteaux 2017).

To make things even more complicated, "race" as a concept is not accepted everywhere in the way we understand it in the United States. In the United States, race is a key way of characterizing people into groups on an official level. For example, the government classifies people by race in the census. However, certain western European countries, which focus more on cultural heritage, use ethnicity or immigration status or generation to classify individuals.

PHOTO 3.2 American writer, intellectual, and civil rights activist James Baldwin in his home in Saint Paul de Vence, France (September 1985). Baldwin moved to France in the 1940s, because he felt more accepted there than in the United States (although he moved back and forth over the years).

Ulf Andersen/Getty Images

DOING SOCIOLOGY 3.1

A Day in the Life

In this exercise, you will reflect on the daily experiences of African Americans who left the United States and lived in or visited another country during segregation.

During the Jim Crow era, state and local laws in the South mandated the segregation of Black and White Americans, legally forcing African Americans to use separate, inferior facilities. Jim Crow permeated nearly every aspect of life, requiring that African Americans learn in separate schools, worship in separate churches, drink from separate water fountains, use separate public bathrooms, eat in designated sections of restaurants, and sit at the back of public buses.

Based on what you know about this period, answer the following questions in writing, and be prepared to share your answers with the class. Your instructor may ask that you work with a partner or a small group.

1. What type of freedoms would African Americans living under segregation in the United States experience in another country during that same time?

2. How do you think African Americans from the South who spent time outside the United States during WWI and WWII felt when they returned to their homes in the United States? Why?

3. How do you think White Southerners treated the returning African American soldiers? Why?

Racism Without Racial Classifications

In France, it is not uncommon to hear that "race does not exist here." In fact, it is illegal to collect statistics that reflect the ethno-racial characteristics of individuals. Most people in France consider even thinking in terms of "Black" and "White," or any other racial categories used in the Unites States, as racist (Salmi 2011). The French unease with race is so deep that the government removed the term from legal texts, including the constitution.

Despite this attitude, however, racism exists in France. For example, reports show that youths ages 18 to 24 who appear Black or Arab are 20 times more likely to be stopped and frisked by police (Défenseur des Droits 2017). The lack of ethno-racial classifications makes it more difficult to combat racism and discrimination, especially institutional and systemic forms of racism rooted in historical oppression. Mainstream antiracism efforts in France focus more on promoting universalism—the idea that France is one and indivisible, and that everyone is the same. In this seemingly benign way, such efforts mask the true experiences of racialized and marginalized groups.

Germany also does not keep track of racial demographics; there is no way to know how many Black people are in Germany. The available data mainly reflect immigration status and country of origin of first- and second-generation migrants. Rather than race, difference is conceptualized around nationality and one's "experience with migration," (i.e., whether an individual or their parents migrated to Germany and hold another nationality) (Mohdin 2019). In other places, like the United Kingdom or Sweden, it is more common to refer to ethnic groups when speaking about racialized groups (European Commission Directorate-General for Justice and Consumers 2019).

As noted earlier, countries like France and Germany that refuse to acknowledge race do so because of the history of World War II and the use of racial hierarchies to justify the Holocaust. After the war, the international community challenged the pseudoscience that supported using race as a way of categorizing people. In the early 1950s, the United Nations Educational, Scientific and Cultural Organization (UNESCO) brought together academics from various fields (sociology, anthropology, genetics) who explicitly denounced the existence of biological races (UNESCO 1969). While some countries—like the United States—held tight to racial categorizations, others used the findings of these experts to drop them to avoid repeating the atrocities of the Holocaust.

CONSIDER THIS

As noted in the preceding section, racism exists even in nations that do not acknowledge race. Would racism in the United States lessen if we stopped using the concept of race? Why?

Hate Crimes

As in France, racism is alive and well in Germany, despite the refusal to think of differences in terms of race. Hate crimes have been on the rise. According to the Organization for the Security and Cooperation in Europe's (OSCE) Office for Democratic Institutions and Human Rights (ODIHR), the most reported hate crimes were motivated by racism, xenophobia, and antisemitism (OSCE-ODIHR n.d.;

Kastner 2019). In June 2019, a far-right extremist confessed to killing Walter Luebcke, administrative chief of the Christian Democratic Union party. Luebcke was pro-immigration and supported German chancellor Angela Merkel's policy of welcoming millions of refugees seeking asylum from violence in the Middle East (Bennhold 2019).

Everyday Racism

In summer 2018, Germans recounted their experiences of everyday racism through the #MeTwo hashtag, a play on the now famous "MeToo" hashtag that brought forward firsthand accounts of sexual harassment and assault on social media platforms. After famous German Turkish soccer player Mesut Özil resigned from the German national soccer team citing "racism and disrespect," writer and activist Ali Can launched this trending discussion. It led many racialized persons—people of color and migrants—to recount the ways in which White Germans make them feel "other" and constantly remind them they are not "really German." Tweets describe how people would often ask where they were "really from," how others would express surprise at their ability to speak German, or how police would frequently stop them for identity checks.

In France in 2019, undocumented migrants organized the *Gilets Noirs* (Black Vests) movement to protest the systemic racism in French society and their exploitative treatment. Many Gilets Noirs are from former French African colonies like the Ivory Coast, Senegal, Mali, Burkina Faso, and Benin. They are calling for more rights in housing, in work, and in dealing with the police as they face increasing challenges because of immigration crackdowns and more frequent deportations (Butterly 2019).

Why Think About Race and Racism on a Global Level?

If race is a social construct, and therefore defined at least somewhat differently from society to society, then why do we need to understand race from a global perspective? First, we can't fully understand race within one location without knowing how worldwide patterns and developments influenced local understandings of race and relations among nations. From imperialism and slavery, to current migratory patterns and transnational relationships between countries, race is a key part of global and national histories.

Second, race and ethnicity continue to impact people's everyday lives around the world. Conflicts and wars based on race and ethnicity persist. For example, in Rwanda, the Hutu ethnic group carried out the mass slaughter of about 800,000 members of the Tutsi ethnic group in 1994. Today, the Rohingya conflict in northern Rakhine State, Myanmar, pitting Rakhine Buddhists and Rohingya Muslims against each other continues. Military operations by the Buddhist-led government—characterized by a United Nations investigation team as crimes against humanity—have forced 740,000 Rohingya women, men, and children to leave their homes and flee, putting pressure on neighboring nations (Amnesty International 2019).

> ### Check Your Understanding
>
> 1. How did some African Americans experience race differently outside the United States during the U.S. Jim Crow era?
> 2. Why do some countries refuse to use the category of race?
> 3. What are examples of racism in countries that refuse the category of race?
> 4. Is it possible to effectively address racism in a nation that does not allow racial classifications?
> 5. Why should we think about race and racism on a global level?

HISTORICAL CONTEXT: RACE AND EMPIRE

To understand global racial dynamics, we need to understand how race and racism were central to imperialism and colonial endeavors, especially in justifying the commodification of human labor in capitalist societies. **Imperialism** refers to the underlying ideology behind efforts to attain control and power over other nations, groups, or territories. Colonialism puts the ideology into action. **Colonialism** is the practice of exerting political, social, and economic control over another territory and its inhabitants. As noted in Chapter 1, race is a modern concept, created to justify European nations' decision to build their empires by forcibly taking lands, enslaving people, and exploiting their resources.

European Imperialism

Imperial endeavors of European nations have shaped our current modern landscape through their conquest of "new" lands and people they "discovered." Starting in the 15th century, Christopher Columbus, Ferdinand Magellan, Vasco de Gama, Francis Drake, Hernán Cortés, and other European explorers set sail to conquer new lands and find riches. The Portuguese exploration of the African coast and Columbus's voyages to the "New World" led to more and more expeditions. European powers—Britain, France, Germany, Belgium, Spain, and Portugal—scrambled to acquire territories vast and far, vying for control over these lands. Four centuries later, they were still at it. At the Berlin West African Conference (November 1884–February 1885), European nations agreed on clear protocols to follow as they divided up Africa among them.

Settler Colonies

While Europeans controlled some territories only administratively through the control of government and public affairs, they also established **settler colonies** across the Americas and later in Africa and Oceania. Large groups of populations from the metropoles—the controlling states—migrated to the colonies to start new lives. Settler colonies sought to dominate the Indigenous populations and take over all aspects of life (social, cultural, political, and economic). In many cases, this involved depopulating the territory of many or most of its inhabitants and imposing their societal structures onto the remaining Indigenous people. By doing so, European colonizers profited from vast natural resources, cheap human labor, and slavery that benefited their economies and allowed them to grow and develop exponentially at the expense of colonized subjects.

The Civilizing Mission

The **civilizing mission** played a key role in imperialism. Europeans' designation of Indigenous people in the colonies as uncivilized people with inferior cultures allowed them to justify their colonialism and efforts to make colonial subjects **assimilate**—to shed their culture and take on the colonizer's culture. For example, in French colonies Indigenous children had to learn French and study French history.

PHOTO 3.3 This 1609 illustration depicts Samuel de Champlain in battle against the Iroquois, who are presented as threatening and uncivilized.

wynnter/Getty

They learned about "their ancestors, the Gauls" while their own culture, language, and religion were trivialized. Today, students in France's overseas territories continue to learn this specific history about mainland France, despite its irrelevance to their lived experience or history.

CONSIDER THIS

Imagine going to school and having to learn the history of your colonists, rather than your own. How might this affect you? How might it affect how the colonists view you?

The civilizing mission is a form of cultural racism that presents the Indigenous cultures as inferior and related to the very *nature or biology* of the Indigenous people. Wielding their power, colonialists—settlers and those living in the metropoles—created both a physical and conceptual distinction between "the West" and "the rest" (Hall 1992) where the settlers were juxtaposed with non-European, non-White "Natives" all lumped together as one entity. Through this lens, colonizers saw Indigenous populations of colonized lands as barbaric, weak, uncivilized, and in need of saving.

Slavery

As noted in the discussion of colonial America in Chapter 1, establishing clear racial demarcations and hierarchies provided a tool for settlers to oppress the Native populations in their colonies and to use them as cheap or forced labor (Marx 2017). For example, in the late 1800s and early 1900s, in the Belgian colony Congo Free State, the Congolese faced horrific violence and exploitation. The French colonists used them as free labor, forcing them to collect rubber for export to Europe and North America. They had to meet unrealistic rubber quotas or suffer abuse and mutilation if they did not. The colonial military, "the Public Force" (*Force publique*), enforced this labor policy by severing hands of offenders. While an exact death toll is hard to establish, historians and anthropologists estimate that 1 to 15 million people perished in the Belgian-controlled Congo Free State from violence, conflict, malnutrition, or disease (Hochschild 1998).

Slavery was an integral aspect of imperialism and colonialism and helped fuel the economies of countries profiting from a global slave trade. While we know that slavery was foundational to U.S. history, the United States was only one part of a wider network. For example, nearly 4 million enslaved people ended up in Brazil (Bourcier 2012). As seen in Figure 3.1, the transatlantic slave trade spanned three centuries (from the 16th to the 19th century) and several regions across the world: Africa, the Americas, the Caribbean, Europe, and the Indian Ocean. An estimated 17 million people were forcibly removed from their homes, transported, and sold as slaves in the colonies (Eltis and Richardson 2010).

Western European countries—France, England, Spain, Portugal, and the Netherlands—were the main traders in the transatlantic slave trade, transporting goods to western Africa, the "Gold Coast," to trade for captured Africans. Traders transported their captives to the colonies in the Americas and sold them into slavery. Their ships then returned to Europe with the crops and agricultural products that enslaved persons produced. Two million enslaved people died during the "Middle Passage," the name given to the trip across the Atlantic (Eltis and Richardson 2010).

Portraying Africans as another race and less than human facilitated the creation of racial hierarchies in legal codes and the very fabric of societies across the world. For example, King Louis XIV ratified the first version of the "Black Code" (*Code Noir*) in 1685 to legally enshrine the subjugated status of the enslaved in French colonies. But racist ideology was not confined to the colonies. Through propaganda and media (Hall 1997), colonialists were able to export the belief in enslaved and colonized peoples' inferiority back to the metropoles—just like crops and goods.

The transatlantic slave trade was not the only slave trading route. As Figure 3.2 shows, the Indian Ocean slave trade involved Africa, the Middle East, and Asia. In the 17th century, traders started taking enslaved people from India and South East Asia to the Dutch Cape Colony in southern Africa. The slave trade in this region grew, widening to include enslaved persons from eastern Africa, Madagascar, the Mascarene Islands, and Indonesia (Williams 2016). In Australia, a slave trade starting in the 1860s, often referred to as "Blackbirding," involved coercing and entrapping Pacific Islanders (the people

FIGURE 3.1 ■ Slave Trade Out of Africa

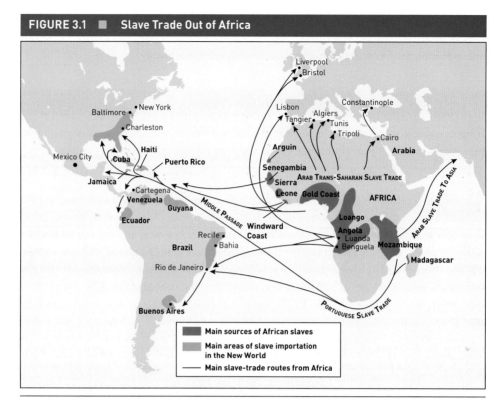

Source: Macmillan Encyclopedia of World Slavery, edited by Paul Finkelman and Joseph C. Miller. Copyright © 1998 by Simon and Schuster Macmillan. Macmillan Reference USA.

FIGURE 3.2 ■ Slave Trading Routes in the Indian Ocean

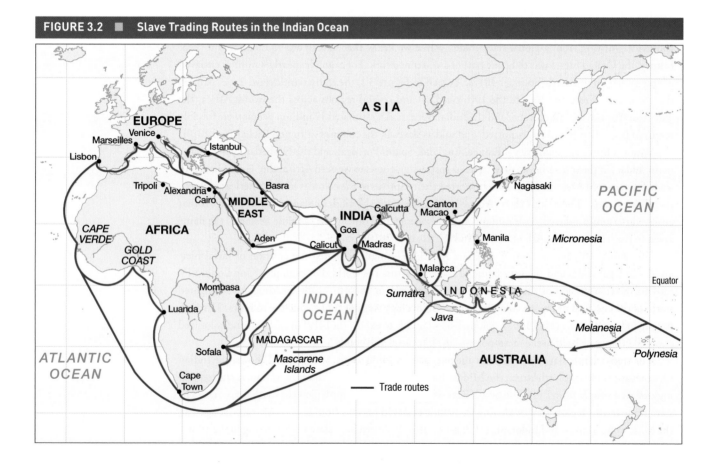

living in Micronesia, Melanesia, and Polynesia) to work on Australian plantations (Higginbotham 2017). This practice ended in about 1904 with the enactment of a 1901 law that called for the deportation of all kidnapped islanders after 1906.

Exhibiting White Supremacy on a Global Stage

Throughout the colonial period, images of and stories about explorers and colonists' encounters with "inferior" and "exotic" races made their way to the general public.

> The progress of the great white explorer-adventurers and the encounters with the Black African exotic was charted, recorded and depicted in maps and drawings, etchings and (especially) the new photography, in newspaper illustrations and accounts, diaries, travel writing, learned treatises, official reports and "boy's-own" adventure novels. (Hall 1997, 240).

From Paris to Amsterdam, from Rio de Janeiro to Chicago, colonizers regularly exhibited and objectified Indigenous and other people of color for popular consumption. These exhibitions promoted European empires, by showing off what they gained through colonialism. They reinforced the idea of White supremacy by presenting colonial subjects as "other" and inferior in relation to Europeans.

On the London stage in the early 1800s, Piccadilly Circus paraded Sara "Saartjie" Baartman, a South African Khoikhoi woman sold into slavery by Dutch colonists. She allegedly signed a contract with an English man, William Dunlop, to be exhibited. Baartman was displayed to expose her "exaggerated" physical features like her buttocks (Hall 1997). In the 1889 Parisian World Fair, the Paris park department led by Jean-Charles Alphand exhibited about 400 individuals in the "Negro village" (Bancel, Blanchard, and Lemaire 2000). King Leopold II's 1897 Brussels International Exposition featured 267 Congolese people in a human zoo "living" in a replica of a Congolese village. These crude displays reinforced notions of European cultural and racial supremacy. Such representations also reinforced standards of beauty that elevated Western aesthetics and body types.

DOING SOCIOLOGY 3.2

Removing Colonial Symbols

In this exercise you will consider the merits of getting rid of statues of colonialists on campuses to challenge the dominant view of history and institutional racism in higher education.

The toppling of colonial figures and symbols of slavery in the 2020 Black Lives Matter protests around the world is reminiscent of earlier protests in South Africa. Students in South Africa led the "Rhodes Must Fall" campaign in 2015 to question the perception of colonial history and challenge institutional racism in higher education. It started at the University of Cape Town and quickly spread to other South African universities. The movement called for the removal of the statue in honor of Cecil Rhodes, the British imperialist businessman who was prime minister of the Cape Colony (present-day South Africa) in the 1890s. Rhodes's imperialism was heavily underpinned by racism:

> *I contend that we are the finest race in the world and that the more of the world we inhabit the better it is for the human race. Just fancy those parts that are at present inhabited by the most despicable specimens of human beings what an alteration there would be if they were brought under Anglo-Saxon influence.* (Rhodes quoted in Flint 1974)

With a partner or individually, answer the following questions in writing:

1. Do you think the presence of statues and buildings in honor of White colonialists is a problem? Why or why not?

2. What do you think is achieved by removing these symbols of colonialism?

3. What additional measures, if any, would support this type of action—considering the goal is to end institutional forms of racism?

> ### Check Your Understanding
>
> 1. What is imperialism?
> 2. What is settler colonialism?
> 3. How was the civilizing mission used to rationalize colonization?
> 4. In what areas of the world were enslaved people of color kidnapped and traded across oceans?
> 5. Why did colonialists exhibit colonial subjects?

LEGACIES OF COLONIAL RACISM

Colonialism has had a lasting impact on former colonies, shaping postindependence relationships with former colonizers. It also created forms of racism and racial hierarchies that still affect people across the world today. This section examines some of the ways colonial racism persists.

Enduring Postcolonial Racial Categories

Colonial empires came crumbling down as waves of independence hit the Americas in the 19th century and countries in the Middle East, Asia, and Africa, during the 20th century. In many colonies in the Americas, rebellions and independence movements challenged the authority and power of their colonizers, Spain and France. For example, Bolivia gained independence from Spain after a long war from 1809 to 1825. Decolonization during the 20th century started during the period between the two world wars. After World War II, most of the remaining colonies in Africa and Asia became independent because of growing calls for self-determination with the creation of the United Nations (UN) and the adoption of the UN Declaration of Human Rights in 1948. For example, Morocco, a French protectorate in North Africa, gained independence in 1956. During the Cold War, the United States and the Soviet Union supported colonies seeking independence to try to ensure the spread of their respective ideologies (U.S. democracy versus Soviet communism) and their interests in newly independent nations (Office of the Historian 2019).

Structural inequalities created by imperialism did not dissipate when colonies became independent nations, however. For example, in India, the British colonists classified different castes and cultural, social, and ethnic groups as either martial or nonmartial races, based on their perceived capacity for fighting and loyalty to the British. They gave those designated as "martial" higher status in colonial Indian society. After India gained independence from Britain these distinctions continued, with groups—such as some Hindu nationalist movements—using the "martial races" distinction to try to gain power (Mahmud 1999).

In some South and Central American countries such as Colombia, Ecuador, and Brazil, the once colonized people tried to dismantle the colonial legacy of racism. In these countries, postindependence nation-building focused on race mixing (*mestizaje/mestiçagem*) to move beyond the strict racial classifications imposed by colonial regimes (Telles and Bailey 2013; Wade 2017). Race-mixing focused on blurring the stark distinctions and inequalities inherent in racial hierarchies by promoting multiracial relationships between groups. These "ideas of mestizaje often began as elite-led projects to unite the frequently divided and scattered Black, Indigenous, White, and mixed-race populations during the nation-making periods throughout the 19th and into the 20th centuries" (Telles and Bailey 2013, 1560).

Racial inequalities persisted (and continue to persist), however. Sociologists and historians explain that, in practice, racial mixing was often a cover for Whitening—the promotion of lighter skin to the detriment of darker skin. In other cases, certain types of racial mixture were promoted over others (e.g., promoting mixing with Indigenous groups rather than with Afro-descendants) (Telles and Bailey 2013; Wade 2010).

In South Africa, which had first been a Dutch and then later a British colony, racial hierarchies took even stronger root *after* South Africa became a sovereign state in 1931. To retain its power, the ruling White minority party (approximately 20% of the population) introduced apartheid, a segregation regime. The 1950 Population Registration Act classified people into four racial categories: White, Black, Colored, and Indian. This legal subjugation of people of color dictated interpersonal relationships, barring interracial marriages and sexual relationships (Prohibition of Mixed Marriages Act 1949; Immorality Amendment Act 1950) and severely restricted the participation of non-Whites in economic and social areas (Black Building Workers Act 1951; Coloured Persons Education Act 1963).

PHOTO 3.4 Comedian, writer, and host of *The Daily Show*, Trevor Noah describes his childhood in South Africa under apartheid. Due to apartheid legislation, his very birth was the result of a "crime."

GP Images/WireImage

Rehousing policies forcibly relocated 3.5 million people of color from 1960 to 1983. Once the government removed Black South Africans from their land, it sold the land to White South Africans at low prices. The government also banned Black South Africans from entering White sections of cities without a permit (South Africa: Overcoming Apartheid n.d.).

Social movements within South Africa and sanctions from the international community helped make apartheid untenable. In the early 1990s, then president F. W. de Klerk took legal steps to dismantle the apartheid system. He released political prisoners like Nelson Mandela and other members of the African National Congress (ANC) and negotiated a new constitution with Black leaders before calling an election in 1994. Despite these dramatic changes, however, structural inequalities established by apartheid continue to impact South African people of color. As Kenny Tokwe, a South African community organizer, says, "South Africa is still a country of two nations: the rich Whites"—he points down the hill—"and the poor Blacks." Tokwe spent his younger years fighting for equal rights for South African Blacks. Today, at 58, he now spends his time trying to get them the basics of life—like a job, decent housing, and access to toilets and sewers (Baker 2019).

PHOTO 3.5 Warning sign that reads "Caution Beware of Natives" in 1956 Johannesburg. These signs were common and helped foment White fear and hostility toward people of color.

Ejor/Getty Images

CONSIDER THIS

Why do you think racial discrimination persists in once colonized but now independent nations?

Colorism and White Standards of Beauty

The centuries-long legal and social institutionalization of racial hierarchies across the globe has had a lasting impact on culture, media, and social interactions. One example is the preference of so-called "Western" standards of beauty. Hierarchies based on skin color are a biproduct of colonialism.

Colorism, a concept we discuss in greater detail in later chapters, is one example of this. It involves prejudice and discrimination against people with darker skin. Women in the Philippines report using skin-whitening products because employers prefer to hire people with lighter skin. As one sociologist explains, "The idea is that your skin tone is directly correlated with some economic value or some social or political value. . . . The lighter you are, the more economic value you have, the better jobs are available to you, the more money you'll make, the better education opportunities are, the better your dating and marriage opportunities are. Skin tone isn't just about skin; it's about class" (Rondilla as quoted in Lebsack 2019).

From South America to Southeast Asia, Western standards of beauty dominate, prioritizing physical features found predominantly in White populations. In 2016, the fair-skin beauty industry was worth $450 million, with the Fair & Lovely skin cream (and its male-targeted counterpart Fair & Handsome) dominating the industry. The industry is projected to reach $24 billion by the end of 2027 ("Skin Lightening" 2018). Such products prey on the long-established idea that lightening your skin can lead to a better life. In Nigeria, similar products, such as the brand Whitenicious launched by Cameroonian artist Dencia and endorsed by American celebrity businesswoman Blac Chyna, are also popular (Banerji 2016; Muzenda 2018). Companies and individuals can profit from perpetuating the notion that lighter skin is better.

Beauty standards that prioritize Western and White physiques play a dual role here. They reinforce racial hierarchies in people's everyday lives in a subtle way, negatively shaping how racialized minorities are seen and how they perceive themselves. As Mamie and Kenneth Clark's famous 1940s "doll test" and more recent iterations of this study show us, children internalize the idea that Whiteness and lighter skin color is better than darker skin (Clark and Clark 1940). This can then impact their perceptions of self-worth and capabilities, which in turn can lessen their chances at leading successful lives.

DOING SOCIOLOGY 3.3

Colorism in Hollywood

In this exercise, you will think about the effects of colorism and ways to end it.

Lupita Nyong'o is a Kenyan Mexican actress who rose to fame for her work in *12 Years a Slave, Black Panther,* and *Star Wars*. In 2015, she delivered a speech at *Essence* magazine's 7th annual Black Women in Hollywood Luncheon. In the speech, she reads part of a letter from a girl who was considering buying skin-lightening cream until she became aware of Nyong'o, who is both dark-skinned and successful. Nyong'o reflects on the painful experience of living in a society that prizes pale complexions, explaining that she used to pray for lighter skin. This changed when she learned about Aleck Weck, a dark-skinned fashion model who was widely praised for her beauty. Nyong'o felt "more seen, more appreciated by the faraway gatekeepers of beauty" as a result.

1. Based on your understanding of colorism and colonialism, reflect on the lasting effects of colonial racism on contemporary ideas of beauty. Write down your reflections and relate them to Lupita Nyong'o's experiences in one or two paragraphs.

2. Share your reflection with a partner and come up with one or two possible ways to end colorism. Be prepared to share your ideas with the rest of the class.

Postwar Migration Perpetuating Colonial Dynamics

At the same time colonialism was fading after WWII, much of western Europe needed laborers to rebuild economies and cities destroyed by the war. Turning to newly independent states and current colonies, European nations encouraged migration to fulfill this need for workers. The United Kingdom, for example, recruited migrants from other European countries, commonwealth countries, and former British colonies in the Caribbean, India, and Pakistan.

This global postwar migration led to higher numbers of racialized ex-colonial subjects living and working in former colonial powers. The colonizer–colonized relationship was no longer dictated by the formal legal colonial arrangements, but racism persisted. For example, the French model of integrating these migrants was assimilation—including the acceptance of social institutions (e.g., education) that perpetuate colonial ideas of cultural racism (Tévanian and Bouamama 2017).

When Black Lives Matter (BLM) protests erupted in the United States in 2020, after the death of George Floyd while in police custody, BLM protests also took place in countries around the world. Some were in solidarity against police brutality and racism in the United States. Others focused on the racism and inequity in their own countries. BLM protestors decried this racism and challenged the colonial legacies that remain in former colonies, toppling down statues and symbols of colonialism and slavery like the statues of notorious slave trader Edward Colston in Bristol, United Kingdom, and King Leopold II, the brutal colonial ruler of the Congo Free State, in Belgium.

Check Your Understanding

1. What happened to racial hierarchies after colonization? In what ways did they persist?

2. What was apartheid in South Africa?

3. How are contemporary forms of colorism rooted in colonialism?

4. What are three impacts of colorism?

CONTEMPORARY EXAMPLES OF SYSTEMIC RACISM AROUND THE WORLD

Today, systemic racism persists in many parts of the world. While some examples are rooted in colonial racism, others have evolved from different dynamics relating to migratory patterns, conflicts, natural disasters, and changing power formations between countries. This section explores some manifestations of systemic or institutionalized racism in examples from around the world.

Education

Race and ethnicity can affect educational opportunities at all levels. In Latin America and the Caribbean, Afro-descendants and non-Afro-descendants have unequal access to education at all levels (see Figure 3.3).

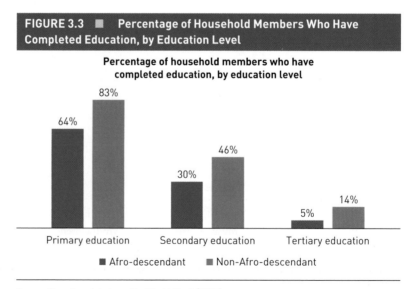

FIGURE 3.3 ■ Percentage of Household Members Who Have Completed Education, by Education Level

Percentage of household members who have completed education, by education level

- Primary education: Afro-descendant 64%, Non-Afro-descendant 83%
- Secondary education: Afro-descendant 30%, Non-Afro-descendant 46%
- Tertiary education: Afro-descendant 5%, Non-Afro-descendant 14%

■ Afro-descendant   ■ Non-Afro-descendant

Source: Based on data from the World Bank (2018).

Politics

Political participation is a crucial element of civic life, and there are few opportunities to gain and wield power without it. Exclusion or marginalization from political life is particularly problematic for racial or ethnic minorities. For example, Roma people, a historically itinerant group, have faced severe discrimination and prejudice in many European countries. In central and eastern Europe, Roma populations are significant but largely erased due to their absence from official registers or the census. This negatively impacts this population's ability to participate in elections, which in turn impedes their ability to influence policy and funding (Open Society Foundations 2019). According to Open Society Foundations (2019), "The Roma face high rates of illiteracy, infant mortality, unemployment, substandard healthcare, and segregation in education."

Health

As mentioned in Chapter 2, racism also contributes to poor health outcomes in disadvantaged racial populations. In Australia, Indigenous people—people of Aboriginal and Torres Strait Islander descent—face disparate health outcomes compared to non-Indigenous populations. Health data from the Australian state of Victoria indicate that institutionalized and individual-level racism negatively impact the health outcomes of all Indigenous people in the state—no matter their economic class or lifestyle (Markwick, Ansari, Clinch, and McNeil 2019).

Around the world, the COVID-19 global pandemic has affected communities of color and racialized groups the most. The United Nations High Commissioner for Human Rights Michelle Bachelet has called on nations to address the systemic racial inequity in health that has led to these disparities. For example, in Sao Paulo, Brazil, and in French and British cities, people of color have a much greater chance of dying from the coronavirus than do White people (OHCHR 2020).

Housing

Race also impacts where and how you live. As Figure 3.4 shows, in Latin America and Caribbean cities people of African descent are more likely to live in slums than other groups. People living in slums often lack access to clean water, adequate sanitation, and secure dwellings (UN Habitat n.d.).

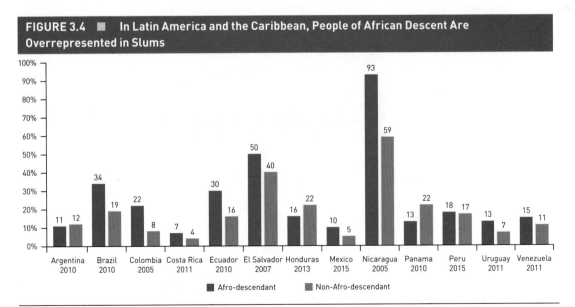

FIGURE 3.4 ■ In Latin America and the Caribbean, People of African Descent Are Overrepresented in Slums

Note: The definition of slums is a simplified version of the UN-Habitat definition, determined by the absences of at least one basic public service (water, electricity, sanitation) in urban areas and/or the presence of dirt floors in the household as a proxy for poor construction materials.

Source: The World Bank. 2018. Afro-descendants in Latin America: Toward a Framework of Inclusion. Washington, DC: World Bank. Licensed through Creative Commons Attribution CC BY 3.0 IGO.

CONSIDER THIS

Aside from inferior housing, sanitation, and water services, how can racism in housing affect people's lives?

According to a World Bank (2018) report, people living in slums also face higher levels of violence and crime. In Brazil, people of African descent, who are overrepresented in urban slums (see Figure 3.4), are 75% more likely to be victims of homicide and violence.

Islamophobia

Islamophobia—the hate, fear, or discrimination of Muslims or people that appear Muslim—has been on the rise in the last two decades. There is a tendency to essentialize Islam and Muslims despite the huge variance across the world, reducing both to one idea. Muslims are lumped together as if there was only one way of Muslim thinking. Often, politicians and social commentators racialize Muslims by associating negative characteristics to the entire Muslim population and assuming they are due to their biological makeup.

In recent years, we have seen a variety of violent attacks and hate crimes against Muslims throughout the world. For example, in January 2017, Islamophobia drove two separate but related attacks on mosques in Cape Town, South Africa (al Jazeera 2017). On March 15, 2019, a gunman murdered 51 worshippers in two mosques in Christchurch, New Zealand. In the Chinese province of Xinjiang, the government represses Uighurs (a predominantly Muslim ethnic group) under the guise of counterterrorism. Since 2014, it has detained more than a million Muslim Uighurs and other Muslim ethnic groups in reeducation camps (Schifrin and Sagalyn 2019). Although China presents the camps as educational facilities, officially referring to them as "Vocational Education and Training Centers," they are internment camps where they try to brainwash Muslims to turn against their religion, as well as monitor and control this population. The international community and human rights organizations have criticized the continued internment of Muslims in China (Sudworth 2019; Tazamal 2019).

PHOTO 3.6 Islamophobic graffiti in Warsaw, Poland, February 2018.

Jaap Arriens/NurPhoto via Getty Images

Islamophobia is also present in several western European countries, where Muslims are viewed as a threat against European ideas and ways of life. Anti-Muslim sentiment intensified with the 2015 refugee crisis that led millions of Middle Easterners (Syrians, Afghans, and Iraqis) to seek refuge in Europe from violence and wars in their countries. As we discuss more in Chapter 11, even though not all Middle Easterners are Muslims, many Europeans conflate Islam and Arabs and the Middle East.

Even before this more recent crisis, first- and second-generation Muslim migrant populations in western Europe experienced racism and Islamophobia due to the perception that they are unable to integrate into the Western world. Over the last decade, these ideas have manifested in the increasing calls for banning symbols of Islam from public life, specifically focusing on the attire of Muslim women. For example, laws ban niqabs and burqas (which cover the entire body and face) in Belgium, Bulgaria, and Sri Lanka. France and Austria have banned hijabs (which typically cover women's hair) in certain school settings, citing general laws prohibiting obvious religious symbols. Studies indicate that the 2004 French ban of headscarves in schools has negatively impacted the educational outcomes of young Muslim women, leading some to drop out of school or take longer to complete their secondary studies. This has a domino effect that hinders their economic and social integration (Abdelgadir and Fouka 2019).

Xenophobia

Another form of racism is xenophobia: the fear, dislike, or hatred of people from other countries. Xenophobia and racism overlap in many ways, but the former does not always rely on physical characteristics in the same way that racism usually does. Xenophobia focuses more on nationality, culture, ethnicity, or religious practices. Migration flows and economic insecurity can exacerbate xenophobic sentiments, as we have seen in South Africa and the United Kingdom. In South Africa, where the economy is weak and unemployment is high, citizens have grown frustrated by migrant workers coming to South Africa for economic opportunities—opportunities that they are struggling to acquire (BBC 2019). Meanwhile the heated debate over Brexit (the withdrawal of Great Britain from the European Union) stoked hatred for immigrants and second-generation immigrants (Reuters 2019).

In some cases, such as in the Dominican Republic, there is a clear overlap between xenophobia and racism. Antihaitianismo *refers to Dominicans' dislike and opposition to Haiti and Haitians.* Antihaitianismo reflects colonial tensions and racialized differences between the two countries that share the island of Hispaniola in the West Indies. In the first half of the 20th century, Dominican dictator Rafael Trujillo massacred thousands of Haitians in his attempts to Whiten the Dominican population by getting rid of the generally darker-skinned Haitians. More recently, in 2015, Dominican politicians amended the constitution to strip children born to Haitian parents of their Dominican citizenship. Since the change in the constitution, the Dominican government has deported tens of thousands of Haitians. Moreover, racist narratives against Haitians in the media and political discourse have fanned the hostility between the two groups (Hall 2017).

DOING SOCIOLOGY 3.4

Losing Your Identity

In this exercise, you will consider how racial appearance affects the lives of people in the Dominican Republic.

Keeping in mind what you just read about antihaitianismo, think about the following questions and write your responses:

1. What is your reaction to what you have learned about the overlap between xenophobia and racism that exists in the Dominican Republic?

2. How do you think the racial appearance of people in the Dominican Republic affects their lives?

3. Imagine you are a lifelong citizen in the nation where you are living. You wake up one day to find your government has taken away your family's citizenship. How would you feel? Would it change how you perceive yourself? How others relate to you?

Indigenous Populations

Settler colonialism devastated Indigenous populations everywhere. The racism and discrimination that Indigenous populations experience today is rooted in the colonial racism that framed encounters between colonialists and Indigenous people throughout the colonial eras. The influence of the institutions and racial attitudes persists today.

In Canada, First Nations people—the Indigenous populations—face stereotyping, stigmatization, violence, and systemic racism. For example, "Indian reserves" receive insufficient funding, resulting in their inhabitants experiencing high levels of poverty. Indigenous people in Canada also experience racial bias and overrepresentation in the criminal justice system (National Collaborating Centre for Aboriginal Health 2014; Wylie and McConkey 2019).

In Australia, Aboriginal and Torres Strait Islander people face inequalities that impact all areas of their lives, including health outcomes (discussed earlier) and access to employment and education (Australian Institute of Health and Welfare 2017; National Agreement on Closing the Gap 2020).

Likewise, Indigenous people in Latin America confront disadvantages due to historical patterns of oppression stemming from colonialism: "They have faced serious discrimination not only in terms of their basic rights to ancestral property, languages, cultures, and forms of governance, but also in terms of their access to basic social services (education, health and nutrition, water and sanitation, and housing) and the essential material conditions for a satisfying life" (Gigler 2015, 88).

New Apartheid Regimes

The international community has explicitly denounced legal segregation based on race or ethnicity. Nonetheless, it remains a problem in many parts of the world. For example, Israel's treatment of Palestinians and other Arabs exemplifies apartheid because of how the state of Israel marginalizes them both in practice and through their laws and legal system. In Israel, Arab citizens face systemic racism and discrimination in areas such as employment, education, and housing (Committee on the Elimination of Racial Discrimination 2012; Dugard 2019; Falk 2014).

> ### Check Your Understanding
>
> 1. What are examples of systemic racism's impact?
>
> 2. Why is Islamophobia considered a form of racism?
>
> 3. What is xenophobia?
>
> 4. How do Indigenous populations experience racism?
>
> 5. What is an example of a new apartheid regime?

RACIALIZED GLOBAL DYNAMICS

When thinking about systems of racism from a global perspective, it is imperative to go outside country-specific examples. By looking at relationships among countries, as well as global migration patterns or international humanitarian efforts, we can identify different ways in which race shapes inequalities. This also involves thinking about differential power arrangements on a global level.

International Movement of People

People leave their home countries for many reasons; some seek economic opportunities, and others need refuge from oppression, conflict, or disasters. Migration is not easy, however, and, increasingly, wealthier countries are tightening and expanding restrictions on who they let into their nations. The resulting migratory patterns of populations reveal different forms of racist systems operating on a global stage.

Migrant Workers

Anti-immigrant rhetoric in the West portrays migrants as unnecessary burdens—people who come to take jobs and resources away from nationals. Yet many countries, like the United Arab Emirates (UAE), actively seek migrants to fill gaps in their workforce. Countries like the UAE that seek workers often set up special visas and conditions for migrant laborers. The UAE and Qatar, for example, recruit migrant workers from Southeast Asia mainly to meet the needs of specific industries (e.g., construction, domestic labor). They live and work under extremely controlled conditions that human rights organizations criticize (ADHRB 2019). Many domestic workers in the UAE reported to Human Rights Watch that their employers took away their passports, exploited their labor, and some even physically abused them. Some countries (Qatar, UAE, and Saudi Arabia) have improved regulations for domestic work, but abuse and mistreatment continue (Human Rights Watch 2014; Secorun 2018).

Fortress Europe and the Global Refugee Crisis

Anti-immigrant sentiment in the United Kingdom results in many disturbing episodes. For example, the UK government had denied services and even deported people with the right to live in the United Kingdom through its "hostile environment" policy targeting undocumented migrants. After World War II, the United Kingdom recruited workers from commonwealth countries, former British colonies still politically affiliated to the United Kingdom, to help rebuild Britain. The term *Windrush Generation* describes the children of these migrant workers who came to the United Kingdom between 1948 and 1971 (most people of color from former British colonies in the Caribbean). Suddenly, in 2013, the UK government required them to prove that they had a legal right to remain in the United Kingdom or face deportation. Many had no way to do so through no fault of their own. They had traveled on their parents' passports, so they did not have any official paperwork, and the government had not kept adequate records. Eighty-three of the Windrush Generation were forced to leave the United Kingdom (BBC 2018).

PHOTO 3.7 In June 1948, the *Empire Windrush* docks in England with Jamaicans onboard, arriving to contribute to postwar efforts and start a new life.

Keystone/Getty Images

This deportation policy in the United Kingdom is but one example of managed migration, an attempt to restrict migration. Migrants receive a description as either good (welcome) or bad (unwelcome). The EU has attempted to guard its external borders from "bad" migrants coming from the Middle East and Africa with a variety of tactics, including erecting over 600 miles of walls and asking countries that border the EU, like Libya or Morocco, to keep migrants away from EU nations and help thwart efforts by migrants to reach EU countries by boat (Stone 2018). Human rights organizations have documented attacks, discrimination, and general hostilities against migrants in these border countries (GADEM 2018). As seen in Table 3.1, many migrants die at sea before they can even reach Europe, and some countries, such as Italy, have closed ports to migrants and prevented nonprofit organizations from attempting to rescue refugees at sea (Lang 2019).

TABLE 3.1 ■ Total Arrivals by Sea and Deaths in the Mediterranean, 2018–2019				
	January 1–September 11, 2018		January 1–September 11, 2019	
Country of Arrival	Arrivals	Deaths	Arrivals	Deaths
Italy	23,370	1,260 (Central Mediterranean route)	5,852	642 (Central Mediterranean route)
Malta	714		2,252	
Greece	20,961	106 (Eastern Mediterranean route)	30,775	58 (Eastern Mediterranean route)
Cyprus	211		1,241	
Spain	32,272	462 (Western Mediterranean route)	15,798	229 (Western Mediterranean route)
Estimated Total	77,528	1,828	55,918	929

Source: International Organization for Migration (IOM) 2019. https://www.iom.int/news/mediterranean-migrant-arrivals-reach-55918-2019-deaths-reach-929.

People seek asylum (refugee status) in another country because of wars, natural disasters, or the fear of persecution. International human rights and humanitarian law grants individuals the right to seek asylum, but by preventing the arrival of would-be refugees, European immigration policy is limiting even the possibility of applying. In 2015, when millions of migrants from the war-torn nations of Iraq, Syria, and Afghanistan tried to get to Europe, a few nations (e.g., Germany) opened their doors while others shut them, and others restricted migrants' rights and movements. Today, many of those migrants are stuck on the Greek island of Lesbos, living in refugee camps under terrible conditions. Across Europe we see increasing numbers of attacks on migrants, particularly those deemed by most nations as "unwelcome" (i.e., Muslims and people of color). Many sociologists have studied the migrant crisis and worked to help address it. Alana Lentin, the sociologist in action featured in this chapter, describes some of her own work on the issue.

CONSIDER THIS

Do you think wealthier countries have a responsibility to accept refugees fleeing disasters and conflict? Why or why not?

SOCIOLOGISTS IN ACTION
Alana Lentin

Transnational Activism, Democratizing Knowledge

PHOTO 3.8

© Alana Lentin

When I first moved to Australia, I was involved in organizing campaigns to increase divestment from the asylum and detention industry. The most successful action that I helped organize was a boycott of the international art festival, the Sydney Biennale, because of its links to Transfield Services, a company profiting from the indefinite detention of refugees and asylum seekers on the islands of Manus and Nauru. The call for the boycott came from the artists themselves. I was part of a collective that provided research to help them in that process. The boycott was successful. In the wake of it, the chair of the board of the Biennale of Sydney, whose family had founded Transfield and were profiting from the detention industry, resigned. We also managed to raise awareness of how some NGOs make money through the pain of would-be migrants.

As a White Jewish woman, I have always seen myself as playing a backup role in antiracism work. For example, when I lived in Italy, I was very involved in the struggles of migrants there. My role was behind the scenes, however, as somebody who had certain resources, access to certain spaces, and sometimes money. I provide that help to support the work migrants themselves are doing.

As somebody who has migrated, worked, and taught in different locations, I can be a kind of interpreter for those seeking information about racial justice issues. For example, I talk to them through social media, such as my blogs. The era of digital communication helps us reach a wider audience more quickly, and we are able to have more direct conversations with people. I think social media works to democratize knowledge.

I am currently the president of the Australian Critical Race and Whiteness Studies Association. We ask how we can make use of concepts like intersectionality and critical race theory outside of a U.S. context, where they were developed in a particular legal context. Colleagues in the association organized a "Critical Race Hackathon," bringing together activists, students, and scholars. The goal behind it was to make sociological concepts about race and racism relevant for the particular places and contexts in which we are located. It was very successful. The participants came up with an online glossary that we can add to over time. Other people who like the idea can replicate it in other spaces. We're doing it in Australia, but people across the world can join in this effort to build up this repository of knowledge.

Alana Lentin is associate professor in cultural and social analysis at Western Sydney University.

Discussion Question

What do you think of the efforts of participants in the Critical Race Hackathon? Before reading this piece, had you ever thought about the need to make sociological concepts useful in a variety of places and contexts? Why?

Global Powers and Racist Stereotypes

In January 2017, President Trump enacted a Muslim ban restricting the travel of people from five predominantly Muslim countries (Libya, Iran, Somalia, Syria, and Yemen), along with North Korea and Venezuela, to the United States. On January 11, 2018, President Trump reportedly asked in a White House meeting on immigration and the temporary protected status of immigrants from El Salvador, Haiti, and African nations, "Why are we having all these people from shithole countries come here?"

(Kendi 2019). When French president Emmanuelle Macron discussed the issues plaguing Africa, he stated it is a "civilizational" problem (Attiah 2017). This type of discourse and legal restrictions against people from certain countries emphasizes that there is still a strict hierarchy splitting the "West" and the "rest." These statements by leading political figures also recall colonial racial hierarchies.

DOING SOCIOLOGY 3.5

What You Know About Africa

Despite Western discourses on the inferiority and homogeneity of Africans, there is incredible variation among the cultures, groups, religions, and people on the continent of Africa. In this exercise you will reflect on what you know about the African continent.

1. List five African countries. For each nation you list, write down a few sentences or phrases relating to what you know about it.

2. How do you rate your own knowledge of Africa?

3. Where does your knowledge of Africa come from? In general, does it confirm or challenge common stereotypes?

4. Why is it important to learn about Africa from the perspective of Africans? How should Americans broaden their knowledge of Africa?

Check Your Understanding

1. Why do migrants leave their homes?

2. What have some European countries done to limit immigration?

3. What is managed migration?

4. What are some discourses about immigrants and other countries that reinforce hierarchies of people?

CONCLUSION

This chapter provides an overview of systemic racism in the world today and how it affects racialized people. Not only can racism impact people's access to opportunities and services within social institutions, but it also affects the relationships of people across nations and people in movement. These racisms are not left without responses, however, and activists and practitioners challenge these forms of oppressions in numerous ways, as we describe in later chapters. The next chapter examines racism in U.S. social institutions.

CHAPTER REVIEW

3.1   How is race socially constructed?

From a global perspective, race is socially constructed according to the respective historical and geographical context. Other countries do not conceptualize race in the same way as does the United States. In some countries, race and ethnicity are not acceptable forms of categorizing individuals into groups. An individual's experience of race will change depending on when and where they live.

3.2 How did imperialism and colonialism enshrine racial hierarchies?

Imperialism and colonialism have played a crucial role in establishing racial hierarchies. Colonialism took different forms, but settler colonialism, in particular, solidified racial hierarchies around the world, with White people on top. Slavery and the civilizing mission were key components of imperialism and relied on racial hierarchies to oppress Indigenous and enslaved populations.

3.3 How are contemporary forms of racism rooted in historical forms of oppression?

The legacy of colonialism, the civilizing mission, and slavery continue to affect societies across the globe. Current issues such as segregation, colorism, and the treatment of postcolonial migration from former colonies to former colonizing countries stem from the institutions and cultures formed from those historical forces.

3.4 What are examples of systemic racism in different parts of the world?

There are many examples of systemic racism around the world today and how it impacts people's access to power, economic opportunities, and living standards. Specific types of systemic racism include Islamophobia, xenophobia, racial inequality experienced by Indigenous populations, and the establishment of apartheid regimes, such as that in Israel today.

3.5 How do transnational relationships and migration issues reflect racial dynamics?

Today, racism is pervasive in relationships among countries, especially those related to migration and asylum. Western countries restrict the movement of people to their lands, with racialized groups tending to fare worst. The dominant discourses about developing countries also reveal racist stereotypes.

KEY TERMS

Antihaitianismo (p. 53)

Apartheid (p. 47)

Assimilation (p. 42)

Blackbirding (p. 43)

Civilizing mission (p. 42)

Colonialism (p. 42)

Colorism (p. 49)

Cultural racism (p. 43)

Imperialism (p. 41)

Islamophobia (p. 52)

Managed migration (p. 56)

Racialization (p. 39)

Settler colonies (p. 42)

Universalism (p. 40)

Xenophobia (p. 53)

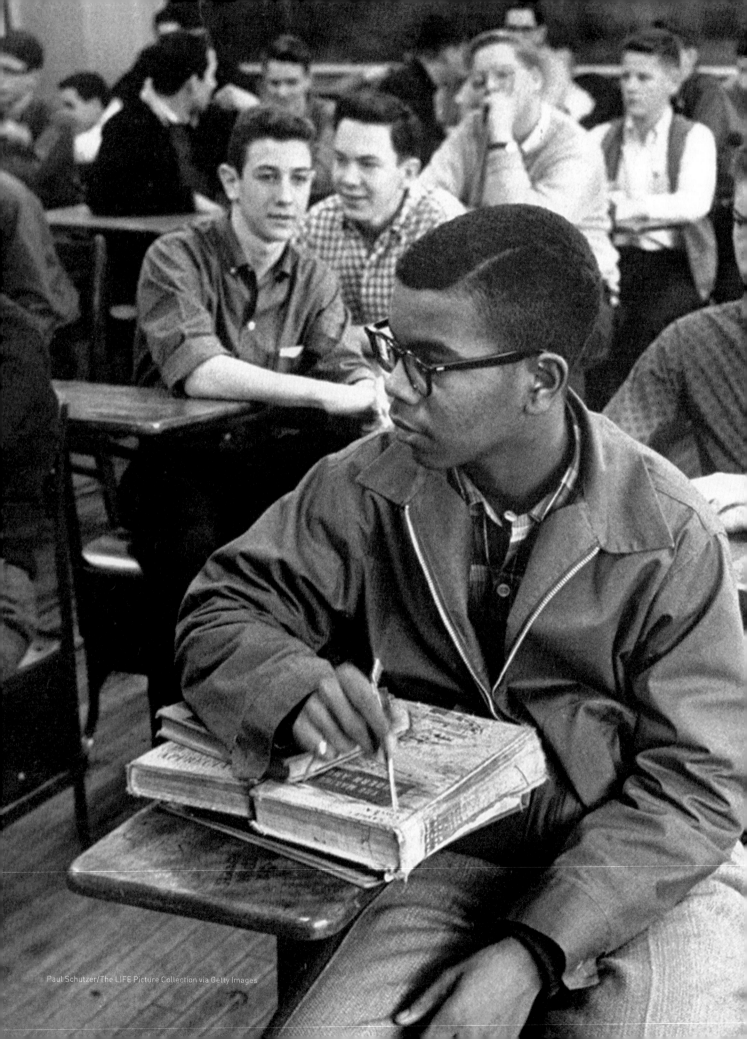

SEEING HOW SOCIAL INSTITUTIONS SUPPORT RACISM

Kathleen Odell Korgen

LEARNING QUESTIONS

4.1 What is the relationship between systemic racism and institutional power?

4.2 What are some current examples of institutional racism in the political system in the United States?

4.3 What are some examples of institutional racism in U.S. government agencies today?

4.4 How do both past-in-present and current institutional racism work to maintain economic disparities among racial groups in the United States?

4.5 How does side-effect discrimination affect racial inequality in education?

4.6 Why do Asian Americans and Pacific Islanders, when considered as one racial group, have higher education levels and incomes than other racial groups?

In a tightly contested election, a candidate trying to become the first woman governor from her disadvantaged racial group was running against a man from the advantaged racial group. The man was also the chief administrator of elections. He refused to step down from his position overseeing elections while he campaigned for the higher office.

As administrator of elections, the male candidate closed hundreds of polling places, making it harder for voters to get to a polling place. The closures also led to longer voting lines at the remaining polling places, increasing the time it took to vote and leaving many voters still in line when the time for voting ended. A majority of the polling places closed were in poor and racially disadvantaged areas of the state.

In addition, the man cut the number of days people could vote early (a popular practice among marginalized racial groups). He also purged thousands of people—almost 10% of all registered voters in the state—from the voting rolls (the official list of voters). As part of the purge, he removed citizens who had registered to vote from the voting rolls if their names on their voter registration forms were not identical matches with their names in other state databases. For example, if they used a middle initial or nickname on one and not on another state form or if an election worker misspelled their name when they registered to vote, he took them off the voting rolls. Most election workers were members of the dominant racial group, and some misspelled names unfamiliar to them but common among marginalized racial groups.

More citizens lost their places on the voting rolls due to a new "use it or lose it" policy the man created that automatically removes people from the official list of voters if they have not voted in previous elections. Still more found themselves removed from the voting rolls if they had moved since registering and not changed their address with the Board of Elections. Seventy percent of the people purged were members of the woman candidate's marginalized group, and just 20% were from the man's advantaged group (Kauffman 2018; Lockhart 2019).

When the final votes were counted, the man had garnered 50.2% of the vote and the woman 48.8%. Would the woman have won if the man had not made it more difficult for people from marginalized racial groups to vote? Many believe that she would have. However, the difference in the percentage of votes received by each of the candidates was not close enough for an automatic recount, and the man—still the chief administrator of elections—quickly declared himself the winner.

A group aligned with the woman submitted a lawsuit, claiming the election system (run by the White advantaged man) created obstacles to voting that disproportionately affected voters from marginalized racial groups (Lockhart 2019). The man, however, was sworn into office and became governor. In what year do you think this election occurred—1958, 1968, 1978, 1988, 1998, 2008, or 2018?

HOW I GOT ACTIVE IN SOCIOLOGY

Kathleen Odell Korgen

When I was a kid, I figured that racism persisted because of either bad or uneducated people. I wanted to be part of the effort to fight and defeat the bad people and educate the uneducated. After delving into sociology, I learned that we must change society—not just wayward and ignorant individuals—to eradicate racism. This entails working with others—across racial lines—to change policies that structure our society to advantage some and disadvantage others. It also requires knowing how society works. I am fortunate to have a career that allows me to use and share the tools to do so.

US INSTITUTIONS AND RACISM

The story in the introduction to this chapter is an example of institutional racism. It happened in 2018 during the governor's election in Georgia. We discussed in Chapter 2 the historical legacy of racism in the United States. But what about today? In Chapter 5, you will see how culture can support systemic racism. In this chapter, however, we focus on the role institutions play in creating and maintaining a racist society.

PHOTO 4.1 Stacey Abrams, former candidate for governor of Georgia, is founder and chair of Fair Fight Action, an organization with a mission to "ensure all voters have access to the polls."

Bill Clark/CQ Roll Call

Remember the definitions of racism and systemic racism. Racism encompasses historical, cultural, institutional, and interpersonal dynamics *that create and maintain a racial hierarchy.* Systemic racism is a set of arrangements and outcomes that provides advantages to one racial group and disadvantages others. Societies with systemic racism use institutional power to maintain racial inequality.

Social institutions consist of ways of acting encoded in laws, policies, and common practices. The major social institutions in a society (e.g., the government, family, education, and economic systems) form the structure of that society and ensure stability by organizing the ways we govern, care for, and educate people, and how we create and share goods. Institutional racism consists of discriminatory laws, policies, and practices carried out by institutions that result in racial inequity. However, as critical race theorists point out, "There is no such thing as a nonracist or race-neutral policy." They are either antiracist and promote and sustain equity, or they are racist and lead to or support inequity among racial groups (and genders, ages, etc.) (Kendi 2019, 18).

CONSIDER THIS

How can sociology help us determine whether a policy is antiracist or racist?

Some racist societies, like the United States before the civil rights movement, have laws that explicitly require institutions to provide differential treatment by race (e.g., state laws that prevented Black people from voting and Japanese immigrants from owning land). This is called *de jure* (enforced by laws) institutional discrimination. It is relatively easy to recognize racism in these societies. It is harder to notice *de facto* (based in fact but not in laws) institutional discrimination in societies without openly racist laws and policies.

Sometimes, de facto institutional discrimination is purposeful (as in the voter suppression example described at the beginning of the chapter) with policies created to hurt racially marginalized groups and help the advantaged one. In other cases, people can create racist policies without malice or conscious intention. This type of discrimination is often hard to discern—even for people working within the racist institutions. The individuals in these systems may have no desire to discriminate, but the way their institution operates (and, in turn, how they operate) leads them to help one racial group and hurt another racial group. By focusing just on what they do and ignoring the results of their actions, they overlook systemic racism.

Recognizing Institutional Discrimination and Side-Effect Discrimination

Let's look at the institution of education. Funding for public schools relies heavily on local taxes. While this system of funding schools could have been designed for reasons other than racial prejudice (e.g., to give local communities more control over the schools in their geographic area), the result is that it leads to racial inequity. When looking at funding for all school districts, researchers show that each year predominantly White school districts receive $23 billion more in funding than predominantly non-White districts with the same number of students (EdBuild 2019). Even if not directly intended, these policies are racist and serve the self-interests of the advantaged race at the expense of disadvantaged racial groups. Just like de jure discrimination, de facto institutional discrimination should and *can* be addressed. As Ibram X. Kendi (2019, 223) reminds us, "Policymakers and policies make societies and institutions, not the other way around.... Only those invested in preserving racist policymakers and policies think that racist policymakers cannot be overtaken and racist policies can't be changed."

DOING SOCIOLOGY 4.1

Reacting to De Jure vs. De Facto Racist Policies

This exercise requires you to think about why people tend not to recognize and challenge de facto systemic racist policies—even if they might oppose de jure systemic racist policies.

Answer the following questions in writing and be prepared to share your response.

1. Explain the relationship between systemic racism and institutional power.

2. Why do you think many people, particularly White people, might oppose de jure systemic racist policies but not de facto racist policies?

3. How would you respond to someone who says only intentionally racist policies should be changed? Why?

Before we can effectively address racist policies and habits of thinking, however, we must recognize them. In later chapters we discuss ways to address racism, once we can see it. In this chapter we shine a spotlight on de facto racial discrimination in the United States today by looking at three primary institutions: politics/government, the economy, and education. As you will see, racial discrimination in one institution tends to lead to inequality in others.

Check Your Understanding

1. What is the relationship between systemic racism and institutional power?

2. What are social institutions?

3. What is institutional racism?

4. How do de jure and de facto discrimination differ?

5. Why can it sometimes be difficult to recognize de facto institutional discrimination?

6. What is side-effect discrimination?

HOW DOES THE POLITICAL SYSTEM SUPPORT RACIAL DISCRIMINATION?

As you saw in the vignette that opened the chapter, the political system today allows states to enact laws and policies that result in advantages for Whites and disadvantages for people of color during elections. As discussed in Chapter 2, however, the Voting Rights Act of 1965 prohibited laws and policies that prevented people of color from voting. So, why is such institutional racism allowed today?

Weakening the Voting Rights Act

Sections 4 and 5 of the Voting Rights Act note the states and local governments that had previously enacted laws and policies that suppressed the votes of marginalized racial groups. These "covered jurisdictions" were Alabama, Alaska, Georgia, Louisiana, Mississippi, South Carolina, Virginia, and certain parts of Arizona, Hawaii, Idaho, and North Carolina. The act mandated that, going forward, these local and state governments must ask for and receive permission from the federal government before making changes in their voting laws or policies that could affect disadvantaged racial groups.

In 2013, however, in deciding the case of *Shelby County v. Holder*, the Supreme Court overturned Section 4 of the Voting Rights Act that indicates which states and locales are covered. In the 5–4 decision, the Court declared that the formula used to determine which areas must receive federal permission to change their election laws needed updating. The majority of the Supreme Court justices reasoned that the United States of 2013 was not the same society as the United States of 1965. Chief

Justice John Roberts wrote that the system to determine what states were covered under the act is "based on 40-year-old facts having no logical relationship to the present day" (Liptak 2013). He and the other four majority justices maintained that racism had diminished in those areas, and there was no longer a need to protect marginalized groups from attempts to suppress their votes.

Today's Style of Voter Suppression

After the Supreme Court ruling, many states—including all of those covered by the Voting Rights Act of 1965—began to create laws and policies that placed restrictions on voting that disproportionately affect people of color. These states are led by the Republican Party.

Examine Figure 4.1. What is the relationship between political affiliation and race and ethnicity?

PHOTO 4.2 Supporters of the Voting Rights Act listen to speakers discussing the Supreme Court's 2013 ruling on the act.

Win McNamee/Getty Images

Which political party benefits if the votes of marginalized racial groups are suppressed? Who is likely to win more elections if there are fewer Black and Hispanic votes?

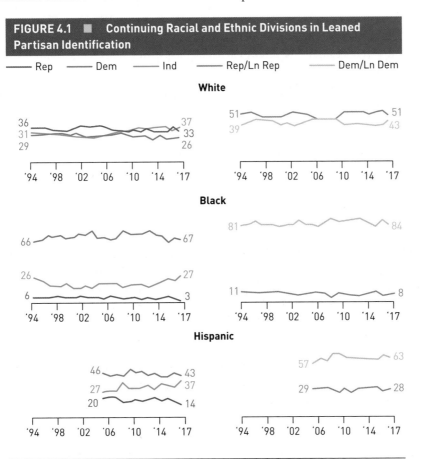

FIGURE 4.1 ■ Continuing Racial and Ethnic Divisions in Leaned Partisan Identification

Note: Based on registered voters. Whites and blacks include only those who are not Hispanic; Hispanics are of any race. Data for Hispanics shown only for years in which interviews were conducted in both English and Spanish.

Source: "Continuing racial and ethnic divisions in leaned partisan identification." Pew Research Center, Washington, D.C. (MARCH 20, 2018). https://www.pewresearch.org/politics/2018/03/20/1-trends-in-party-affiliation-among-demographic-groups/2_3-14/.

Voter identification laws that require voters to present identification before they can vote are the most popular form of voter suppression today. Just like many of the laws that prevented Black people from voting before the Voting Rights Act of 1965, these laws and policies apply to all voters, but in practice they hurt marginalized racial groups and benefit the advantaged group. For example, in states with voter ID laws, White citizens are more likely to have the required ID than other voters (Ansolabehere and Hersh 2017). A study in Texas revealed that Hispanics (5.7%) were more likely and Blacks (7.5%) were more than twice as likely as Whites (3.6%) to have IDs that don't match those in state or federal identification databases or no form of identification at all (Ansolabehere and Hersh 2017).

To gain support for new voter suppression laws and policies, state leaders use the false claim that they are needed to combat rampant voter fraud. The fact, however, is that in-person voter fraud, what voter ID laws are designed to deter (when people who are unregistered or from outside a voting precinct pretend to be a registered voter in that precinct so that they can vote), is very rare. For example, the state board of elections in North Carolina conducted an investigation in 2016 to determine the extent of in-person voter fraud in their state. The result? They found just one credible case among every 4.8 million votes cast (Campbell 2017). Studies also indicate little risk for fraud when citizens mail in their ballots, as many people did during the pandemic. Fortunately, "there is no evidence that mail ballots increase electoral fraud" (West 2020).

The fact that voter fraud is almost nonexistent has not stopped some politicians from using this myth as an excuse to enact voter identification laws that advantage Whites and disadvantage people of color. While talking on a conservative radio show, the Republican attorney general of Wisconsin described the effect voter ID laws had in the 2016 election when he said, "How many of your listeners really honestly are sure that Senator [Ron] Johnson [a Republican] was going to win reelection or President Trump was going to win Wisconsin if we didn't have voter ID to keep Wisconsin's elections clean and honest and have integrity?" (Marley 2018).

By 2021, 37 states had voter identification requirements. Most other states require just a signature. Figure 4.2 indicates the states that have voter ID laws.

FIGURE 4.2 ■ Voter Identification Requirements by State

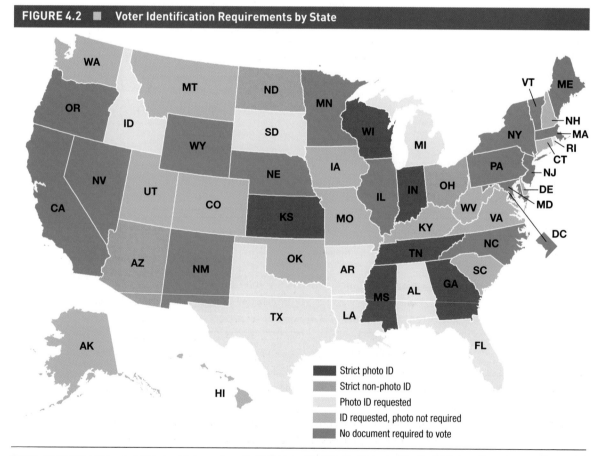

Strict photo ID
Strict non-photo ID
Photo ID requested
ID requested, photo not required
No document required to vote

Source: National Conference of State Legislatures, June 16, 2020. Voter Identification Laws in Effect in 2020, http://www.ncsl.org/research/elections-and-campaigns/voter-id.aspx.

As the Republican attorney general of Wisconsin noted, the results of these efforts have proven effective. Remember the story about the two candidates running for governor? Figure 4.3 shows that every step of the voting process is more difficult for people of color than for Whites. From being able to get off work to vote to being harassed at the polls, the voting process is easier for Whites and harder for Black and Hispanic citizens (Jones et al. 2018).

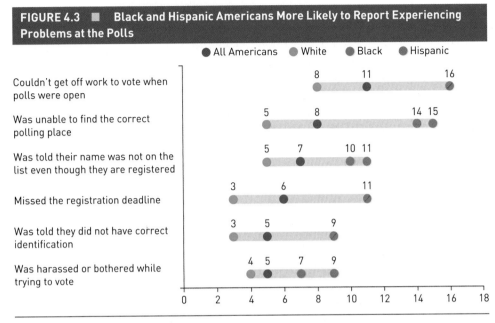

FIGURE 4.3   ■   Black and Hispanic Americans More Likely to Report Experiencing Problems at the Polls

Credit: PRRI/The Atlantic 2018 Voter Engagement Survey.

CONSIDER THIS

Looking at Figure 4.3, what policies can you think of that might help alleviate race-based impediments to voting?

Fighting Back

Disadvantaged racial groups have reacted to these racist laws by mobilizing and voting in greater numbers than usual. For example, before the 2018 midterm elections, North Dakota passed a law requiring voters to present identification showing a street address in order to vote. Most Native Americans living on reservations do not have street addresses. This blatant attempt to suppress their vote galvanized these Native Americans, and they rapidly worked to create street addresses and new ID cards for those without them. The result? They broke the record for highest turnout among Native American voters in those areas of North Dakota.

Alexis Davis, a 19-year-old member of the Turtle Mountain youth council, describes how the law spurred the people on the reservations to take action as she explains why she became a leader in the effort despite having little interest in politics before: "But then this voter ID law came, and then I was paying attention, and then I started seeing quotes about how this election is so important and this election is going to make history," she says. "They were trying to take a right away from us. It made us want to go in there and vote twice as much and make a statement" (Reilly 2018).

Likewise, as Figure 4.4 shows, *many* people of color voted for the first time in the 2018 elections. Compared to Whites, far more Hispanic citizens voted for the first time in a midterm election (Krogstad, Flores, & Lopes, 2018). They also tended to vote for Democratic candidates. Among the newly elected members of the House of Representatives, 34% of Democrats and just 2% of Republicans identified as members of racially marginalized groups (Panetta & Lee, 2019). For the first time ever, more than one-third of newly elected representatives in Congress were people of color (see Figure 4.5).

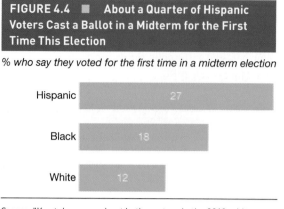

FIGURE 4.4 ■ About a Quarter of Hispanic Voters Cast a Ballot in a Midterm for the First Time This Election

% who say they voted for the first time in a midterm election

Hispanic 27

Black 18

White 12

Source: "Key takeaways about Latino voters in the 2018 midterm elections." Pew Research Center, Washington, D.C. (9 November 2018) https://www.pewresearch.org/fact-tank/2018/11/09/how-latinos-voted-in-2018-midterms/

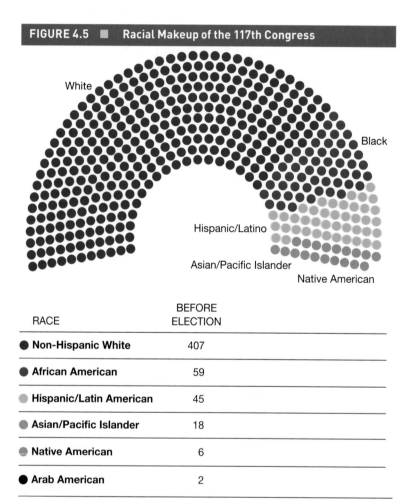

FIGURE 4.5 ■ Racial Makeup of the 117th Congress

White

Black

Hispanic/Latino

Asian/Pacific Islander

Native American

RACE	BEFORE ELECTION
● **Non-Hispanic White**	407
● **African American**	59
● **Hispanic/Latin American**	45
● **Asian/Pacific Islander**	18
● **Native American**	6
● **Arab American**	2

Source: Adapted from Korgen and Atkinson 2019; Panetta and Lee 2019; and partly data from https://thehill.com/homenews/house/527890-incoming-congress-looks-more-like-america.

DOING SOCIOLOGY 4.2

Voter Suppression and You

This exercise requires you to think about how voter suppression efforts affect you.

Answer the following questions in writing and be prepared to share your answers.

1. Does knowing about voter suppression efforts today make you more or less committed to voting? Why?

2. If no one in your racial group(s) votes in the next presidential election, how might it affect you? Why?

In the 2020 special election in historically red Georgia, effective voter mobilization, particularly of Black voters, allowed the Democrats to flip the state to gain control of the Senate. Raphael Warnock is the first Black person to represent Georgia in the United States Senate. He and fellow Democrat Jon Ossoff became the 49th and 50th Democrat to win Senate seats in the 2020 voting cycle, assuring Democratic control of all three branches of government (at least from 2020 to 2022).

Check Your Understanding

1. How did the *Shelby County v. Holder* Supreme Court decision weaken the Voting Rights Act?

2. Which political party gains advantages from policies that result in lowering the number of votes of people of color? Why?

3. What is the most popular form of voter suppression today?

4. Is in-person voter fraud widespread?

5. What are some ways the voting process is more difficult for Black and Latinx than White voters?

6. What are two examples of how disadvantaged racial groups have fought back against voter suppression efforts?

EXAMPLES OF INSTITUTIONAL RACISM IN OTHER PARTS OF THE U.S. GOVERNMENT

Suppressing the vote of people of color is just one way a government can practice institutional racism. Many of the institutions and agencies the U.S. government controls (e.g., the criminal justice system, educational system, Federal Housing Administration, and Environmental Protection Agency) also work in racially discriminatory ways. Let's look at the criminal justice system and two federal government agencies, the Environmental Protection Agency (EPA) and the Federal Housing Administration (FHA).

Criminal Justice System

The criminal justice system—the arm of government charged with protecting citizens and keeping order—has a well-known history of treating people differently based on race. No doubt you have heard of or seen videos of police killings of unarmed Black men and women. Maybe you participated in some of the massive protests against the disproportionate use of deadly force against Black Americans led or inspired by the Black Lives Matter movement. It is important to understand that the criminal justice *system*, not just a few police officers, acts in racially discriminatory ways.

Racial disparities exist at every step in the criminal justice system (Pierson et. al 2019). For example, a review of 100 million U.S. traffic stops by police revealed that the phrase *driving while Black* is based in fact. The police are more likely to pull over Black drivers than any other drivers. Police are also more likely to search Black and Latinx drivers despite the fact that they find more contraband when searching White drivers (Pierson et al. 2019).

Walking while Black may become a new term. A study in Jacksonville, Florida, found that Black residents are 3 times more likely than White residents to receive a pedestrian citation (for crossing against a red or yellow light, not walking on the right-hand side of the road when there are no sidewalks, etc.). Another study revealed that Black men are punished with a 20% longer sentence than White men who committed the same crimes—even when controlling for past violent offenses (U.S. Sentencing Commission, 2017). The evidence shows that White people are less likely than racially disadvantaged groups to be arrested and, if arrested, charged with a crime and then found guilty of that crime (Pierson et al. 2019).

The movie *When They See Us* vividly illustrates one example of racial discrimination in the criminal justice system. In 1989, a White woman jogging in Central Park was raped and viciously beaten. Five teenagers, Black and Hispanic boys, were intimidated into confessing to the crime—confessions they soon recanted—and portrayed as violent rapists by the district attorney and the media. Thirteen years later, the person who did commit the crime confessed, and the verdict against them was overturned. By then, the time they had spent in prison ranged from 6 to 13 years (Dwyer 2019). Comparisons of often violent police reactions to Black people at Black Lives Matter protests and to the largely hands-off approach to White insurgents who stormed the Capitol in 2021 provide another powerful example that Black Americans face much harsher treatment from our criminal justice system.

While the number of incarcerated people, particularly Black people, has decreased over the past decade, Blacks and, to a lesser extent, Hispanics are still overrepresented, and Whites are underrepresented in the prison system. The "school-to-prison pipeline" is one reason why. Students of color—especially African American boys—are much more likely to be arrested for school-related infractions than White students (LDF 2018). This is one example of how racial discrimination in the criminal justice system affects treatment in other institutions, leading to side-effect discrimination.

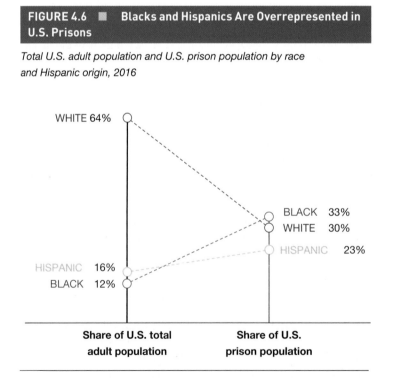

> **FIGURE 4.6 ■ Blacks and Hispanics Are Overrepresented in U.S. Prisons**

Total U.S. adult population and U.S. prison population by race and Hispanic origin, 2016

Source: "The gap between the number of blacks and whites in prison is shrinking." Pew Research Center, Washington, D.C. (30 April 2019) https://www.pewresearch.org/fact-tank/2019/04/30/shrinking-gap-between-number-of-blacks-and-whites-in-prison/.

Most employers are reluctant to hire people with prison records. This contributes to the relatively high levels of unemployment and low average earnings for Black Americans (Ajunwa and Onwuachi-Willig 2018). "In the first full calendar year after their release, only 55 percent [of former prisoners] have any reported earnings. Among those with jobs, their median annual earnings is $10,090" (Looney and Turner 2018, 1). We will discuss institutional racial discrimination in the economy in more detail later in this chapter. We now look at how two federal agencies operate in ways that support racial inequality.

The Environmental Protection Agency

In 2018, Environmental Protection Agency (EPA) scientists published a study on the distribution of particulate matter air pollutants such as smog, automobile exhaust, soot ash, and oil smoke in the United States. This pollution is linked to many serious illnesses, including heart attacks, asthma, low birth weights, and high blood pressure (EPA 2019). Their findings showed that, compared to the overall population, people of color breathe 30% more emissions and Blacks, alone, 50% more particulate matter air pollutants than the average person in the overall population. These findings controlled for poverty status and showed consistency across geographic areas.

The findings also indicated that the same types of emissions are found at higher rates in non-White than White neighborhoods—a sign that businesses in non-White areas face less regulation enforcement (Mikati et al. 2018). This is an example of environmental racism—when environmental hazards are disproportionately borne by racial and ethnic minority groups (Bullard 1990, 1993). Robert Bullard (1990), the first sociologist to effectively publicize environmental racism in the United States, explains that governments and private industries seek the "path of least resistance" in distributing pollutants. This means that "companies tend to site facilities that negatively impact human health in these communities because they lack the political clout and resources necessary to fight siting decisions" (U.S. Commission on Civil Rights, 2016, p. 6). State regulatory agencies rarely, if ever, grant permits for high-polluting businesses in White areas. In the Sociologist in Action feature, sociologist David Pellow describes his participation in a project to fight this type of environmental injustice in California's Central Coast.

SOCIOLOGISTS IN ACTION
David N. Pellow

Confronting Institutional Racism by Working to Promote Energy Justice

Energy justice (fair access to and democratic participation in the governance of energy systems) is part of the effort to dismantle institutional racism. Government and corporate institutions in my region, California's Central Coast, regularly target population areas with high percentages of immigrants and other people of color to build and expand dangerous energy projects. To help address this problem, I recently co-led an initiative at the University of California, Santa Barbara (UCSB), to develop critical and creative research practices in energy justice.

We focused on the ways in which scholars can collaborate with community members who are leading energy justice struggles. In doing so, we guided students as they worked on group projects focused on developing relationships with local communities and working with them on energy justice campaigns. Our community collaborators were members of the Climate Justice Network (CJN), a coalition of social movement organizations working together to build power and momentum to achieve climate, environmental, food, and energy justice.

To enable our collaboration with CJN, we organized a class to work with the activists on the following campaigns:

1) Opposing a proposal by ExxonMobil to transport oil on local highways
2) Opposing a major local oil well drilling proposal
3) Articulating a fair and just transition for fossil fuel workers
4) Promoting a ban on oil well drilling on agricultural terrain in Ventura County

To advance these campaigns, students conducted critical analyses of the environmental impact reports (EIRs) prepared for the first two projects and distilled them into plain language for our CJN partners. In collaboration with CJN activists, the students also

1) determined the risks associated with the spillage of hazardous materials on the ExxonMobil trucking route and their impacts on local ecosystems, plants and animals, and public health;
2) examined the CO_2 emissions the projects would release (which would exceed Santa Barbara County's threshold);
3) attended public hearings to testify against the projects, in written and oral form; and
4) advocated for a "no project alternative" instead of the usual choice between the proposed fossil fuel project and a slightly scaled back version.

In addition, students met and conducted interviews with local fossil fuel workers. They sought to understand what kind of future workers would like to see in the county, their concerns regarding actions associated with climate justice movements, and where we share common ground on energy topics. Finally, a subset of the students worked with local NGOs to mobilize residents to attend a county supervisors meeting.

The groups' efforts led to an extension of a ban on oil and gas drilling in Ventura County—a community with a high percentage of immigrants, Indigenous populations, and other people of color. I am proud of what we accomplished fighting environmental injustice.

Professor David Pellow is Department Chair, Dehlsen Chair of the Environmental Studies Program, and Director of the Global Environmental Justice Project at UCSB. His latest book is What Is a Critical Environmental Justice?

Discussion Question

What is energy justice? Why is there energy injustice in the United States, a society that believes in equality under the law?

Established in 1970, the EPA has a mission "to protect human health and the environment." Its Civil Rights Office is supposed to enforce Title VI of the Civil Rights Act, which prohibits organizations or agencies that receive federal funding from favoring one racial group and discriminating against people because of their race (and color and place of origin).

Given its mission—and the findings of environmental racism by EPA scientists—you might expect the EPA's Civil Rights Office to step in and stop the inequitable pattern of distributing permits. However, the practices of this office have worked to tacitly support, rather than alleviate, environmental racism. Through a combination of delays (in some cases, decades) and dismissing or rejecting 90% of the complaints they receive, the Civil Rights Office of the EPA has not fulfilled its mission to enforce Title VI of the Civil Rights Act.

One of the most appalling dismissals of a civil rights case by the EPA comes from Uniontown, Alabama. Alabama serves as "the dumping ground of the US, with toxic waste from across the country typically heaped near poor, rural communities, many with large African American populations" (Milman 2019). In Uniontown, 90% of the residents are Black, and the average household's income is below the poverty level. Right above Uniontown sits the Arrowhead landfill—a mountain of trash, including 4 million tons of toxic coal ash sent there from a predominantly White county in Tennessee. Since the landfill opened in 2007—against the wishes of the Uniontown community—33 states have sent their garbage to Arrowhead, and 15,000 tons of garbage comes in every day (Millman 2018).

Residents have long complained about a smell akin to rotten eggs and a wide range of health and environmental problems they believe are related to the coal ash on the site. Esther Calhoun, who has lived in Uniontown most of her life, says, "That smell... it makes you want to vomit. The pecan trees, they don't bear any more. Even the garden that I had, we don't use it anymore"(Pillion 2018).

PHOTO 4.3 A truck moves across a large mound of coal ash carried from the site of a spill in Tennessee to a landfill in the rural, largely minority community of Uniontown, Alabama.

John L. Wathen/MCT/Tribune News Service via Getty Images

CONSIDER THIS

Imagine you own a corporation that produces more waste than you can handle. You need to build a new incinerator. Where would you try to place it? Why? How might your choice affect your chances of getting a permit to build the incinerator?

Local residents formed a group, Black Belt Citizens Fighting for Health and Justice, to fight the landfill and the pollution emanating from it. In 2013 they filed a complaint with the EPA, saying that the Alabama Department of Environmental Management (ADEM) had violated Title VI of the Civil Rights Act. After holding the case for 14 years without a decision—during which time the landfill continued to operate—in 2017 the EPA's External Civil Rights Compliance Office ruled there was "insufficient evidence" that ADEM discriminated against the people of Uniontown.

Upon hearing of the dismissal, Ben Eaton, the vice president of Black Belt Citizens, said, "If EPA can't see that what we experience are civil rights violations, then EPA will never protect people from discrimination" (Pillion 2018). New Jersey senator Corey Booker, who had visited Uniontown, declared:

The EPA has abdicated its responsibility to protect people of color and low-income communities from blatant discrimination…. I saw with my own eyes how the residents of Uniontown struggle on a daily basis with a massive industrial garbage dump that's been planted in their backyards…. Access to clean air, clean water, and clean soil shouldn't be a privilege—it's a right and the EPA has failed to protect this right for the people of Uniontown…. This issue goes to the core of a larger movement for equal justice in this country that we're unfortunately still struggling with. (Pillion 2019)

Under the Trump administration, the EPA did little to fight environmental racism. In fact, President Trump focused on using the EPA to deregulate business and allow companies to pollute *more*, adding to climate change and environmental racism. A 2019 report shows that the increased levels of pollution allowed by Trump will lead to "thousands more premature deaths, hundreds of thousands more asthma attacks, and countless additional missed school and workdays" (The State Energy & Environmental Impact Center, NYU School of Law, 2019, p. 5). While everyone will suffer from this additional pollution, people of color will face more of these harms than the overall population.

DOING SOCIOLOGY 4.3

Poor Air Quality: An Example of Racist Policy Making?

In this exercise, you will examine statistics on pollution and demographics as they relate to clean-air policies.

San Bernardino County had the third worst air quality in the country in 2019. The air quality has deteriorated considerably over the past several years, leading to poorer health outcomes for its residents. According to the *Los Angeles Times*, smog regulators in Southern California set a goal to raise $1 billion a year until 2031 to pay for greener vehicles and equipment. So far, though, they have only raised 25% of the necessary funds.

Review the demographics of San Bernardino provided in Table 4.1. Then answer the following questions.

1. Based on the racial and ethnic composition of the population of San Bernardino, would you consider this to be a case of environmental racism? Why or why not?

2. Why do you think the regulators are falling so short of their financial goal?

TABLE 4.1 ■ Racial, Ethnic, and Immigrant Status of Residents of San Bernardino, California	
Race, Ethnicity, and Place of Birth	**Percentage of San Bernardino Population**
Born outside the U.S.	24%
Latinx	64%
White alone	15%
Black or African American	13%
Asian	4%
American Indian and Alaska Native	0.2%
Native Hawaiian and other Pacific Islander	0.2%
Two or more races	2.5%
Some other race	0.17%

Source: Data USA 2019. https://datausa.io/profile/geo/san-bernardino-county-ca.

The Federal Housing Administration and Enforcement of the Fair Housing Act of 1968

As discussed in Chapter 2, President Franklin Roosevelt established the Federal Housing Administration (FHA) in 1934 to help spur the economy during the Great Depression. The FHA did so, in part, by supplying FHA-approved banks with government-backed mortgage insurance. This insurance assured banks that if people who received loans defaulted on them the government would repay their loans to the bank. This made banks feel comfortable lending more money and helped save the economy from collapse.

The establishment of the FHA worked out well for both the housing market and for White people who wanted to buy a house, but it did not help people of color. In fact, it led to the creation of what historian Richard Rothstein (2017) describes as a "state-sponsored system of segregation." To ensure that it did not have to pay banks large sums of money because of defaults, the FHA came up with maps indicating neighborhoods whose residents it thought posed little risk of forfeitures and a decline in housing values (White neighborhoods) and those where banks should not give loans (neighborhoods with high percentages of people of color). They marked the maps with red pens—the advent of redlining. It was not until passage of the Fair Housing Act in 1968, which "prohibited discrimination concerning the sale, rental, and financing of housing based on race, religion, national origin, and sex" (and, as amended later, handicap and family status), that de jure racial discrimination in housing ended (HUD.gov, 2019).

Redlining by the FHA, as well as discrimination by individuals and communities of homeowners, is an example of past-in-present discrimination, which occurs when discrimination in the past affects people in the present. During the decades before the Fair Housing Act became law, home prices rose dramatically, allowing homeowners to gain wealth and making it more difficult for those who did not yet have a house to buy one. The result was that few people of color could "avail themselves of what is arguably the most significant route to family and personal wealth-building in the 20th century, which is homeownership" (Nelson as quoted in Domonoske 2016). This past discrimination plays a direct role in the racial "wealth gap" today.

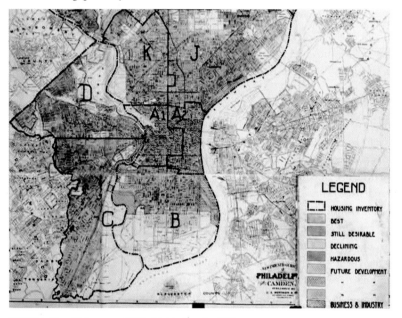

PHOTO 4.4 A redlining map of Philadelphia from the 1930s.

Volgi archive / Alamy Stock Photo

Check Your Understanding

1. What are some examples of racism in the criminal justice system?

2. How does racism in the criminal justice system relate to racial inequality in employment?

3. What is environmental racism?

4. Why is the EPA decision in Uniontown, Alabama, a good example of environmental racism?

5. How is redlining by the FHA an example of past-in-present racial discrimination?

RACIAL DISCRIMINATION IN THE ECONOMIC INSTITUTION

Along with racism in law and policy comes racial inequality in the economic system and other social institutions. The economic institution includes the wide range of activities that provide us with the means to create and distribute goods and services. In a capitalist system, some people gain more from the economic institution than others. Past as well as present racist laws and government policies affect wealth inequality in the capitalist economic system in the United States today. That inequality, in turn, affects the resources people can use to gain a good education, attain a well-paying job, and give their children an advanced education or a down payment for a house.

You can see the influence of past-in-present racism at your school right now. This year, many grandparents will help pay for their grandchildren's college expenses. No doubt some of that money comes from house sales and home equity loans. This same support is not available to students whose grandparents could not get a mortgage or were forced to buy homes in areas with declining housing values. Hence, a higher percentage of White students than students of color receive college money from their grandparents. In turn, this gives White students more college options, saves them from burdensome college loans, and gives them a better chance of attaining a high-paying job and being able to provide their own children and grandchildren with a good education.

Loss of Land Equals Loss of Wealth

Land distribution has also contributed to wealth inequality. As we discuss in Chapter 6, White people took all the land now known as the United States from Native Americans. African American farmers also lost most of their land to White Americans and, with it, much wealth. Through a combination of violence, mistrust of government, the chicanery of some White people, and lack of information about inheritance laws, African Americans were forced to give up 90% of their farmland by the end of the 20th century (Presser 2019). More are still losing their property today.

The Reels Brothers and Land Loss

Melvin and Licurtis Reels lived on land their great-grandfather purchased one generation after the end of slavery. The 65 acres of swampy land on the North Carolina shore was the site of tent revivals and a beach for Black people when they were not allowed to use other beaches. The brothers' sister described it as "our own little Black country club."

Their grandfather, Mitchell, did not trust the White-dominated Southern courts and, therefore, did not want to establish a legal will that would rely on the enforcement of such a court. So, he let his land become "heirs' property." Heirs' property land leaves descendants with an interest in the land, similar to owning stock in a business. The widespread practice of leaving land as heirs' property began shortly after the Civil War and continues even now. Today, White Americans are twice as likely as African Americans to have a will. Three out of four African Americans do not have one. Lissie Presser (2019), a journalist who wrote about the brothers' experience, notes the following:

> *Many assume that not having a will keeps land in the family. In reality, it jeopardizes ownership. In the course of generations, heirs tend to disperse and lose any connection to the land. Speculators can buy off the interest of a single heir, and just one heir or speculator, no matter how minute his share, can force the sale of an entire plot through the courts.*

The removal of Native Americans from their land and the forced sales of most of the farmland owned by Black Americans has deprived these racial groups of sources of great wealth and contributes to the great wealth divide today. As Figure 4.7 shows, the wealth gap exists across all education levels. White people also have advantages in the job market, which we look at next.

Racial Discrimination in Employment Today

As discussed further in Chapter 7, field experiments conducted over the last several decades reveal that White applicants have advantages when seeking employment. Among applicants with resumes identical in every way except race, "since 1989, Whites [have received] on average 36% more callbacks than African Americans, and 24% more callbacks than Latinos" (Quillian, Pager, Hexel, and Midtbøen 2017, 1). Systemic racism is apparent in the persistent disparities in unemployment rates over the past several decades. Note that the data in Figure 4.8 show continually high unemployment rates for American Indians, as well.

Racism in economic institutions affects employed people, as well. As seen in Table 4.2, even when controlling for education levels, Whites earn higher incomes than Blacks and Hispanics. From high school grads to master's degree recipients, Whites have higher average incomes than Blacks and Hispanics.

FIGURE 4.7   ■   Household Net Worth Varies by Race

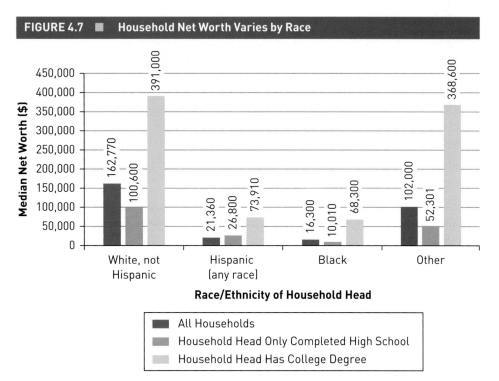

Race/Ethnicity of Household Head

- ■ All Households
- ■ Household Head Only Completed High School
- ■ Household Head Has College Degree

Source: Board of Governors of the Federal Reserve System, 2016 Survey of Consumer Finances. September 2017. Compiled by PGPF. Peter G. Peterson Foundation. 2018 Household Net Worth Varies By Race. https://www.pgpf.org/chart-archive/0259_net_worth_by_race.

FIGURE 4.8   ■   Patterns of Unemployment by Race

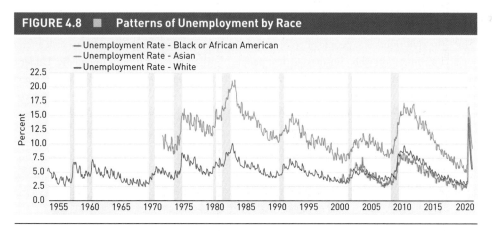

Sources:

U.S. Bureau of Labor Statistics, Unemployment Rate: Black or African American [LNU04000006], retrieved from FRED, Federal Reserve Bank of St. Louis; https://fred.stlouisfed.org/series/LNU04000006, August 15, 2019.

U.S. Bureau of Labor Statistics, Unemployment Rate: Asian [LNU04032183], retrieved from FRED, Federal Reserve Bank of St. Louis; https://fred.stlouisfed.org/series/LNU04032183, August 15, 2019.

U.S. Bureau of Labor Statistics, Unemployment Rate: White [LNU04000003], retrieved from FRED, Federal Reserve Bank of St. Louis; https://fred.stlouisfed.org/series/LNU04000003, August 15, 2019.

Bureau of Labor Statistics, U.S. Department of Labor, The Economics Daily, Labor market trends for American Indians and Alaska Natives, 2000–17 on the Internet at https://www.bls.gov/opub/ted/2018/labor-market-trends-for-american-indians-and-alaska-natives-2000-17.htm (visited August 15, 2019).

TABLE 4.2 ■ Income by Education and Race/Ethnicity			
Education			
	White Income	**Black Income**	**Hispanic Income**
High school degree/ GED	$32,399	$27,490	$30,198
Associate degree	$40,484	$35,747	$35,454
Bachelor's degree	$54,004	$48,878	$46,298
Master's degree	$65,499	$56,880	$60,866

Source: U.S. Census Bureau 2017. https://www.bls.gov/spotlight/2017/educational-attainment-of-the-labor-force/home.htm.

Housing and Racism Today

Racism in the mortgage and housing market also still exists. Even (unofficial) redlining persists. An analysis of mortgage lending in 48 cities revealed that, compared to their treatment of White applicants, banks are significantly more likely to reject members of one or more non-White racial groups in all 48 cities (Blacks in 48, Latinx in 25, Asian Americans and Pacific Islanders in 9, and Native Americans in 3 cities) (Glantz and Martinez 2019; Reed and McGregor 2019).

Today, the homeownership rate for Black Americans is the lowest it has been in 50 years. Among people seeking to buy a house, Whites have advantages at every step of the process—from working with realtors to mortgage approval and appraisal (Korver-Glenn 2018). The result is that Whites who can afford a house can get a mortgage and buy one wherever they would like. People of color, on the other hand, are much more likely to be turned down or offered higher-interest mortgages by banks and, if they get a mortgage, steered by realtors into neighborhoods with many non-White people. Most also will find that their house value grows at a much slower rate than a comparable house in a White neighborhood.

Since the civil rights era, people of color and their representatives have been able to seek a remedy for racial discrimination when businesses treat people of different racial groups unequally. Under this *disparate impact standard*, if a bank gives loans to one racial group but does not give loans to another

PHOTO 4.5 The HUD website urges people to file a complaint if they face "discrimination in renting or buying a home, getting a mortgage, seeking housing assistance, or engaging in other housing-related activities." Proposed rules, however, would make proving discrimination almost impossible.

Andrew Harrer/Bloomberg via Getty Images

one, even if they have similar incomes, this is discriminatory behavior for which the government can punish the bank. The Trump administration, however, made rule changes that made it much harder to prove that a landlord or bank is guilty of racial discrimination. The added requirements for those trying to prove discrimination placed "an incredible and extraordinary burden" on them and made it "virtually impossible to prevail." The rule changes even include tips for banks on how to win a racial discrimination case brought against them (Fadulu 2019; Meckler and Barrett 2021). President Biden moved to reverse these changes shortly after he took office.

Under President Trump's rules, a business could avoid a charge of discrimination if it used a computer algorithm not directly tied to race to determine to whom they should give loans. So, "a hypothetical bank that rejected every loan application filed by African Americans and approved every one filed by White people, for example, would need to prove only that race or a proxy for it was not used directly in constructing its computer model" (Glantz and Martinez 2019). Moreover, a company could beat a charge of discrimination if it could provide evidence that the algorithm it uses is standard in its field. "This means that if an entire industry is engaged in discrimination, it essentially insulates the discriminatory conduct of an individual actor" (Ifill, as quoted in Glantz and Martinez 2019).

CONSIDER THIS

How do past-in-present and current discrimination in housing affect the wealth of people of color? Why do you think the Trump administration has pushed to make it harder to prove racial discrimination in housing?

Where you live in the United States affects your life in many ways, including your education. Racism in housing supports systemic racism in the educational system. We now look at how the institution of education supports and strengthens racism in the United States.

DOING SOCIOLOGY 4.4

Algorithmic Bias

In this exercise, you will consider how racism can be embedded in the technology used by organizations.

An algorithm is essentially a series of instructions that a computer uses to process data, perform calculations, and make determinations. Though some might think that computer code is unbiased, the reality is that algorithms often produce biased outcomes. This phenomenon is sometimes referred to as algorithmic bias.

Answer the following questions in writing and be prepared to share your answers.

1. How does algorithmic bias relate to institutional racism?

2. How is it possible that a computer algorithm could make racist determinations, for example?

3. What responsibility do organizations have to prevent algorithmic bias?

4. Are you aware of other examples of racist—or antiracist—technology? If so, what examples have you learned about?

Check Your Understanding

1. What function does the economic institution serve for a society?

2. How has land loss affected the racial wealth gap?

3. How do we know there is systemic racism in employment today?

RACISM IN EDUCATION

Segregated neighborhoods lead to segregated schools. This is an example of side-effect racial discrimination, as racial discrimination in one institution (or area of an institution) leads to racial discrimination in another institution or area. While they *may* not be intentional, the effects of side-effect discrimination are just as detrimental as those of direct discrimination. We can see this in how school funding leads to racial inequality in the education institution.

School Funding

Despite the 1954 *Brown v. Board of Education* Supreme Court decision that declared separate schools are unequal and mandated that they must be racially integrated, segregated schools are just as common today as they were in 1954. Moreover, as Supreme Court justice Thurgood Marshall pointed out as a young attorney arguing the case, they are still not equal.

As noted earlier, schools with predominantly White students have advantages over schools with mostly students of color because of the way U.S. funding for public schools works. U.S. public schools receive funding from their town or city (about 45%), their state (about 45%), and the federal government (about 10%). Local funding tends to be tied to property tax revenues. Wealthier (and Whiter) areas have higher property values and thus more local funding. Some states give more funding to low-income school districts, but, even in those cases, the state funds do not make up for the lower local tax funds. That is why the average predominantly White school districts get about 30% more funding than predominantly non-White school districts (EdBuild 2019).

Even when controlling for class, White students still have an advantage. Poor White school districts get approximately $150 less per student less than the average school district in the United States but almost $1,500 *more* than the average poor non-White school district (EdBuild 2019). This relates to the fact that homes in White neighborhoods tend to be worth more than those in non-White neighborhoods, leading to more local funding for predominantly White schools.

DOING SOCIOLOGY 4.5

School Funding and Your Education

In this exercise you will consider how the funding system for public schools has affected your ability to succeed in college.

Answer the following questions in writing and be prepared to share your answers.

1. Has the funding system for public schools in the United States helped or hurt your chances of achieving academic success in college? How so?

2. Do you think your educational experience relates to that of other members of your racial group(s)? Why?

White students in the United States also go to schools with more qualified teachers. This has led to different qualities of education among high school graduates of different racial groups—and even some dramatically different percentages of high school graduates. The high school graduation rate for American Indians and Alaska Natives (72%) is considerably lower than the national rate (85%). The 8% who attend poorly funded schools on reservations have an even lower graduation rate—53%. The Bureau of Indian Education has pledged to reorganize itself and provide better education for reservation students. However, in describing the reasons behind the reorganization, the bureau notes that the students they serve have had to deal with "failing schools, crumbling infrastructure, failure to include tribal nations in the decision-making process and lack of access to broadband, and teachers and principal shortages" (Bureau of Indian Education 2019; National Center for Education Statistics 2019).

Other than American Indians and Alaska Natives, most students finish high school or get a GED (85%), and of those, most enroll in college (67%). However, as noted, poorly funded schools tend not to offer the same quality of education as well-funded schools. High school graduates have wide ranges of preparation, which makes college success much easier for some than others (National Center for Education Statistics 2019). As you can see in Figure 4.9, far less than half of American Indian/Alaska Native (39%) and Black students (40%) who start college at a 4-year school leave with a college degree. Just half of Pacific Islanders graduate within 6 years. Whites have the second highest (64%) and Asian students have the highest graduation rate (74%) (we explain why Asians have a higher rate later in this chapter).

The wealth and income gap among racial groups also plays a factor in the different college graduation rates. If you come from a family with low income and little wealth, you probably have to take out loans and spend much of your time in college working. Financial pressure, plus a lack of educational preparation, plays a large role in the high dropout rate among Black, Latinx, Pacific Islander, and American Indians and Alaska Natives.

FIGURE 4.9 ■ Graduation Rates From First Institution Attended for First-Time, Full-Time Bachelor's Degree–Seeking Students at 4-Year Postsecondary Institutions, by Race/Ethnicity and Time to Completion: Cohort Entry Year 2010

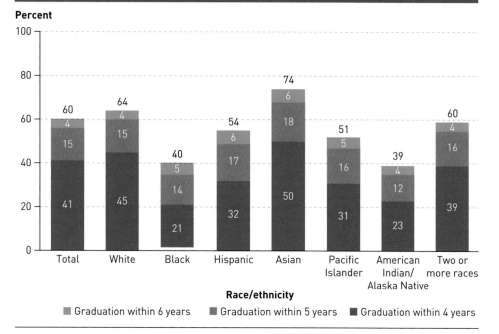

Source: National Center for Education Statistics, Integrated Postsecondary Education Data System (IPEDS), Winter 2016–17, Graduation Rates component. See *Digest of Education Statistics 2017*, table 326.10. https://nces.ed.gov/programs/raceindicators/indicator_red.asp.

Milliken v. Bradley

During the 1974 case of *Milliken v. Bradley*, the makeup of the justices on the Supreme Court was very different from that of the Court that decided *Brown v. Board of Education* in 1954. In 1974, there were four new justices—all appointed by President Richard Nixon. A lower court had ruled for the plaintiffs, parents of students in Detroit who argued that the state must implement desegregation policies across district lines to integrate schools. At the time, due to the segregation in housing discussed earlier, Detroit was about 75% Black and struggling economically. Most White people had moved to the suburbs and were putting lots of money into their school districts. The disparity was striking—and almost a perfect illustration of the term *separate and unequal*.

The suburban districts said they understood their schools and those in Detroit were clearly racially segregated. They argued, however, that this segregation was not intentional. They had not created their school districts to segregate themselves—that was just an unintended result. In a 5–4 ruling, the

Court decided the Milliken v. Bradley case by agreeing with the suburban districts, saying that, since they had not intended to racially segregate the Detroit schools, they should not have to do anything to desegregate them. The Court did not consider the fact that redlining and other forms of intended economic racial discrimination had allowed Whites, but not Blacks, to move out of Detroit and create new suburbs around it. The Court told Detroit that it must somehow desegregate its schools itself—an impossible task given the paucity of White students in the city.

In his dissent, Supreme Court justice Thurgood Marshall declared that "the Detroit-only plan simply has no hope of achieving actual desegregation. Under such a plan, White and Negro students will not go to school together. Instead, Negro children will continue to attend all-Negro schools. The very evil that Brown was aimed at will not be cured but will be perpetuated" (Quoted in Nadworny and Turner 2019).

CONSIDER THIS

How do the Brown v. Board of Education and Milliken v. Bradley decisions illustrate why antiracists must work to elect antiracist policymakers?

Marshall was right. The racial segregation of schools that *Brown v. Board* said must be eliminated persists. Although the Supreme Court did not acknowledge it, the endurance of school segregation is a direct result of institutional racism and decisions to let it go unaddressed. As was the case in 1974, Whites may no longer openly discriminate against Black people, but they can use their advantages in the housing market and the economic system to buy houses in neighborhoods with few non-White people but plenty of well-funded schools. The result is racial inequality.

Check Your Understanding

1. How does the system for funding public schools lead to racism in the educational institution?

2. How does racism within the education and economic systems affect high school and college graduation rates among racial groups?

3. What has been the state of schools on American Indian reservations?

4. How did the *Milliken v. Bradley* Supreme Court decision affect efforts to desegregate public schools?

ASIAN AMERICANS AND PACIFIC ISLANDERS—AN EXCEPTION?

You may be wondering why Asian Americans and Pacific Islanders (AAPI), as a group, clearly surpass all other racial groups—including Whites—in educational achievement. As Figure 4.7 reveals, the percentage of AAPI people with a graduate or professional degree is *double* that of the total population. However, as we discuss more in Chapter 9, the ethnic groups that comprise the AAPI population in the United States are diverse, and some AAPI groups have much higher education levels and incomes than others.

Inequality Among AAPI Ethnic Groups

If you look at immigrants to the United States from the largest five AAPI groups, you will see that the average member came to the United States with a much higher level of education than that of the average person in their country of origin (from 3 to 4 times higher for Koreans and Filipinos to 18 times higher among Chinese immigrants). As Figure 4.10 shows, all but Vietnamese immigrants came with much higher rates of college education than people in the United States, as well. Knowing this, it makes sense why AAPI people, in general, have higher levels of education than other U.S. racial groups. Again, however, as Figure 4.11 reveals, education levels among AAPI groups vary tremendously.

Likewise, the relatively high average income of all AAPI Americans masks the wide range of incomes among AAPI groups, as seen in Figure 4.12.

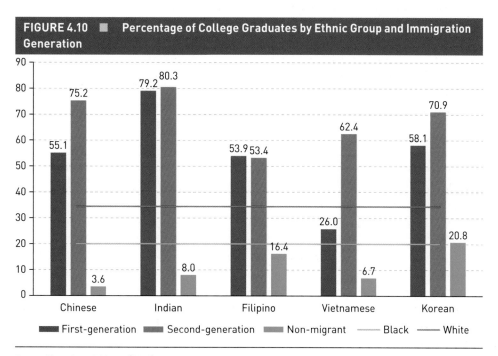

FIGURE 4.10 ■ Percentage of College Graduates by Ethnic Group and Immigration Generation

Source: Tran, Lee, & Huang (2019).

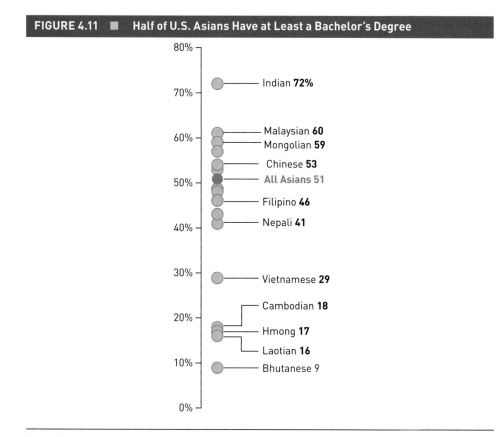

FIGURE 4.11 ■ Half of U.S. Asians Have at Least a Bachelor's Degree

Note: Chinese includes those identifying as Taiwanese. Data not available for all Asian origin groups. See methodology for more.

Source: "Key Facts About Asian Groups in the United States." Pew Research Center, Washington, D.C. (22 May 2019) https://www.pewresearch.org/fact-tank/2019/05/22/key-facts-about-asian-origin-groups-in-the-u-s/

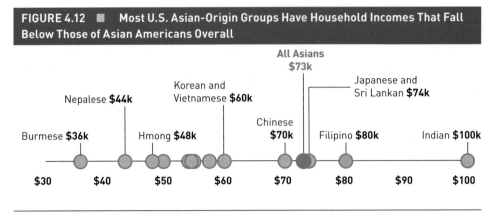

FIGURE 4.12 ■ Most U.S. Asian-Origin Groups Have Household Incomes That Fall Below Those of Asian Americans Overall

Notes: Bhutanese, Malaysian and Mongolian estimates not shown due to small sample size. The household population excludes persons living in institutions, college dormitories and other group quarters. Households are classified by the race or detailed Asian group of the head. Incomes are not adjusted for household size. See methodology for more detail.

Source: "Key Facts About Asian Groups in the United States." Pew Research Center, Washington, D.C. (22 May 2019), https://www.pewresearch.org/fact-tank/2019/05/22/key-facts-about-asian-origin-groups-in-the-u-s/.

Hitting the Asian American Glass Ceiling

Despite their relatively high levels of education, second-generation AAPI Americans (with the exception of Chinese Americans) tend to fare no better than Whites in the work world. In fact, despite *much* higher levels of education, Vietnamese and Filipino Americans are not more likely than Whites to attain managerial or professional positions. Indian and Korean Americans are *less* likely than Whites and no more likely than African Americans to attain these high-level jobs (Tran et al. 2019).

Many hit a barrier (like the "glass ceiling" women hit) of racial discrimination that prevents AAPI people from advancing into management and CEO positions. In fact, among professional workers, AAPIs are less likely than any other racial or ethnic group to receive promotions to management positions. Simultaneously, White professionals are almost twice as likely as AAPI Americans to gain such promotions (Gee and Peck 2018). As seen in Table 4.3, a quarter or more of AAPI Americans report being personally discriminated against when it comes to applying for jobs (27%), being paid equally or considered for promotion (25%), or when trying to rent a room or apartment or buy a house (25%).

TABLE 4.3 ■ Asian Americans Reported to Have Been Personally Discriminated Against Due to Their Race in Each Situation

Situation	Percentage
Applying for jobs	27
Being paid or promoted equally	25
Trying to rent or buy housing	25
Applying to or attending college	19
Interacting with police	18
Going to doctor or health clinic	13
Trying to vote or participate in politics	7

Source: Adapted from NPR, Robert Woods Foundation, and Harvard T. H. Chan School of Public Health (2017).

CONSIDER THIS

Based on the information in this section, how would you prove—despite their overall educational and financial success—that Asian Americans experience discrimination in the workplace?

DOING SOCIOLOGY 4.6

Demographics and Work Experiences

In this exercise, you will look at how demographic characteristics affect work experiences.

Answer the following questions in writing and be prepared to share your answers.

1. Have you faced or are you worried about facing discrimination when seeking a job or a promotion? Why?

2. Which of the following demographic characteristics are true for you?

   • I am a person of color.

   • I am White.

   • I am a person who uses a wheelchair.

   • I am a man.

   • I am straight.

3. How do you think your demographic characteristics affect your response to the first question?

4. Do you think you would answer the first question differently if your demographic characteristics were different from those you just selected? Why?

Institutional Discrimination and Racist Beliefs

The discrimination Asian Americans face in employment and housing, like all forms of institutional racial discrimination, finds support in beliefs that people of color are inferior to White people, which, in turn, encourages and maintains institutional racial discrimination. Laws, policies, and practices described as "race neutral" that lead to racial inequities naturally lead people to believe that the inequities must be due to people of color themselves, rather than the institutions in society. They assume that if few Asians rise to management positions that must be because they are not natural leaders, as racist ideologies maintain, not because of discriminatory hiring practices.

Check Your Understanding

1. How can you explain why AAPIs as a group have higher incomes and education levels than other racial groups?

2. What are some examples of inequality among AAPI ethnic groups?

3. Why, despite their relatively high levels of education, do second-generation AAPI Americans (with the exception of Chinese Americans) tend to fare no better than Whites in the work world?

4. What is the relationship between racist beliefs and racist laws and policies?

CONCLUSION

Intentional and unintentional de facto institutional racism continue to support systemic racism in the United States. Unintended racism leads to the same results as intended racism. Knowledge of these results, however, does not necessarily lead to action. Remember, the five Supreme Court justices who decided the *Milliken v. Bradley* case *knew* that their decision would lead to segregated schools and negate the intent of the *Brown v. Board of Education* ruling. To address institutional racism, we must dismantle *all* racist laws and policies.

In the next chapter, we look at how culture supports systemic racism. As you will see, racist cultures support and encourage racist institutions, and, in turn, these institutions influence culture. We need to change both to eradicate systemic racism.

CHAPTER REVIEW

4.1 What is the relationship between systemic racism and institutional power?

Societies with systemic racism use institutional power to maintain racial inequality. The racial group that controls the institutions has the power to enact either racist or antiracist laws and policies.

4.2 What are some current examples of institutional racism in the political system in the United States?

Voter suppression efforts today are one key form of institutional racism in the U.S. political system. Techniques to suppress the votes of people of color include new voter ID laws, purging of voter rolls, requiring Native Americans living on reservations to have street numbers on their identification, and reducing the number of polling places. Enacted in states controlled by Republicans (whose voters tend to be White), these policies and practices disproportionately hurt voters of color.

4.3 What are some examples of institutional racism in U.S. government agencies today?

Many of the institutions and agencies the U.S. government controls (e.g., the criminal justice system, educational system, Federal Housing Administration, and Environmental Protection Agency) work in racially discriminatory ways. For example, in the criminal justice system, Black people are more likely to be arrested; if arrested, charged with a crime; if charged, convicted; and, if convicted, given longer prison sentences than White people. Other examples include the federal government allowing de facto racial discrimination in mortgage lending and the housing market and the EPA allowing environmental racism to persist, leading to more pollution-related illnesses and deaths among people of color than White people.

4.4 How do both past-in-present and current institutional racism work to maintain economic disparities among racial groups in the United States?

Past-in-present institutional racism is racism practiced in the past that continues to hurt people today. People of color, primarily Black Americans, were denied the chance to attain wealth through home ownership due to racist policies and practices in the past. Lack of trust in government created by a lack of government protection from racist Whites after the Civil War led many Black landowners to avoid making wills recognized by the state. For many, this led to their family members losing the land after they died. The loss of land and house-based wealth in the past supports the racial wealth gap today.

4.5 How does side-effect discrimination affect racial inequality in education?

Side-effect discrimination occurs when discrimination in one institution leads to inequality in other institutions. Past and present racist practices in the mortgage and housing market have created segregated neighborhoods. School funding policies based in part on local taxes lead to poorer neighborhoods, particularly those with predominantly people of color, receiving less money for their schools. In turn, this leads to the average White student (even poor White students) receiving a better education and having a better chance of attending and graduating from college than most students of color.

4.6 Why do Asian Americans and Pacific Islanders, when considered as one racial group, have higher education levels and incomes than other racial groups?

Among the five largest AAPI groups, the average immigrant came to the United States with a *much* higher level of education than the average person in their country of origin and in four out of the five groups, much higher than people in the United States. This education allowed them to find relatively high-paying jobs and provide their children with a good education. The average educational and income levels of AAPI people, however, tends to hide the educational and income inequality within the overall AAPI group. Also, even those who have high incomes and much education tend to face a "glass ceiling" in the workforce and are less likely to be promoted to managerial and other leadership positions than White workers due to racism.

KEY TERMS

Economic institution (p. 75)

Environmental racism (p. 71)

Institutional racism (p. 63)

Milliken v. Bradley (p. 81)

Past-in-present discrimination (p. 75)

Side-effect racial discrimination (p. 80)

Social institutions (p. 63)

Richard 🦃 Spencer
@RichardBSpencer

...ng to @tomperriello

...ot re-fighting the C...

...nting for a White ...

...defeat weaklin...

...13, 2017 · Twitter fo...

...0 Likes

WA
SU
CO
INC

5 CULTURAL SUPPORTS FOR SYSTEMIC RACISM IN THE UNITED STATES

Nikki Khanna

LEARNING QUESTIONS

5.1 How and why does American media maintain and perpetuate systemic racism?

5.2 In what ways does the American educational system maintain and perpetuate systemic racism?

5.3 What are two American cultural ideologies that support systemic racism, and how do they do so?

At the movies, you notice that most of the central characters are White. At the library, you find that the majority of books are written by and about White people. In school, you read about the accomplishments of Europeans and White Americans. You learn about European art and architecture, European history, and how White ingenuity and grit built the United States of America. You read literature written primarily by White authors. At home, you are taught that hard work is the key to success, with the implication that the poor are poor because they simply don't work hard enough. You are also taught that talking about or noticing one's race is impolite or wrong, and that only by ignoring race will we end racism. Does any of this ring true for you? These are just some of the many ways that racism is embedded in American culture in the United States.

Although the United States is a multiracial society, the privileging of Whiteness is pervasive and deeply embedded in American social structures and culture. This chapter focuses on three areas of American culture to illustrate the ways in which it privileges Whiteness: (1) the media, (2) the educational system, and (3) widely shared cultural ideologies.

HOW I GOT ACTIVE IN SOCIOLOGY
Nikki Khanna

I grew up in a multiracial, multiethnic, and multinational family. My mother is White and from Tennessee, and my father immigrated from India in the early 1970s. I grew up in White suburbia just outside of Atlanta, Georgia, and as a mixed-race child, I was interested in all issues of race and ethnicity. I was fascinated by interracial and interethnic relations and, as I grew older, racial justice.

I took my first sociology course in college (having no idea what sociology was at first!), and I quickly realized that I found my "home." I continued on to graduate school, and my first research projects examined attitudes toward interracial dating and identity among biracial Americans— both were close to my heart and personal. Today I research and teach on a broad variety of topics related to race and ethnicity, and I am passionate about my work. The history of and contemporary issues regarding race and ethnic relations in the United States are both painful and fascinating, and through my research and teaching, I feel like I am contributing to something important.

THE IMPACT OF AMERICAN MEDIA

The term media is broad and refers to the various channels of mass communication in a society—including (but not limited to) film, television, books, Internet, music and music videos, newspapers, magazines, advertising, and product and sporting logos. Through these various outlets, Americans are constantly bombarded with racialized messages from White-centric media that privilege the voices and representations of White Americans, typically at the expense of people of color. The two primary reasons American media privileges Whiteness are the following: (1) the majority of Americans are White (60.1% of the U.S. population in 2019 according to the U.S. census), and as such, American media, for the most part, is geared toward and caters to White audiences, and (2) powerful White people own most major media outlets in the United States; hence, they are the ones deciding whose images and stories should be represented and portrayed.

White-centricity in American media matters because the media (such as television and books) provides a "view" into the lives of people of other races. For some people, it is their only window into the lives of Americans with different racial identities. While White Americans are often depicted in a myriad of ways (think of the range of White characters in your favorite television shows), people of color are often missing, underrepresented, or presented in ways that reinforce American racial stereotypes.

Often, it takes a person of color in power to rectify these problematic images. For instance, historically, few Black women appeared in lead roles in American prime-time television. In 2012, however, Shonda Rhimes, a Black female producer and writer, produced the hit television series *Scandal*, which was quickly followed by her next hit, *How to Get Away with Murder*; both prime-time shows cast Black women in lead roles. Further, the lead characters are complex, dynamic, highly intelligent, and powerful, providing a counternarrative to persistent negative stereotypes of Black women. Despite these recent advances, however, a close examination of media outlets reveals that, despite a few exceptions, the media still maintains a mostly White-centric focus.

Sociologists, like Dr. Marisela Martinez-Cola, the Sociologist in Action featured in this chapter, have helped uncover and explain the detrimental effects of these racist patterns in the media. Dr. Martinez-Cola describes how she helps college students of color recognize that portrayals of non-White people in White-centric media follow a pattern detrimental to *all* people of color. This knowledge helps students of color recognize common challenges all people of color face—despite their differences—and see opportunities to work together to combat systemic racism.

SOCIOLOGISTS IN ACTION

Marisela Martinez-Cola, JD/PhD

Seeing and Using Connections to Fight Against Injustice

My first professional position in higher education was as a director of multicultural affairs at a variety of predominantly White colleges across the United States. At each, I would advise students of color in leadership positions. When I introduced myself, I would tell them I was like that little kid in the movie *The Sixth Sense*. But instead of dead people, I see connections. I see connections everywhere.

I noticed that the student organizations I encountered seemed to function separately, each doing their own thing. They acknowledged one another's existence but did not quite recognize each other's shared goal of trying to survive the challenging world of studying at a predominantly White institution (PWI). I saw my role as helping them to find meaningful connections and support for one another, while still recognizing their distinct differences.

My staff and I created a program called Dangerous Distortions: Racial Stereotypes in Film. We gathered clips from documentaries about the history of racial stereotypes in film such as *Ethnic Notions*, *The Bronze Screen*, *Reel Injun*, *Slaying the Dragon*, and *Reel Bad Arabs*. We printed out the images of famous actors in blackface, brownface, redface, and yellowface. The films featured actors such as Marlon Brando in *The Teahouse of August Moon*, Natalie Wood in *West Side Story*, and Judy Garland in *Everybody Singing*. The discussions we had after showing the movie clips were electric! Students were not surprised to see that racial caricatures exist but were surprised that each group had their own mimicked, exaggerated, distorted stereotypes.

Now, after becoming a sociology professor at a PWI, I have the privilege of teaching students. Those documentaries have now become part of my Race & Ethnicity syllabus. As I present them, I give students the sociological language to describe the patterns behind these dehumanizing stereotypes and show how these patterns emerge from and support systemic racism.

I designed a course called Civil Rights of a Different Color in which students compare the civil rights movements of Black, Latinx, Asian American, Indigenous, Middle Eastern, disability rights, and LGBTQ+ communities throughout history. We look for patterns in how they organize and gain the power needed to fight against forces that work to marginalize them. As we search for these connections, however, I point out that finding patterns among them does not mean that all these groups are exactly alike and have the same experiences. It does mean, however, that they can learn from one another and work in collective, as well as individual, ways for social justice. From university administrator to professor, my sociology training allows me to see connections everywhere—and to use them to help marginalized groups work together to achieve shared goals.

Marisela Martinez-Cola is an assistant professor of sociology at Utah State University. She is currently working on The Bricks before Brown v. Board of Education, *an examination of race, class, and gender in Mexican American, Native American, and Chinese American school desegregation cases argued before* Brown v. Board of Ed.

Discussion Question

Why is it important for marginalized groups to recognize patterns among them?

Film and Television

American film and television have a long history of privileging White actors, White characters, and White storylines. In early American entertainment when characters of color were present, they were typically played by White actors and often portrayed in stereotypical and disparaging ways for the entertainment of White audiences. Before the advent of film and television, stage entertainment was popular throughout the United States. Popular variety shows, called minstrel shows, included comic skits and musical numbers with White actors in blackface (they literally blackened their faces, donned wigs, and painted their lips wide and bright white). In doing so, they portrayed Black Americans as cartoonish caricatures who were lazy, ignorant, and buffoon-like in order to garner laughs from White audiences.

As American entertainment turned to film, White characters continued the blackface tradition in popular movies such as *The Birth of a Nation* (1915) and *The Jazz Singer* (1927). Both films (and others that would follow) featured stereotypical blackface characters. *The Birth of a Nation*'s portrayal of the Ku Klux Klan as heroes protecting White Southerners—particularly White Southern women—from savage Black people led to a revival of the KKK. The effects of its stereotypical racist images were strengthened when President Woodrow Wilson, after screening it in the White House, declared it an accurate portrayal of the South during Reconstruction (Shiff 2017; Simons 2016).

Blackface was popular in American media until the mid-20th century. Even today, however, many Americans are unaware of why dressing up in blackface is offensive. In 2018, while apologizing for her on-air defense of blackface, television personality Megyn Kelly asserted that "back when [she] was a kid, that was okay" (Battaglio 2018). In 2019, the governor of Virginia, Ralph Northam, issued a public apology after a 1984 yearbook photo surfaced of him dressed in blackface and standing next to a fellow student dressed in a Ku Klux Klan robe. In the same year, the prime minister of Canada, Justin Trudeau, similarly apologized after multiple pictures from the 1990s and 2001 showed him dressed in blackface. Blackface is considered offensive and racist because White men and women have used it since around 1830 to mock, ridicule, and dehumanize African Americans for their own entertainment.

Popular vaudeville-type shows in the 19th century, branded as Wild West shows, caricatured Native Americans. Crisscrossing the United States, they showcased Native Americans in extravagant rodeo performances (Young 2015) and presented them as wild savages who needed Whites to tame

PHOTO 5.1 A crowd waits outside a theater to see Al Jolson in *The Jazz Singer* (1927).

Bettman/Contributor

them. Like the early portrayals of African Americans, these images soon made their way to the silver screen to reach even wider audiences. American films, like the earlier traveling shows, depicted Native Americans as bloodthirsty and wild—perhaps not surprising given that the films' producers, directors, and writers were White and had little understanding or respect for Native American peoples and cultures. Furthermore, although Native Americans would play bit parts in these films, the main roles (such as the "Indian chief") typically went to White actors (Young 2015).

The practice of casting White actors to play characters of color or whitewashing roles originally intended for people of color by reracing the character as White continues in recent movies (see the 2016 *Washington Post* article titled "100 Times a White Actor Played Someone Who Wasn't White"). Some examples include *Aloha* (2015), in which White actress Emma Stone played the mixed-race White, Chinese, Native Hawaiian lead; *Pan* (2015), in which White actress Rooney Mara played a Native American princess; *Dr. Strange* (2016), in which White actress Tilda Swinton played a Tibetan mystic; and *Ghost in the Shell* (2017), in which White actress Scarlett Johansson played the Japanese lead (Simons 2016). Moreover, while White Americans are presented in a variety of roles and characterizations in both film and television, people of color, if seen at all, are more likely to appear in monolithic, stereotypical, and disparaging ways. In 2015, 12 Native American actors walked off the set of Adam Sandler's comedy *The Ridiculous Six* because of the stereotypical depiction of Native Americans as dirty and animalistic (Young 2015).

CONSIDER THIS

What are the first 10 words that come to mind when you think of Native Americans? From where do you get these thoughts about Native Americans?

The power of film and television to shape ideas about race cannot be understated, especially given that for many White Americans, their only exposure to people of color is at their local movie theater or on television.

Brian Young (2015), a Navajo director, writes about the power of film to perpetuate stereotypes:

During my orientation week freshman year [of college] in 2006, many of my classmates, when they discovered my Navajo heritage, seemed to think I lived in a teepee and hunted buffalo. . . . Further, they wanted to know why I didn't wear any feathers or have long, black hair. I was shocked by how little my fellow students knew about American Indians and how much they based their perceptions of me and my heritage on what they had seen in westerns.

Despite these problems, Hollywood has made progress in recent years. When, in 2015, an overwhelming number (94%) of Oscar voters nominated only White actors in the categories of lead and supporting actor many people in and out of the film industry protested. You probably remember seeing the hashtag #OscarsSoWhite all over social media. In response to the social media backlash, the Academy invited the largest and most diverse class of new Oscar voters in its history. Just over 40% percent of its 683 new members were people of color (Keegan 2017).

Hollywood has also made strides in diversifying characters and story lines to appeal to an increasingly diverse society. Films such as *Black Panther* (2018), which featured a majority Black cast, and *Crazy Rich Asians* (2018), with its all-Asian cast, were undoubtedly anomalies in White-centric Hollywood—and a risk for a historically White-centric business. They proved, however, that such movies can attract a wide audience and be big money-makers—which should lead to more such films in the future.

Some consumers of film and television, however, do not welcome increased diversity. In 2019, Disney cast Halle Bailey, a Black actress, as the lead in a live-action remake of *The Little Mermaid*. Though many fans applauded the decision (as it was the first time Disney had cast a person of color in a traditionally White role and one of the rare times that Disney's lead was Black) (Joyner 2019), others took to Twitter to express their anger that an African American actress would play the role (Cummings 2019). Though there exist no readily available statistics to show just how many dissenters there actually were, the online uproar garnered much media attention and revealed the obstinate resistance by some Americans to the racial diversification of characters in the media.

Racial Bias in News Media

Finally, racial bias is even evident in news media. For example, studies show that news outlets report more often on crime committed by people of color (particularly, African Americans) than crime committed by Whites. A 2014 analysis of late news in New York City found that news outlets more often ran stories on crimes committed by Blacks than those committed by Whites; in doing so, they starkly overrepresented Black crime (Desmond-Harris 2015; Sun 2018). According to New York City Police Department statistics, African Americans were suspects in 54% of murders, 55% of thefts, and 49% of assaults. News coverage, however, presented them in 74% of murder stories, 84% of theft stories, and 73% of assault stories. The uneven reporting overrepresents Black criminals, giving viewers a false impression that crime is primarily a Black problem. Further, research reveals that news media tends to focus on crimes that involve Black perpetrators and White victims, though most crime, including violent crime, occurs within racial groups (i.e., Black on Black or White on White) (Ghandnoosh 2014). An analysis of crime news in Philadelphia, for instance, found that 42% of crimes reported over a 14-week period involved Whites who were victimized by Blacks, though crime data for that period reveal that Black-on-White crime made up only 10% of all crime (Ghandnoosh 2014).

An examination of news coverage of mass protests and riots shows that the racial makeup of participants has often colored the coverage they receive. For example, when White rioters at the Keene Pumpkin Festival in 2014 damaged property, threw bottles at police, set multiple fires, and overturned and smashed cars, media outlets tended to depict them as "kids" engaged in "youthful debauchery"; by contrast, when Blacks protested and rioted shortly thereafter as part of the Black Lives Matter (BLM) movement, media stories often portrayed them as "criminals" and "thugs" (Greenwald and Jones 2016).

Despite this bias, news media can also be used as a vehicle to challenge systemic racism in America. The egregious murder of George Floyd (an unarmed Black man who died at the hands of police in 2020) and the racially diverse protests that followed led some outlets to portray BLM protestors as justified, persuasive, and mostly peaceful. This shift in reporting promotes and supports changing public attitudes about the Black Lives Matter movement and increased awareness of systemic racism in policing. A 2020 Monmouth University poll found that most Americans, 57%, believed that anger over the murder of Blacks by police was "fully justified." Most (57%) also agreed that police are more likely to use excessive force on Blacks than Whites (even when in similar situations), an increase from 33% just 4 years earlier (Monmouth University 2020). Public opinion is changing, and no doubt, media plays a powerful role in this shift.

Children's Books

Like film and television, books also help shape beliefs about race—particularly for children. Though children's literature has made great strides over the decades in moving away from explicit racist imagery and blatant stereotypes, there remains an underrepresentation of characters of color in children's book and an overrepresentation of White characters, especially as main characters. Consider your favorite books as a child—if the characters were human, what were the races of the key characters?

In 2018, the Cooperative Children's Book Center (CCBC) at the University of Wisconsin-Madison analyzed American children's books and found that half of all books featured White characters (in particular, as primary or secondary characters important to the storyline). Books with primary or secondary characters of color were far fewer in number (only 10% of books had African or African American characters, 7% Asian Pacific Islander/Asian Pacific Islander American, 5% Latinx, and 1% American Indian/First Nations). The remaining 27% featured animals or objects (e.g., trucks) rather than people. Though a striking increase in the number of characters of color from just 3 years prior (73% of books featured White primary and secondary characters in 2015), much work needs to be done. Approximately 80% of those working in the children's book world (such as authors, illustrators, editors, publishing executives, marketers, and reviewers) are White (Slater 2016)—and as noted previously, this affects how and whose stories are told.

The "pervasiveness of whiteness" in children's books contributes to the notion that White is "the norm or default," with other races consequently perceived as a deviation from the norm (Welch 2016). Even in cases where a character's race is not explicitly stated by the author, readers may, by default, imagine the character as White (especially if they are White themselves). For example, author Suzanne Collins did not specify the race of the characters in her *Hunger Games* book series. However, when the film adaptations of the books portrayed three of the central characters as Black, some White fans took to social media to express their anger. Similar to critics of the casting of a Black woman for *The Little Mermaid* (described earlier), some fans were shocked, resentful, and enraged over the casting of people of color in *The Hunger Games* movies. Even when the media makes strides to diversify characters, some audiences fight back.

DOING SOCIOLOGY 5.1

Who Holds Power in American Media?

In this exercise you will examine the demographics of some of the most powerful positions in American media.

Racial-ethnic minorities are underrepresented throughout the media industry.
In "The Faces of American Power, Nearly as White as the Oscar Nominees," the *New York Times* provides the following statistics regarding the number of people of color in top leadership positions:

- Hollywood executives: 1 out of 20
- Music executives: 1 out of 20
- Book publishing executives: 2 out of 20
- Television executives: 2 out of 29
- News executives: 2 out of 13

Answer the following questions in writing and be prepared to share your answers with the class:

1. Why does a lack of representation of people of color matter?

2. How might American media change if more people of color were in leadership positions in these various parts of the industry?

The Internet

The Internet adds another layer to the perpetuation of systemic racism. Social media, for example, allows people to easily spread racial stereotypes and racist material through online connections. As like tends to attract like, people's online connections tend to share similar demographics and beliefs. For example, in 2019, an examination of public profiles of police officers discovered "thousands of Facebook posts and comments that ran the gamut from racist memes to conspiracy theories to bombastic expressions of violence" posted by current and former police officers across the country (Epstein 2019). The discovery shows how social media contributes to racism by acting as an echo chamber. In this case, it allowed officers to post and share racist material with like-minded individuals. Through their online connections, they were able to find support for their racist beliefs, which may influence how they police communities and interact with people of color.

In some cases, users can share racist posts anonymously or under pseudonyms, especially in comment sections of news articles, YouTube videos, and online forums. The anonymity allows for racist behavior to flourish, exemplifying what social psychologists term **deindividuation**—when individuals lose their sense of self, lose their sense of personal responsibility and accountability, and engage in antisocial behavior because they feel anonymous. During Barack Obama's presidency, for instance, he and his family were targeted online by racist critics (some critics operated openly, others anonymously). Pictures of the Obamas as monkeys, President Obama with watermelons, and other racist tropes flooded the Internet. Once these racist posts, pictures, memes, and videos were shared, they were easily reshared and retweeted hundreds and thousands of times, allowing for their rapid spread and replication.

CONSIDER THIS

Consider the people you are connected to on social media (via Snapchat, Instagram, Facebook)—do you share particular traits with the majority of your connections (think race, political leanings, region of country, nationality, religion)? How do those similarities or differences affect what you choose to post and share?

The Internet also provides hate groups with easy access to potential recruits. Websites such as Stormfront.org, run by a White nationalist group, have a centralized place to make their racist claims, recruit new members, and "educate" their followers in racism. Many hate groups have large followings on Twitter and "amassing followers heightens visibility to their hateful agendas" (Safehome.org 2017). Hate groups on Twitter, in particular, are on the rise, as are the number of likes given to tweets and comments by hate groups (Safehome.org 2017).

However, while the Internet provides racist organizations a platform to promote their agendas, people can also use it as a tool to organize and recruit people to combat systemic racism. For example, social media is integral to Black Lives Matter, a movement whose prime focus is to protest police violence against Black Americans. Also, in recent years, people have posted and shared a barrage of photographs and video clips that illustrate the perils of living as a Black person in America. Examples include images and videos of African Americans arrested while waiting for friends at a Starbucks, police responding to a call when a Black child mowed the wrong yard, Black women harassed by white men for golfing too slowly, and police called when an 8-year-old Black child sold bottled water on a public street (Lockhart 2018). Likely, most of these interactions would have gone unnoticed without the aid of social media; instead, they went viral on social media platforms such as Facebook and Twitter, drawing the attention of mainstream news outlets and the American public.

> **Check Your Understanding**
>
> 1. What are two explanations for why American media is White-centric today?
>
> 2. In what ways were people of color portrayed in early American traveling shows, television, and film?
>
> 3. In what ways is American film and television racially biased today?
>
> 4. What aspects of children's literature remain White-centric today?
>
> 5. How do "like attracting like" and deindividuation online contribute to systemic racism?
>
> 6. How can people and organizations use the Internet to combat racism?

THE AMERICAN EDUCATIONAL SYSTEM

As explained in Chapter 4, systemic racism affects the education system in the United States in several ways, including through racial inequality in funding and segregated housing. The education system also works to support systemic racism. For example, cultural norms within schools maintain and perpetuate racial inequality.

How did your race affect your experience in school? Racially toxic environments in some schools, as well as low academic and behavioral expectations of students of color by many educators yields very different school experiences for children of color and White children across the nation. A Eurocentric-focused curriculum privileges European/White accomplishments and perspectives, while simultaneously downplaying or ignoring the contributions of people of color and the atrocities in the nation's racist past. School culture also maintains systemic racism through student dress codes targeted disproportionately at children of color—especially Black girls.

Racial Toxicity, Racialized Expectations, and Consequences for Children of Color

A growing body of research reveals racial bias in American schools and the detrimental effects on children of color (Swaak 2018). Racial bias can come in many forms, including explicit and implicit bias. Explicit bias is overt and blatant, such as the use of racial slurs and bullying from classmates and peers. It also occurs when educators ignore students' and parents' complaints about this harassment (Branigin 2018). For example, in 2019, the American Civil Liberties Union (ACLU) filed a complaint against an entire district in Wisconsin, alleging that district officials did little to stem the atmosphere of hostility toward Black students and dismissed the concerns raised by their parents (Hughes 2019; Rose 2019). In the same year, students at a prestigious New York City private high school barricaded themselves in a school building overnight to protest what they alleged was a racist culture (E. Shapiro 2019). In 2017, the Tribal Executive Board of Fort Peck in Montana filed a civil rights complaint contending that the nearby off-reservation public school system routinely discriminated against Native American students. The complaint alleged that a coach at an area high school used derogatory slurs such as "dirty Indians" in front of Native students. They also said the school system blatantly treats Native American students differently than their White counterparts—such as providing fewer opportunities and academic and social supports to Native children as compared to White children (Green and Waldman 2018).

CONSIDER THIS

Reflect on the schools that you attended before college: how would you describe their school culture(s) regarding race? How do you think your classmates (especially those of other racial groups) would answer this question?

An uptick in bias reports in recent years suggests that these cases are not mere anomalies but indicative of school cultures in many districts across the nation. The spike in racial bias claims aligns with the "nationwide amplification of white supremacist rhetoric, as well as the growing number of hate groups in the US," as reported by the Southern Poverty Law Center (Swaak 2018). The racial climate in schools cannot be divorced from the racial climate of the larger society. "Our schools are places that encapsulate and reflect the national climate" (Klein 2018).

Though media attention often focuses on explicit bias in schools, bias also occurs implicitly. People who hold **implicit biases**, or subconscious biases, are not aware of their biases and how they influence their perceptions and behavior. Teachers and school administrators, like all people, can hold implicit racial biases. Moreover, while teachers of *all* races may hold implicit biases toward students of color, the racial imbalance between educators and students in American schools is also problematic. Eighty percent of all public school teachers are White, while students of color make up slightly more than half of the public school population (Dwyer 2017).

Teachers' biases (whether explicit or implicit) can affect the *expectations* they have of their students, both in terms of academics and behavior. For example, research shows the following:

- Public school teachers have lower academic expectations for Black and Latinx students than White students—even before these students ever set foot in their classrooms (Dwyer 2017).

- Non-Black teachers have lower expectations of their Black students than Black teachers, illustrating the benefit of matching teachers and students by race (Gershenson, Holt, and Papageorge 2016).

- Black female students believe their White teachers have higher expectations of their White peers and that they hold these expectations even before getting to know them (Joseph, Viesca, and Bianco 2016).

- Even names can affect teacher expectations. Students with distinctly Black names are subject to more "disrespect, stereotypes and low academic and behavioral expectations" by educators (A. Shapiro 2019).

PHOTO 5.2 Studies show that teachers tend to hold implicit racial biases, which affect their interactions with and behaviors toward students.

Maskot

While educators may hold low expectations for Black, Latinx, and Native American students, studies show that they often hold high expectations for Asian American students (Cherng and Liu 2017). Consider the stereotypes you hold about Asian Americans. The model minority stereotype (also called the model minority myth) portrays Asian American students as "whiz kids" and overachievers, and these stereotypes contribute to high expectations by administrators, teachers, and school counselors.

High expectations by educators may lead to academic opportunities, but they may also place unrealistic pressures on some Asian American students and obscure wide disparities among Asian American ethnic groups. For instance, while some Asian American ethnic groups have stellar high school and college graduation rates, others (such as Cambodians, Hmongs, and Laotians) have extremely high dropout rates—even higher than rates for Latinx and African Americans (Southeast Asia Resource Action Center 2020). Educators influenced by the model minority myth may assume Asian American students need little assistance and consequently fail to meet the needs of those who struggle academically.

Racial Bias in Tracking

Different expectations by educators have important implications for student performance and educational opportunities. For instance, studies show that teacher expectations affect how students perform in school, and even influence students' scores on IQ tests (Spiegel 2012). Teacher expectations also affect **tracking**, the process of placing students into different educational programs within schools. Even after controlling for standardized test scores, Black children are less likely to be tracked into gifted programs than White students—especially if they have White teachers (Grissom and Redding 2016). Moreover, Black students make up more than half of all remedial students across the nation (53%) (Pirtle 2019) and are more than 2 times more likely than White students to be labeled as "cognitively deficient" (Mazama 2015).

Because tracking is racialized, it creates "separate and unequal education systems *within* single schools" (Pirtle 2019) (i.e., White and Asian students in gifted and honors courses, while Black, Latinx, and Native American students languish in remedial courses). Tracking also has far-reaching consequences. Children placed in higher tracks are more likely to graduate high school and gain college degrees than those put in lower tracks. As such, racial biases by educators reproduce inequality and maintain a social structure that privileges Whiteness.

Racial Bias in Punishing

Teachers' expectations of students based on race may also explain uneven discipline in American schools. Consider how you and your classmates were punished at school—what types of punishments were typical? Black students are 3 times more likely to be suspended or expelled from school than their White peers, and studies show that Black children face harsher discipline than White students for *the same infractions* (Gordon 2018; Nittle 2019).

Even in preschool (where students are typically 3 and 4 years old), Black children are 3.6 times more likely to be suspended than their White counterparts (Turner 2016). A recent study of 132 preschool teachers may help explain why. Using cutting-edge eye tracking technology, researchers at Yale University found that preschool teachers watched Black boys (42% of the time) more than White boys (34%), White girls (13%), and Black girls (10%). According to the researchers, teachers may watch Black boys more closely and punish them more often because they assume that Black boys are more likely to misbehave than other children.

Educators' biases also effect *how* they discipline students for infractions. Black students are much more likely than White students to attend schools patrolled by police. This contributes to a nationwide pattern of Black students facing arrest at school at disproportionately high rates. For example, Black boys are 3 times more likely than White boys to find themselves arrested at school (Blad and Harwin 2017).

In 2019, a 6-year-old African American girl was arrested, handcuffed, and then transported in a police car to a local juvenile detention center where she was then fingerprinted and photographed for a mugshot. Her offense? She threw a tantrum at school (Meara 2019). While her story is extreme, it reflects a pattern of racial inequality in the punishment of students.

Eurocentric Curricula and the Invisibility of People of Color

The American educational system also maintains systemic racism in the school curricula. Whether the subject is history, art history, literature, geography, or science (this list is not exhaustive), the educational focus in America is Eurocentric and one that privileges the accomplishments and perspectives of

Europeans or European-descended peoples. By contrast, students of color tend to see few people who look like themselves in the curricula, and when they do, they find their stories presented from the perspective of the dominant White group.

Racism expert and psychology professor Beverly Daniel Tatum points out that a key problem with the Eurocentric focus is that it leads many students, of all races, to believe that people of color have contributed little to American society. She writes of a White male student enrolled in one of her college-level courses who complained in a writing assignment: "It's not my fault that Blacks don't write books." She questions whether any of his teachers had ever told him that there were no Black writers but concludes, "Probably not. Yet because he had never been exposed to Black authors, he had drawn his own conclusion that there were none" (Tatum 2017, 85).

Further, in history and social studies courses across America, America's racist past is often white-washed, downplayed, and in many cases, erased altogether. Textbooks in schools often gloss over or omit important historical events when minorities were oppressed by the White majority. How much did you learn about slavery in school?

Many students do not learn about slavery until high school, and often they never learn the complete history. In a survey of high school seniors, nearly 70% did not know that a constitutional amendment formally ended slavery, and less than 25% could explain how provisions in the U.S. Constitution supported slavery (Chavez 2018). Moreover, in many cases, crucial events in American history are erased altogether—including the internment of Japanese Americans, the forced assimilation of Native American children in boarding schools, Juneteenth, the wave of anti-Black violence during the Red Summer, the Tulsa Race Massacre, the brutal history of lynching, sundown towns, and the role the U.S. government played in perpetuating systemic racism via widespread policies such as redlining. Looking back, did you, as a student, learn about these important historical events?

Distorted History and Maps

Also problematic in American schools is the reframing and distortion of history and geography in ways that often favor the dominant White group. Some examples include the following:

- Many students learn in elementary schools that Christopher Columbus discovered America, despite the fact that thousands of Native peoples were already living in the Americas and despite the fact that Christopher Columbus never actually set foot in what is now the United States. Further, students rarely learn about the atrocities committed by Columbus and his men (e.g., that Columbus allowed his men to rape Native women and that he supported the dismemberment of Native peoples) (Cutler 2017).

- In 2015, publisher McGraw Hill came under fire for its history textbook, which referred to enslaved African peoples as "workers" brought over from Africa to work on plantations (Wong 2015). Many critics were outraged that slavery and the forced movement of people from Africa to the United States was so blatantly misrepresented. Though the publisher fixed the wording, the book had already been distributed to many school districts across the nation, including all public schools in Texas. In 2016, a fourth-grade textbook that similarly minimized the brutality of slavery was pulled from a Connecticut school district. The text, which had already been in use for nearly a decade, read that owners of enslaved peoples "cared for and protected [enslaved people] like members of the family" (Grochowski 2016).

- Many textbooks used in American classrooms, especially those in the South, teach children that the Confederate states left the Union over the issue of states' rights, not because they wanted to protect slavery in their states. This is a remarkably brazen falsehood, considering that the declarations of secession by Confederate states proclaimed that they were seceding to protect the institution of slavery (Wong 2015).

- Most world maps hanging in American schools are "Mercator maps" that provide a Eurocentric view of the world. They use a projection devised centuries ago to convert the spherical Earth's surface into a flat map. They depict South America and Africa proportionally but greatly magnify the size of northern Europe. During the colonial era, it was politically expedient to exaggerate the prominence of European nations. For example, on traditional Mercator maps the United Kingdom and its former colony of India appear approximately the same size, even though India is approximately 13 times the size of the United Kingdom. Colin Rose, Boston's assistant superintendent of opportunity and achievement gaps, noted that the traditional Mercator map is "one of the most insidious examples of how schools perpetuate racism." Boston is one of the few cities in the nation to use a new set of maps that more accurately reflect world geography (Mahnken 2017).

PHOTO 5.3 World maps commonly found in classrooms and textbooks in American schools are Eurocentric. For example, in this map Africa and Greenland appear the same size even though Africa is 14 times the size of Greenland (Bendix 2017).

Przemyslaw Klos / Alamy Stock Photo

The Eurocentric focus in American schools is particularly problematic because research shows that the "overwhelming dominance of Euro-American perspectives leads many [non-White] student to disengage from academic learning" (as cited in Depenbrock 2017). Conversely, when students of color take courses that connect to their lived experiences, their "engagement increases, as do literary skills, overall achievement and attitudes towards learning" (Depenbrock 2017).

CONSIDER THIS

Did you know that enslaved people helped to build the White House and that the transcontinental railroad was built on the backs of exploited Chinese laborers? In what ways were the accomplishments of people of color in American society or world history incorporated into your high school curriculum? If they were absent, why do you think that is?

DOING SOCIOLOGY 5.2

Whose History?

In this exercise you will reflect on the history you learned in high school and how you might change it, if given the chance. As you do so, consider the information you just read in this chapter.

Imagine you were just put in charge of the history curriculum at your high school and answer the following questions in writing:

Would you change the curriculum? If no, explain why it is the best possible curriculum possible. If yes, what changes would you make? What material would you delete? What would you add? Why?

Alternatives to Public School Curricula

To combat the Eurocentric education provided in American schools, some non-White parents have chosen homeschooling for their children in lieu of traditional education (Mazama 2015; PBS News Hour 2018). In 2015, Black children made up 10% of all homeschooled children in the United States. Most of their parents chose homeschooling "due to White racism" in the American school system and "to provide their children the history and social context they say can't be found in public schools" (Mazama 2015; PBS News Hour 2018). One parent who homeschools notes that most American schools teach limited history about African Americans and says, "the history that all kids, Black and White, learn about Black people" is either nonexistent or focused on slavery (PBS News Hour 2018). Through homeschooling, Black parents can expand the history curriculum to include information about non-White racial groups in the United States. Of course, few parents can afford to give up paid work time and homeschool their children. Homeschooling may help some children, but it is not a solution to systemic racism in the American public education system.

Promoting Eurocentric Norms in American Schools: The Policing of Clothing and Hair

Did you have dress codes in the schools you attended growing up? Pressure for Euro-conformity is evident in dress codes used by many schools—public, private, and charter—across the nation. Many of these dress codes are both sexist and racist, and according to the Barrett (2018), they often enforce a "White male default." In short, they favor White boys, while often penalizing children of color and girls. For instance, many schools prohibit particular styles of clothing, such as sagging pants, baggy clothing, and hoodies. Because these styles are associated with African American culture, these rules disproportionately target Black boys, while prioritizing White American cultural norms. One teacher observes that "dressing as most White young men do seems to be what is encouraged" (Barrett 2018).

Moreover, because dress code rules tend to favor White cultural norms and males, they often pose a double-whammy for girls of color, especially for African American girls. According to a study of schools in Washington, DC, Black girls were 17.8 times more likely than White girls to be suspended for dress code violations, and one reason is because "adults often see Black girls as older and more sexual than their [W]hite peers" (National Women's Law Center, as cited in Reese 2018). When one student who attends a Baltimore City public school brought up this racial disparity in her school with a male administrator, he responded that it was because "[W]hite girls don't have as much to show" (Barrett 2018). These gender-biased dress codes and their race-biased enforcement lead many Black girls to miss days of school and face more obstacles to academic success than other students (Barrett 2018).

In 2019, one Texas high school came under fire for the racially discriminatory dress code they imposed on *parents*. In what some described as a "condescending" letter sent home to families of its 1,600 students, the principal warned parents that administrators would turn them away if they wore sagging clothing, pajamas, hair rollers, satin caps, or bonnets. Forty percent of the student body is Black, and the final two items target Black women, who often wear satin caps and bonnets to protect their hair. One mother told a local television station that the new code had prevented her from registering her child for class (Gold 2019). The principal is an African American woman, illustrating that one does not need to be White to support systemic racism.

Policing Black Girls' Hair

Many schools have implemented policies targeting Black students, especially Black girls, for their hair. According to a 2018 study, 68% of DC public high schools banned hair wraps or head scarfs, which Black girls often wear (Reese 2018). Also, some schools ban Black girls from wearing their hair naturally and prohibit hairstyles common in Black culture—including hair extensions, puffs, braids, and dreadlocks. For example, in 2013, one Ohio school banned "afro-puffs and small twisted braids," which are styles typical of Black girls (Klein 2013). In 2016, a Kentucky high school banned cornrows, twists, and dreadlocks. One parent noted that the school policy stated that students' hair must be "neat and clean," implying, she argued, that Black hairstyles are not (Quinn 2016). In 2017, Black girls at a Massachusetts charter school were pulled from class, served multiple detentions, and were threatened with suspension for wearing box braids because administrators charged that their hairstyle violated the school's dress code. Though the girls were good students, school administrators also banned them from afterschool sports activities and attending prom (Lazar 2017). The good news is that organized protests of unjust rules can be successful. After facing backlash from parents and negative media attention, these three schools changed their policies.

PHOTO 5.4 Butler Traditional High School in Louisville, Kentucky, banned dreadlocks, twists, cornrows, and braids. Braids, like those pictured on the left, were prohibited because administrators deemed them to be "distracting and "extreme" (Wilson 2016).

Nick David

These dress code and hair policies exemplify systemic racism in American schools. Even if school rules do not mention race explicitly, they can disproportionately target students of color and assume that all students should follow White cultural norms (Lattimore 2017). In 2019, California became the first state to legally protect Black people from natural hair discrimination. The law, called the CROWN Act (an anacronym for "Creating a Respectful and Open World for Natural Hair"), prohibits workplace and school policies that ban hairstyles such as afros, twists, cornrows, dreadlocks, and other styles commonly worn by African Americans. Within one year of California's law, six additional states followed suit by passing similar laws—including New York, New Jersey, Maryland, Virginia, Colorado, and Washington. Despite this progress, however, Black women and girls continue to face hair discrimination in much of the nation (Glamour 2020; Willon and Diaz 2019).

Check Your Understanding

1. How do schools maintain and perpetuate systemic racism through both explicit and implicit bias?

2. What is the model minority stereotype, and what is problematic about the stereotype?

3. What is tracking in schools, and how are racial groups differentially affected by the practice? How might tracking affect students' future trajectories?

4. How does the American education system maintain and perpetuate systemic racism through its curricula?

5. How are Eurocentric norms maintained and perpetuated in school dress codes and policies regarding hair?

AMERICAN CULTURAL IDEOLOGIES

In addition to media and schools, some widely shared cultural ideologies support systemic racism in the United States. A cultural ideology refers to the ideals, principles, and shared sets of beliefs held by a given society or culture. You are no doubt familiar with two beliefs that provide powerful support for systemic racism: (1) America is a meritocracy, and (2) colorblindness is the answer to racism and racial inequality.

The Myth of the American Meritocracy: "If You Just Work Hard Enough. . ."

Do you believe that America is a meritocracy—a place where if people work hard enough they can prosper? This belief is a cornerstone of American culture and one that imparts a "pull yourself up by your own bootstraps" lesson to Americans and newcomers alike. The meritocratic belief was popularized in the second half of the 19th century by author Horatio Alger Jr., who wrote more than a hundred novels replete with "rags to riches" stories (Steinberg 1989). His books titled *Sink or Swim, Strive and Succeed, Brave and Bold*, and *Struggling Upward* (to name some examples) told promising tales of new immigrants (always from Europe) who worked hard to succeed in the New World. They had the right values. They had talent. They sacrificed. They persisted despite obstacles. In all Alger's stories, the protagonist perseveres to achieve the coveted American Dream.

Unfortunately, the widespread idea that the United States is a meritocracy is a myth. One area that illustrates its pretense is college admissions. Students may believe, for example, that they gained admission into an academically competitive college based on their unique abilities, talent, and hard work (in other words, based on their own merit). While students may believe that they *deserved* admission, the reality of college admissions is that the system is rigged toward the middle and upper classes. Affluent parents, for instance, can afford to live in areas with good public schools. Money gives them the ability to choose areas with schools that have rigorous academic programs (e.g., honors and AP courses), an array of extracurricular opportunities, and resources such as college counselors. In some cases, affluent parents may even give their child a leg up over other applicants by paying for elite private education, expensive SAT preparatory courses, and/or private tutors for their children.

Moreover, if college applicants are legacies (children of alumni) they have an even greater advantage in admission decisions at many colleges and universities, including many of the most prestigious in the nation. A survey of college admissions directors reveals that 42% of private colleges and universities considered legacy status as a factor in admissions, and at Harvard legacy students made up 14% of undergraduates in 2018. Six percent of public colleges and universities also consider legacy status in admissions (Larkin and Aina 2018). Some critics describe legacy admissions as an affirmative action program for wealthy Whites, privileging families who have a multigenerational history of college education.

CONSIDER THIS

Think about advantages some students have that help them attend college (that may be unavailable to others). Is the playing field level for all Americans with regards to going to college?

PHOTO 5.5 Books by Horatio Alger Jr., such as the one seen here, were popular in the late 19th century and promoted the view of America as a meritocratic society.

Buyenlarge/Getty Images

Prioritizing legacies is problematic because it disadvantages first-generation college or university students, many of whom are students of color. In particular, it disadvantages African American students whose ancestors were prohibited from attending many U.S. colleges and universities before desegregation. Many southern state universities, for example, did not admit Black students until the 1960s.

Wealthy parents can also donate to colleges to secure spots for their children. Egregious examples include wealthy politicians and celebrities who donate large sums of money to elite schools. Charles

Kushner, for example, donated $2.5 million to Harvard in 1998, not long before his son (and son-in-law of former president Donald Trump), Jared Kushner, gained acceptance into Harvard (Menon 2019). In 2019, Dr. Dre received pushback when he bragged on social media about his daughter getting into the University of Southern California "all on her own"; he deleted the post after critics reminded him that he donated $70 million to the school just 6 years prior (Aswad 2019). In some cases, wealthy parents have also blatantly cheated and broken the law to snare coveted spots for their children at prestigious schools, hence further rigging a system that already advantages them in many ways. In 2019, 50 people faced charges in a nationwide college admissions scheme for allegedly using their wealth to bribe officials and, in some cases, to alter test scores to gain their children seats at elite schools such as the University of Southern California, UCLA, Stanford, Georgetown, and Yale (Bryant 2019).

Despite the realities of college or university admissions, the myth of the meritocracy persists—perhaps because it supports a deeply held value in American culture: the importance of hard work (Garber 2017). The belief in America as a meritocracy is problematic, however, because it downplays inequality and provides Americans with a false impression of a level playing field for all.

This illusion allows those who succeed in American society to believe that they alone are responsible for their successes, while simultaneously blaming others for their own so-called failures (e.g., "Well, they didn't work hard enough"). In doing so, they ignore or downplay the ways U.S. society has systematically advantaged them and disadvantaged people of color (e.g., slavery, genocide, Jim Crow segregation and voter suppression, redlining, public school funding).

Colorblindness: "I Don't See Race"

A second popular American cultural ideology, the colorblind ideology, posits that the best way to end prejudice, racism, and discrimination is to ignore race altogether. It is exemplified in statements such as, "I'm colorblind, I don't see race," or "I don't see color." For some, these assertions arise from an upbringing in a culture where they learned that noticing or noting a person's race is wrong or racist and that "racism would disappear if we just quit talking about it." For others, it is a way to try to convey their aversion to racism.

Though seemingly innocuous, there are at least three problems with this ideology. First, it is disingenuous for someone who can see to say, "I don't see color." Antiracist educator Jon Greenberg (2015) describes his skepticism upon hearing such statements and says, "I just don't believe you. Essentially, you are saying that you don't notice any difference between [Black actress] Lupita Nyon'o and, say, [White actress] Anne Hathaway, two similarly aged actresses who I'm betting have never been confused for each other . . . let's just be honest." Additionally, ignoring a person's race may well invalidate or treat as problematic a major part of a person's identity. Greenberg points out that doing so "implies that color is a problem, arguably synonymous with 'I can see who you are *despite* your race.' As evidence, note that the phrase is virtually never applied to White people. In over 40 years of life and nearly 15 years as an antiracist educator, I have yet to hear a White person say in reference to another White person, 'I don't see your color; I just see you.'"

Second, the colorblind ideology is a form of racism, one that is particularly insidious. Sociologist Eduardo Bonilla-Silva (2010) notes in his book *Racism Without Racists* that the colorblind ideology is really "colorblind racism." It allows the racially dominant group (Whites) to maintain their own racial privilege by drawing attention *away* from race and ignoring systemic racial inequality and bias.

Finally, the colorblind ideology has a detrimental effect on programs designed to combat racial inequality—such as affirmative action in hiring and higher education—programs that require Americans to acknowledge race. As noted in Chapter 4, policies that disregard race typically maintain the status quo, which benefits the dominant group and disadvantages people of color. For example, in 1996 Californians voted to remove race from consideration in college admissions and banned affirmative action in the state. Supporters of the ban argued that students should be judged without regard to skin color, drawing on colorblind language to make their case. In response, critics argued that American society is not colorblind and predicted that prohibiting universities from considering race would likely most disadvantage Black and Latino students at elite campuses such as UC–Berkeley and UCLA. They were right. Black and Hispanic enrollment dropped significantly, while White enrollment increased.

Thus, ignoring race did nothing to level the playing field in college admissions; in fact, it simply preserved the status quo and perpetuated racial inequality in higher education.

DOING SOCIOLOGY 5.3

Actively Responding to the Colorblind Ideology

In this activity, you will respond to colorblind statements.

Imagine a friend or family member saying one or more of the following statements in casual conversation with you. How would you respond to each statement based on what you have learned? Write a response to each statement.

1. "I don't see color; I just see people."

2. "It's racist to see race."

3. "If everyone would just stop talking about race, racism would disappear."

Check Your Understanding

1. What is the ideology of the American meritocracy?

2. Using college admissions as an example, how can you show that this ideology is a myth?

3. What are "legacies," and how do legacy policies maintain and perpetuate systemic racism?

4. What is the colorblind ideology, and how does it support systemic racism?

CONCLUSION

Racism is widespread in American society and deeply embedded in our culture. In our media and educational systems, Whiteness is pervasive and privileges the voices, perspectives, and stories of White Americans. Widely shared cultural ideologies, such as the myth of the American meritocracy and colorblindness, further contribute to racism by perpetuating beliefs that privilege White Americans at the expense of people of color. In the next chapter, we examine Native Americans and Alaska Natives and genocide in America. As you read, consider what cultural supports continue to support the systemic racism that continues to disadvantage Indigenous peoples in the United States.

CHAPTER REVIEW

5.1 How and why does American media maintain and perpetuate systemic racism?

American media, such as films, television, and children's books, maintains and perpetuates racism by privileging representations and perspectives of White people and underrepresenting people of color or portraying them in stereotypical ways. The Internet—especially social media—provides racists groups and individuals an avenue to connect online. It enables the rapid and easy spread of racist material and provides racist groups a platform to easily recruit and spread their messages of hate. At the same time, however, social media also allows antiracist groups to connect, recruit, organize, and spread a counternarrative to racist messaging.

5.2 In what ways does the American educational system maintain and perpetuate systemic racism?

Ways in which the educational system maintains and perpetuates systemic racism include racial bias (both explicit and implicit) among school administrators and teachers. For example,

- Teachers typically hold high expectations for White and Asian students, and low expectations for Black, Latinx, and Native American students (academically and behaviorally).
- Eurocentric curricula privilege the accomplishments and perspectives of White Americans and Europeans, whitewash America's racist past, and—for the most part—omit people of color.
- Discriminatory dress codes and hair policies maintain White cultural norms in American schools.

5.3 What are two American cultural ideologies that maintain and perpetuate systemic racism, and how do they do so?

First, the myth of the American meritocracy assumes an equal playing field for all Americans, allowing Whites to believe they alone are responsible for their own successes. It allows them to ignore the ways in which Whites benefit from systemic racism and people of color are disadvantaged. Second, the colorblind ideology maintains that the best way to end prejudice and racism is to ignore race. This benefits the dominant racial group (Whites) by drawing attention away from racial inequality.

KEY TERMS

Blackface (p. 91)

Colorblind ideology (p. 105)

Cultural ideology (p. 103)

Deindividuation (p. 95)

Explicit bias (p. 96)

Implicit bias (p. 97)

Legacy (p. 103)

Media (p. 90)

Meritocracy (p. 103)

Minstrel shows (p. 91)

Tracking (p. 98)

Wild West shows (p. 91)

LOVE IS AMONGST US

RECLAIM INDIGENOUS PEOPLES RIGHTS

TAÍNO

6 AMERICAN INDIANS AND ALASKA NATIVES: SURVIVING GENOCIDE

Kathleen Odell Korgen

LEARNING QUESTIONS

6.1 Why were so few Native Americans around when the "Pilgrims" landed in 1620?

6.2 What did White people desire that led to Indian removal?

6.3 How did the idea of "manifest destiny" influence the removal and attempted destruction of American Indians?

6.4 Why does the United States' treatment of American Indians fall under the label of genocide?

6.5 What were some key resistance actions led by the "Indians of All Tribes" and the American Indian movement?

6.6 How do the experiences of the Native peoples in Alaska correspond to those in the lower 48 states?

6.7 How does historic trauma relate to the challenges facing American Indian and Alaska Native people today?

Let's see what you know about Thanksgiving in the United States. How many of the following questions can you answer?

- Why do some people see Thanksgiving as a joyful holiday during which we should give thanks for all we have while others experience it as a day of mourning?

- Did you know that the Wampanoags helped the colonists in Plymouth, Massachusetts?

- Why were the Wampanoags interested in helping the colonists at that time?

- What is the name of the Wampanoag leader who made the decision to aid them?

- Why—50 years later—did the colonists put the head of the leader's son on a pike and leave it there for 20 years?

If you have a hard time answering these questions, why do you think that is? If you could answer most or all of them, how did you learn that information? Did you gain it from your history textbooks in your K–12 schooling? What do your answers tell you about your knowledge of the history of American Indians in what is now the United States?

This chapter focuses on the experiences of American Indians and Alaska Natives (AIAN). We cannot relay a detailed history, in one chapter, of the many hundreds of Indian nations in what is now the United States. We do, however, look at some key experiences they share. In doing so, we pay attention to their continual resistance to the genocidal efforts of White people. In the process, we answer the "why" questions posed previously.

HOW I GOT ACTIVE IN SOCIOLOGY

Kathleen Odell Korgen

I was a history major in college. I was drawn to study sociology in graduate school, in part, because it enables me to explore why past events occurred—and how they affect society today. Every semester, I show my students two maps of what is now the United States. The first shows the locations of Native American nations across the continent before contact with Europeans. The second shows Native American territory in the United States today. Each time, I hear gasps from my students. Most have never before seen a map showing what is now the United States as a populated land *before* the arrival of Whites. The comparison of the two maps makes it clear that Whites did not "discover" and settle an empty wilderness. Whites seized land belonging to hundreds of Native nations, practicing genocide as they did. We then talk about why—and how it relates to current events. Sociology helps us uncover, recognize, and understand patterns in the past—and make use of that knowledge today.

REPERCUSSIONS OF CONTACT

Separatists (people only started calling them "Pilgrims" in the late 1700s) landed in Massachusetts in 1620. They were seeking a place where they could start a new life guided by strict religious rules and beliefs. Separatists gained their name because they had separated themselves from the Church of England, which they viewed as corrupt (Kidd 2019).

By the time the Separatists landed in Massachusetts, Europeans had been exploring parts of what is now the United States for more than a century and had already established some colonies. For example, Spain and France fought over what are now South Carolina and Florida in the second half of the 1500s (Havard and Vidal 2003). English colonial settlers inhabited Roanoke island in North Carolina in 1587. Three years later, however, the colony and colonists had vanished and were never seen again. In 1607, a group of English profiteers searching for gold started the Jamestown colony in Virginia. It, too, almost ended in failure but managed to survive with the help of the Powhatan Indians.

Our history books, written through the ethnocentric lens of White people, usually focus on Plymouth and the Separatists. The feel-good story of Separatists and American Indians sharing a meal together portrays European settlers and American Indians as friends—rather than adversaries who temporarily used each other. The protagonists in this story—propagated by Whites—are the colonists, rather than the Wampanoags, upon whose land they settled.

PHOTO 6.1 A typical painting of the first Thanksgiving. Note who is in the front and who is in the background.

Barney Burstein/Corbis/VCG via Getty Images

Before and After Contact

By the late 1500s, millions of American Indians (estimates range from 4 million to 40 million) lived in North America. They had resided there for about 14,000 years before the arrival of Europeans (Calloway 2008; Dunbar-Ortiz 2014). During that time, the Native Americans created many hundreds of various societies as they adapted to their geographic locations. For example, Northeast Indians fished and gathered fruits and berries from forests. Plains Indians relied on the buffalo for most of their food, clothing, and housing needs. Southwest Indians created impressive irrigation systems so they could grow corn and a wide variety of other crops in their dry lands. The Aleut (from the Aleutian Islands in Alaska) relied on fish and other animals from the sea (Calloway 2008).

Disease and Death

All American Indian nations faced the disease and death that came with Europeans. Even before the Separatists arrived, European diseases began to kill them. They had no resistance to these illnesses, and the results were catastrophic. English explorer and Jamestown settler, John Smith, visited New England before the first plague that began in 1614. When he went back in 1622, he could scarcely believe his eyes. After noting that 90% to 95% of the American Indian population there had died, he thanked the Lord, saying, "God had laid this country open for us." Another plague from 1616 to 1618 almost decimated the Wampanoag and, as Smith noted, left their lands open for the Separatists. The governor of Plymouth, William Bradford, wrote that so many Wampanoags became sick and died that they could not bury their dead: "They not being able to bury one another, their skulls and bones were found in many places lying still above the ground" (New England Historical Society 2018).

Just a few years before the Separatists arrived, Massasoit, the leader of the Wampanoag, controlled a confederation of tribes consisting of more than 20,000 people. However, fewer than 1,000 of that 20,000 withstood the European diseases. With so few followers left alive, Massasoit knew they were vulnerable to their enemy, the Narragansett nation, who had lost far fewer people. The tensions between the two Indian nations resulted in little interaction between them. This lack of interaction made it possible for the Narragansett to mostly avoid the disease decimating the Wampanoag (they were not so lucky when smallpox hit them in 1633) (Mann 2005).

Fearing that the Narraganset would attack and overwhelm the Wampanoag, Massasoit decided to accept the presence of the Separatists and set up an alliance with them. This alliance included teaching the Separatists how to grow crops and survive in their new surroundings.

CONSIDER THIS

Do you think we would celebrate Thanksgiving today if the Wampanoags were not exposed to European diseases? Why?

The pact between the Wampanoag and the Separatists lasted until 1675, when one of the sons of Massasoit known as King Philip gathered about a dozen other tribes and attacked the Europeans. The number of Europeans had increased steadily since they first landed in 1620, and King Philip realized that if Native people didn't unite and try to rid their land of the White people, they would lose it. Outnumbered and outgunned, the confederation under King Philip lost, but their attacks were bloody and scary for the colonists, which is why they put his head on a pike and left it there for two decades.

DOING SOCIOLOGY 6.1

In Massasoit's Shoes

In this exercise, put yourself in Massasoit's shoes and think about how you would respond to the disease-related deaths of your people and the Separatists' arrival.

Based on what you read about Massasoit, the leader of the Wampanoag, and his decision to ally with the Separatists, write answers to these questions and be prepared to defend them.

1. Do you think Massasoit should have attacked or helped the Separatists? Why?

2. What would you have done if you were Massasoit—and what might have been the repercussions?

3. Explain how answering these questions affects your opinion of Massasoit.

Iroquois League

Long before the American Revolution and the creation of the U.S. government, a confederation of Northeast Indians formed their own government and showed the power of united Indian nations. Between 1100 and 1400, in what is now New York state, the Mohawks, Oneidas, Onondagas, Cayugas, and Senecas created the **Iroquois League**, also known as the Great League of Peace. A desire to unite against their common enemies and maintain peace among themselves led the tribes to form the league. Representatives from all five tribes met regularly for over a year as they created their government. They distributed power between individual nations and the league, which would conduct diplomacy and trade policies for all five tribes (the Tuscarora joined the league in 1722). Until the Revolutionary War, when the confederacy split up, with some supporting the British and others the revolutionaries, the Iroquois were the dominant American Indians in the region—forcing other nations to submit and pay tribute to them (Calloway 2008).

The Five "Civilized" Tribes

While the Iroquois were breaking up, some Indian nations in the Southeast were doing their best to assimilate into the White population. The Cherokees, Choctaws, Chickasaws, Creeks, and Seminoles were farmers in the southeastern area of what is now the United States. White Americans dubbed them "civilized" because they adopted much of the culture of White people. For example, most became Christians, believed in private property (some even owned plantations and enslaved people), established a democratic government, created a written language, and dressed like White people. These "civilized" attributes would not save them from land-hungry Whites, however.

Check Your Understanding

1. What Indian nation helped the Separatists—and why?

2. Who attacked the Separatists—and why?

3. What was the Iroquois League?

4. Why did the five "civilized" tribes gain that name?

RELATIONSHIPS WITH THE UNITED STATES

Every American Indian nation has its own relationship and experiences with the U.S. government. However, just as all were susceptible to European diseases, all had to deal with White people after their land. The Framers of the U.S. Constitution realized that the United States would have to deal with the American Indians around them and gave this power to the federal government. Article I, Section 8, of the U.S. Constitution states, "The Congress shall have the power to... regulate commerce with foreign nations, and among the several states, and with the Indian tribes" (National Conference of American Indians 2019).

President Andrew Jackson, Indian Removal, and the Trail of Tears

President Andrew Jackson entered the White House in 1828 determined to clear out Indian nations from east of the Mississippi. He pushed through Congress the Indian Removal Policy of 1830. This policy gave him permission to exchange land west of the Mississippi for the land of Indian nations east of the Mississippi. It also stated that the United States would never take the "Indian land" in the West away from Indian nations.

PHOTO 6.2 President Andrew Jackson, known as the "Indian fighter." During his presidency, he engineered the removal of almost all Native Americans east of the Mississippi.

Bettman / Contributor

Meanwhile, White settlers had been complaining for some time about the continued presence of Cherokee people in Georgia. They coveted their land and the gold discovered under it in 1828. Emboldened by the election of Jackson (the "Indian fighter"), the state leaders in Georgia revoked the constitution of the Cherokee nation, declaring that the Cherokee were subject to the laws of the state of Georgia.

DOING SOCIOLOGY 6.2

The Forced Removal of Civilized Tribes

In this exercise you will examine why "civilized" tribes were deported.

Write answers to the following questions and be prepared to share them.

1. Why were even "civilized" tribes forced to leave their homeland for an unknown land in "Indian Country"?

2. What does it indicate about Whites' reception to American Indian assimilation efforts?

3. If you had the opportunity to gain the land of a deported Cherokee, would you? Why?

In 1832, the Cherokee nation took the state of Georgia to the Supreme Court, arguing that it was an independent nation and, as such, not subject to the authority of the state of Georgia. In Worcester v. Georgia, Chief Justice John Marshall, representing the majority opinion, said that the state of Georgia had no power over the Cherokee, pointing out that the Cherokee were a sovereign nation and only the federal government had authority over them. Jackson heard the decision of the Supreme Court, ignored it, and allowed Georgia to continue to establish laws damaging to the Cherokee and other Indian nations in Georgia (Indian Removal 1999).

CONSIDER THIS

Why do you think President Jackson was able to ignore the Supreme Court (one of the three equal branches of the U.S. government)?

The Indian nations who resisted orders to give up their land in the Southeast for some unknown land in the West (in what is now Oklahoma) were forcibly taken from their homes and rounded up. Troops captured American Indians and put them into holding pens, so they couldn't escape before the journey now referred to as "**the Trail of Tears**." Poorly planned and executed by the military, many died along the way to "Indian land" from hunger, disease, cold, exhaustion, and heartache. Among the 17,000 Cherokee forced to march west from 1838 to 1839, somewhere between 4,000 and 8,000 died during the trip (Indian Removal 1999).

Check Your Understanding

1. What was the Indian Removal Policy of 1830?

2. Why did White people want to force the Cherokee (one of the "civilized" nations) to move out of Georgia?

3. What was the Trail of Tears?

INDIAN WARS

President James K. Polk (1845–1849), Andrew Jackson's protege, built his administration under the ideology of **manifest destiny**, the belief that the United States has a God-given obligation and inevitable destiny to expand and take over territories occupied by inferior peoples (e.g., Mexicans and American Indians). Polk used disagreements with Mexico over where, exactly, the Mexican–U.S. border lay to start a war. Going into an area Mexico claimed as its own, U.S. troops started a skirmish with Mexican troops. Polk immediately declared that Mexico had invaded and attacked the United States, using it as a reason to begin the **Mexican–American War** (1846–1848) (Hietala 2003).

The Treaty of Guadalupe Hidalgo, which ended the war in 1848, forced Mexico to cede 55% of its land to the United States. Today, that area includes all or parts of the states of Wyoming, Utah, Nevada, New Mexico, Colorado, Arizona, and California (Hietala 2003). This seizure of vast amounts of land encouraged those who embraced the idea that the United States had a calling to take over and "civilize" the land from sea to sea. They would not let the "inferior" people already there stop their "destiny."

Opening the West for Whites

Shortly after the Mexican–American War, the California gold rush of 1849 increased White migration (the "49ers") through territory of American Indian nations west of the Mississippi. Seeking to protect the 49ers and other Whites passing through, the U.S. government signed a treaty with the Indian nations in the area. The U.S. government promised 50 years of payments if the American Indians promised not to attack White people traveling through their lands and to keep the peace among themselves (Calloway 2008). This treaty, the First Treaty of Fort Laramie (1851), quickly fell apart as Indian nations started fighting among themselves. A scarcity of resources caused by increasing numbers of White migrants and the U.S. government's forcing many Indian nations to live near each other prompted fights for survival. Even more White people entered Indian Country in 1859 during the Pike's Peak gold rush (the 59ers) in what is now Colorado (Calloway 2008).

The Black Hills and the End of the Indian Wars

As part of the **2nd Treaty of Fort Laramie (1868)** the U.S. government established the Great Sioux Reservation, which included the Black Hills—a sacred place for the Sioux in what are now South Dakota and Wyoming. In the 2nd Treaty of Fort Laramie, the U.S. government declared that it would never allow White people to settle in the Black Hills (Calloway 2008). So, what do you think happened next?

Yes, the pattern continued. In 1874, Lieutenant Colonel George Armstrong Custer discovered gold in the Black Hills, and Whites poured into them. Under pressure from gold seekers, the U.S. government took over the Black Hills and allowed White people to occupy them. This prompted the **Black Hills War of 1876**, the last of the big wars on the Great Plains. After defeating the Lakota Sioux and their allies, the Cheyenne and Arapaho, the U.S. government forced the Lakota to move to relatively small, separate reservations in the western area of South Dakota (Centre Communications 1988).

Indian nations in the western part of the United States continued to fight, however. Although they had some success (including killing Custer and almost all his men in the **1876 Battle of Little Bighorn** in the territory of Montana), by 1890 the resistance became untenable. The Indians were outmanned, outgunned, and starving (encouraging the decimation of the buffalo was a tactic of the U.S. government). While a few individuals refused to submit, by 1890 almost all Native Americans were confined to reservations and dependent on the U.S. government for food rations. The U.S. government also separated many parents from their children, whom it forced to go to White-run boarding schools (we discuss boarding schools later in this chapter).

Desperate, many Indians started to take solace through participating in the **Ghost Dance**. A Paiute holy person claimed the dance would bring back loved ones and the buffalo from the dead and return the dancers to a time before Europeans arrived. The dancers wore special shirts when they danced that they believed would protect them from bullets. After dancing in a circle for hours, some people would fall and black out. This was when they could be with their dead loved ones. Everyone wanted an opportunity to have this experience, so people would dance day and night.

White leaders looked at the Ghost Dance with alarm and feared that it signified an imminent revolt. U.S. military leaders ordered the arrest of the few American Indian leaders and their followers still off reservations. Hearing this and news that military police had killed Sitting Bull, a fellow Lakota leader who had helped lead the Battle of Little Bighorn, one of those leaders, Big Foot, realized the fight was over. He had just 350 Lakota under him, and 230 of them were noncombatants (women, elderly people, and children). Big Foot decided it was time to lead his followers to a reservation, lay down arms, and surrender.

DOING SOCIOLOGY 6.3

The Narrative of Manifest Destiny

In this exercise, you will examine American Progress, an 1872 painting by New York-based artist John Gault that was widely reproduced at the end of the 19th century.

PHOTO 6.3 Manifest Destiny

George A. Crofutt. Courtesy of the Library of Congress.

Consider Photo 6.3. Write answers to the following questions and be prepared to share them:

How does the painting justify and glorify the notion of manifest destiny?

Columbia, the robed woman at the center of the painting, sweeps across the western frontier. What do you think she represents?

How does the painting portray the Native American population?

As Big Foot and his people were on their way (in subzero temperatures) to turn themselves in, U.S. troops intercepted the group of Lakota and forced them to a military campsite in the Pine Ridge reservation in South Dakota called **Wounded Knee**. The troops surrounded them and ordered Big Foot and his followers to hand in all their weapons. One Lakota resisted, a shot went off, and the troops opened fire with rifles and machine guns. When the smoke cleared, 300 Indians lay dead in the snow. Twenty-five soldiers also died after being hit by their fellow soldiers' bullets (they fired in a circle). This massacre of unarmed Lakota marked the end of the Indian Wars. The U.S. government rewarded 20 of the soldiers with Medals of Honor for their actions at Wounded Knee (Dunbar-Ortiz 2014).

PHOTO 6.4 Mount Rushmore in the sacred Black Hills. How do you think the Sioux feel about its presence in the Black Hills?

Jean-Marc Giboux/Liason

The Sioux continued to fight for their sacred Black Hills, however. They sued the federal government, and in 1980, after decades of effort, the Supreme Court agreed that Congress had broken the 2nd Treaty of Fort Laramie. In *United States v. the Sioux Nation of Indians*, the Court ruled that Congress must pay the Sioux $102 million in compensation. However, the Sioux refused to take the money (now about $1.3 billion), arguing that they want the *land* back—not money (Zotigh 2018).

CONSIDER THIS

Life on Sioux reservations is difficult, with high rates of alcoholism and poverty and low rates of employment. If you were living on one of these reservations, would you want to take the settlement money? Why?

Check Your Understanding

1. What does "manifest destiny" mean?

2. How did the Mexican–American war start?

3. What did the Treaty of Guadalupe require Mexico to give to the United States?

4. What did the Sioux get from the 2nd Treaty of Fort Laramie?

5. What prompted the Black Hills War of 1876?

6. Why did many American Indians participate in the Ghost Dance?

7. What happened at Wounded Knee in 1890?

GENOCIDE

If you are thinking that all this sounds genocidal, you are correct. The U.S. government's action against American Indians encompass all five acts that the International Criminal Court (ICC) deems genocidal. We now turn to how the U.S. actions meet the definition of genocide.

What Is Genocide?

According to the ICC, **genocide** consists of "any of the following acts committed with intent to destroy, in whole or in part, a national, ethnical, racial or religious group:

- Killing members of the group

- Causing serious bodily or mental harm to members of the group

- Deliberately inflicting on the group conditions of life calculated to bring about its physical destruction in whole or in part

- Imposing measures intended to prevent births within the group

- Forcibly transferring children of the group to another group (ICC 2019).

We now review the evidence for each of these genocidal acts.

Killing Members of the Group

Europeans spread various diseases, including "measles, smallpox, influenza and the bubonic plague across the Atlantic," both unintentionally and intentionally (e.g., giving Indians "gifts" of blankets infected with smallpox) (Koch, Brierley, Maslin, and Lewis 2019). Exposure to these European diseases had devastating consequences for the Indigenous populations.

Causing Serious Bodily or Mental Harm to Members of the Group

As noted, European diseases killed many millions of Native Americans, causing bodily harm for those who caught the diseases and mental harm for those who survived. The survivors had to live with the death of family members, friends, and, for some, their nation. The forced removal of Indians at gunpoint from fertile to uninviting land and their children to White-run boarding schools resulted in more harm—both mental and physical. Finally, regularly broken treaties meant that American Indians could not feel secure, even after the United States repeatedly promised they would be.

Deliberately Inflicting on the Group Conditions of Life Calculated to Bring About Its Physical Destruction in Whole or in Part

As discussed earlier, the U.S. policy to wipe out the buffalo was part of a deliberate plan to starve Indians into capitulation. White soldiers and civilians killed 10 million buffalo, and by the 1880s only a few hundred remained. Forcing the Indigenous population onto crowded reservations also prevented them from gathering enough food to feed themselves (Dunbar-Ortiz 2014).

Imposing Measures Intended to Prevent Births Within the Group

Forced sterilization of American Indians was rampant in the early 1970s. Doctors regularly sterilized women without their consent to curb the relatively high birthrate of Native American women. In fact, "studies revealed that the Indian Health Services (IHS) sterilized between 25% and 50% of Native American women between 1970 and 1976" (Lawrence 2000, 410).

Forcibly Transferring Children of the Group to Another Group

Part of the 2nd Treaty of Fort Laramie required American Indians to send their children to schools in Indian territory from the ages of 6 to 16. A decade later, however, forced assimilation into the dominant White society became the norm. In order to "kill the Indian and save the man" boys and girls were brought—often forcibly—to military-like boarding schools. Taking the children away from their parents helped the U.S. government to control the parents, who wouldn't cause trouble for fear of what would happen to their kids far away in White-run boarding schools (Dunbar-Ortiz 2014).

Forced Assimilation, Theft of Land, and Cultural Genocide

We now look at some other U.S. policies that resulted in great harm to American Indians.

The **General Allotment Act of 1887**, for example, was an attempt to turn Indians into individual farmers—like White people. The U.S. government broke up reservations and assigned a plot to each Indian household. The hope was that American Indians would start seeing themselves as individuals, rather than as members of a collective. After establishing the allotments, the U.S. government stole the unassigned land (about three-fourths of all Indian territory) and opened it up for White settlers.

The results were more broken treaties and less land for Native peoples. Indian nations fought against allotments with lawyers, and then, when that failed, some took up arms. For example, one Creek leader in Oklahoma, known as Crazy Snake, refused to accept the U.S. government's declaration that the Creek government was illegitimate and that they must follow the Dawes Act. Crazy Snake and a few thousand traditional followers kept their government going, moving from place to place as needed to keep safe. After a skirmish in 1909, the military tried to catch Crazy Snake, but they never did. Most people think he died in 1911. His efforts, however, still inspire American Indians today (Dunbar-Ortiz 2014; Harring 1990).

The Indian Reorganization Act—A Reprieve

In 1924, in another assimilation effort, the U.S. government unilaterally gave American Indians citizenship. Meanwhile, the process of allotment continued. President Franklin Delano Roosevelt finally stopped allotment in 1934 with the **Indian Reorganization Act (IRA)**. In a change of pace, John

Collier, Roosevelt's U.S. Commissioner of Indian Affairs, consulted with Native nations to create an act that stopped the allotment process, gave reservations some additional land, and encouraged nations to create their own governments with limited autonomy (Dunbar-Ortiz 2014).

The Termination and Relocation Acts

Trying to prompt greater assimilation and less reliance on the U.S. government, President Dwight Eisenhower signed the Termination Act in 1953 and the Relocation Act in 1956. The first stopped payments promised American Indian nations in treaties. The second provided moving expenses to any Indian willing to move off a reservation to an urban area. The goal was to freeze government expenditures for people on reservations, force them to move to poor neighborhoods in cities, and break the connection between individual Indians and their tribal culture (Dunbar-Ortiz 2014).

Boarding Schools

Boarding schools were one of the most powerful and heartbreaking forced assimilation efforts. In 1879, Captain Richard Henry Pratt (known for his famous quote "Kill the Indian and save the man") established the Carlisle Indian Industrial School, the first boarding school for American Indians. He located the school in Carlisle, Pennsylvania, far away from Indian land (Carlisle Indian School Digital Resource Center n.d.).

In these schools, far from home, American Indian boys and girls had to cut their hair, wear clothes worn by White people, speak English, and embrace Christianity rather than the religion of their people. The teachers at these schools beat the children if they violated the rules, and many boys and girls faced sexual assault from teachers and administrators (Edwards 2016). The result? Traumatized children and families. When the children graduated and returned to their families, they could not understand or speak the language of their parents. Neither could they remember the culture of their Indian nation. They were lost people—estranged from their families and still not accepted by White people (Dunbar-Ortiz 2014).

PHOTO 6.5 Chiricahua Apaches on their first day at the Carlisle Indian School in 1886.

John N. Choate/MPI/Getty Images

PHOTO 6.6 The same Chiricahua Apache children after being at the Carlisle Indian School for 4 months.

John N. Choate/MPI/Getty Images

DOING SOCIOLOGY 6.4

Boarding School Horrors

In this exercise, you will put yourself in the shoes of Indian children at the Carlisle school.

Consider what you have read about the Carlisle school, and then write answers to the following questions:

1. What do you think Pratt meant when he said, "Kill the Indian and save the man"? What does his statement indicate about how he ran the Carlisle Indian Industrial School?

2. Many of the Indian children sent to the school were sons and daughters of chiefs. Why do you think that was the case?

3. Nearly 200 students died and were buried at the school due to the strenuous journey and their poor treatment. Many of the gravestones are marked "Unknown," contain misspellings, or are missing birth date information. What do you think this symbolizes?

4. Imagine you are a child who just arrived at the Carlisle school. How would you feel? Now, imagine it's 8 years later. You arrive home dressed in White people's clothes, with your hair short, and unable to communicate with your family because you no longer speak their language. How will you interact with your family? How do you think your family will react to you?

The U.S. government, although aware of the problems at boarding schools, did not address them for many years. For example, a federal investigation of Indian boarding schools released in 1928 stated that "children at federal boarding schools were malnourished, overworked, harshly punished and poorly educated" (Bear 2008). Another investigation ordered by President Kennedy in the early 1960s revealed that "when asked to name the most important things the schools should do for their students, only about one-tenth of the teachers mentioned academic achievement as an important goal. Apparently, many of the teachers still see their role as that of 'civilizing' the native.... [The] school environment was sterile, impersonal and rigid, with a major emphasis on discipline and punishment, which is deeply resented by the students" (Bear 2008).

CONSIDER THIS

Why do you think assimilation-focused boarding schools kept operating for so many years—even when the U.S. government knew of the harm they were doing?

In the late 1970s, Indian nations finally gained control of their educational systems. Today, the few boarding schools in existence teach students their Indian culture. For many students, this is the only way they will learn it. If their parents went to boarding schools, they were unable to learn about their Native American culture in school. This lack of education means that many young Indians did not get to gain knowledge about their native culture from their parents (Bear 2008).

Check Your Understanding

1. How does the ICC define genocide?

2. What were the Termination and Relocation Acts?

3. What percentage of Native American women did the IHS sterilize without their permission in the 1970s?

4. What happened to Indian children when they were in boarding school? Once they went home?

RESISTANCE

Ironically, the Termination and Relocation Acts helped Native Americans to make connections and organize across nations. Moved to cities, they found people from other tribes whom they never would have met otherwise. Today, just one out of five (22%) American Indians live on reservations. Many of the Native people relocated to urban areas found inspiration in the social movements active in the 1960s and 1970s. San Francisco is an area where many Indians settled and one of the centers of urban Indian resistance.

Resistance Actions

One of the first and most well-known resistance actions organized by Native Americans in San Francisco was the takeover of Alcatraz, an island off the coast of San Francisco. For 19 months from 1969 to 1970, people from at least 12 tribes participated in the occupation of the island. They called themselves "Indians of All Tribes."

In 1963, the federal government closed the famous prison on Alcatraz (the "Rock") and declared the island surplus land (Treuer 2019). Citing a section of the 2nd Treaty of Fort Laramie that declared that the Lakota could claim unused federal land, the protestors took over, saying, "We will purchase said Alcatraz Island for twenty-four dollars in glass beads and red cloth... a precedent set by the White man's purchase of a similar island about 300 years ago. We know that $24 in trade goods for these 16 acres is more than was paid when Manhattan Island was sold, but we know that land values have risen over the years" (quoted in Treuer 2019).

"The occupiers' list of demands included the return of Alcatraz to American Indians and sufficient funding to build, maintain, and operate an Indian cultural complex and a university" on the island (Cooper 2016). These demands were not met, but the occupation became known internationally, brought attention to American Indians and their struggles, and sparked more protests (Blue Cloud 1972). It also encouraged President Richard Nixon to end the Termination Act in 1970—shortly after the end of the occupation.

PHOTO 6.7 An occupier of Alcatraz in front of a tepee on the island with the Golden Gate Bridge in the background.

Bettmann / Contributor

Relocation efforts also ended in 1972, after 100,000 Native Americans had moved from reservations to cities. Note that these efforts ended 14 years after the General Accountability Office's 1958 evaluation of the program noting that "(1) the areas selected for relocation did not offer adequate opportunities for Indians, (2) Indians were not adequately prepared for relocation, and (3) no standards for selecting relocatees had been established by the BIA" (NativeAmericanNetroots 2010).

DOING SOCIOLOGY 6.5

Alcatraz

In this exercise, you will consider the effect of the occupation of Alcatraz by the Indians of All Tribes.

Recall what you learned about the 1969–1970 occupation of Alcatraz by the Indians of All Tribes and answer the following questions in writing.

1. Why do you think the occupiers called themselves "Indians of All Tribes"?

2. Richard Oakes, a Mohawk activist who helped lead the Alcatraz occupation, once wrote, "Alcatraz is not an island. It's an idea." Given what you've learned about this act of resistance, what do you think he could have meant by that?

3. Were you previously aware of the Native American occupation of Alcatraz? What other acts of Native American resistance—if any—have you learned about?

Other Native Americans created another cross-tribal organization, the American Indian Movement (AIM), in 1968. Some AIM members participated in the siege of Alcatraz. In 1972, they organized caravans of Native Americans and headed to Washington, DC. Referring to their trip as the "Trail of Broken Treaties," they descended on the Bureau of Indian Affairs in Washington. After security guards tried to eject them, more than 1,000 Native people from over 250 tribes (from both urban areas and reservations) took over the building for 6 days. Their demands included closing the BIA (citing its corruption and paternalistic relationship with Indians), stopping employment discrimination against

Native Americans, having stolen land returned, protecting their water rights, and lowering the tuberculosis and infant mortality rate on reservations. When the government agreed to a meeting to discuss these demands and promised amnesty for the protestors, the Indians left the building (Simpson 1972).

In 1973, AIM organized the 71-day occupation of Wounded Knee to protest (primarily) the corrupt tribal government on the Pine Ridge Reservation where Wounded Knee is located. They wanted to create a new tribal government not connected with the BIA. As noted, Wounded Knee was the sight of the Lakota Sioux massacre in 1890. Both the occupiers and federal forces shot at each other regularly, resulting in the death of two Indians and the paralyzing of a U.S. marshall. While their demands were not met, this protest also gained the attention of the media, which regularly gave updates on the stand-off between U.S. government troops and the Indians occupying the area.

Probably the greatest achievement of AIM and other organized American Indian groups seeking greater autonomy was the **Indian Self-Determination and Education Assistance Act of 1975**. This act allows tribes to control their own education and teach through their cultural lens. It also lets them run programs formerly led by federal agencies. "In effect, tribes step[ped] into the shoes of the federal government by assuming the responsibility for operating programs formerly provided by federal agencies" (Strommer and Osborne 2014, 21). Noting the paternalism of the former system in which the federal government controlled all Indian programs, the act allowed for "an orderly transition from federal domination of programs for and services to Indians to effective and meaningful participation by the Indian people in the planning, conduct and administration of these programs and services" (Northern Plains Reservation Aid n.d.).

The most well-known recent actions by Indian activists are the protests of the Dakota Pipeline, designed to transport oil from Canada and North Dakota. The Sioux and allies attempted to stop it, arguing the following:

- They had not been properly consulted before U.S. government approved permissions for the pipeline.

- This is a case of environmental racism. The original design for the pipeline had it near a water source for White people. The U.S. government moved it so it would endanger the water supply of the Standing Rock Indians, rather than the city of Bismarck in North Dakota.

- The construction of the pipeline would damage and destroy a culturally important site the Sioux deem sacred (LaPier 2017).

Thousands of Indians and hundreds of environmentalists from around the United States joined residents of the Standing Rock reservation. As well-known actors such as Mark Ruffalo and Shailene Woodley joined the protests, they gained media attention around the world.

While the Standing Rock tribe achieved a victory when President Obama halted the construction of the pipeline, they eventually lost when President Trump signed an executive order to allow work on it to continue. The pipeline began operating in 2017, but the battle hasn't ended. President Biden ordered a thorough environmental review, reversing President Trump's order to waive it. As of 2021, however, oil still flowed through the pipeline, endangering the Standing Rock water supply and spewing the equivalent of 23 new coal power plants into the atmosphere (Lakota People's Law Project 2019).

For many younger people in the United States and around the world too young to remember the heyday of the American Indian movement, the Dakota pipeline protests provided their first look at Native Americans uniting and challenging the U.S. government. Standing Rock continues to be a symbol of both the continued injustices facing Native Americans and the ability of Indians from different tribes to work together, rally non-Indian allies to their cause, and gain attention from people across the world (Hill 2019; Thorbecke 2016). Sociologists also participate in efforts to show the resilience and strength of Indigenous communities today. Sociologist Andrew Jolivette, of Indigenous descent himself, describes in the Sociologists in Action feature how he uses sociology to show that his tribe "and the hundreds of other tribes across the United States are not only still here but thriving."

SOCIOLOGISTS IN ACTION
Andrew Jolivette

Thrivance Circuitry and Indigenous Belonging

I was born in 1975 in the unceded territory of the Ramaytush in the city of Yelamu (San Francisco) to Annetta Donan and Kenneth Louis. As the descendant of mixed-race people of Atakapa-Ishak, West African, French, Spanish, Italian, and Irish descent, I was often forced into the margins of society. Being Native American/Indigenous was an invisible experience in many ways because people generally knew nothing about Native Americans and were especially confused by my mixed-race background. The fact that my tribe is not federally recognized also made my background somewhat confusing to others. My descendants come from the Tsikip/ Opelousa/Heron band of the Sunrise People of the Ishak nation in southwest Louisiana.

PHOTO 6.8

© Andrew Jolivette

Today, in my sociological writing and research, I show how, despite a history of trauma, colonization, genocide, and removal, my tribe and the hundreds of other tribes across the United States are not only still here but thriving. For example, working with other Native and Indigenous scholars on the *Handbook for Indigenous Sociology* (Oxford University Press), I use sociology to document the social and cultural experiences of Native peoples from our own perspectives and in our own voices.

In *American Indian and Indigenous Education for the 21st Century* (Cognella, 2019), I define thrivance as "the ability to use pre-colonial, settler-colonial, and contemporary experiences (both negative and positive) to adjust, reset, build, and center Indigenous histories, languages, intellectual traditions and relationships with a focus on self-determination, collective wellness, and joy" (Jolivette 2019). With thrivance circuitry, these means of resistance and (re)construction of Indigenous ways of life spread to other Native peoples. Through this lens, I examine how Indigenous, queer, and queer Afro-Indigenous communities center our lived experiences, cultural traditions, and practices from a place of joy, strength, and active engagement with our own world views—despite anti-Black, antiqueer, and anti-Indian policies and practices.

Today, we can see more people using the tools of sociology in Indigenous communities across the world. Their efforts, too, are forms and results of thrivance circuitry. They are sharing and spreading positive parts of individual tribal communities to support the health and productivity of the collective tribal groups that make up the Indigenous world.

Andrew Jolivette is professor and senior specialist in Native American and Indigenous studies in the Department of Ethnic Studies at UC San Diego and the author or editor of six books, including the Lammy Award finalist Indian Blood: HIV and Colonial Trauma in San Francisco's Two-Spirit Community *(University of Washington Press, 2016).*

Discussion Question

How can the concept of thrivance (as opposed to concepts like trauma) support a more balanced and comprehensive sociological understanding of contemporary life in Native American and Indigenous communities in the United States and globally?

Native Americans won victory in 2020 with the *McGirt v. Oklahoma* Supreme Court decision that declared the state of Oklahoma does not have jurisdiction over crimes committed by Native Americans in territory granted to Indian tribes by the federal government. Writing for the majority in the 5–4 decision, Justice Neil Gorsuch declared that approximately half of the state of Oklahoma is Native land, according to the treaty Congress established with the Creek nation in 1833 that "fixed borders for a 'permanent home to the whole Creek Nation of Indians.'" Gorsuch said, "Today we are asked whether the land these treaties promised remains an Indian reservation for purposes of federal criminal law. Because Congress has not said otherwise, we hold the government to its word" (*McGirt v. Oklahoma* 2020). This decision means that crimes conducted on reservations and involving a Native American are under the jurisdiction of the respective Indian government or (for certain major crimes) the federal government, rather than state governments. Reacting to the decision, the Creek Nation stated that "the Supreme Court today kept the United States' sacred promise to the Muscogee (Creek) Nation of a protected reservation.... [This] decision will allow the Nation to honor our ancestors by maintaining our established sovereignty and territorial boundaries" (Wamsley 2020).

CONSIDER THIS

If you were asked to join any of the protests described in this chapter, would you? If so, which one(s)? Why?

Check Your Understanding

1. What percentage of American Indians live on reservations today?

2. What were three acts of resistance led by AIM in the 1970s?

3. What does the 1975 Indian Self-Determination and Education Assistance Act allow Native Americans to do?

4. Why do Indians and their allies disapprove of the Dakota Pipeline extension?

5. What were the reactions of Presidents Obama and Trump to the Dakota Pipeline protests?

ALASKA NATIVES: FROM RUSSIAN COLONIZATION TO TODAY

Alaska has a population of 740,000 people, including 120,000 (15.4% of the population) Native Alaskans (Iggiagruk Hensley 2017). The U.S. census combines American Indians and Alaska Natives into one racial category (AIAN). The federal government recognizes 224 Native Alaska tribes in Alaska, and there are 20 Indigenous languages spoken in the state.

Alaska Natives and American Indians in Alaska are different groups of people with their own cultures. Two key commonalities, however, are their location (Alaska) and their experiences with White people (U.S. Census Bureau 2018). Unlike Native people in the mainland United States, most Alaska Natives live where their people have resided for thousands of years (University of Alaska 2019). This does not mean, however, that they were treated well by White people who entered Alaska.

Colonization by Russians

Russians first set foot in Alaska in 1741. While there, these explorers gathered fur seals and brought them back to the great delight of Tsar Peter the Great. This started a brisk fur trade among Russians and throughout other parts of Asia and Europe (University of Alaska 2019).

In 1784, the Russians established a colony in the Aleutian Islands in Southeast Alaska (see Figure 6.1). They then proceeded to enslave the Aleut, making them catch fur seals for them. The Russians killed those who fought back or refused to work for them.

The Russians also gave the Aleut and other Alaskan Natives diseases to which they had no immunity. Before the Russians arrived, there were approximately 100,000 people living in Alaska, with 17,000 on the Aleutian Islands. Fifty years later, when almost all the seals were gone and the Russians abandoned their colonies in Alaska, only 50,000 Native people had survived in all of Alaska and just 1,500 on the Aleutian Islands.

CONSIDER THIS

Compare the Russian colonization of Alaska with how Whites treated Native people in the lower 48 states. Was one better than the other?

In 1867, low on funds and unable to defend Alaska from attack, Russia sold Alaska to the United States. While many people could not see what the United States would gain from Alaska, William Seward, the secretary of state (under the spell of manifest destiny), persevered through years of negotiations with Congress to purchase it. Shortly after the United States acquired Alaska, missionaries teamed up with the BIA to destroy the culture of Native Alaskans to "kill the Alaskan and save the man." Many Alaskan Native children found themselves far apart from their families in boarding schools. Some attended boarding schools thousands of miles away in the lower 48 states—including the Carlisle school in Pennsylvania (Alaska State Archives 2019).

Meanwhile, White Americans poured into Alaska during several gold rushes. Many stayed, put down roots, and treated Native Alaskans as inferior, unwanted neighbors. Before they became citizens in 1924, Natives in Alaska were not allowed to vote or own property. Even after that, they had to face signs in stores like "No Dogs or Natives Allowed." This type of overt discrimination remained legal until **Alaska's Anti-Discrimination Act of 1945.**

The Aleuts and World War II

After the Japanese attacked some of the Aleutian Islands about 6 months after Pearl Harbor, the lives of Aleuts were never the same. The Japanese captured and imprisoned some Aleutians, many of whom died from disease and hunger. Meanwhile, the U.S. government forced others to relocate thousands of miles away in cold, disease-ridden, unsanitary conditions, with little or no medical assistance. On some Aleutian Islands, the U.S. Army destroyed homes and towns in order not to leave anything to the Japanese, if they invaded. That also meant nothing was left for those Alaska Natives to return to after the war.

The Permanent Fund Dividend and the Alaska Native Claims Settlement Act (ANSCA)

The discovery of oil in 1969, 10 years after Alaska became a state, changed Alaska dramatically. The once-poor state became flush with cash. State leaders decided to place one-quarter of the oil and mineral profits into a Permanent Fund that would invest it and use the proceeds to give every Alaskan a guaranteed dividend every year. These dividends and jobs in oil and mineral excavation have helped many Alaskans survive and rise out of poverty. The dividend for 2020 was $992 (Alaska Department of Revenue 2020; Alaska Permanent Fund Corporation 2019).

The Alaska Native Claims Settlement Act (ANSCA) of 1971

The Alaska Native Claims Settlement Act (ANSCA) of 1971 created a relationship among Alaska Natives, Alaska, and the federal government that differs in some important ways from that of Native people and state and federal governments in the lower 48 states. Through ANSCA, Alaska Natives agreed to give up their claims on most of the land in Alaska in exchange for $962.5 million and one-ninth of the state's land. They also agreed to create 200 Alaska Native village corporations and 12 Alaska Native land-owning, for-profit, regional corporations (a 13th was created for those living outside of Alaska but is not active now).

The regional corporations make money for the villages within their regions, and the village corporations decide how to use the money. Due to expensive minerals (e.g., zinc, gold) and oil under the Alaskan earth, most of these corporations have made a lot of money, which they use to give dividends to their villages. The villages then invest in needed infrastructure such as sewer lines, schools, and hospitals, and provide dividends to individuals in the villages. While the downturn in oil prices in recent years has hurt the regional corporations because of their investments in it, overall, the corporations have done well and continue to provide dividends to their members (Lasley 2019; Stricker 2017). The size and place of each corporation is roughly based on the languages and cultures of the people in the respective regions. Figure 6.1 shows the region of the state for each corporation.

FIGURE 6.1 ■ The 12 Regional Corporations of Alaska.

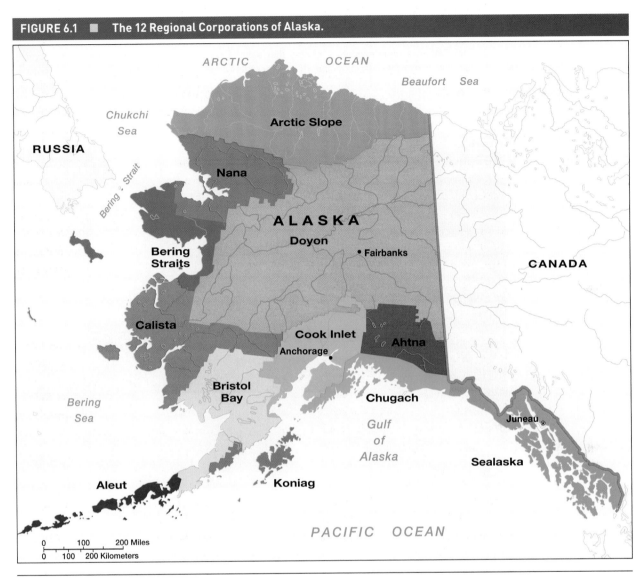

Source: Courtesy of Shane Lasley, Noth of 60 Mining News.

DOING SOCIOLOGY 6.6

Environmental Injustice in Alaska and the Lower 48 States

In this exercise, you will consider the pros and cons of establishing a mine near a pristine lake in Alaska.

Alaska Natives and American Indians on the U.S. mainland often have to decide between jobs and income and the health of their sacred environment (Gilio-Whitaker 2019). In Iliamna, Alaska, the cost of living is high—a half gallon of milk can cost over $13—and there are few job opportunities. A proposed gold, copper, and molybdenum mine could provide financial means for the community but at the risk of permanently polluting the pristine waters of Iliamna Lake and its watershed, one of the world's last spawning grounds for wild salmon.

Imagine you live near the proposed mine. Then write answers to the following questions using information from the chapter and your perspective as someone who (a) lives in a village downstream and depends on salmon for a living, (b) would gain a job selling food to miners, (c) is a village elder and activist who believes the lake is sacred, and (d) is the regional leader of the mining corporation.

1. What might people from each of the four perspectives say about the mine? Write a paragraph for each perspective that includes your reaction to the proposed mine and information to support your reaction.

2. Which of the perspectives do you agree with most? Why?

3. Tom Collier, a mine executive, claims that a mine can boost the economy without harming Iliamna Lake and its surroundings: "It's really a false choice when people say you've gotta choose between environmental protection and natural resource development. You can in fact do both." Do you think there is any truth to his claim? Why or why not?

PHOTO 6.9 Global warming caused in part by the oil and gas Alaska produces now threatens Alaskan villages as ice and permafrost melt and waters rise. Pictured is Kivalina, Alaska, a village 83 miles above the Arctic circle.

Joe Raedle/Getty Images

Check Your Understanding

1. When and from whom did the United States purchase Alaska?

2. What did the Alaska Native Claims Settlement Act (ANSCA) of 1971 do?

3. How did Russians treat Alaska Natives?

4. Why was Alaska's Anti-Discrimination Act of 1945 necessary?

5. What happened to many Aleuts after the Japanese attacked Alaska?

CHALLENGES FACING AMERICAN INDIANS AND ALASKA NATIVES TODAY

Today, many American Indians and Alaska Natives still feel the effects of past—as well as present-day—racism. While situations vary among tribes and villages, overall, high rates of alcoholism, suicide, and violence against women are some of the key challenges facing AIAN people today, particularly those who live on isolated reservations. Why?

Historical Trauma

Research shows us that trauma experienced by our mothers and earlier generations of mothers "can influence the structure of our genes, making them more likely to 'switch on' negative responses to stress and trauma" (Pember 2017). **Historical trauma** affects people in three stages. "In the initial phase, the dominant culture perpetrates mass trauma on a population in the form of colonialism, slavery, war or genocide. In the second phase the affected population shows physical and psychological symptoms in response to the trauma. In the final phase, the initial population passes these responses to trauma to subsequent generations, who in turn display similar symptoms" (Pember 2017). This helps explain why AIAN people have the following characteristics:

- 2 times the national average of child abuse

- 1.5 times the national average of PTSD

- Twice the rate of diabetes as White adults

- 2.5 times more sexual assaults against women than any other racial group

- Relatively high rates of alcoholism

- High rates of car accidents

- High rates of mental health disorders

- The highest rate of suicide among people 15 to 24 years old (Alcohol.org 2019; Sunrise House 2019)

The American Psychiatric Association (APA) lists the following substance abuse risk factors:

- Family history of substance abuse

- A mental health disorder

- Being male (In most cases, males are more susceptible to developing substance abuse disorders than females.)

- History of trauma or stress, particularly as a child

- Being in a lower social economic status group

- Poor health or chronic medical conditions

- Being poorly educated

- Exposure to substance use at an early age and developing an attitude that substance usage is a proper coping mechanism

- Peers who regularly engage in substance use (Alcohol.org 2019)

As you can see, American Indians—especially those on reservations—tend to have all or almost all these risk factors, making them particularly vulnerable to substance abuse.

CONSIDER THIS

Had you heard of the effects of historical trauma before? Does it make you view the present situation of AIAN people in a different light than before you learned about it? Why?

PHOTO 6.10 A mural at the Cheyenne River Reservation tells people how to prevent fetal alcohol syndrome disorder.

Andrew Lichtenstein/Corbis via Getty Images.

Violence Against Native American Women

In the United States, violence against Native women on tribal lands and in Alaska Native villages is pervasive. More than 4 in 5 American Indian and Alaska Native women experience violence, and more than 1 in 2 are victims of sexual violence. Alaska Native women suffer the highest rate of forcible sexual assault (Indian Law Resource Center n.d.).

Since the Oliphant v. Suquamish Indian Tribe *Supreme Court decision in 1978,* U.S. law has stripped Native nations of all criminal authority over non-Natives. Therefore, non-Native men who commit the vast majority (96%) of sexual violence against Native women cannot be prosecuted in tribal courts—and off-reservation law enforcement rarely prosecutes them. The result is that non-Native men can do almost anything to women on reservations without worrying about arrest or imprisonment. With intermarriage, there are many non-Indians living on Native land. Non-Indians now make up 76% of the population on reservations and 68% of the population in Alaska Native villages (Indian Law Resource Center n.d.).

Indian Health Services

A report on the Indian Health Services (IHS), the treaty-mandated provider of health services for AIAN people, reported that "the number of doctors, nurses, and dentists is insufficient. Because of small appropriations, the salaries for the personnel in health work are materially below those paid by the government in its other activities concerned with public health and medical relief" (Siddons 2018). This report from 1928 could just as well have today's date on it.

Chronically underfunded, the IHS spends about one-third of what Medicare and the Veterans Health Administration spends per person. It also lacks an adequate number of doctors and mental health workers (Mathews and Weaver 2019). Lawmakers who oversee the IHS agree that it has had and continues to have incompetent leadership and a lack of funding (Siddons 2018). For example, Senator Lisa Murkowski, who looks over funding for IHS, complains that the IHS hospitals are "severely troubled" and that she is "singularly unimpressed" with those running the organization. Representative Markwayne Mullin, the head of a Congressional group inspecting the IHS says the organization is "a mess" (Siddons 2018).

Given these known problems, it is no surprise that American Indians have suffered from the COVID-19 pandemic more than any other racial group in the United States. Native Americans are 5 times as likely as White Americans to be hospitalized for the coronavirus. Meanwhile, a federal judge had to force the secretary of the treasury under former president Trump, Steve Mnuchin, to disperse the stimulus money Congress allocated to Native American nations during the pandemic (Beitsch 2020).

DOING SOCIOLOGY 6.7

Moving the IHS From a "Mess" to an Effective Program

In this exercise you will create policies to reform the IHS.

Using what you just learned about the Indian Health Services, write answers to the following questions:

1. If you were president and received this information about the IHS, how would you react? Why?

2. List at least three policies you would propose to fix the IHS. How would you gain public support for your suggested policies?

The good news is that AIAN people have repeatedly shown that their organized efforts can attract the world's attention to their continued existence and the racism they still face. Their most recent actions, such as the Dakota Pipeline Extension protest, indicate that they will continue to use their power to fight for their rights as both Native people and U.S. citizens.

Check Your Understanding

1. What are some of the key challenges facing AIAN people today?

2. How does historical trauma relate to these challenges?

3. What is a key reason violence among women is so prevalent on American Indian reservations and Alaska Native villages?

4. What are three problems with the IHS today that have existed for approximately 100 years?

CONCLUSION

Despite having to deal with the challenges they face today and the historical trauma from the genocidal actions of the past, Native Americans have survived. That is a testament to American Indians and Alaska Natives' fortitude, grit, and continual resistance to racial injustice. American Indians endured disastrous efforts by White people to force them to assimilate into White society. Many European immigrants—despite years of discrimination—*have* assimilated into the White-dominated United States. In the next chapter, we look at how various European ethnic groups became White.

CHAPTER REVIEW

6.1 Why were so few Native Americans around when the "Pilgrims" landed in 1620?

When the Separatists (now known as Pilgrims) came to what is now the United States, they landed where the Wampanoags lived. Right before then, the Wampanoags lost almost all their people to diseases brought over by European explorers.

6.2 What did White people desire that led to Indian removal?

Whites wanted the land and precious materials underneath it (e.g., minerals, oil, and gas).

6.3 How did the idea of "manifest destiny" influence the removal and attempted destruction of American Indians?

Manifest destiny is the idea that the United States has a God-given obligation and inevitable destiny to expand and take over territories occupied by inferior peoples (e.g., Mexicans and American Indians). This belief provided White people with an excuse to push Indians out of their way and to gain new territory (all land east of the Mississippi, the majority of Mexico, Alaska.)

6.4 Why does the United States' treatment of American Indians fall under the label of genocide?

According to the International Criminal Court (ICC), genocide consists of "any of the following acts committed with intent to destroy, in whole or in part, a national, ethnical, racial or religious group:

- Killing members of the group
- Causing serious bodily or mental harm to members of the group
- Deliberately inflicting on the group conditions of life calculated to bring about its physical destruction in whole or in part
- Imposing measures intended to prevent births within the group
- Forcibly transferring children of the group to another group (ICC 2019).

The United States has carried out all these actions against American Indians.

6.5 What were some key resistance actions led by the "Indians of All Tribes" and the American Indian movement?

Indians of All Tribes and the American Indian movement led many protests, including the occupation of Alcatraz (1969–1970), the "Trail of Broken Treaties" takeover of the Bureau of Indian Affairs building in 1972, and the occupation of Wounded Knee in 1973.

6.6 How do the experiences of the Native peoples in Alaska correspond to those in the lower 48 states?

Natives in Alaska and the lower 48 states faced White people who took over much of their valuable land, discriminated against and killed many of their people, coveted their lands, and trained them (particularly their children) to abandon their Native culture and act like Whites.

6.7 How does historic trauma relate to the challenges facing American Indian and Alaska Native people today?

Scientists now realize that historical trauma affects many generations—not just the one that experienced it firsthand. This leads American Indians—especially those on reservations—to be particularly vulnerable to problems such as substance abuse, suicide, and other mental health issues.

KEY TERMS

The Alaska Native Claims Settlement Act (ANSCA) of 1971 (p. 126)
Alaska's Anti-Discrimination Act of 1945 (p. 126)
Battle of Little Bighorn (1876) (p. 115)
Black Hills War of 1876 (p. 115)
Boarding schools (p. 119)
General Allotment Act of 1887 (p. 118)
Genocide (p. 117)
Ghost Dance (p. 115)
Historical trauma (p. 129)
Indian Removal Policy of 1830 (p. 113)
Indian Reorganization Act (IRA) (p. 118)
Indian Self-Determination and Education Assistance Act of 1975 (p. 123)

Iroquois League (p. 112)
King Philip (p. 111)
Manifest destiny (p. 114)
Massasoit (p. 111)
Mexican–American War (p. 114)
Permanent Fund (p. 126)
2nd Treaty of Fort Laramie (1868) (p. 115)
Separatists (p. 110)
Takeover of Alcatraz (p. 121)
Termination Act of 1953 and Relocation Act of 1956 (p. 119)
The Trail of Tears (p. 114)
Worcester v. Georgia (p. 114)
Wounded Knee (p. 116)

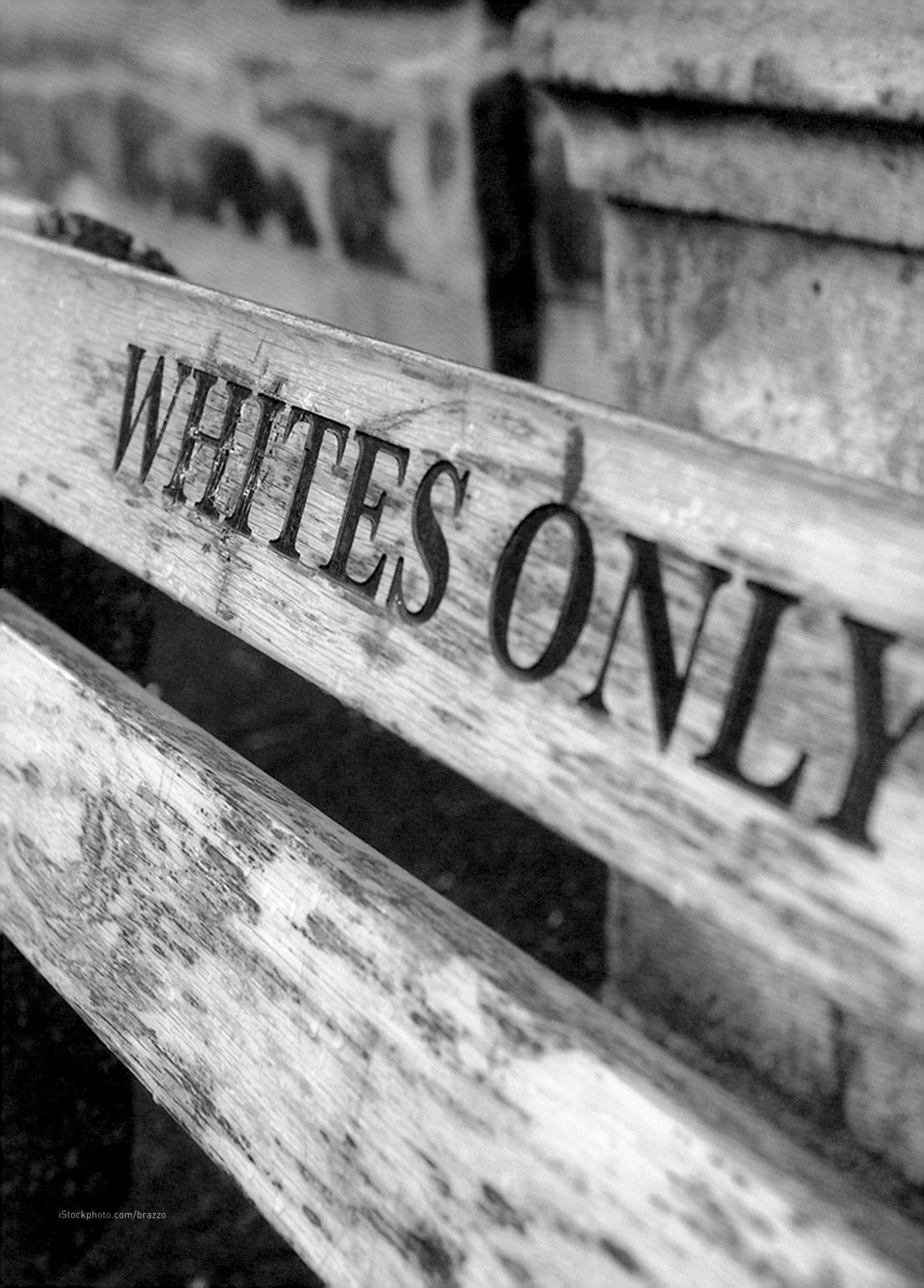

iStockphoto.com/brazzo

7 DEFINING, ATTAINING, AND BENEFITTING FROM WHITENESS

Daniel Herda

LEARNING QUESTIONS

7.1 Why is Whiteness a social construction that often goes unacknowledged?

7.2 What is the connection between racial categories and the distribution of political, social, and economic power?

7.3 What is White privilege, and how does it provide advantages to White people?

7.4 Why are some White people in the United States resentful of people of color?

How often have you discussed how racism influences the experiences and opportunities of White people? Topics like racial inequality, racial discrimination, racial segregation, and racism usually focus on the disadvantages people of color experience. Most of the time, when we hear the word *race*, we think of people of color, not White people. Yet, with the renewed #BlackLivesMatter protests, you may have heard people using the phrase "White privilege" and wondered what they mean. This concept changes the focus of racial discussions and encourages people to think about Whiteness and the ways that White people have benefited from segregation, discrimination, stereotypes, and racism. In this chapter we focus on White people as a racial group. We consider how White people constructed racial categories, shaped them over time, and benefitted from them throughout the history of the United States. In doing so, we show how Whiteness matters for individuals and society.

HOW I GOT ACTIVE IN SOCIOLOGY

Daniel Herda

I didn't really know what sociology was when I started at St. Joseph's College in New York, but I enrolled in a class anyway because my freshman seminar professor was teaching it. I was quickly impressed. I had never taken a class that was so relevant for understanding my own life. I remember using the sociological imagination, and concepts like deviance and role conflict, to understand my relationship with my girlfriend at the time (she would later become my wife). And then the idea of our reality being socially constructed completely changed my worldview. At that point there was no turning back. I majored in sociology with my interest lying mostly in the study of religion. However, it wasn't until my first graduate seminar at the University of California–Davis that I realized that studying immigration and race relations was my true passion. These topics helped me to understand where I fit into society and where my biography fits within the context of history. I am fascinated by intergroup dynamics and how individuals think about and act toward people they perceive as different. These have become my primary areas of teaching and research, and I find them very rewarding.

WHITE: THE SOCIALLY CONSTRUCTED DEFAULT RACE

Dominant groups tend to avoid putting their advantages up for public discussion. When they feel compelled to comment on inequality, they tend to keep the spotlight on disadvantaged groups. For example, when we talk about gender, we usually refer to women. When we bring up sexuality, we usually refer to gay men, lesbians, or bisexuals. This works to center the **dominant group**, making them the norm, while simultaneously making other groups deviant and somehow "less than." It also works to hide the history of the dominant-status groups; their impact on society; and how gender, sex, or racial group membership affects the life chances of the people in the respective groups.

DOING SOCIOLOGY 7.1

How Many White People?

In this exercise, consider the accuracy of your perceptions of the White population of the United States.

Write your answers to the following questions:

1. According to the U.S. Census Bureau, about 60% of individuals in the United States classified themselves as White (non-Hispanic) in 2018. Is this roughly what you would have guessed? Or is it lower or higher than you expected?

2. Think about your answer to Question 1. Why do you think you responded the way you did?

3. Research finds that most people overestimate the White population in the United States. Why do you think this is the case?

4. What does this tendency to overestimate the White population say about the visibility of Whiteness in the United States?

Whiteness as a Social Construction

As discussed in Chapter 1, Whiteness, like all other racial categories, is socially constructed. Its **boundaries**—the social dividing lines indicating who is part of the category and who is not—do not correspond to an objective biological truth. They are not God-given, inevitable, or natural but rather a determination made by a particular society at a given time. We know this because throughout U.S. history, our definition of the White racial category has changed. Its boundaries have expanded over time, incorporating some but continuing to keep others out.

Who Was "White" in American History?

To see how our definitions of Whiteness have changed, you can look back to one of the first large immigrant populations to arrive in colonial America after the initial British settlers: Germans. By today's definition, Americans of German descent fit into the White category. They have all the physical features that we currently use to classify individuals as White. However, if we consider some of the writings of Benjamin Franklin, one of our Founding Fathers, we will see that he recognized racial differences that we no longer see today:

> *Why should the Palatine Boors be suffered to swarm into our Settlement, and by herding together, establish their Language and Manners, to the Exclusion of ours? Why should Pennsylvania, founded by the English, become a Colony of Aliens, who will shortly be so numerous as to Germanize us instead of our Anglifying them, and they will never adopt our Language or Customs, any more than they can acquire our Complexion?* (Franklin 1751)

The word *Palatine* refers to a region in southern Germany from where most of these early immigrants originated. Beyond lamenting a perceived refusal to culturally assimilate, Franklin notes that they are unable to acquire his complexion. Here he implies that the Germans and English looked different (complexion refers to the color, texture, and appearance of skin) and, thus, were racially distinct. Franklin continues:

> *Which leads me to add one Remark: That the Number of purely White People in the World is proportionably very small. All Africa is Black or tawny. Asia chiefly tawny. America (exclusive of the new Comers) wholly so. And in Europe, the Spaniards, Italians, French, Russians and Swedes, are generally of what we call a swarthy Complexion; as are the Germans also, the Saxons only excepted,*

who with the English, make the principal Body of White People on the Face of the Earth. I could wish their Numbers were increased. . . . But perhaps I am partial to the Complexion of my Country, for such Kind of Partiality is natural to Mankind. (Franklin 1751)

Here, Franklin clearly states that Germans (save for Saxons who occupy regions in northern Germany), are swarthy, meaning they have a dark skin color or complexion. He similarly distinguishes French, Swedes, Russians, Italians, and Spaniards from Whites as well. Only the English and the Saxons fit into this definition of White. Today, we have constructed a different definition of White. The distinguishing physical characteristics that were obvious to Franklin in 1751 no longer seem so obvious today.

CONSIDER THIS

In what ways are Franklin's concerns about German immigrants in 1751 similar to peoples' concerns about immigrants today?

Other groups we now see as White also faced racial prejudice and discrimination. For example, Irish immigrants faced racial boundaries that kept them lower on the racial hierarchy than Whites. The political cartoons in the United States during the mid-1800s reveal the exaggerated perceived racial differences. The Irish, as seen in Photo 7.1, were frequently portrayed as a monstrous, subhuman species with animalistic features and exhibiting wild and unpredictable tendencies.

THE IGNORANT VOTE—HONORS ARE EASY.

PHOTO 7.1 A 19th-century caricature of an Irish American on the right being equated with a caricature of an African American on the left.

Stock Montage/Getty Images

According to Noel Ignatiev, author of *How the Irish Became White*, many drew comparisons between Irish Americans and Black Americans. Photo 7.1 does exactly this, placing a Black man and an Irish man on a scale indicating equal weight and implying similarity. The top of the scale reads "South" and "North," suggesting that these minority groups are analogous across the regions. People frequently referred to the Irish as "White negros." Similarly, Blacks were sometimes referred to as "smoked Irish" (Ignatiev 1995). The boundaries that the White majority drew between themselves and the Irish led to discrimination, as seen in "No Irish Need Apply" signs attached to some storefronts and classified job ads.

As time progressed, the sources of immigration changed. During the mid to late 1800s, Chinese and Japanese arrived in increasing numbers on the West Coast. This prompted the first immigration laws aimed at particular nationalities—The Chinese Exclusion Act of 1882 and the Gentlemen's Agreement of 1907. These acts, respectively, halted almost all immigration from China and Japan. As noted in Chapter 2, Asian immigrants who came to the United States before these acts were not eligible for naturalization (the process of becoming a citizen) because they were not White. The Naturalization Act of 1870 expanded the right of naturalization to those of African descent or origin but to no other people of color.

By the early 1900s the United States began to receive large numbers of immigrants from southern, central, and eastern Europe—places like Italy, Poland, the Austro-Hungarian Empire, and Russia. These groups, like the Germans and Irish before them, were viewed as distinct from Whites. People saw them as incompatible with American society and values. They were subject to stereotypes portraying them as criminal, unintelligent, and possessing dangerous ideologies like communism and anarchism, making them unassimilable. White people feared the effects of these groups so much that in 1924 the United States changed its immigration policies to block their entry. The Johnson-Reed Immigration Act halted nearly all immigration from these new sources. According to Calvin Coolidge (the president who signed the act into law),

> There are racial considerations too grave to be brushed aside for any sentimental reasons. Biological laws tell us that certain divergent people will not mix or blend. The Nordics propagate themselves successfully. With other races, the outcome shows deterioration on both sides. Quality of mind and body suggests that observance of ethnic law is as great a necessity to a nation as immigration law. (Coolidge 1921).

President Coolidge believed that these "divergent people" to which these "biological laws" pertain must be kept from the United States and prevented from "mixing" or "blending" with White Americans. As discussed in Chapter 1, his ideas reflected the "scientific" research findings of his time, which created these "biological laws."

Changing Definitions of Whiteness

Today, it is easy to see the fallacy of efforts to develop "scientific" racial classification schemes. But from the 19th to the first half of the 20th century many scientists devoted countless hours trying to show that humans were of different races and to sort groups of people by race. One major clue that this task was impossible is the remarkable disparities in the "scientists'" racial classifications.

> Linnaeus had found four human races; Blumenbach had five; Curvier had three; John Hunter had seven; Burke had sixty-three; Pickering had eleven; Virey had two "species," each containing three races; Haeckel had thirty-six; Huxley had four; Topinard had nineteen under three headings; Desmoulins had sixteen "species"; Deniker had seventeen races and thirty types. (Gossett 1963, 82)

These conflicting racial classification systems led famous anthropologist Ruth Benedict to conclude that "in all modern science there is no field where authorities differ more than in the classification of human races" (1959, 22). The reason for such variation is that these scientists were searching for something that did not exist. Again, the racial categories we use are not objective but socially constructed during a particular time and in a particular place.

Whiteness Today

After decades of shifting and evolving the boundaries of the White category in the United States, we have now expanded it to include all European ethnicities. The distinctions between White people that once motivated us to close the doors to immigrants in 1924 are barely recognized today. Assimilation has occurred so completely that many White Americans are unfamiliar with their ancestral origins or unaware that they have ethnic surnames.

PHOTO 7.2 A symbolically ethnic St. Patrick's Day celebration in the United States. Why do you think Americans celebrate their ethnic heritage in such a way?

wundervisuals

Except for recent immigrants, most Whites have only superficial connections to their ancestral origins. Perhaps they occasionally eat foods or celebrate holidays associated with their ethnic homelands, but ethnicity tends not to be a major part of their identity. Herbert Gans (1979) coined the term **symbolic ethnicity**, which is the maintenance of a nostalgic connection to the cultural traditions of one's ancestors. Often, however, the symbolically ethnic traditions differ from anything practiced in the home country. St. Patrick's Day parades and celebrations in the United States provide an illustrative example. Up until a few decades ago, St. Patrick's Day was not celebrated in a similar way in Ireland. It is now—but only thanks to the influence of Irish American visitors from the United States (Klein 2019)!

Symbolic ethnicity allows White Americans the luxury of choosing to identify as ethnic in certain contexts (e.g., holidays) or not, without any consequences. Alternatively, they can simply identify as American. This ethnic option, according to sociologist Mary Waters (1990), is a privilege not available to many people of color. For example, in the United States the physical traits characteristic of Asian Americans are frequently associated with foreignness—no matter how many generations the person's family has lived in the United States (Tessler, Choi, and Kao 2020). Sometimes just having a "foreign-sounding" name can lead some people to accuse you of not being "truly" American. We observed this with the "birther" movement's insistence that President Barack Hussein Obama was a foreigner, despite evidence to the contrary (he was born in Hawaii).

Occasionally we still see ethnic-based stereotypes attached to individuals of specific European backgrounds in the United States. For example, many people still associate the Irish with alcohol consumption, and Italians with mobsters, and some people still tell "Polish jokes." However, it is unlikely that any of these characterizations have much of a negative impact on the lives of individuals in these categories today. Antisemitism is an unfortunate and persistent exception as Jewish Americans remain one of the most common targets for hate crimes (Cherelus 2018). We discuss this in Chapter 11.

Whiteness in the Future

You have probably heard of demographic projections that indicate that the relative proportion of White individuals in the United States is in decline. The U.S. Census Bureau predicts that non-Hispanic Whites (Whites without ethnic origins in Spanish-speaking nations) will no longer be the majority by the year 2044 (Colby and Ortman 2015). If this projection is true, Whites will become a plurality, which is the largest group among several with none exceeding 51%.

Of course, this forecast assumes a static, unchanging definition of Whiteness, which the previous sections demonstrate has never existed. If history is a guide, then it is possible that Whiteness will change again. For example, what will happen to people of Hispanic heritage who appear White and speak English? Will they remain part of a distinct Hispanic ethno-racial category? Or will they follow the Germans, Irish, Italians, and Polish before them and become absorbed into the White category? Sociologists predict the latter for light-skinned, English-speaking Hispanics (Bonilla-Silva and Glover 2004).

Check Your Understanding

1. What evidence indicates that Whiteness is socially constructed?

2. In what ways were most European ethnics excluded from the early definitions of the White category?

3. How is Whiteness defined in America today?

4. What happened to the "obvious" differences between White ethnic groups in the United States?

5. How does the socially constructed nature of Whiteness complicate the demographic projections of a shrinking White population?

HISTORIC ADVANTAGES TO WHITENESS

American history provides many examples of groups fighting to be classified as White, since Whiteness comes with various political, social, and economic advantages. Take access to citizenship as an example. Attaining citizenship is the key to gaining political power. It provides one the right to vote and hold political office. At certain times in history it has also brought economic privileges, like the right to own property or to avoid certain penalties like the Foreign Miners Tax, a tax specifically designed to hurt Mexican and Chinese residents in California during the 1800s. The original naturalization laws in the United States made citizenship accessible only to immigrants classified as "free Whites." Who, however, is a "free White" person? For many, that was a matter of fierce debate.

In 1908 the Minnesota district attorney argued that Finnish immigrants were not White and therefore ineligible to naturalize (Huhta 2014). Their participation in labor strikes in the mining industry earned Finns a negative reputation as radical, anti-American rabble-rousers, which citizens interpreted as racial proclivities. Some argued that the Finnish immigrants were Asian because Finland is closer to Asia than the rest of Europe and the Finnish language is unrelated to other Indo-European languages. However, the courts eventually classified the Finnish immigrants as free Whites, allowing them to naturalize and become citizens. Similar cases involving Arabs, Syrians, Armenians, and others who wished to gain citizenship and share in the advantages reserved only for Whites reached the United States Supreme Court, with many eventually gaining recognition as legally White through the process. In

Chapter 11 we discuss the more recent trend in the opposite direction for Americans of Middle Eastern and North African (MENA) descent (Arab American Institute 2015).

While several of these cases ultimately expanded the boundaries of Whiteness, others crystallized boundaries and excluded certain groups. The Supreme Court case of *Ozawa v. United States* (1922) involved a Japanese immigrant named Takao Ozawa in the territory of Hawaii. He had lived in the United States for 20 years, was educated in America, and spoke English at home with his American-born family. He argued that he was an assimilated American whose skin was Whiter than many European ethnicities. However, the Court disagreed, insisting that the term *White* refers exclusively to the "Caucasian" race (a term from one of the many pseudoscientific racial classification systems), which did not include Japanese people. Thus, the Supreme Court ruled that Japanese Americans were not "free White" persons and ineligible for naturalization.

A few months later the Supreme Court decided the case of *United States v. Bhagat Singh Thind* (1923). Thind was a Sikh man from northern India. He similarly argued that his group should be classified as free White, and he had the backing of the same "science" that the Court used to deny Ozawa. Thind argued that there were racial classification systems that grouped Europeans and northern Indians together in the "Caucasian" or "Aryan" race. However, the Court disagreed, saying the typical American with "common sense" would not view a Sikh from northern India as White. Thus, another legal racial boundary became crystallized, and the consequences of a socially constructed reality became real for Indian Americans. They, like other immigrants deemed non-White, would be officially barred from citizenship and the ballot box.

PHOTO 7.3 The Supreme Court ruled that according to "common sense," Bhagat Sing Thind, pictured here, and other Sikh immigrants from northern India were not White.

Unknown author, Public domain, via Wikimedia Commons

Racism and the Preservation of White Advantages

The naturalization laws reserving citizenship for Whites only were clearly racist. As noted in earlier chapters, racism is not something that exists solely in an individual's mind or actions but at the level of an entire society and culture. Racism encompasses historical, cultural, institutional, and interpersonal dynamics that create and maintain a racial hierarchy that advantages Whites and hurts people of color. Yes, it identifies Whites as the sole beneficiaries of racism and people of color as the victims of racism. Whites have commanded political, social, and economic power for the entirety of U.S. history. This outcome is not accidental. It is the result of many purposeful actions by the dominant group.

To illustrate, we can go all the way back to the beginnings of race in America. White elites created the distinction between Black and White—the famous "color line"—as a strategy to entice poor Whites to identify along racial lines rather than social class lines (see Davidson Buck 2001). In colonial America, prior to the 1700s and the establishment of slavery as the norm across the country, poor White Europeans and many Africans labored together as indentured servants. They entered into labor contracts for a set period of time and gained their freedom when the contract expired. These individuals lived as neighbors, sometimes married each other, and liked or disliked one another based on individual personalities and not on race as we view it today. Occasionally they rebelled alongside one another, which posed a clear threat to wealthy White landowners.

To exercise more effective control over the labor force, landowners began enacting laws that drew clear distinctions between racial categories. These included banning interracial marriage and extending Black—but not White—indentured servitude into permanent slavery. Notions of racial superiority and inferiority between Blacks and Whites arose through this process among both elite and poor Whites. Most colonizers justified their participation in the horrors of slavery by this social construction of an "inferior" race.

Racism and the Concentration of Political, Social, and Economic Power Among Whites

American history provides many other examples of racist policies that gave White people advantages while disadvantaging people of color. As discussed in the previous chapter, U.S. policies have caused genocidal-level damage to the first inhabitants of the land. Also, remember that before the United States closed the doors to European immigrants deemed biologically unfit in 1924, it barred Chinese and Japanese immigration. In both cases, Whites perceived immigrants from Asia residing on the West Coast as economic competitors, which made them a target for discrimination.

The postbellum American South during the era of Jim Crow provides another example of White people passing laws that gave them advantages over people of color. Jim Crow laws established the segregation of schools and public buildings, including separate White and colored entrances and water fountains. It wasn't just laws that upheld racism, however. The former Confederate states created an all-encompassing system of racial oppression that involved informal rules of racial etiquette designed to keep Blacks in a position of subordination. The rules were violently enforced through intimidation and lynchings. This provides a clear example of a racist system designed to concentrate economic, social, and political power in the hands of Whites. We discuss it more in the next chapter.

Racism also played a role outside of the American South, allowing Whites to accumulate wealth while excluding people of color from the same opportunities to do so (Conley 1999; Massey and Denton 1993; Oliver and Shapiro 2006). For most Americans, their house is their most important form of wealth. However, as described in Chapter 4, it was not until shortly after the Second World War that the opportunity to purchase a home arrived for working- and middle-class Americans. During the 1930s the Federal Housing Administration (FHA) rewrote the rules for mortgage loans by reducing interest rates, lowering the minimum down payment, and stretching the life of the mortgage to 30 years. This made home ownership more affordable, allowing Americans to build equity and accumulate wealth. At the same time, the FHA also recommended that real estate developers build and maintain racially segregated neighborhoods to preserve stability and housing values.

Developers followed the FHA guidelines and built properties in suburban areas almost exclusively for White home buyers. After the return of the troops from the Second World War, Whites flocked to the suburbs en masse. People of color, however, particularly African Americans, were excluded. Anthropologist Karen Brodkin (1998, 27) calls this amazing opportunity for Whites the "biggest and best affirmative action program in the history of our nation" as it turned out to be a financial boost reserved primarily for Whites. The racist policies of the FHA and real estate developers worked to concentrate economic power among Whites, while disadvantaging people of color.

CONSIDER THIS

In what ways might America be different today without this history of advantaging Whites and disadvantaging people of color?

The Legacy of Centuries of Racism

Civil rights legislation during the 1960s gave people of color the same *legal* access to social, political, and economic power as Whites. They eliminated the direct forms of racism mentioned previously, but instances of illegal discrimination still occurred and continue to happen. Also, the civil rights legislation did not bring people of color up to the same economic, political, and social level as Whites, leaving them to overcome three centuries of accumulated disadvantage after they finally gained legal equality.

Direct racism practices of the past manifest themselves today in indirect racism. For example, what happened to housing after the racist housing practices described earlier were outlawed? The Fair Housing Act of 1968 officially prohibited the aforementioned FHA and real estate practices that produced racial segregation in America and deprived many people of color from gaining wealth through homeownership, as seen in Figure 7.1. The Fair Housing Act, however, did nothing to rectify the fact that Whites, but not Blacks, were able to acquire house-based wealth during the period of racialized suburbanization. As described in Chapter 4, White homeowners could pass this wealth to their children and grandchildren, but most Black people (and many other people of color) did not have house-based wealth to give to their children and grandchildren. These racist policies and practices of the past helped create a wide racial wealth gap that persists in the United States today, as seen in Figure 7.1. While illegal now, patterns of racial discrimination related to housing and the mortgage and real estate industries persist (Glantz and Martinez 2018; Marte 2017).

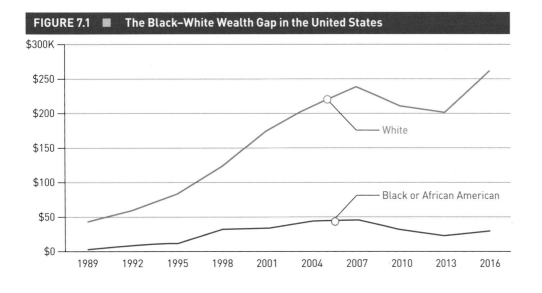

FIGURE 7.1 ■ The Black–White Wealth Gap in the United States

Note: All dollar figures are in 2016 dollars. Nominal dollars are deflated by consumers price index for urban consumers research series. Sample includes a cohort of nonretired households as they aged from between 23 to 38 years in 1989 to between 50 and 65 years in 2016.

Source: This material, "Systematic Inequality: How America's Structural Racism Helped Create the Black–White Wealth Gap," by Angela Hanks, Danyelle Solomon, and Christian E. Weller, was published by the Center for American Progress (https://www.americanprogress.org/issues/race/reports/2018/02/21/447051/systematic-inequality/).

Imagine two young children, one White and one Black, growing up in America just after the Second World War. Thanks to FHA policies, the White child's parents were able to buy one of the newly available homes in the suburbs. The Black child's parents were blocked from this opportunity because of the racist policies of the FHA and real estate developers. After 30 years of paying off the mortgage, the White child's parents now own a valuable asset. The Black child's parents have been paying rent across this same period and have not accrued any equity. The White child will inherit an asset valued at potentially hundreds of thousands of dollars when his parents pass away, while there is no comparable asset for the Black child. The White child, while not benefitting directly from the racist policies, will benefit indirectly decades after the fact—even today. Similarly, the Black child, while not affected directly by the racist policy, is still harmed by it indirectly decades later.

Since no official policy mandates the Black–White wealth gap in the United States today, it is easy to miss that racism is still at play. Your sociological eye, however, will allow you to recognize both present-day racial practices and the cause and effects of indirect, past-in-present racism. In doing so, it will help you to notice the advantages Whites have in U.S. society today.

Racism and White Advantage in the Normal Functioning of Society

As you can see, racism is embedded within our society and often manifests itself in ways that are difficult to recognize. Hidden patterns such as these are what make discussions of racism so difficult today. Many Whites will not understand the frustrations of #BlackLivesMatter protestors if racism is invisible to them. If you can't see it, it's easy to deny its existence. Hence, we often hear counterarguments claiming that "all lives matter"—implying that White and Black people are treated—and valued—equally.

Yet social scientists have uncovered mountains of evidence that prove racism continues to advantage Whites and disadvantage people of color. For instance, in her well-known study, "The Mark of a Criminal Record," Devah Pager (2003) used an approach known as an **audit study** to identify racism that would normally go unnoticed or be difficult to prove. Pager was interested in whether race and a criminal record mattered in shaping one's chances of getting a callback after a job interview. To test this, she recruited individuals to act as auditors to play the role of job applicants. They were all 23-year-old college males from Milwaukee, Wisconsin. Some of them were Black and some were White. They were given fake biographies that differed only in terms of race and criminal record (four scenarios: White with no record, White with a record, Black with no record, and Black with record). Everything else (e.g., education, job experience) was the same. They were each assigned 15 entry-level job openings per week, with Black and White testers assigned to different openings. They would visit the employers, fill out an application, and participate in an interview if they had the opportunity to do so on the spot. Potential employers interacted only with one of the auditors, meaning they did not have the opportunity to see both a White and Black applicant.

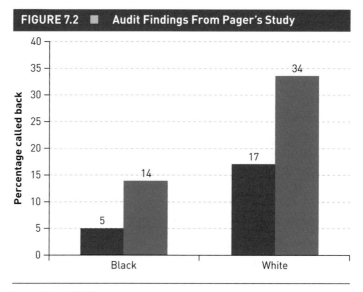

FIGURE 7.2 ■ Audit Findings From Pager's Study

Source: Pager (2003).

Over the course of 350 audits (150 from the White applicants and 200 from the Black applicants), Pager found that Whites, regardless of criminal record, were more than twice as likely to receive a callback compared to the Black applicants.

Figure 7.2 shows Pager's results. In the non–criminal record comparison, 34% of Whites received a callback, while the same was true for only 14% of Blacks. This demonstrates an advantage experienced by Whites *on average*. Specifically, with all else being equal, Whites can expect a more than 50% greater likelihood of being called back for a job simply by virtue of being part of the dominant group (see also Bertrand and Mullainathan 2004; Gaddis 2014; Pager, Bonikowski, and Western 2009). Pager found the same pattern among those listing a criminal record; 17 Whites but only 5 Blacks were called back. In fact, White individuals with a felony on their record were more likely to be called back for a job than a Black applicant *without* one.

Pager's study reveals racism, but where are the racists? Remember, the employers only saw one auditor. They did not decide between the Black auditor and White auditor at the same time. Rather, this study uncovered a pattern of racism on average across hundreds of observations. There is no single person who can be blamed for this racism. Rather, this is a manifestation of systemic racism within our society and helps reveal the historical, cultural, institutional, and interpersonal dynamics that create and maintain a racial system that advantages Whites and hurts people of color.

Other studies using the audit methodology have uncovered racism when people buy a car (Rice and Schwartz 2018), select a new church (Wright et al. 2015), seek the services of a mental health professional (Kugelmass 2016; Shin et al. 2016), ask election officials about voting locations and voter IDs (White, Nathan, and Faller 2015), contact their congressperson (Gell-Redman et al. 2018), crowdfund over the Internet (Younkin 2018), and even when they take a bus (Mujcic and Frijters 2013). In the lattermost example, the researchers sent a racially diverse set of auditors to use a public bus system. They would hop on the bus, tell the driver that they forgot their pass, and ask if they could simply ride for a few stops. Drivers of all races allowed the White passenger to ride for free 2 times more often than the Black passenger. Remember, these are *current* examples of racist practices that give Whites advantages over people of color.

DOING SOCIOLOGY 7.2

Always Check Your Understanding!

In small groups, write your answers to the following questions. Be prepared to share your answers.

Check Your Understanding

1. Why does the White racial category tend to remain in the background during discussions about race?

2. What are the consequences of focusing discussions of race on people of color, rather than on White people?

3. Why did so many groups in the early 1900s fight to gain legal classification as White?

4. What are some examples of the direct forms of racism from American history that advantaged Whites and disadvantaged people of color?

5. How do direct forms of racism from the past still advantage Whites indirectly today?

6. What is an audit study, how does one design one, and what can it measure?

WHITE PRIVILEGE

Another way to think about how White people benefit from racism is through the concept of White privilege. This idea, popularized by Peggy McIntosh and used widely today, encourages people to think about the taken-for-granted advantages of being part of the dominant group. Most often when we think about stereotypes, discrimination, and racism, we consider the ways they harm victims. The concept of privilege allows us to focus on the advantages Whites gain by being able to avoid facing stereotypes, discrimination, and racism. To take an example from outside the realm of race, consider the phenomenon of gay and lesbian individuals "coming out of the closet." Going public with one's sexual orientation can be stressful and bring consequences. Rejection by family and friends is still a risk for many, but a risk that straight people never have to face. There is no need for straight individuals to "come out of the closet." It's as if they have a free pass allowing them to avoid the stress and risk of rejection that gays and lesbians endure. This is a privilege.

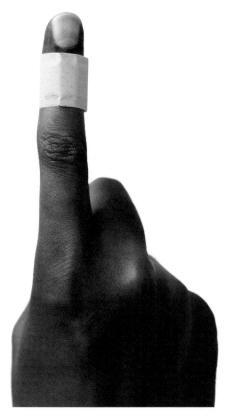

PHOTO 7.4 This person is using a bandage that is significantly lighter than their skin tone. Why are bandages so often manufactured in this color?

iStockphoto.com/Cunaplus_M.Faba

McIntosh (1988, 30) defines privilege as "an invisible weightless knapsack of special provisions, maps, passports, codebooks, visas, clothes, tools and blank checks." If we want to end racism, a key step is helping the dominant group recognize their privileges. McIntosh shines a light on a long list of specific areas of White privilege, a few of which we describe next.

Being the Social Norm Is a Privilege

One place where we can observe advantages is in the fact that the dominant group constitutes the social norm in society. They are viewed as typical and expected. In probably her most famous example, McIntosh states, "I can choose blemish cover or bandages in 'flesh' color and have them more or less match my skin" (1988, 33). Photo 7.5 illustrates this issue effectively. As discussed in Chapter 5, the most easily accessible color of bandages is in a tone that more closely matches White complexion. While, today, some bandages are manufactured in other colors that might more closely match the skin of the individual in the photo, they are more difficult to find. Not having to go through the extra effort necessary to procure products that match your skin tone is a privilege.

In the act of purchasing Band-Aids, it would probably not cross the mind of a White individual that the same task might be more challenging for a person of color. Yet this is exactly what the concept of White privilege is designed to highlight. Privilege is often invisible for the dominant group. For them to see it, they must compare their experiences to someone in a different social status. In addition, this particular privilege is small if viewed in isolation. However, it exists well beyond bandages, and the effects are cumulative. It is easier in our society for Whites to find toys (dolls and action figures), greeting cards, and many other products that reflect their group (McIntosh 1988). Similarly, as discussed in Chapter 5, it is easier for Whites to find their group represented in television, film, children's books, and other media (Smith, Choueiti, Pieper, Case, and Choi 2018).

Avoiding Stereotypes Is a Privilege

Our society often attaches different characteristics to our socially defined racial groups. We associate some groups with positive attributes (e.g., hardworking, intelligent, capable) and others with negative characteristics (e.g., criminals, lazy, uneducated). These stereotypes are bad generalizations about a particular group that are fixed and persist over time. Typically, stereotypes of the dominant group are positive, and being able to avoid negative characterizations is a privilege. McIntosh states, "I can go shopping alone most of the time, pretty well assured that I will not be followed or harassed by store detectives or customers" (1988, 31). Meanwhile, Black Americans are followed so often when shopping, the experience is dubbed "shopping while Black" (Pittman 2017). It is something that Whites will rarely, if ever, experience. Similarly, Whites generally avoid the heightened police suspicion that leads to disproportionate stops (Dunn and Shames 2019) and deaths of unarmed Black Americans (McPhillips 2020). Avoiding this suspicion and the stereotypes that motivate it is a privilege.

DOING SOCIOLOGY 7.3

The Privilege of Avoiding Negative Stereotypes

This exercise asks you to think about the privilege of not having to deal with negative racial stereotypes.

The uncomfortable experiences of "shopping while Black" and "driving while Black" are two examples of how African Americans are negatively affected by stereotyping. Because our culture maintains many racist stereotypes, African Americans frequently face greater suspicion in various areas of social life.

Write your answers to the following questions:

1. What is another example of a common scenario in which African Americans are negatively affected by stereotyping?

2. Would a White individual under similar circumstances arouse as much suspicion or fear? Why or why not?

3. Why is avoiding incidents like these a form of privilege?

Not Having to Wonder Is a Privilege

Living in a racist society can make people wonder if people are viewing them through a racist lens. Peggy MacIntosh states, "If my day, week, or year is going badly, I need not ask of each negative episode or situation whether it has racial overtones" (1988, 33). If a person of color is pulled over by the police, fired from their job, or has an unfriendly interaction, they may find themselves wondering if their race was a factor. For White individuals, who do not have the same history of discrimination, the possibility of racism rarely crosses their mind. Not having to think about racism is a privilege.

CONSIDER THIS
When do you think about your race on your campus? Why?

Unpacking the invisible knapsack of privilege allows people in dominant groups (e.g., White, cisgendered men; middle or upper class people) to start to understand what it is like for those in marginalized groups. It also helps them see that patterns of behavior that create inequality must change if we are to make a more just society. Often, changing such patterns can be difficult—but it is impossible if the patterns are invisible. Nathaniel Porter and H Smith, profiled in our Sociologists in Action feature, describe how Smith helped Porter recognize his participation in patterns that create inequality. They also describe how, together, they flipped the script to expose those behaviors to others—and to change them.

SOCIOLOGISTS IN ACTION
Nathaniel Porter and H Smith

Flattening or Flipping

I am intersectionally privileged: a cisgender male, married, White, middle-class U.S. citizen and homeowner with multiple graduate degrees and a secure job with benefits. I didn't focus on race, gender, or other marginalizations in my classes or research, but I tried to be an ally.

As a data consultant in the University Libraries at Virginia Tech, I secured funding for a graduate assistant (GA) with the topic "Data Equity and Justice." I figured we'd get someone from the social sciences or engineering, do a study and symposium about an issue like minority health data or algorithmic policing, and at the end of the day, we could feel like we'd helped make things a little less unfair.

My GA, H Smith, is not a social or data scientist. They were a gender nonbinary counseling student with passions for listening to other people's stories and seeking justice. H wanted whatever we did to help people experiencing intersectional disadvantage, so we started looking at "flat" event models where discussion replaces speeches and people are treated as peers.

After weeks of feeling nothing was quite right but not knowing why, I figured it out. Just flattening the format of events or research would leave all the prestige, social cues, and habits of relationship—I as faculty would get to attend on the clock, but the people I wanted to invite into conversation, working hourly or by the gig, would have to arrange time off and lose pay to come—intact.

The only way we found to truly address power differences was to flip, not flatten, the relationships. The format replaces senior researchers with marginalized community members as speakers to share their stories. Those speakers work with attendees to brainstorm projects to answer the questions these stories inspired and are paid to lead teams of experienced researchers to carry the projects out, publish them, and share them with the community.

Our fellow (mostly White) academic elites generally supported the idea in theory but sometimes faltered when asked to commit university resources to paying outsiders or to entrust others to have the final say on everything, reflecting paternalistic assumptions that (we) experts know what (you) masses need. But our stories are built on their backs. No flattening of equality or charity will upset generational power imbalance until elites intentionally trade their privilege, control, and comfort for the lives of the marginalized.

Nathaniel Porter is a data educator and consultant in the Virginia Tech University Libraries with a passion for storytelling that creates change. His research and teaching apply nontraditional methods and diverse data to address big social and cultural questions.

H Smith is a master's student in Virginia Tech's Counselor Education program. They serve marginalized communities, including leadership roles in Virginia and national associations for LGBT Issues in Counseling (ALGBTIC). They are passionate about serving marginalized rural individuals.

Discussion Question

What are some other types of invisible privilege that prevent equality of opportunity? What would it take to flip the script on those privileges?

Check Your Understanding

1. What is White privilege, and what can it help us understand?

2. How does occupying the normal or expected category constitute a privilege?

3. How can avoiding negative stereotypes constitute a privilege?

4. How is not having to think about racism a form of privilege?

WHITE ANGER AND WHITE SUPREMACIST ORGANIZATIONS

While the concept of White privilege is useful for understanding the taken-for-granted benefits of being part of the dominant group, many Whites would argue that their lives are far from privileged. Over the past few decades, working-class and poor Whites have been hit particularly hard by deindustrialization, the outsourcing of manufacturing jobs, stagnant wages, rising health care costs, and most recently the opioid crisis (Russell Hochschild 2018, 2019; Skocpol and Williamson 2013).

We simultaneously exist within many social hierarchies and can be privileged and underprivileged at the same time. As you will recall from earlier discussions about intersectionality, while one may reap the benefits of White privilege, they may be underprivileged based on their gender, sexual orientation, physical abilities, or social class status. Often, arguments about White privilege will find little traction among White people who believe they are underprivileged themselves. In fact, they may feel threatened by people of color as they observe the shifting demographics and influx of people with different cultural backgrounds. Thanks to the White-dominated curricula in public schools discussed in Chapter 5, most do not know the history of racism in the United States or the ways in which people of color still face disadvantages because of systemic racism. The combination of lack of knowledge about racism and economic hardships leads many Whites to believe that the government has treated them unfairly by allowing people of color to cut in line ahead of them with policies like affirmative action and refugee assistance programs (Russell Hochschild 2019).

It is no wonder that former president Trump's "Make America Great Again" slogan resonated with so many White people. Critics argue that Trump worked to rile up working-class Whites using racialized tactics, starting with his "birther movement" during President Obama's presidency. He opened his presidential campaign in 2015 with anti-immigrant comments about Mexicans, calling them criminals, drug dealers, and rapists (Lee 2015). Racist statements like these can also embolden White supremacists who may see a kindred spirit in the White House (O'Brien 2019; Simon and Sidner 2018).

White Supremacist Organizations

As noted earlier, for most Whites today, race and ethnicity do not represent salient components of their identity. However, there is a small but frightening group of individuals who identify strongly with Whiteness and in turn are hostile toward people of color. Organizations like the Ku Klux Klan, neo Nazis, and White nationalist groups maintain ideologies that promote the superiority of Whiteness (and non-Catholic Christianity). They have recently made their presence known to the American mainstream with events like the Unite the Right rally in Charlottesville, Virginia, in 2017 during which crowds chanted "Jews will not replace us" and "White lives matter" as they carried tiki torches and swastikas (McEldowney 2018). The rally ended in horrific violence after a White supremacist drove his car into antiracist protestors, killing one and injuring many. Other recent acts of terrorism by White supremacists include the mass shooting at the Tree of Life synagogue in Pittsburgh in which 11 people were murdered; the 2019 mosque attacks in Christchurch, New Zealand, in which 50 people were murdered; the 2019 mass shooting of 22 people in El Paso, Texas; and the attack on the Capitol in 2021.

The Center for Strategic and International Studies reports that terrorist attacks perpetrated by far-right extremists, which include White supremacists, more than quadrupled from 2016 to 2017 (Jones 2018). According to the Southern Poverty Law Center (SPLC), fears about the aforementioned changing demographics and increases in immigration help explain the heightened White supremacist activity and violence (Beirich 2019).

The Trump Effect

Trump's reticence, at times, to condemn the violent acts of White supremacists, as when he said there were "very fine people on both sides" at the Unite the Right rally, seems to have emboldened some racists (Coaston 2019; Klein 2018). A recent study identifies a **Trump effect** in which counties that hosted a Trump rally in 2016 saw a 226% increase in hate crimes relative to counties that did not (Feinberg, Branton, and Martinez-Ebers 2019). Other researchers found a correlation between Trump's tweets about Islam and anti-Muslim hate crimes, and the El Paso shooter echoed the former president's anti-immigrant rhetoric in his manifesto (Baker and Shear 2019; Muller and Schwarz 2018).

Twitter and other social media sites terminated Trump's account two days after his followers attacked the Capitol on January 6, 2021. Twitter explained it's decision in the following statement: "After close review of recent Tweets from the @realDonaldTrump account and the context around them—specifically how they are being received and interpreted on and off Twitter—we have permanently suspended the account due to the risk of further incitement of violence."

CONSIDER THIS

In what ways might the Internet and social media help to spread White supremacist ideas? Should we do anything to prevent this?

At the same time, Trump has publicly downplayed the problem of White supremacy hate groups. Following the Christchurch attack, Trump responded to a reporter asking if White nationalism is a growing problem by dismissing the idea, saying, "I don't really. I think it's a small group of people that have very, very serious problems" (Reilly 2019; Sherman 2019).

While Trump is correct that these individuals remain a small minority of White people, data from the SPLC indicate that these movements are more numerous—and active—than they have been in decades. According to the Anti-Defamation League (ADL) (2019), White supremacist propaganda efforts (which include the dissemination of literature and public events) increased 182% from 2017 to 2018, reaching an all-time record.

DOING SOCIOLOGY 7.4

Examining White Supremacist Extremist Organizations

In this exercise, you will consider the prevalence and threat of White supremacist activity in the United States.

White supremacist groups are a persistent problem in American society, and they are now more influential than they have been in many years.

Write your answers to the following questions and be prepared to discuss in class:

1. Why is it problematic for people to identify strongly with Whiteness?

2. What are some of the racist myths that White supremacists spread?

3. Why do you think it is necessary for antiracist groups like the ADL to catalog White supremacist activity? How might society benefit from understanding racial hatred?

4. What should be done about these groups? Should they be permitted to hold rallies and distribute propaganda? Should freedom of speech protect hate speech?

Check Your Understanding

1. What factors explain the increase in White anger over the past few years?

2. What does it mean to describe privilege as intersectional?

3. What are White supremacist organizations, and why has their influence increased in recent years?

4. What influence has the Trump effect had on White nationalism, and why is it potentially dangerous?

CONCLUSION

By examining Whiteness through a sociological lens, the many ways Whiteness brings advantages and privileges become clear. Simultaneously, the disadvantages people of color face from past and present discrimination also become obvious. Some of these were touched on in this chapter. Many others will constitute the focus of subsequent chapters. Chapter 8 looks at the experiences of people who fall under the Black racial category from the era of slavery until today.

CHAPTER REVIEW

7.1 Why is Whiteness a social construction that often goes unacknowledged?

Whiteness is a social construction often pushed to the background in racial discussions because it is viewed as the norm. Our current definition, which includes all European ethnicities, is not a natural or God-given category but rather something created by society. We can see this because previous definitions have excluded Americans of German, Irish, Italian, and Polish descent. In the past, the differences between these groups and Whites were obvious. Today, we see little difference at all. The frequently changing definition of Whiteness complicates the demographic projections indicating that Whites will no longer be a majority of the American population as we move into the future.

7.2 **What is the connection between racial categories and the distribution of political, social, and economic power?**

Throughout American history, Whites have used racism to concentrate social, political, and economic power among their group. There are many examples of direct racism that have established legal obstacles for people of color and that have advantaged Whites. These include the Jim Crow laws in the American South; racist suburbanization and real estate practices in the American North, Midwest, and West; naturalization laws that reserved citizenship for Whites only; and many others.

7.3 **What is White privilege, and how does it provide advantages to White people?**

White privilege is a useful philosophical tool for recognizing the taken-for-granted ways in which society advantages Whites. Privilege can play out in many ways, including being considered the social norm, by avoiding the burdens of occupying nonprivileged statuses, and by not having to wonder if your status is harming you. An understanding of privilege can give Whites a better insight into how people of color experience the world.

7.4 **Why are some White people in the United States resentful of people of color?**

There is much evidence that anger and resentment toward people of color has increased among Whites. Much of this has to do with structural changes in our society that have left poor and working-class Whites economically vulnerable. President Trump propelled himself to the White House by stoking these feelings. His efforts may have also paved the way for the frightening increase in White supremacist activity in the past few years. These groups espouse an ideology of hatred toward people of color and are more common today than they have been in decades.

KEY TERMS

Audit study (p. 144)

Boundaries (p. 136)

Direct racism (p. 143)

Dominant group (p. 136)

Fair Housing Act (p. 143)

Federal Housing Administration (p. 142)

Indirect racism (p. 143)

Johnson-Reed Immigration Act (p. 138)

Naturalization (p. 138)

Racism (p. 141)

Social construction (p. 142)

Social norm (p. 146)

Symbolic ethnicity (p. 139)

Trump effect (p. 149)

White privilege (p. 145)

8 BLACK AMERICANS: FACING SLAVERY AND FIGHTING FOR JUSTICE

Richard Maurice Smith

Did you know that some scholars believe African people traveled to the Americas at least 22 generations before Columbus? Or that the first Black people in the Americas were not enslaved but explorers? In fact, African explorers "participated, in some way, in virtually all of the Spanish expeditions in the New World in the 16th century" (Gates and Yacavone 2016, 3). Juan Garrido, the first known African to travel in what is now the United States, accompanied Spaniards Ponce de Leon and Hernán Cortés on their expeditions across the Americas in 1513. Another African, Estevanico (also known as Esteban de Dorantes), explored 15,000 miles across what is now the United States in 1528 (Gates and Yacavone 2016).

Slavery, however, brought the most Africans to the Americas. The enslaved Africans came from diverse groups with different cultures, traditions, religions, languages, and values. In this chapter, we discuss slavery, but we also look at how, generation after generation, Black people have challenged the status quo, overcome incredible odds, and made lasting changes to U.S. society.

HOW I GOT ACTIVE IN SOCIOLOGY

Richard Maurice Smith

Ever since I was a teenager, I loved to read about African Americans who rejected racist narratives about who they were and what they could do. They exceeded social expectations, often not just for African Americans but all Americans. In the face of societal pressures, unjust laws, and even death, many African Americans exemplified resilience and excelled regardless of the problems they faced. That fascinated me because I was living in an onslaught of negativity. I grew up during a time when the war on drugs was being pushed with negative images of people who looked like me flooding TV screens. I saw how vastly different the living standards were across racially divided neighborhoods in Baltimore where I grew up. I also saw the way that people looked down on me.

I had so many questions by the time I reached college that centered around why our society was like this to begin with and why it continued to be this way. It seemed like sociology was a way to navigate those questions and find many of those answers. As a result, I have done research and taught courses on race and racism in the United States; racial and ethnic relations; African American culture; and race, crime, and justice. I still have questions, but now I can help to find answers.

CREATING SLAVERY

In 1619, an English pirate ship landed in Jamestown, Virginia, and brought 20 Africans to what would become the United States of America. While they were forcibly brought to the colony, many were freed after providing involuntary labor for a number of years. For example, in 1622, "Antonio" was listed in the historical record as an enslaved African. However, by 1625, the census described him as a "Negro servant." After he gained his freedom, he changed his name to Anthony Johnson and became a landowner himself. After purchasing his freedom, Johnson married an enslaved African woman named Mary. By 1650, the Johnsons owned 250 acres of land on the eastern shore of Virginia. After Johnson died in 1670, however, an all-White jury ruled that his land should be seized "because he was a Negro and by consequence an alien." By this time, the colonists viewed all Black people as enslaved peoples.

In 1656, Elizabeth Key, another enslaved African, sued for her and her son's freedom. She argued that they were wrongfully enslaved because her father was a free White man. She won her case and became the first woman of African descent to sue for her freedom from slavery and win. However, in 1662, the colony of Virginia passed a law stating that a child would be "held bond or free according to the condition of the mother" instead of the father. Colonists referred to the law as partus sequitur ventrem, which means "that which is brought forth follows the womb." As a result, White men who would rape and impregnate enslaved African women were not expected to support, recognize, or free their offspring from a life of slavery (Morgan 2003).

Slavery and the Creation of Blackness

As mentioned in Chapter 1, the conceptualization of Blackness and Whiteness helped justify slavery. Distinguishing "superior" White people from "inferior" Black people provided a rationale for Whites to enslave Blacks.

The creation of different racial groups also helped White elites maintain their high-class position by dividing the working class by race: White and Black. Bacon's Rebellion (1666–1667), the first rebellion in the American colonies, helps reveal the reasoning for this strategy to divide those outside of the White elite. The rebellion arose from a dispute between Nathaniel Bacon and the governor of Virginia, Sir William Berkeley. Bacon, and those who followed him, wanted to take the land of local Native Americans and possibly enslave them. However, the governor and many in the colony's legislature were not interested in the war that action would surely bring about. Bacon, frustrated by the lack of support from the wealthy and powerful government officials, built a militia of both White and enslaved African American men to rebel against the government of Virginia. While successful at first, the rebellion petered out when Bacon died from dysentery toward the end of 1667.

While Bacon's Rebellion was not a rebellion to end slavery, it was a multiracial uprising against the merchant class. In response, the merchant class strengthened the racial caste system by creating new laws and codes, including the slave codes of 1705, that made it illegal for Black people and White people to do anything together. Slave codes defined the position of enslaved Black people, solidified their subjugation, and prevented poorer Whites and Black people from uniting against the White upper class.

This racial caste system also provided a "public and psychological wage of Whiteness" for lower-class Whites. A **wage of Whiteness** refers to the social status provided to poor Whites simply because they are White and not Black (Du Bois 1935/1998). It encouraged poor Whites to identify themselves with the rich because of their mutual connection to Whiteness. As a result, instead of economic class positions, racial categories became the primary means of identifying difference. After this time, the terms *White* and *Black* became common in public documents to describe, respectively, people of European descent and people of African descent.

CONSIDER THIS

Do you think the "wage of Whiteness" did more to hurt or help poor White people? Why?

Slavery in Northern States

White people in northern, as well as southern, parts of what is now the United States enslaved Black people. In fact, slavery existed in all 13 colonies when they declared their independence from Britain in 1776. A combination of revolutionary beliefs in the inalienable right of "life, liberty, and the pursuit of happiness" and a lack of widespread economic dependence on enslaved labor led leaders in northern states to abolish slavery by the early 1800s. Many did so gradually, however, and up until the middle part of the 19th century some northern states had enslaved people residing within their borders (Miller and David 1997).

DOING SOCIOLOGY 8.1

How Slavery Made America

In this exercise, you will examine the formation of race-based slavery and how it drastically impacted the lives and status of Black people in the United States.

When *The White Lion* arrived at the Jamestown colony in 1619, the colonists bartered for the 20 Africans aboard the Dutch slave ship. At this point, the institution of slavery had not yet been established in the colony. The kidnapped Africans were forced to work as indentured servants alongside White indentured servants already living in Jamestown. As the colonists' profits grew, they were loath to give up the free labor the Africans provided; slavery was legalized in 1641.

   With this in mind, write answers to the following questions, and be prepared to share your answers with the rest of the class.

1. What is the difference between indentured servitude and slavery?

2. Why do you think European settlers in North America decided to enslave the Africans but not the White indentured servants?

3. Imagine if racial categories were never created. Is it difficult or easy to imagine this? Why?

4. Without the concept of race, how might have relations between the offspring of European settlers and of kidnapped Africans differed?

Chattel Slavery

You may have heard the term *chattel slavery* and wondered what *chattel* means. The term chattel refers to personal property that owners can do with as they wish. Slave owners in colonial and U.S. society had complete power over the people they enslaved because they were considered property. The slave owners had control of subjects' bodies as well as their work. Many enslaved women faced repeated rape with no recourse. Slave owners forced the women and men to work and serve regardless of how they felt or the surrounding physical climate. Anything produced by their hands and even the babies they gave birth to belonged to the White owners. While any form of slavery is horrible, "American chattel slavery was often brutal, barbaric, [and] violent." In addition to sexually exploiting enslaved people, many owners maimed or killed them for offenses such as working too slowly, visiting relatives on nearby plantations, and learning to read and write (Stevenson 2015).

Check Your Understanding

1. How did Bacon's Rebellion shift the status of Black people in the United States?

2. Why was the creation of "Black" and "White" necessary for the existence of slavery in the United States?

3. What is chattel slavery?

RESILIENCE AND RESISTANCE OF AFRICAN AMERICANS WITHIN THE INSTITUTION OF SLAVERY

Slavery was clearly an oppressive institution for African Americans. Slave masters attempted to control every aspect of the lives of the people they enslaved. On most slave plantations, the enslaved could not read or write, gather together in a meeting, or even marry. There were cruel penalties for violating written and unwritten rules, such as refusing to work, trying to run away, or speaking out of turn. Enslaved people faced the threat of being whipped, hung by their feet, dismembered, forced to wear heavy iron masks and weights around their necks, or killed. There was nowhere enslaved Africans could turn for protection.

To justify this brutality, subjugation, and assigned inferiority, some people turned to belief systems, such as religion and pseudoscience. For example, those who supported slavery pointed to a story in the Bible that describes Africans as descendants of Noah's youngest son Ham. According to this story, God supposedly cursed him with Black skin because he looked at his father Noah's nakedness. Later "scientists" would use unscientific research to "prove" the existence of a racial hierarchy with Whites on top and Blacks on the bottom. Even in the midst of this brutality, subjugation, and anti-Black beliefs, however, Black people exhibited agency through resilience, resistance, and rebellion.

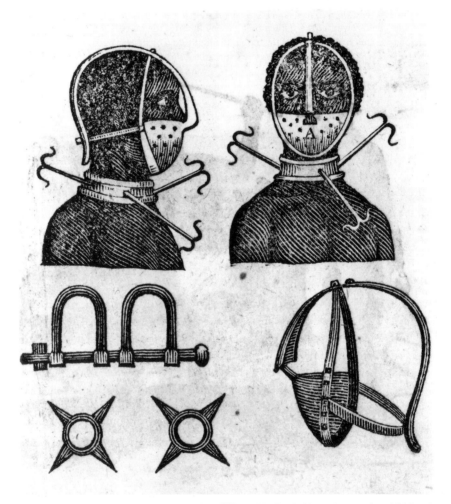

PHOTO 8.1 Shown is an iron mask and collar, circa 1750, used by slaveholders to keep enslaved field workers from running away and to prevent them from eating crops such as sugarcane. The mask made breathing difficult and if left on too long would tear away at the enslaved person's skin when removed.

MPI/Getty Images

Forms of Resilience

Enslaved peoples were not passive, docile, content, and submissive actors in the institution of slavery. Many found ways to be resilient and to resist the oppressive institution. For example, they created songs—later known as Negro spirituals—to send messages among each other without the slave owners and overseers knowing they were doing so. This strategy allowed them to circumvent strict rules about gathering together. Through these songs they could warn one another of impending danger and share information about travel routes for enslaved people trying to escape.

Enslaved people used humor to lift their spirits and make fun of White people, particularly their owners. They might talk about the mistress, joke about the hypocrisy of White Christian slave owners, and make fun of how their owners looked. Du Bois (1940/2007) called it a "delicious chuckle" because the enslaved used comedy at their slave master's expense. These moments gave the enslaved some agency and power in the midst of a disempowering institution.

Many enslaved people held on to the traditions from their African roots as closely as they could. From the way they sang songs to the items they created and the food they made, the enslaved expressed their own cultural traditions. They passed down stories from generation to generation that helped to keep their ancestors' traditions alive.

Even though many slave owners' families prohibited marriages, enslaved Africans found ways to marry and start families. Jumping over a broom, for example, signified and consecrated a union within the community of the enslaved. They maintained their dignity in many other ways, as well, and many envisioned more for their lives than their conditions and positions indicated. Some taught themselves to read, learned all they could about the land, and sharpened their skills to be ready for freedom.

Forms of Resistance

Not only were enslaved Black people resilient, many resisted the practice of slavery—at great peril. One form of resistance was escaping. Enslaved people who ran away often did so to connect with loved ones or to gain the freedom they believed was rightfully theirs. They were willing to face the well-known risks, which included receiving severe whippings where their wounds would be filled with salt, pepper, or some other substance that would make an already painful punishment exponentially harsher and more agonizing. Some knew they faced dismemberment or branding if caught, but they still planned for the right moment to escape the harsh realities of living confined within the brutal and unrelenting slave system.

Harriet Jacobs hid in an attic for close to 7 years and then made the journey north for freedom in 1835. Henry Brown, who would gain the nickname "Box," stowed away in a box that his friend then mailed from Richmond, Virginia, to a Philadelphia, Pennsylvania, abolitionist. Harriet Tubman personally led hundreds of people to freedom through a system of underground networks known as the Underground Railroad. With numerous conductors, including formerly enslaved African Americans, free African Americans, and some White abolitionists (those who fought for the abolishment of slavery), the Underground Railroad helped as many as 100,000 enslaved people make their way to freedom between 1800 and the start of the Civil War (Yellin 2005).

Rebellions

Rebellions by enslaved peoples composed another form of resistance. They were an incredible source of fear for slave owners. There were at least 250 rebellions by enslaved peoples in the United States before the abolishment of slavery in 1865. The Stono Rebellion of 1739 in South Carolina, about 20 miles outside of Charleston, was the largest rebellion by enslaved peoples in the 13 colonies. Twenty enslaved Africans raided a gun shop, armed themselves, and marched along the Stono River shouting "Lukango!" ("liberty" in their native language). Other enslaved peoples joined them until their number reached approximately 60. Before being killed or captured, they killed 20 White people. The surviving—and terrified—Whites in the area publicly executed the surviving rebels (Gates and Yacavone 2016).

CONSIDER THIS

Did you know that many enslaved people rebelled in the United States? If no, why not?

In 1831, Nathaniel Turner led another rebellion and slaughtered many of the White slave owners in Southampton County, Virginia. After capturing or killing most of the rebels, the Whites who eventually put down the revolution executed Turner. They then took his body, skinned it to make purses and belts, gave other pieces of it to onlookers, cut off his head, and rendered the rest of his remains into grease. It is possible that his skull and a purse made from his skin still exist today (Rodriguez 2006).

Nonviolent Acts of Resistance

The enslaved also resisted in many nonviolent ways. For example, some would play into stereotypes that they were unintelligent. They would pretend not to understand instructions or how to do a certain task. Others would act like they were clumsy, hard of hearing, almost blind, or sick. Some destroyed farm equipment or sabotaged other parts of their owners' plans of building wealth by losing tools or purposely destroying crops (Foner 2019).

DOING SOCIOLOGY 8.2

Violent and Nonviolent Resistance

This exercise asks you to consider two forms of resistance to slavery: violent and nonviolent.

Think about the different forms of resistance enslaved Black people used in the United States. Then, write down the benefits of each. Compare answers with a classmate and be prepared to share your answers with the class.

Civil War

Approximately 200,000 Black men escaped from the South to fight for the Union in the Civil War (1861–1865). Robert Smalls was one such man. In 1839, he was born into slavery on a South Carolina plantation. Due to his impressive skills and knowledge of steering boats and ships, he was forced to steer the *C.S.S. Planter*, a Confederate military transport ship, in Charleston Harbor. Smalls carefully planned his escape while acting as a reliable enslaved person. On a night in 1862, while the White crew members were off the ship and the captain had entrusted it to him to watch over, Smalls commandeered

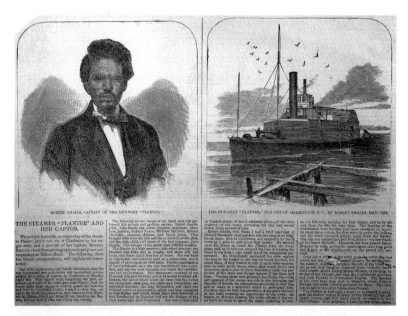

PHOTO 8.2 Left: American naval hero and politician Robert Smalls (1839–1915). Right: The gunboat *Planter*, run out of Charleston, South Carolina, by Robert Smalls, May 1862. Undated engravings.

Bettmann / Contributor

the ship, picked up his family, and wearing the Confederate uniform and mimicking the manners of the captain, he sailed through several checkpoints. Through all these steps, he fooled Confederate onlookers from the shore and the forts. They did not suspect anything was amiss. He then piloted the *C.S.S. Planter* right to Union ships and surrendered it to their commanders. Through his harrowing escape, Smalls secured freedom for himself and the other enslaved men and women onboard. He would eventually become one of the first African American members of the U.S. House of Representatives (Lineberry 2017).

Check Your Understanding

1. How did enslaved African Americans use comedy as a form of resilience?

2. What were some ways African Americans escaped from slavery?

3. How were enslaved people who rebelled punished?

4. Approximately how many African American men fought in the Civil War?

AFTER SLAVERY: RECONSTRUCTION AND MIGRATION

The Civil War ended in 1865; later that year, the Thirteenth Amendment abolished slavery in the United States and any territory under its jurisdiction. But where did formerly enslaved people fit in U.S. society? In this section we look at Reconstruction, the decade or so after the Civil War when Black people used their new rights to become leaders and landowners. We also look at what happened to Black people after Reconstruction ended.

Reconstruction

Shortly after the Civil War two more constitutional amendments (the Fourteenth and Fifteenth) gave citizenship to formerly enslaved peoples and the right to vote to Black men. With the support of Union troops in the South, Black people began to vote and gain elected office (at this time many Confederate soldiers had not yet regained their right to vote). Many ran for public office and won seats in local and national government bodies. For this brief period called Reconstruction (1865–1877), the future looked bright for the formerly enslaved. However, as soon as Black people started to make these gains, they faced backlash from White southerners. In Tennessee, during the winter of 1865–1866, former Confederate general Nathan Bedford Forrest formed the Ku Klux Klan and led an onslaught of terror on African American communities.

The ascension of Andrew Johnson to the presidency after the assassination of Abraham Lincoln in 1865 also hindered the progress of Reconstruction. A racist, Johnson focused on strengthening the South and moving African Americans into a second-class citizenry that made them, in a sense, slaves of the state. His administration gave confiscated lands meant for the formerly enslaved to the former land—and slave—owners.

Meanwhile, a political coalition of elite White southerners called Redeemers came together to help roll back the gains of Reconstruction. Their goals were to regain political power and reestablish what they saw as the natural order in the United States. The natural order for them was to maintain a government for White people only, subjugate Black people by any means, and restore the "glory" of the South. Through threats, terrorism, ideology, and political negotiations, they helped bring about a legal end to Reconstruction.

The demise of Reconstruction came with the Hayes-Tilden Compromise of 1877—a secret negotiation between Republican presidential candidate Rutherford Hayes and Southern Democrats. The election results were uncertain. The Democratic candidate, Samuel Tilden, seemed to have more votes (though some states' vote tallies were disputed), but he needed one more electoral vote to win. The Southern Democrats agreed to give the election to Hayes if he promised to remove federal troops from the South. He took the deal and gained the presidency.

The removal of federal troops from the South left Black people at the mercy of those who wanted to roll back the clock and ensure that Black people lost the rights they had gained through Reconstruction. Democrats quickly took control of the entire South and began to establish laws and policies that deprived Blacks of their constitutional rights. African Americans who had gained political office lost their positions and influence. More were thrown into jail for violating newly created laws such as loitering, not having a job, and being in the wrong area, or simply for "disrespecting" a White person.

Many of those arrested faced convict leasing, the selling or renting of prisoners to a White person or the government for forced labor. Even though the Thirteenth Amendment officially ended slavery in the United States and its territories, it allowed for an exception—slavery as punishment for a crime. W. E. B. Du Bois summarized this period this way: "The slave went free, stood a brief moment in the sun, then moved back again towards slavery" (1935/1998, 15).

The First Black Migration (1915–1940)

In the post-Reconstruction South, almost all African Americans—even those not arrested—lived in slavelike conditions doing work for little to no pay. Most were sharecroppers. Sharecropping involves landowners allowing families to use part of their land to live and cultivate crops in return for a share of their crops. Often, however, White landowners (almost all former slave owners) would take so many of the crops that the tenants could not afford food or other necessities. Then, the African American tenants would have to borrow money from the landowner, which kept them in a perpetual state of debt.

Many southern Blacks managed to escape those conditions by leaving the South and pursuing work elsewhere. The first Black migration officially began in 1915 and lasted until about 1940. After the start of World War I in 1914, immigration slowed dramatically and led to a shortage of laborers in northern industrial areas. The 1924 Immigration Act, which reduced immigration to just a trickle, also contributed to a lack of workers in industrial cities outside the rural South. Industrialists recruited southern Black people, enticing them to go north for better work and treatment. Black newspapers like the *Chicago Defender* published advertisements encouraging African Americans to leave the South to find work in the North and West. It was clear to many African Americans that they could have a better life and earn much more money if they moved out of the South. During the first Great Migration, approximately 1.6 million Black people left the South, the majority seeking opportunities in the North.

The Harlem Renaissance

The Great Migration led to northern cities becoming hotspots for African American exploration, education, and expression. The Harlem Renaissance sprouted up from the migration. Harlem, a neighborhood in Manhattan, gained the most migrants, and Black social, intellectual, and artistic expression exploded there throughout the 1920s. Theater, literature, music, and art dealt with the problems of racism, the Black experience, and the hopes and dreams of African Americans. Some called this the New Negro movement, inspired by the 1925 anthology *The New Negro*, edited by Alain Locke, a prominent African American and "dean" of the Harlem Renaissance. The new Negro—educated, literate, and middle class—differed markedly from the traditional view of Black people as uneducated and incapable of progress.

Backlash

With success, however, came backlash. For many Whites, "black success was an intolerable affront to the social order of white supremacy" (Hirsch 2002). Many poor Whites, in particular, resented successes of Black people. Greenwood, a neighborhood in Tulsa, Oklahoma, known as Black Wall Street due to the many African American businesses and financially successful families in the area, provides a gruesome example. This neighborhood, purposely segregated by Tulsa leadership, was known as "America's wealthiest Black neighborhood." In 1921, a White mob, angered by the success of African Americans and disgruntled about their own economic state, beat and killed many African Americans and burned down numerous Black-owned businesses in Greenwood. Police helped and even deputized White mob participants. Whites in airplanes (some owned by police departments) flew over and threw bottles of gasoline down on the neighborhood. Much of Greenwood was destroyed, and it has never fully recovered (Anderson 2017).

CONSIDER THIS

How does the attack on Greenwood relate to the "wage of Whiteness"?

The Second Black Migration (1940–1970)

The second Black migration began after 1940 and lasted until around 1970. During the Great Depression in the 1930s, agricultural employment declined with the drop in prices of major crops such as sugar, tobacco, and cotton. White planters received subsidies through New Deal programs, but African American sharecroppers did not. With the subsidies they received from the government, White southern farmers began using tractors and mechanized cotton pickers, dramatically decreasing the need for human laborers. As a result, many African Americans moved from southern rural areas to urban areas outside the South. Approximately 6 million Black people moved out of the South between the start of the first and the end of the second Black migration.

DOING SOCIOLOGY 8.3

What Have You Learned?

In this exercise, you will check your understanding of the section you just read.

Write your answers to the Check Your Understanding questions at the end of this section. Then, share and compare your answers with a classmate. Which question was the most challenging for you? Were there any answers that you and your partner disagreed about?

Check Your Understanding

1. What was the goal of Reconstruction?

2. Why did Reconstruction end?

3. Why did many African Americans feel it was necessary to move from the South?

4. What was the importance of the Harlem Renaissance?

RESILIENCE: RELIGION AND EMPOWERMENT GROUPS

Black churches have been the center of the Black community throughout the history of the United States. During slavery, Black slaves formed small churches, even though they were often disbanded and the pastor whipped or beaten for having a following. In the North, Richard Allen and Absalom Jones formed the Free African Society of Philadelphia. Later, Allen started the African Methodist Episcopal denomination. Many Black pastors spoke for the abolition of slavery and later for the full citizenship of the formerly enslaved. It was through the church that many Black people found—and continue to find—inspiration, enrichment, spiritual and professional development, and support (Lincoln and Mamiya 1990).

Black religious groups formed in the United States include Christian denominations (e.g., African Methodist Episcopal Church, African Methodist Episcopal Zion Church, National Baptist Convention, Church of God in Christ), Muslim groups (e.g., Moorish Science Temple of America, Nation of Islam, Five-Percent Nation), and the Black Hebrew Israelites. Today, a little over 80% of African Americans are Christian.

DOING SOCIOLOGY 8.4

Abolition, Black Power, and Black Churches

In this exercise, you will consider the debate surrounding Black Power teachings in Black churches.

In 1967, Reverend James Cone wrote *Black Theology and Black Power*. In the book, he describes a Black theology that supports the teachings of the Black Power movement, which emphasizes the need for Black liberation and rejects less assertive integrative measures. In 2003—in response to the question "Is the Black church too political?"—Cone urged his audience to consider the church's mission:

> Is its mission primarily saving souls? Or is it saving bodies? Or is it both together? I think if you see them both together, I think you would have to see that the Black church [has] to be political because politics is a part of life. It also has to be concerned about saving souls, because full meaning in life is not simply found in politics.

Consider Cone's response. Then write answers to the following questions:

1. What do you think Cone meant when he said that the Black church can focus on "primarily saving souls," primarily "saving bodies," or saving "both together"?

2. Cone sees the mission of the Black church as saving "both together." How do you think Black ministers who saw the mission of the Black church as "primarily saving souls" viewed the abolitionist movement?

3. Do you think this religious debate is still relevant today? Why or why not?

PHOTO 8.3 Marcus Garvey, circa 1920. Jamaican-born African American nationalist Marcus Garvey (1887–1940), founder of the Universal Negro Improvement Association (UNIA), promoted the back-to-Africa movement.

MPI/Getty Images

African American Empowerment Groups

In addition to churches, African Americans created groups and organizations focused on Black empowerment, self-preservation, and economic development. W. E. B. DuBois developed the Niagara movement, an equal rights movement, after a meeting of leading Black men near Niagara Falls in 1905. The Niagara movement led to the founding of the **National Association for the Advancement of Colored People (NAACP)** in 1909, an organization of women and men, both Black and White. Its cofounders included sociologists W. E. B. DuBois and Jane Addams. The NAACP shared the goals set forth in the Niagara movement to promote racial equality and respond to violence and injustice toward Black Americans. For example, it focused much of its early efforts on fighting lynching. The NAACP also arranged protests, such as the one against President Woodrow Wilson's segregation policies in the federal government. In 1914, the NAACP won the right for African Americans to serve as officers in the military.

While the NAACP fought for racial equality and the end of violence against African Americans, the United Negro Improvement Association (UNIA), which created a branch in Harlem in 1916, connected with African Americans who believed those goals were unrealistic and impossible to achieve. Goals of the leader of the UNIA, Marcus Garvey, included instilling pride in Black people, helping them to support themselves economically, and getting African Americans to move to Africa and establish an independent Black nation in Africa. The UNIA quickly became a pan-African movement, attracting Black people in over 40 countries by 1920. A forerunner to the Black pride and Black Power movements, the UNIA ended in 1923 when the U.S. government deported Garvey (Grant 2010).

CONSIDER THIS

Imagine if you were a Black person living in the United States in 1920. Do you think you would be a follower of W. E. B. Du Bois or Marcus Garvey? Why?

Check Your Understanding

1. Why were Black churches so important to African American communities?

2. What was the purpose of the NAACP?

3. What was one of the victories achieved by the NAACP?

4. What were the goals of the United Negro Improvement Association?

THE CIVIL RIGHTS MOVEMENT

While African Americans fought for their rights throughout U.S. history, the murder of Emmett Till in 1955 sparked a more organized national civil rights movement. At the time of his murder, Till was 14 years old. A few days after being accused of whistling at a White woman, the woman's husband and his brother abducted him from his uncle's house in Mississippi, where he was visiting. They beat Till, mutilated his body, shot him in the head, and then threw his body in the river. While this type of violence was not rare, it gained national and international attention when his mother insisted that his casket be open during the public funeral service, so people would see what happened to him. Several Black-owned media outlets displayed pictures of Till's mutilated and bloated body in their newspapers and magazines. People all over the world saw the image of Emmett Till's body and, through it, the treatment of Black people in the United States and the devastation of racism. The death of Emmett Till and the subsequent acquittal of his killers provided a powerful catalyst for the civil rights movement.

Boycotts and Sit-ins

The Montgomery, Alabama, bus boycott also took place during 1955. Jo Ann Robinson, the president of the Women's Political Council (WPC) in Montgomery, Alabama, had been working to improve the treatment of African Americans on public transportation. In 1953 she wrote to the mayor on behalf of the WPC and threatened a boycott if the city did not meet three demands: (1) end racial segregation on buses, (2) end the practice of asking Black people to pay in the front of the bus and then enter through the rear, and (3) have buses stop at every corner in Black areas as well as White areas. Robinson further made clear in her letter that "three-fourths of the riders of these public conveyances are Negroes. If Negroes did not patronize them, they could not possibly operate" (Robinson, found in Jeffries 2019, 133). There was no reply to the letter.

When Robinson heard of Rosa Parks's arrest in 1955—for not giving up her bus seat for a White person—she printed and distributed 35,000 flyers that announced the boycott would start on December 5, 1955. Due to the initial success of the boycott, civil rights leaders formed the Montgomery Improvement Association (MIA) to continue to oversee the boycott. They selected the Reverend Dr. Martin Luther King Jr. to lead the boycott, preside over the MIA, and become their spokesperson. After roughly a year, the Montgomery bus boycott ended in victory for the MIA (Williams and Greenshaw 2007).

There were many other racial injustices to address, however. **Jim Crow laws**, state and local laws that legalized and enforced racial segregation and discrimination, continued in the South into the 1960s. Civil rights leaders and activists led various peaceful demonstrations and nonviolent direct actions to put an end to these unjust laws. For example, Clara Shephard Luper successfully led the 1958 Oklahoma City sit-ins. The Oklahoma City sit-in protests at racially segregated downtown drugstore lunch counters brought about the end of segregation policies in Oklahoma City. Thanks in part to these efforts, Congress passed and President Lyndon B. Johnson signed two landmark civil rights acts. The **Civil Rights Act of 1964** outlawed discrimination based on race, color, religion, sex, or national origin, and the **Voting Rights Act of 1965** prohibited voter suppression. With these two acts, the federal government prohibited discrimination in voting, education, employment, public accommodations, and services.

Black Pride and Black Power

Other movements during the 1960s addressed the effects of negative racial stereotypes on Black people. Instead of trying to get White people to value and accept them, many Black people focused on self-acceptance.

PHOTO 8.4 Singer Diana Ross poses in 1975 with her hair styled in an Afro. California.

Harry Langdon/Getty Images

The "**Black Is Beautiful**" slogan became popular during the 1960s and counteracted the prevailing perception in the United States that Black features are undesirable and less attractive than White characteristics. African Americans stopped perming or conking their hair and accepted their hair's natural curly texture. The Afro became the hairstyle of choice for both women and men to exemplify full acceptance of themselves. The Black Is Beautiful slogan coincided with James Brown's song and declaration, "Say it loud, I'm Black and I'm proud." The Black Is Beautiful movement was a way to resist the dominant White perception of beauty.

Also, in the 1960s, Nation of Islam minister Malcolm X taught people that being Black is powerful and that African Americans should have pride in who they are due to their rich heritage. He argued that Black people should gain equal rights through any means possible, saying, "Nobody can give you freedom. Nobody can give you equality or justice or anything. If you're a man, you take it" (found in Breitman 1973, 122).

The teachings of Malcolm X influenced the **Black Power movement**. Popularized by Stokely Carmichael (he later changed his name to Kwame Ture), the term *Black Power* became recognized throughout the United States. At a march in 1968, Carmichael declared, with his fist clenched in the air, "This is the twenty-seventh time I have been arrested and I ain't going to jail no more! The only way we gonna stop them White men from whuppin us is to take over. What we gonna start sayin' now is Black Power" (found in Horowitz, Bond, and Theoharis 2021, 299).

Carmichael would later make clear that he saw Black Power as Black people coming together to form a political force and elect politicians to meet the needs of Black people. A Black gloved raised fist symbolized Black Power. Olympic medal winners Tommie Smith and John Carlos shocked the world and embarrassed U.S. government officials by each raising a Black gloved fist while on the podium at the Olympics in 1968.

Black Panther Party

In 1966, several African American students at Merritt College in Oakland, California, protested the omission of the role of African Americans in the college's annual celebration of the founding of California. Two of these students, Bobby Seale and Huey Newton, formed the Black Panther Party soon after. Originally called the Black Panther Party for Self-Defense, the goals of the group were to encourage self-empowerment; create and run community programs; and practice their constitutional right to carry firearms to patrol their neighborhoods, monitor the actions of racist police officers in the Oakland police department, and challenge police brutality. They patrolled African American neighborhoods to protect the residents from police brutality. They also started and ran breakfast programs for children and free health care clinics in 13 African American communities.

DOING SOCIOLOGY 8.5

Perceptions of Black Groups

In this exercise, you will look at the influence of the media's portrayal of the Black Panthers.

Examine Photo 8.5 and Photo 8.6 and answer the following questions in writing. Then, share your answers with another person in the class, compare your answers, and discuss why you each responded as you did. Be prepared to share your answers with the class.

PHOTO 8.5 A line of Black Panther Party members demonstrates outside a New York City courthouse in April 1969.

David Fenton/Getty Images

PHOTO 8.6 Kansas City Black Panther Bill Whitfield serves breakfast to local children as part of the Panther free breakfast program in April 1969.

GRANGER.

1. What words first come to mind while viewing each photo?

2. Which photo exemplifies what you were taught about the Black Panthers?

J. Edgar Hoover, the head of the FBI at the time, described the Black Panthers as "one of the greatest threats to the nation's internal security" and implemented a counterintelligence program to dismantle the party (Jones 1998, 336). Hoover focused on disrupting the free breakfast program and other social programs the party ran, causing friction within and outside the group, and capturing and/or assassinating leaders such as Fred Hampton and Mark Clark. Under constant threat, the Black Panther Party dissolved in 1982. Its legacy remains today, however, and its slogan, "All Power to All the People" continues to influence and motivate many people working for racial justice (Bloom and Martin 2013).

> **Check Your Understanding**
>
> 1. Why did the murder of Emmett Till help spark the civil rights movement?
>
> 2. How did African Americans change the narrative about Blackness for themselves?
>
> 3. Why is the Black Power movement important to the history of African Americans?
>
> 4. What did J. Edgar Hoover do to the Black Panther Party?

BLACK ETHNIC GROUPS IN AMERICA

As we discuss in earlier chapters, *Black* refers to a race of people, but there are numerous ethnic groups within that race, such as African American, Jamaican American, Haitian American, and Nigerian American. All these ethnic groups have both shared and distinct histories in the United States. Each of the Black ethnic groups has also influenced our society and helped diversify the Black population in the United States.

The Immigration Experiences of African, Afro Latinx, and Caribbean Immigrants

Prior to 1965, there were so few Black immigrants in the United States that they did not even make up 1% of the population. However, due to more opportunities available in the United States and the passing of the Immigration and Nationality Act of 1965, by the 1990s, the population had increased to approximately 400,000 from countries in Africa, and close to 1 million from the Caribbean. As seen in Figures 8.1 and 8.2, the Black immigrant population continues to rise, reaching 4.2 million by 2016. Immigrants from African countries make up close to 40% of the Black immigrant population while almost half of all Black immigrants living in the United States are from the Caribbean, with the largest groups coming from Jamaica and Haiti (Anderson and López 2018). Today, 1 in 10 Black Americans are immigrants.

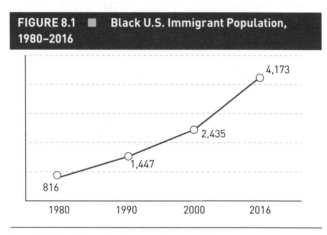

FIGURE 8.1 ■ Black U.S. Immigrant Population, 1980–2016

Note: In 2000 and later, foreign-born Blacks include single-race Blacks and multiracial Blacks, regardless of Hispanic origin. Prior to 2000, Blacks include only single-race Blacks regardless of Hispanic origin since a multi-racial option was not available.

Source: "Key facts about black immigrants in the U.S." Pew Research Center, Washington, D.C. (24 January 2018) https://www.pewresearch.org/fact-tank/2018/01/24/key-facts-about-black-immigrants-in-the-u-s/.

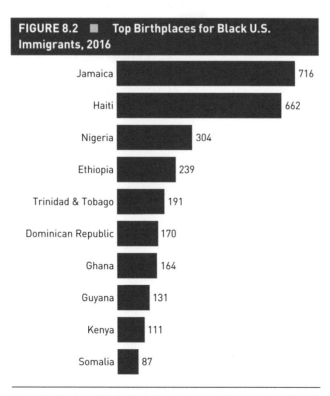

FIGURE 8.2 ■ Top Birthplaces for Black U.S. Immigrants, 2016

Note: Foreign-born blacks include single-race blacks and multiracial blacks, regardless of Hispanic origin. Top 10 largest black immigrant groups shown.

Source: "Key facts about black immigrants in the U.S." Pew Research Center, Washington, D.C. (24 January 2018) https://www.pewresearch.org/fact-tank/2018/01/24/key-facts-about-black-immigrants-in-the-u-s/.

Some of the most affluent and educated Black people in the United States come from African nations (Anderson and López 2018; Zong and Batalova 2017). For example, as seen in Figure 8.3, compared to the overall U.S. population, a higher percentage of immigrants from Nigeria, Kenya, and Ghana have college degrees.

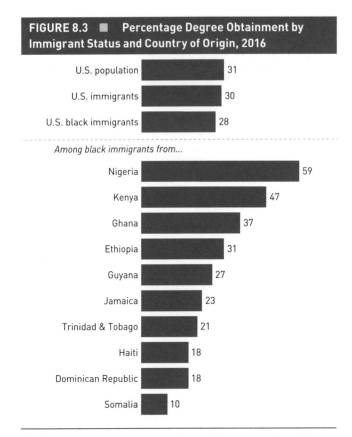

FIGURE 8.3 ■ Percentage Degree Obtainment by Immigrant Status and Country of Origin, 2016

Note: Foreign-born blacks include single-race blacks and multiracial blacks, regardless of Hispanic origin. Top 10 largest black immigrant groups shown.

Source: Anderson and López 2018. "Key facts about black immigrants in the U.S." Figure 5. "Overall, 28% of black immigrants have a college degree, but this varies widely by country of origin" Pew Research Center tabulations of the 2016 American Community Survey (IPUMS). https://www.pewresearch.org/fact-tank/2018/01/24/key-facts-about-black-immigrants-in-the-u-s/.

Not only do some immigrants from African nations have a higher education than the average person in the United States, they also have more economic power. African immigrants make substantial contributions to the U.S. economy. According to Andrew Lim (2018), the associate director of research at New American Economy, "Overwhelmingly the evidence shows that [African immigrants] make a significant, positive economic contribution to the U.S. economy. They contribute more than $10.1 billion in federal taxes, $4.7 billion in state and local taxes, and most importantly, they have significant economic clout to the point of $40.3 billion in spending power."

Black immigrants and their children, as well as African Americans, however, must deal with the U.S. legacy of slavery and racism. Sociologist Mary Waters (2001) looks at the experiences of West Indian immigrants and their children in the United States. She explains that first-generation immigrants tend to find success due to their lack of attention to racism and their focus on education, desire to save, and willingness to do difficult work. They believe there's greater opportunity in the United States than in their homeland and are willing to deal with or ignore the racist treatment they receive. However, while West Indian immigrants may put up with low pay, poor working conditions, and racist practices, their children are less likely to do so. Their expectations differ from those of their immigrant parents who were raised in a different—non–African American—culture.

CONSIDER THIS

Why, in general, are children of West Indian immigrants to the United States less likely to put up with racist practices than their parents?

Black immigrants, however, also face other forms of discrimination—based on their status as Black immigrants. According to the Black Alliance for Just Immigration, deportations of Black immigrants increased 140% since the 2016 presidential election of Donald Trump. Trump's disparaging comments about African countries, and his efforts to make the Immigration and Customs Enforcement (ICE) detain and deport more undocumented immigrants and those with criminal records of any kind (even for minor crimes), contributed to the spike in deportations among immigrant Black communities (Foer 2018).

DOING SOCIOLOGY 8.6

Attitudes Toward the United States

In this exercise, compare the attitudes of Black immigrants and African Americans toward U.S. society.

Answer the following question in writing and be prepared to share with the rest of the class:

1. Why do you think Black immigrants tend to have a more positive attitude toward the United States than African Americans?

Check Your Understanding

1. Which nations do most Black immigrants come from today?

2. Why do Black immigrants tend to have more economic success than their children?

3. Why might it be easier for Black immigrants than their children to ignore the racism they encounter in the United States?

4. Why did deportations of Black immigrants increase after the election of Trump?

THE FIGHT FOR RACIAL JUSTICE AND RESILIENCE TODAY

The civil rights movement of the 1960s provided necessary change in the United States. However, as discussed in earlier chapters, Black Americans still face persistent racial injustice. From the war on drugs to mandatory sentencing, Black Americans face more surveillance and disproportionate chances to be arrested and sentenced to long prison terms than other racial groups. Moreover, as we describe in Chapters 4 and 5, they continue to encounter (and push back against) discrimination in housing, political representation, employment, the media, and schools.

War on Drugs

On June 18, 1971, President Richard Nixon called drug abuse "public enemy number one" in a message to Congress and officially declared the "war on drugs" (Sherman 2016). However, according to a 1994 interview with President Nixon's domestic policy chief John Ehrlichman, the war on drugs was not initiated to combat drugs but to disrupt groups and communities not likely to vote for Nixon—"the antiwar left and Black people." Ehrlichman says,

> We knew we couldn't make it illegal to be either against the war or Black, but by getting the public to associate the hippies with marijuana and Blacks with heroin, and then criminalizing both heavily, we could disrupt those communities. We could arrest their leaders, raid their homes, break up their meetings, and vilify them night after night on the evening news. Did we know we were lying about the drugs? Of course, we did. (Sherman 2016)

While President Nixon started the war on drugs, it was President Ronald Reagan who fully funded the war, expanded the policy, and emphasized what Patricia Hill Collins (2005) calls **controlling images** of Black people to create support for the war. Controlling images are stereotypes and negative images that provide an ideological justification for race, class, and gender inequality. One example is the "crack babies," images of babies of women who used crack (cocaine).

Another example of a controlling image that targeted and harmed Black women was that of the "welfare queen." The Reagan presidential campaign created the idea of the welfare queen (e.g., a woman on welfare driving a Cadillac) to give the impression that Black women on welfare were living well off the government. According to Collins,

> With the election of the Reagan administration in 1980, the stigmatized welfare mother evolved into the more pernicious image of the welfare queen. To mask the effects of cuts in government spending on social welfare programs that fed children, housed working families, assisted cities in maintaining roads, bridges, and basic infrastructure, and supported other basic public services, media images increasingly identified and blamed Black women for the deterioration of US interests. Thus, poor Black women simultaneously become symbols of what was deemed wrong with America and targets of social policies designed to shrink the government sector. (1999/2008, 80)

The negative depiction of African Americans and the war on drugs devastated the Black community. From overpolicing to mass incarceration, African American communities were stigmatized and criminalized.

PHOTO 8.7 Activists hold a rally to demand an end to the war on drugs and mass incarceration.

Alex Wong/Getty Images

President Clinton also adopted a tough-on-crime stance, and it helped him win the presidency. Many in the African American community who lived in urban centers and suffered from the devastation of drugs and crime supported tougher laws and more police, thinking it might improve their neighborhoods. Clinton put into place mandatory sentencing laws, such as the three strikes policy for repeat offenders. Regardless of what the third strike (arrest) was for, if convicted, the person would get life in prison. These mandates impacted those who committed victimless crimes such as drug possession and drug use as well as those who carried out more serious crimes.

Mandatory sentencing remained until the presidency of Barack Obama. Obama also reduced the racial disparity in punishments for crack cocaine (used by more Black Americans) versus powder cocaine (used by more White people) through the 2010 Fair Sentencing Act. Before Obama's presidency, punishments for possession of crack cocaine were 100 times harsher than those for possession of power cocaine. During the presidency of Donald Trump, however, former attorney general Jeff Sessions reactivated mandatory sentencing and refused to support efforts to legalize marijuana (Reinhard 2017).

In *The New Jim Crow*, Michelle Alexander (2012) details how the war on drugs and tough-on-crime laws led to overpolicing, racial profiling, criminalization of minor offenses by African Americans, and the mass incarceration of women and men of color. She argues that these racially discriminatory policies are similar to the Jim Crow laws that used to pervade the South. As noted in earlier chapters, racial segregation also persists in neighborhoods and schools throughout the United States. Today, a new civil rights movement has spurred more widespread knowledge of these problems and demands to address them.

DOING SOCIOLOGY 8.7

The New Jim Crow

In this exercise, consider Michelle Alexander's assertion that the discriminatory policies described are similar in effect to Jim Crow laws.

Write your answers to the following questions:

1. What similarities do you see between the Jim Crow laws of the past and the criminal justice system of the present?

2. Do you think our society uses the criminal justice system as means to justify racial inequality? Why or why not?

Black Lives Matter

Alicia Garza, Patrisse Cullors, and Opal Tometi founded the Black Lives Matter movement (BLM) in 2014 after the police killing of unarmed teenager Michael Brown in Ferguson, Missouri. Since then Black Lives Matter has been a leader in protesting police brutality and shootings of Black men and women.

The Black Lives Matter movement inspired former NFL quarterback Colin Kaepernick's "Take a Knee" protest, which led many to look at patterns of police brutality against Black Americans. People of all races began taking a knee at sporting events to protest mistreatment of Black people by the police and other forms of racial injustice. BLM grew exponentially in response to the recorded police killing of George Floyd Jr., an unarmed Black man. Video shows a White police officer kneeling on Floyd's neck for over 8 minutes, eventually choking and killing him, despite Floyd telling the officer he could not breathe. People throughout the United States and the rest of the world viewed this recording with horror and participated in protests against racial injustice. Businesses and organized groups of all kinds proclaimed that Black lives matter and that

PHOTO 8.8 Protesters stretch for more than five blocks during demonstrations over the death of George Floyd near the White House in June 2020.

Samuel Corum/Getty Images

they support racial justice. The mayor of Washington, DC, even renamed the street leading to the White House as Black Lives Matter Plaza and had the words *Black Lives Matter* painted boldly in large letters on a street within sight of the White House. More people than ever in the United States and throughout the world are now discussing the racial issues we cover in this book.

Black Lives Matter and other racial justice organizations, social media, and cell phone videos bring the reality of racial injustice into people's living rooms. In the process, they make more and more people aware of dangers related to "living while Black"—the injustices Black people in the United States face because of their race. They also reveal the continued resistance and resilience of Black Americans. Many sociologists like Nina Johnson, the Sociologist in Action featured in this chapter, also work for racial justice.

SOCIOLOGISTS IN ACTION
Nina Johnson

Collaborating in Pursuit of Racial Justice

As a sociologist who works at the intersections of race, class, politics, cities, culture, and public policy, folks are not surprised to hear that I am interested in carceral (prison) policy and its impact on city residents. They are often surprised, however, to learn that I teach many of my advanced seminars inside prison walls and that I find them the most rewarding and intellectually rigorous learning environments.

I bring on-campus students together with incarcerated men and women for semester-long college courses. We create opportunities for people inside and outside of prison to have transformative learning experiences together that emphasize collaboration and dialogue and generate possibilities for creating wider, more systemic change through civic agency and human connection. These courses combine scholarly inquiry with facilitated dialogue and student collaboration in seminars with intensive reading and writing that culminate in inside and outside students working together in small groups to design research projects that have real-world applicability.

We create spaces within correctional institutions for incarcerated and nonincarcerated people to learn together as peers, preparing them through study, dialogue, and collaboration to become leaders in making communities more inclusive, just, and socially sustainable. In short, we facilitate the building of an intellectual community in spaces that otherwise impose and amplify the dislocation that is so prevalent in our shared world. The impact on student learning has been immensely gratifying.

This collaborative approach informs not only my and my colleagues' pedagogy but also our research practice. We don't do work *on* communities and neighborhoods; we are in community and do our work collaboratively and collectively. Radical inclusivity is our method for democratizing knowledge production. Our research team includes currently and formerly incarcerated scholars, community-based organizations, community members, and undergraduate students and graduate researchers from underrepresented groups who, along with their families and communities, have been most directly impacted by the policies and practices we examine and make known. In this way, we act out our values and make our research more rigorous and our recommendations more helpful.

Our current project examines the impact of mass incarceration policies at the neighborhood level. It highlights how macrostructural changes impact communities and individuals, and how those changes are described, experienced, and understood. This work promises to provide carceral policymakers with broader insight into the effects of their policies and how communities might help improve them. Most importantly, we think it has gotten us closer to achieving the change we want to see in the world.

Dr. Nina Johnson is an assistant professor of sociology and Black studies at Swarthmore College. Her research addresses the impact of the war on drugs and mass incarceration on neighborhoods in Philadelphia.

Discussion Question

If criminal justice policymakers sought suggestions from African American communities with high crime rates, what ideas might they hear? If these suggestions were implemented, in what ways might those neighborhoods change?

CONCLUSION

From the time of race-based slavery to today, Black Americans have faced racist laws, practices, violence, and ideology. However, Black people have continued to pursue equality, get their voices heard, and redefine themselves through protests and movements. The struggle for full equality will continue thanks to the resilience of Black Americans. In the following chapter, we look at the history of Asian Americans, including their own stories of resistance and resilience in the face of racial injustice.

CHAPTER REVIEW

8.1 What is race-based slavery, and how did it develop in the United States?

Slavery was a harsh and oppressive system through which Africans were brought forcibly to the United States. Whites redefined the enslaved Africans and their offspring as property and labeled them as members of a distinct "Black" race.

8.2 What forms of resilience did Black groups use to survive the institution of slavery?

Even though slavery was extremely oppressive for Black people, they found ways to survive and have a sense of agency. They created songs to send messages of encouragement or instructions to each other. The enslaved also used humor to lift spirits and make fun of the White people that oppressed them. Many held on to traditional African beliefs and practices and formed families secretly. Additionally, many ran away, and some took part in rebellions.

8.3 What were the benefits and backlashes from Reconstruction and the Great Migration?

When slavery ended in 1865 after the Civil War, African Americans received rights they never had before. Through the decade or so after the Civil War, known as Reconstruction, the formerly enslaved gained the right to vote, run for office, and own land. Federal soldiers patrolling the South gave them some protection during this period. When Reconstruction ended in 1877, southern Whites immediately created new rules that took away most of the rights of African Americans and enforced them through terror.

8.4 Why were Black organizations, such as churches and empowerment groups, important for African Americans?

African American religious and civic organizations provided a space for African American representation and freedom. Some groups were sources of encouragement and empowerment while others focused on antiracist activism. All sought to improve the lives of African Americans.

8.5 How do the results and reputation of the civil rights and Black Power movements compare to one another?

The civil rights movement helped bring down Jim Crow laws, including those that enforced racial segregation and deprived African Americans in the South the right to vote. Using a strategy of peaceful, nonviolent protests, it gained more widespread acceptance than the Black Power movement. Refusing to say they would remain nonviolent when confronted with violence, Black Power organizations promoted the ideology that Black people should gain power through whatever means necessary. One organization, the Black Panthers, combined efforts to provide direct service to their community (such as free breakfasts and other social services) and protect them with physical force when necessary. Both movements faced violence and government efforts to weaken them. The Black Power movement helped thousands of people and continues to inspire many but receives less credit and positive attention than the civil rights movement.

8.6 How have Black immigrants influenced U.S. society?

Since the Immigration Act of 1965, immigration from Africa and the Caribbean increased dramatically. These immigrants have contributed to the economy and culture of the United States. They carry out low-level and professional work needed in the United States.

8.7 What are some persistent problems that impact Black Americans today?

Today, Black Americans continue to deal with systemic racism in various social institutions. For example, laws and policies in the criminal justice system disproportionately target and punish Black communities. The war on drugs, mandatory sentencing, police use of violence, and racial segregation and other race-based patterns negatively affect Black communities.

KEY TERMS

Black Is Beautiful (p. 164)

Black Lives Matter movement (BLM) (p. 171)

Black migration (p. 160)

Black Power movement (p. 164)

Chattel (p. 155)

Civil Rights Act of 1964 (p. 164)

Controlling images (p. 170)

Convict leasing (p. 160)

Harlem Renaissance (p. 160)

Hayes-Tilden Compromise of 1877 (p. 159)

Jim Crow laws (p. 164)

Living while Black (p. 172)

National Association for the Advancement of Colored People (NAACP) (p. 162)

Partus sequitur ventrem (p. 154)

Reconstruction (p. 159)

Voting Rights Act of 1965 (p. 164)

Wages of Whiteness (p. 154)

9 FOREVER FOREIGNERS? ASIAN AMERICAN ETHNIC GROUPS

SunAh M. Laybourn

LEARNING QUESTIONS

9.1 What is the connection among early Asian immigration, anti-Asian immigration policies, and Asian activism?

9.2 What were key events that shaped an "Asian American" consciousness?

9.3 What are the similarities and differences between the "Yellow Peril" and "model minority" stereotypes?

9.4 How does Asian American–created media challenge stereotypical portrayals of Asians in America?

I was the only Indian on a ship that was carrying hundreds of Chinese passengers in the third class.... On the August 25, 1949 morning, as the American coastline appeared on the horizon, I and hundreds of others went up on the deck to survey the first glimpse of America. I had read many books dealing with America and its people. I had talked to many Americans who had tried to give me some ideas about things to come. I had listened to "The Voice of America" and had formed a mental picture of America. Yet seeing a country with your own eyes is an entirely new experience. So as our ship approached the Golden Gate Bridge, my pulse rate was quickening as I surveyed the first magnificent work of American labor. I had seen many bridges... but the sight of the Golden Gate Bridge, set against the blue sky over the expansive Pacific Ocean was a stunning experience. The bridge looked like a real gateway to an heaven on earth. (First Days Project n.d.)

We open this chapter with the words of Roshan Sharma, who immigrated from Bhumbli, India, to the United States, arriving in San Francisco when he was 22 years old. He would begin the fall semester at UCLA but not before finding a Sikh temple in Stockton, California, that welcomed him, offering a place to stay, food, and connections in his new country.

Roshan's story is one of many of those who came to the United States for school or work. Other Asians immigrated to the United States for different reasons—some because of war or natural disasters, others as military brides, some as colonial subjects, and still others as adoptees. Currently there are over 20 million Asian Americans with origins tracing to more than 20 countries in East Asia, Southeast Asia, and the Indian subcontinent. Asian Americans comprise about 6% of the total U.S. population and are one of the fastest-growing racial groups in the United States. Despite their long history and contributions to the United States, however, many Americans still see Asian Americans as foreigners. In this chapter, we examine the history of Asian immigration and how Asian American activism and U.S. immigration policies have shaped Asian America.

HOW I GOT ACTIVE IN SOCIOLOGY
SunAh M. Laybourn

Growing up as one of the few Asian American students in my K–12 classes, I knew that race mattered, even though I often did not know how or why it affected my life and the lives of my classmates in the way that it did. I watched as the racial composition of my neighborhood changed from predominantly White to predominantly Black. I answered questions regarding my racial, ethnic, and national identity more times than I could count. I experienced vastly different educational resources and expectations at my predominantly White (and academically selective) middle school versus my predominately Black local high school. But I didn't have a way to make sense of it all, at least not until I took my first sociology class in undergrad. From those initial courses, it seemed like sociology had the answers to many of my questions about race, ethnicity, and inequality. Of course, sociology does not have all the answers, but it provided me with the tools to critically examine the world we live in and to address inequality.

ASIANS IN AMERICA: EARLY IMMIGRATION, ANTI-ASIAN POLICIES, AND RESISTANCE

Most of the first Asian immigrants to the United States were male laborers enticed by promises of fortune. Although many U.S. businesses actively recruited Asian men, they were often met with hostility and suspicion, which eventually fueled anti-Asian immigration policies. However, at every turn, Asians in America fought for their social and legal citizenship.

Initial Immigration Waves

In 1834, 19-year-old Afong Moy became the first Chinese woman recorded as arriving in the United States. Afong traveled to New York Harbor by way of Nathaniel and Frederick Carne's *Washington*, a trading vessel bringing an array of Chinese goods. Afong was brought to attract buyers to the Carnes' goods and sat on display for 8 hours a day. Paying viewers watched her eat with chopsticks and speak in Chinese. Like other Chinese wares brought from "the Orient," Afong was an "exotic" commodity.

During the 1830s and 1840s most Asian immigrants were crewmembers from transatlantic ships. Chinese, Japanese, and Filipino men served aboard U.S. shipping vessels, and some eventually made their home in cities on the eastern U.S. coast. There were also small numbers of Asians in the South. In the 1840s, about 100 Filipino men resided in a fishing village in St. Malo, Louisiana, and in the 1850s, a number of Filipino men made New Orleans, Louisiana, home.

The largest waves of Asian migration began with news of the California Gold Rush (1848), which lured gold seekers from around the world, including China. Beginning in 1849 Chinese men immigrated to California. While a few hundred came initially, in 1851 over 2,700 arrived and in 1852 over 20,000. "By 1870, there were 63,000 Chinese in the United States, most of them (77 percent) in California" (Lee 2015, 59). Though few struck gold, most continued to stay in the United States finding jobs on the railroads or starting small businesses catering to other Chinese immigrants.

Though we may not think about the importance of railroads much today, in the 1800s and early 1900s railroads were a crucial component of the U.S. economic system and a primary mode of transportation for individuals and families traveling cross-country. Chinese labor was critical to the creation of the railroad system.

After the legal end of slavery, employers looked to China for cheap and exploitable labor. In 1865, the Central Pacific Railroad Co. began recruiting Chinese workers to work on the California Central Railroad, bringing male laborers directly from China. By late winter 1865, approximately 4,000 Chinese men were working around the clock, clearing tunnels through the Sierra Nevada Mountains. This was dangerous work.

As Chinese workers began to comprise the majority of the railroad workforce, White railroad workers became angry. White workers attacked Chinese laborers and set fire to their living quarters.

In June 1867, two thousand Chinese railroad workers went on strike for a week, demanding an end to beatings by railroad employers, increased wages, and work hours equal with Whites. The Central Pacific Railroad broke the strike by withholding food supplies to the Chinese who were isolated in the high mountains of the Sierras.

During this time, Asians were seen as threats to White labor and, because scientific racism prevailed, as culturally and biologically inferior. Many Whites thought they would cause the degeneration of the "superior" White race through miscegenation (interracial marriage). These fears of a "Yellow Peril," a stereotype introduced in the 1870s to describe the threats of Asian immigration, led the government to bar Asians from legal citizenship and any legal protections. Passage of the Chinese Exclusion Act (1882) created a moratorium on Chinese labor immigration, effectively banning all Chinese immigration as it was difficult for nonlaborers to prove they were not laborers. The Chinese Exclusion Act was unique in that it engaged in class- and race-based discrimination—something new to U.S. immigration legislation.

THE ONLY ONE BARRED OUT.
ENLIGHTENED AMERICAN STATESMAN.—" We must draw the line *somewhere*, you know."

PHOTO 9.1 A political cartoon illustrates anti-Asian attitudes and exclusionary policies aimed at Chinese immigrants.

Interim Archives/Getty Images

Throughout the late 19th century Chinese laborers in America often faced boycotts, intimidation, and violence. The Chinese Exclusion Act of 1882 sought to prevent them from competing in the U.S. labor force altogether. The Chinese immigrant community fought for their rights, developing organizations such as the Zhonghua Huiguan, which provided financial support and legal defense for Chinese laborers.

Similar to Chinese immigrants, Japanese migrated to the United States after hearing tales of great fortunes there. U.S. businesses saw them as another exploitable source of labor that could take the place of the banned Chinese. Shortly after the Chinese Exclusion Act of 1882, Japanese men, and small numbers of women and children, immigrated to the continental United States and Hawai'i, then an independent nation (but controlled by U.S. businesses).

From 1891 to 1900, 27,440 Japanese, mostly male laborers, were admitted into the United States. Over the next seven years, 53,457 more were admitted.... Japanese filled the jobs that Chinese immigrants once had. Labor contractors sent them to railroads, mines, lumber mills, fish canneries, farms, and orchards throughout the Pacific Coast states. In the cities, Japanese worked as domestic servants. (Lee 2015, 116)

Japanese were a cheap labor source and economically beneficial to West Coast businesses, but most White Americans viewed them as they did the Chinese—threats to White labor. This fear existed even though Asian immigrants could not become citizens and Alien Land Laws prohibited them from owning land.

As Japanese immigrants began to establish themselves in the United States, creating ethnic enclaves in larger cities, like Los Angeles, San Francisco, and Seattle, with thriving businesses and assimilating to Western customs, they faced Whites' increasing resentment and racial discrimination. Japan's victory over Russia in the Russo-Japanese War (1904–1905) heightened fears of Japanese immigrants. The *San Francisco Chronicle*'s 1905 headline, "Yellow Peril – How Japanese Crowd Out the White Race" captured White Americans' anxieties (Daniels 1993) and helped spur violent attacks on Japanese and the U.S. government to create policies limiting Japanese immigration. The Gentlemen's Agreement (1907) sharply reduced the number of Japanese immigrants. It did not bar them completely, however, as the Chinese Exclusion Act did to the less militarily powerful Chinese. It prohibited more Japanese laborers from immigrating to the United States, but those already here could move between the nations freely and have family members join them in America.

Due to the gender imbalance among Japanese in the United States and the restrictions on Japanese immigration, with the exception of family members, the next wave of Japanese immigration came in the form of Japanese "picture brides." **Picture brides** were women promised in marriage via matchmakers through a process that included the exchange of pictures between the potential bride and groom. In the early 20th century, about 20,000 picture brides traveled from Japan to the United States and Hawai'i.

PHOTO 9.2 Four Japanese picture brides on their way to arranged marriages in the United States in 1931.

Bettmann/Contributor

Immigration from East Asia continued as Koreans sought not only riches but to escape Japanese control at home. Japan officially annexed Korea in 1910 after gaining control of it over a decade earlier. The Japanese colonization of Korea continued until 1945. Japanese policies made living conditions harsh for Koreans and included stripping families of their land and homes and promoting religious intolerance and cultural genocide. As a result, many Koreans fled their home country, with some making their way to the United States

Beginning in 1902, Korean men began to immigrate to Hawai'i, finding work on sugar plantations. Koreans were a welcome source of new labor as the 1882 Chinese Exclusion Act had cut off immigration from China, and Japanese workers were organizing and demanding increased wages. Most Koreans escaping political persecution were young men who were students. They tended to arrive in the United States through Angel Island in San Francisco. About a thousand Korean women also immigrated to Hawai'i and the continental United States as picture brides.

Although small numbers of Filipinos migrated to the United States earlier, it was not until after the Philippines became a U.S. colony in 1898, after the Spanish–American War, that Filipinos immigrated in higher numbers. Under the Pensionado Act of 1903, elite Filipino students, or "pensionados," were encouraged to attend American universities. The expectation, however, was that they would return home after their studies to become leaders in the Philippines. Hawai'i sugar plantation recruiters drew larger waves of immigration. Beginning in 1906 and continuing through 1929, approximately 60,000 Filipino workers arrived in Hawai'i.

The Johnson-Reed Act (1924) barred "aliens ineligible for citizenship"—basically all Asians except Filipinos. Aa you might expect, farm owners on the West Coast of the United States began to recruit new workers from the Philippines. By 1930, there were 56,000 Filipinos in the United States. Around 60% of the Filipinos in California worked as migrant farmworkers, as did the Chinese, Japanese, and Korean immigrants before them, rotating up and down cities in California, such as Delano, Stockton, and Salinas, following the various harvest seasons. The work was grueling, the conditions hazardous with dust from the fields filling laborers' lungs, and exploitation was rampant. As a result, Filipinos began to organize. In 1928 they created the first formal Filipino American labor organization, Anak ng Bukid, or Children of the Farm. More unions followed as did strikes for higher wages and better working conditions.

Although Chinese, Japanese, Korean, and Filipino migrations to the United States were the most significant Asian immigration waves, South Asians came also, though in much smaller numbers, in the early decades of the 1900s. Although fewer than 10,000 South Asians migrated to the United States in the early 20th century, those numbers were still enough to fuel threats of a "Hindu invasion." The Immigration Act of 1917 halted South Asian immigration along with other Asian immigration (aside that from the Philippines, which was then a U.S. colony). The 1924 Immigration Act reaffirmed the inadmissibility of all Asians except for Filipinos.

Although their numbers were low, South Asians created community organizations such as the Pacific Coast Khalsa Diwan Society in Stockton, California; Sikh temples along the Pacific Coast; the Moslem Association of America in 1919 in Sacramento; the Hindustani Welfare and Reform Society of America in 1919 in El Centro; and the Hindu American Conference in 1920 in Sacramento. These organizations provided community support, housing, and employment along with a space to practice their faith. It was one of these Sikh temples where Roshan, from this chapter's opening excerpt, found a welcoming community.

U.S. Territories

Asians in America came by way of migration but also through U.S. colonization and cession. The U.S. annexed Hawai'i in 1898 and made it a territory in 1900 (it became a state in 1959). When Hawai'i became a U.S. territory its population was 154,001, including 37,656 Native Hawaiians, 25,767 Chinese, and 61,111 Japanese (Schmitt 1968).

In April 1898, the United States declared war against Spain, supporting Cubans' and Filipinos' struggle against Spanish colonization. At the time, Spain controlled Cuba, the Philippines, Guam, and Puerto Rico, as well as some smaller islands. When the United States won the war, Spain relinquished sovereignty of its overseas empire. As a result, the Philippines, Guam, and Puerto Rico became U.S. territories (the United States gave Cuba its independence), making their residents U.S. nationals, though not citizens. Woodrow Wilson granted residents of Puerto Rico U.S. citizenship in 1917.

Due to its location in the Pacific, the Samoa Islands were a desirable and strategic military and trading outpost. In 1857, German trading company J.C. Godeffroy and Son established an outpost on the Samoan island of Upolu, making it one of the most popular trading posts in the Pacific. In 1872, the United States established a naval base in the harbor of the Samoan island of Tutuila and promised to protect the Samoan people from civil war and foreign threats. However, civil wars convulsed the Samoan Islands from the late 1870s through the late 1890s, and Germany and the United States fought over who should control the islands. In 1899, Germany and the United States divided the islands into what is now Samoa and American Samoa.

On February 19, 1900, President Roosevelt signed an executive order that placed American Samoa, the islands of Tutuila and Manu'a, under a U.S. military–controlled government. The Samoans (approximately 5,600 people at the time) became U.S. nationals. Currently, American Samoa is the only territory whose inhabitants are U.S. nationals and not citizens. As U.S. nationals, Samoans have the right to reside and work in the United States without restriction, apply for a U.S. passport, and apply for U.S. citizenship via naturalization under the same regulations as permanent residents. However, U.S. nationals cannot vote in any election or hold an elected office, making some American Samoans feel like second-class citizens (Simmons 2018).

Executive Order 9066

Immigration policies reflected the United States' changing alliances abroad as well as attitudes toward Asians at home. Executive Order 9066 (1942), a legislative response to the Japanese attack on Pearl Harbor, authorized the internment of American citizens of Japanese descent and resident aliens of Japan. The misguided assumption was that Japanese Americans were enemies of the United States. President Roosevelt signed this order; he also froze Japanese Americans' assets, such as homes, businesses, and property. The Japanese internment order entailed the forced removal, relocation, and incarceration of Japanese Americans and Japanese nationals on the West Coast of the United States. Over 117,000 men, women, and children were sent to makeshift facilities, such as converted livestock pavilions and former military camps, across the interior United States. Families remained incarcerated from 1942 to 1945.

PHOTO 9.3 Newspapers across the United States announced the removal of Japanese Americans and Japanese nationals following the attack on Pearl Harbor.

Buyenlarge/Getty Images

Early in 1943 the U.S. government, through the War Relocation Authority, released a questionnaire for interned men 17 years old and over. It was titled "Statement of U.S. Citizenship of Japanese American Ancestry." Question #27 asked, "Are you willing to serve in the armed forces of the United States on combat duty, wherever ordered?" Question #28 asked, "Will you swear unqualified allegiance to the United States of America and faithfully defend the United States from any or all attacks by foreign or domestic forces, and forswear any form of allegiance or obedience to the Japanese emperor, or other foreign government, power or organization?" (Nittle 2020).

In response to draft notices, Frank Emi and six other interned men created the Fair Play Committee. In March 1944, they signed a declaration challenging the internment policy and their conscription as shameful affronts to the Constitution and American ideals. They wrote,

> We, the members of the FPC, are not afraid to go to war.... We are not afraid to risk our lives for our country. We would gladly sacrifice our lives to protect and uphold the principles and ideals of our country as set forth in the Constitution and the Bill of Rights, for on its inviolability depends the freedom, liberty, justice, and protection of all people, including Japanese-Americans and all other minority groups. But have we been given such freedom, such liberty, such justice, such protection? NO!!" (Downes 2010)

More than 300 men across 10 camps joined the Fair Play Committee's resistance. They were mocked by other Japanese Americans as "no-no boys," and the Japanese Americans Citizens League denounced them as seditious. All were prosecuted and sentenced to prison (Downes 2010).

The End of Exclusionary Asian Immigration Policies

Individual acts such as the following began dismantling anti-Asian legislation:

- The Magnuson Act (1943) repealed the Chinese Exclusion Acts, made Chinese eligible for U.S. citizenship, and gave China an annual immigration quota of 105. Note that this was after China and the United States became allies during World War II.

- The Luce-Celler Act (1946) ended exclusion and extended immigration and naturalization rights to South Asians and Filipinos in anticipation of their imminent independence from colonial rule: India from Great Britain and the Philippines from the United States (in 1947 and 1946, respectively).

- The McCarran-Walter Immigration Act of 1952 changed exclusionary Asian immigration policies by allowing immigration from China and Japan, albeit in small numbers. Importantly, the McCarran-Walter Act included naturalization rights for Asians, making Asians eligible for citizenship for the first time. More than 40,000 first-generation Japanese Americans became U.S. citizens from 1952 to 1965—many had waited decades to do so.

While the McCarran-Walter Act also introduced preferences for the immigration of highly skilled laborers and family reunification, the Hart-Celler Immigration and Nationality Act (1965) solidified changes in immigration policy. Notably, it abolished the national origins quota system that had governed U.S. immigration policy since the 1920s. It prioritized family reunification, encouraged employment-based or skills-based immigration, and welcomed refugees. This legislation drastically changed immigration to the United States with ramifications for the perception of Asians (as we discuss later in this chapter).

CONSIDER THIS

How did perceptions of Asians in America and immigration policy go hand in hand? What are some contemporary examples of attitudes toward specific ethnic groups affecting immigration policies?

Did You Know? Asian American History and Resistance

In this exercise you will examine your prior knowledge of Asian American history and resistance.

Write answers to the following questions and be prepared to share them with your classmates.

1. Prior to this class, what did you know about Asian American history?

2. Did you know much about Asian American resistance to the racism they face(d)? If yes, what are some examples of Asian American resistance that you knew? If not, why do you think that was the case?

Check Your Understanding

1. What spurred early Asian immigration to the United States?

2. Why were Asian immigrants seen as a threat and to whom?

3. What are some examples of Asian American resistance?

4. What made the Chinese Exclusion Act unique from other earlier immigration policies?

5. What was Executive Order 9066?

6. Why did some interned Japanese men create the Fair Play Committee?

7. How did the Hart-Celler Immigration and Nationality Act of 1965 change immigration to the United States?

THE BEGINNINGS OF CONTEMPORARY ASIAN AMERICA: BECOMING "ASIAN AMERICAN"

The term *Asian American* may now be part of the everyday lexicon in the United States, but that was not always the case. Up until the 1960s, Asian Americans primarily identified themselves by their particular ethnic group (e.g., Chinese, Korean, Japanese). This makes sense, given the following:

- Many Asian nations held great animus toward one or more other Asian countries.

- U.S. businesses pitted different ethnic Asian laborers against one another.

- Exclusionary U.S. immigration policies distinguished among Asian sending countries.

However, as waves of activism across many marginalized groups transformed U.S. society in the 1960s, a pan-ethnic Asian student movement was also taking shape. This student movement joined other forms of activism, helping shape an "Asian American" consciousness.

Coining the Pan-Ethnic Asian American Race

During the summer of 1968, Japanese American Yuji Ichioka and Chinese American Emma Gee, both student activists at UC Berkeley, created the first interethnic pan-Asian American political group, the Asian American Political Alliance (AAPA), thereby introducing the term Asian American. The name not only signified a pan-ethnic Asian unification of traditionally separate groups of Asian students but also challenged the derogatory term *Oriental*. Like the Orient, which was a historic Eurocentric term used to describe the "Far East" and implied that people, commodities, and cultures from Asia were exotic and subordinate to "the West," Oriental was a pejorative label applied to people from Asia emphasizing their inferiority to and difference from people in Western nations. The term *Asian*

American was a signal of "yellow power," a power for self-determination and a call against racism, imperialism, and inequality.

In fall 1968, AAPA supported the San Francisco student strike (more details in the following section). Shortly thereafter, Ichioka became a founding member of UCLA's Asian American Studies Center and taught the first Asian American studies class at UCLA. In the years that followed, student groups on other college campuses adopted the term *Asian American* to define their own pan-ethnic Asian groups. In 1980, the U.S. census began to use the term, though it was not until 2016 that the U.S. government banned the word *Oriental* and required the use of *Asian American*.

San Francisco State College Strike

"On strike! Shut it down!" was the daily rallying cry across San Francisco State College. From November 1968 through March 1969, a coalition of students of color, including the Black Student Union and the Third World Liberation Front, marched on the college administration building to demand changes to admissions practices that limited the admissions of non-White students and curriculum that mini-mized the histories and experiences of racial and ethnic minorities. Even set against the backdrop of the wave of student-led anti–Vietnam War protests on college campuses across the United States, the San Francisco State College strike quickly gained national attention. This strike was noteworthy for a num-ber of reasons, including the guerilla tactics students used to disrupt the campus and gain the attention of the administration (e.g., stink bombs, clogging toilets, interrupting classes). The extreme response of the college, which included bringing police tactical units to campus daily, resulted in over 400 arrests during the strike, with the pan-ethnic coalition of students leading the protests (Whitson 1969).

PHOTO 9.4 Student demonstrators march in front of the San Francisco State College (later San Francisco State University) administration building in 1968 to protest the school's lack of minority studies programs, as other students and media, some on the roofs, watch.

Garth Eliassen/Getty Images

The Black Student Union (BSU) at San Francisco State was closely linked to the Black Panther Party, which shaped the community activities and political goals of the BSU. The Third World Liberation Front (TWLF) was an alliance of the Latin American Student Organization (LASO), the Mexican American Student Confederation, the Philipino American College Endeavor (PACE), and the Intercollegiate Chinese for Social Action (ICSA). These students, like most of the San Francisco State students, were primarily commuters from working-class backgrounds and active in their home communities.

The San Francisco State College strike remains the longest student strike in history and changed the landscape of higher education across the country. The strike resulted in the creation of San Francisco State College's School of Ethnic Studies, including American Indian studies, Asian American studies, Black studies, and La Raza studies (focusing on Chicanos and Latin Americans). Thanks to the strike, ethnic studies programs began to appear not only in the Bay Area but across the United States.

CONSIDER THIS

Would you be willing to participate in a similar strike on your campus? Why? If yes, for what? If no, why not?

DOING SOCIOLOGY 9.2

Pros and Cons of the Term Asian

In this exercise you will think about the pros and cons of the term Asian *for Asian Americans.*

Write answers to the following questions. Then, share your answers with a group of your classmates and work together to make a list of the pros and cons. Prepare yourselves for a class debate on whether the pros outweigh the cons.

1. Are you surprised that the term *Asian American* has activist roots? Why or why not?

2. Which Asian cultures do most people in the United States think of when they hear the word *Asian*? Are there some Asian cultures that are often overlooked?

3. Why do you think some Asian Americans have a complicated relationship with the word *Asian*? What are the pros and cons of the term?

Gidra, "Voice of the Asian American Movement"

In 1969, just around the time of the San Francisco student strikes and the creation of AAPA, five Japanese American UCLA students—Mike Murase, Dinora Gil, Laura Ho, Tracy Okida, and Colin Watanabe—created *Gidra*, a newspaper-magazine. At the time, the University of California, Los Angeles (UCLA), did not have an ethnic studies department. It did, however, give students approval to create informal study centers and provided funding for student publications. The students approached the UCLA administration about starting an Asian American community newspaper. However, when they were told that receiving funding from the school required agreeing to give the university final editorial rights, the five students decided to fund the paper themselves and each contributed $100 toward the publication.

Initially, the students located the *Gidra* office in the Asian American Studies Center at UCLA and focused on the fight for ethnic studies programs on college campuses and other local, on-the-ground activism. When they moved *Gidra* off campus to an office in the Crenshaw District of L.A., they broadened its coverage to include international Asian movements as well as the Black Power and Chicano movements. In addition to news coverage, the students also included poetry, art, and political cartoons in the paper.

A volunteer-led paper, *Gidra* was truly a community-based, grassroots, activist-oriented publication. Groundbreaking in its structure and coverage of issues that most mainstream news media ignored, it created a collective identity and sense of community by and for Asian Americans. *Gidra* had neither an editorial board nor a hierarchical structure. As the "voice of the Asian American movement," *Gidra* publicized stories about Asian American activism and reclaimed narratives about Asians in America, particularly Japanese Americans, through refuting the "model minority myth" and putting attention on the long-term detrimental effects of the Japanese internment.

Gidra had a monthly circulation of about 3,000 and more than 200 Asian American contributors, including students, community organizers, and Vietnam veterans, during its 5-year run from 1969 to 1974. Its reach extended far beyond UCLA and the Bay Area. Asian American activists from New York City and other cities across the United States incorporated *Gidra* into their local activism and teaching. For example, reflecting on the role of *Gidra* at that time, artist and activist Fay Chiang shared, "I had started an Asian American studies course at Hunter College (in New York City) and our friends were pushing for a department at City College, but we had no curriculum.... So I was just collecting all the mimeograph sheets and ditto sheets [of the *Gidra* that] I could get my hands on" (Lee 2018). Although the last published issue came out over 45 years ago, *Gidra*'s reach continues to grow as new readers access its online digitized archives.

International Hotel Protests

The 9-year anti-eviction protest (1968–1977) surrounding the International Hotel (I-Hotel) in Manilatown in San Francisco also played a major role in the emergence of an Asian American consciousness. A 10-block Filipino ethnic enclave located on the edge of Chinatown, I-Hotel provided low-income housing to approximately 150 residents, the majority of whom were elderly Filipino and Chinese men. Because previous immigration policies limited immigration of Asian women and anti-miscegenation laws prevented Asian men from marrying cross-racially, this was a primarily male population.

Urban renewal and an encroaching Financial District threatened the I-Hotel. On November 27, 1968, both the residents and the businesses located on the first floor received eviction notices. The businesses included Everybody's Bookstore, the first Asian American bookstore in the nation, as well as the Asian Community Center, Chinese Progressive Association, and Kearny Street Workshop. The I-Hotel was more than just a home and a refuge to the 150 or so residents. It was a community hub contributing to the social, political, and cultural life of Manilatown and the bordering Chinatown area of San Francisco.

Soon after word of the eviction notices spread, the Third World Liberation Front students from San Francisco State and UC Berkeley, along with other college students and members of activist groups across the Bay Area, participated in I-Hotel protests. *Gidra* covered the events. As Ling-chi Wang, an activist and professor emeritus of Asian American studies at UC Berkeley, notes, "I-Hotel became a symbol of... [the] struggle not only for dignity, [but] for identity, for a community to defend itself and protect its own destiny" (Franko 2007).

On August 4, 1977, police removed the remaining 50 or so tenants. In a demonstration of cross-generational, interracial, and interethnic solidarity, 3,000 nonviolent protesters met the 300 riot police sent to remove the lingering residents. However, the protests did not end there. Tenants and community members continued to lobby for low-income housing and the preservation of the Filipino community for the next two decades. In 2005, a new I-Hotel opened, providing 100 units of low-income housing for seniors, including some original I-Hotel residents, and a museum commemorating the community activism.

Who Was Vincent Chin?

In 1982, the murder of Vincent Chin mobilized Asian American social justice organizations, and Asian pan-ethnic solidarity soared across the United States. It also thrust the term *Asian American* out of the primarily academic and activist circles and into the mainstream. People of all Asian ethnicities realized they all faced racial discrimination aimed at any Asian ethnic group.

On June 19, 1982, 27-year-old Vincent Chin, a Chinese American man, was celebrating at his bachelor party in a local Detroit strip club when he got into an altercation with two White male patrons, Ronald Ebens and his stepson, Michael Nitz (a recently laid off Chrysler automobile worker). At this time, many people blamed the decline of the Detroit auto industry on the rise of Japanese auto imports, including Ebens and Nitz who were both autoworkers. Assuming he was Japanese, Ebens and Nitz saw Chin as a symbol of their economic fears. They exchanged words with Chin and the three started to fight. The club threw all the patrons out of the club. However, Ebens and Nitz were not done. They searched the area for Chin, finding him at a nearby McDonald's. While Nitz held him down, Ebens bludgeoned him with a baseball bat, cracking his skull. Chin died 4 days later from the severe head injuries (Asia Society 2017).

In a Michigan county court, the two plead guilty to manslaughter but appealed their sentences. The appeals judge, Charles Kaufmann, sentenced them to just 3 years' probation, a $3,000 fine, and $780 in court fees. Judge Kaufmann explained the light sentence by saying, "These aren't the kind of men you send to jail. You fit the punishment to the criminal, not the crime" (Wang 2010).

The circumstances around Chin's murder made public the type of racism Asian Americans experienced. Asian American activists pushed for the case to be tried by the U.S. Department of Justice as a hate crime, citing racial discrimination as the cause for Chin's murder. It was the first application of hate crime charges against people who committed a crime against an Asian American. Although the courts cleared Ebens and Nitz from the hate crime charge, the case became a rallying cry for stronger hate crime legislation.

Check Your Understanding

1. Who created the term *Asian American* and why?

2. How and why did Asian American students engage in activism?

3. What was an outcome of the San Francisco State College strike?

4. What made the San Francisco State College strike noteworthy?

5. What distinguished *Gidra* from other forms of news coverage at the time?

6. What were the policy implications of the Vincent Chin case?

(MIS)REPRESENTATION

As discussed in Chapter 4, Asian Americans are overrepresented in stories about achieving the American Dream and underrepresented in stories about poverty, educational disparities, health disparities, and other social disparities. However, as the data presented in Chapter 4 show, educational attainment and income vary widely by Asian ethnic group, something the broad umbrella term of *Asian American Pacific Islander* (AAPI) obscures. The census began using the label *Asian and Pacific Islander* in the 1980s, grouping these distinct groups together. However, in the 2000 census, "Asian" and "Native Hawaiian and other Pacific Islander" were listed as two separate racial categories. This change was a response to Native Hawaiians' objections to being grouped under the umbrella category of "Asian and Pacific Islander," as it provided "inadequate data for monitoring the social and economic conditions of Native Hawaiians and other Pacific Islander groups" (Office of Management and Budget 1997, 8). One of the key goals of the census is to provide accurate and comprehensive data on race and ethnicity for statistical purposes and program administration. The separation of "Asian" and "Native Hawaiian and other Pacific Islander" was an important step toward acknowledging the varied histories, socioeconomic conditions, and Indigenous populations of Hawaii and the Pacific islands, such as Guam and Samoa. However, stereotypes that portray Asian Americans and Pacific Islanders as one monolithic group persist.

Media Portrayals

Just as socioeconomic data obscure the realities of many Asian ethnic groups within the United States, so do media representations, both past and present. Some of the United States' earliest depictions of Asians in America (mis)characterized Chinese men as a "Yellow Peril." This stereotype was first deployed in the 1870s, as White men had an economic fear of losing jobs to "filthy yellow hordes." As discussed earlier in this chapter, the Chinese Exclusion Act followed, limiting the immigration of Chinese male laborers. The idea of a "Yellow Peril" or "Asian menace" resurfaced after Japan won the Russo-Japanese War (1904–1905) (Tchen and Yeats 2014).

In the 1930s and 40s, American audiences were introduced to the movie character Fu Manchu. Derived from a series of novels by British writer Sax Rohmer in the early 20th century, Fu Manchu was "the yellow peril incarnate in one man" (Frayling 2014, 9). An evil genius and inexplicably foreign threat, Fu Manchu projected Western fears onto the silver screen. Performed by a rotating cast of European men and written by a man who had never been to China, Fu Manchu movies—five in all—played on Western fears of a Chinese takeover of American society and intermarriage.

PHOTO 9.5 Poster for *The Return of Fu Manchu* (1940), the fourth of five Fu Manchu movies that played on White America's fears of a "Yellow Peril" that threatened Americans' way of life.

After the Japanese attack on Pearl Harbor in 1941, White Americans immediately viewed Japanese people (and by extension Japanese Americans) as a foreign threat. Similar to how Chinese people were viewed in the 1800s, the media portrayed Japanese people as dangerous and subhuman. However, because China was allied with the United States during WWII, so to, by extension, were Chinese Americans. Popular U.S. magazines like *Time* ("How to Tell" 1941) and *Life* ("How to Tell" 1941) published stories instructing White Americans on "how to tell friend [Chinese] from foe [Japanese]."

After WWII, to diminish White America's fears of Japanese people (Japan was now an ally, not an enemy), the media began to portray Japanese Americans in a positive light. During this time, in the 1950s and 60s, the model minority myth took shape. Newspapers ran stories on Japanese and Chinese Americans' exemplary American values such as family, education, and hard work. Even though internment was only a decade earlier, journalists pointed out how Japanese Americans were able to restart their lives quickly and integrate into (White) America. This was credited to their inherent "cultural values." The implied message was that other racialized minority groups should be able to do what these non-White Americans had done. If they could not, it was due to cultural inferiority or moral failure. These media depictions served not only to craft an image of Asian Americans but of other racialized minority groups as well.

Even after the creation of the model minority myth and its use as a wedge against other racialized groups, however, Asian American acceptance was conditional. While their cultural values made them acceptable enough, their immutable foreignness made Whites reluctant to fully incorporate them into the fabric of U.S. society. Similar to the Yellow Peril stereotype, the model minority myth also emphasized Asian Americans' inherent difference from White Americans. For example, it was not until the mid-1990s that the first television show featuring an Asian American family aired (ABC's *All American Girl*, which ran for 19 episodes from 1994 to 1995). The same decade saw the release of the first Hollywood movie to feature a majority Asian American cast (*The Joy Luck Club* in 1993). A few years later, a MSNBC headline from the 1998 Winter Olympics figure skating competition reminded readers of the assumption that Asian Americans are immigrants. The headline summarized the competition's results as "American beats out Kwan" (Sorensen 1998). Though both were American competitors, the "American" in the headline referred to Tara Lipinski and thereby inferred that Michelle Kwan was not an American.

Stereotypes about Asians' immutable foreignness and distinct cultural values around family and education continue to endure. In 2011, Amy Chua's novel, *Battle Hymn of the Tiger Mother*, garnered the spotlight for its portrayal of Chinese motherhood; tiger moms are overbearing, strict, authoritarian parents with an extreme focus on achievement, have exceedingly high standards, and show no reluctance to use razor-sharp criticism on their children. This portrayal of Chinese mothers exacerbated stereotypes about Asian Americans as emotionless people with little personality and intense educational ambition for their children.

CONSIDER THIS

How can the model minority myth affect Asian American students?

DOING SOCIOLOGY 9.3

Asian Americans in the Media

In this exercise, you will examine contemporary portrayals of Asian Americans in the media.

Reflect on and write answers to the following questions:

1. Define the Yellow Peril and model minority stereotypes.

2. What was the last television show or movie you watched with Asian Americans represented? If so, what was their role? Were they a main character, minor character, or background actor? Are

they portrayed as part of a Yellow Peril, model minority, or some other stereotype about Asian Americans? If the only ideas you had about Asian Americans were based on the portrayal, what would you believe about Asians in America (e.g., personality, values, occupation, education)?

3. How do media portrayals of Asian Americans compare to those of other racial and ethnic groups? Are they similar or different in frequency of portrayals, significance (e.g., main character, minor character, background), and type (e.g., negative, positive, neutral)? Why are they similar or different?

4. Are media representations of Asian Americans stereotypical? Provide an example. Are there mainstream media representations that are not stereotypical? Provide an example.

"Bamboo Ceiling" and Education

The stereotype of Asian Americans as hardworking yet lacking personality is reflected in the idea of the "bamboo ceiling." Coined by Jane Hyun in her 2005 book *Breaking the Bamboo Ceiling*, **bamboo ceiling** refers to the specific obstacles Asian Americans face in attaining senior leadership positions. As mentioned in Chapter 4, these obstacles are often tied to Asian American stereotypes about personality traits and lack of "soft skills," particularly communication styles. Although overrepresented in people with BA degrees, Asian Americans are underrepresented in management positions. In fact, Asian Americans account for just 3.7% of total board seats for *Fortune* 500 companies (Alliance for Board Diversity 2018).

The focus on Asian American educational attainment shows up in how Asian Americans are used in affirmative action debates around college admissions. Even though educational attainment by Asian American ethnic groups is uneven, there are attempts by conservative interest groups to dismantle affirmative action by casting Asian Americans as "victims." In this case, the belief is that elite schools discriminate against Asian American applicants, holding them to higher standards or limiting the numbers admitted. While some Asian Americans, Chinese Americans in particular, have been vocal about their opposition to affirmative action, their objections are not shared across the many Asian American ethnic groups. Research finds that 66% of registered Asian American voters support affirmative action (AAPI Data 2018). Chinese Americans are the only Asian American ethnic group with declining support for affirmative action. Figure 9.1 shows attitudes toward affirmative action programs among various Asian American groups.

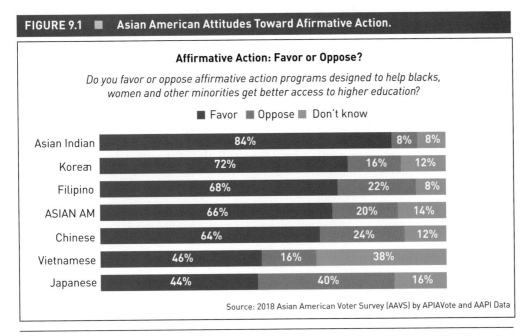

FIGURE 9.1 ■ Asian American Attitudes Toward Affirmative Action.

Affirmative Action: Favor or Oppose?

Do you favor or oppose affirmative action programs designed to help blacks, women and other minorities get better access to higher education?

■ Favor ■ Oppose ■ Don't know

	Favor	Oppose	Don't know
Asian Indian	84%	8%	8%
Korean	72%	16%	12%
Filipino	68%	22%	8%
ASIAN AM	66%	20%	14%
Chinese	64%	24%	12%
Vietnamese	46%	16%	38%
Japanese	44%	40%	16%

Source: 2018 Asian American Voter Survey (AAVS) by APIAVote and AAPI Data

Source: "Infographic – 2018, Affirmative Action Favor" 2018. https://aapidata.com/infographic-2018-affirmative-action-favor/.

> ### Check Your Understanding
>
> 1. What were the effects of the Yellow Peril stereotype?
>
> 2. What is the model minority myth?
>
> 3. Do Asian Americans support affirmative action?

ASIAN AMERICA ONLINE

More nuanced media portrayals of Asian Americans began in 1980, with the creation of the Center for Asian American Media (CAAM), formerly the National Asian American Telecommunications Association (NAATA), one of the longest-standing Asian American media entities. CAAM (n.d.) "has exposed audiences to new voices and communities, advancing our collective understanding of the American experience through programs specifically designed to engage the Asian American community and the public at large." CAAM worked within mainstream media to create change from the inside out, benefiting from government-funded initiatives meant to increase ethnic media. However, as technological advances made user-generated media more accessible, especially with the rise of the Internet, Asian Americans created alternate forms of media, affecting change from the outside in.

From Print Magazines to Blogs

While Asian American print magazines such as *Jade* (1974–1987), *A.* (1989–2002), and *Yolk* (1994–2004) were unable to sustain themselves due to printing costs and difficulties in attracting advertisers, Internet-based publications have the potential for more widespread distribution without the costs of traditional print media. One of the first Asian American blogs, *AARising* (1990–2015), began from a record label but became the go-to site for Asian American Pacific Islander entertainment news. Then in 2001, Jenn Fang, a Chinese Canadian who lives and works in the United States, founded *Reappropriate.co*, now one of the oldest Asian American and Pacific Islander feminist and race activism blogs.

Around that same time, Phil Yu, cofounder of now-defunct *A.* magazine, began blogging at blog.AngryAsianMan.com. As the "About" section succinctly states, "This is a blog about Asian America." In an interview with the *Huffington Post* (Yam 2019), Yu goes into more detail about Asian America, saying,

> *There is no one way to be Asian American. People try to put you in a box... and unfortunately, the way that that plays out is a lot of us are silenced or made to feel that we need to shut up.... It's OK to speak up and have a voice and say something, even when it goes against the grain and when people tell you to sit down and shut up.... The other side of that is that you don't have to wait for permission to tell your story, and don't let anyone else tell your story.*

Through *AngryAsianMan*, and now a podcast titled *They Call Us Bruce* cohosted with Jeff Yang, Yu and other Asian Americans voice the unique and wide-ranging stories of Asian America. Blogs and other online media are not just for entertainment. Fang, reflecting on the role of these forms of media, shared, "I think Asian American bloggers—like Angry Asian Man, and (hopefully) Reappropriate, as well as others—are a form of activism because we help to foster a diverse, online AAPI voice that I believe has helped to both incite and organize subsequent activism within the AAPI community by fostering greater passion in AAPI readers towards social change" (Angry Asian Man 2014).

Asian America YouTube

While blogs and early social networking sites, like Xanga, were connecting Asian Americans from coast to coast, YouTube provided a unique space for traditionally marginalized communities to create their own programming and see themselves reflected in a way missing from other media. In 2003, three college friends at UC San Diego, Ted Fu (Taiwanese American), Wesley Chan (Chinese American), and Philip Wang (Chinese American), created Wong Fu Productions. The trio began with short skits about college life including their popular 2006 15-minute short *Yellow Fever*, a comedic take on interracial dating. They created Wong Fu's YouTube channel in 2007. Soon short films turned into full-length features and a YouTube series on YouTube Red (now YouTube Premium). Wong Fu Productions has become a space to promote other Asian American creatives, redefining and also publicizing the multi-faceted experiences of Asian America.

In the early years of YouTube, before commercial musical artists and mainstream television shows began using the platform, Asian Americans were among the top 20 YouTubers. In 2010, comedian Ryan Higa (Japanese American) (YouTube channel: nigahiga) became the first person to reach 3 million YouTube subscribers (VanDeGraph 2016). Other high-ranking Asian American YouTubers included comedian Kevin Wu (Chinese American) (YouTube channel: kevjumba) with 1.2 million subscribers and makeup artist Michelle Phan (Vietnamese American) (YouTube channel: Michelle Phan) with 1 million (VanDeGraph 2016). Although legacy media used to act as a gatekeeper, with YouTube, Asian Americans can sidestep racial barriers and create their own media on their own terms, resulting in wide-ranging portrayals that appeal to both Asian American and non–Asian American audiences. Kevin Wu distills the appeal of Asian American–created media, stating, "I'll talk about things that Asians don't like to talk about. We're a new breed of Asian-American, and I'm a representative of that" (Considine 2011).

Through YouTube, Asian American users contribute to an Asian American *racial* identity, shaping Asian American consciousness alongside the Asian ethnic identities they may have already developed through home, family, and community life. Similar to the origins of the pan-ethnic label of the 60s, more contemporary Asian American identity reflects a shared consciousness around similarities in experiences across Asian ethnic groups while still serving as a rallying point for advocacy.

The effects of YouTube can be seen in the introduction of more mainstream media portrayals. "Today with Wong Fu, traditional media is open to us in a way it wasn't before," Wang says. "It's not like there are green lights everywhere, but we are getting into the room and people are starting to think, 'We should take a meeting with these guys. We should take this seriously'" (Lanyon 2018). Traditional media are taking Asian American stars and stories more seriously as evidenced by prime-time television shows featuring Asian American families. For example, ABC's *Fresh Off the Boat* (2015–2020) is the first network show about an Asian American family since *All American Girl* aired in 1994 and is based on chef Eddie Huang's memoir of the same name. Set in the 1990s, *Fresh Off the Boat* follows an adolescent Eddie and his family as they relocate from Washington, DC's, Chinatown to suburban Orlando. *Kim's Convenience*, a Canadian TV show picked up by Netflix, delves into the complexities of familial relationships across generations and immigration status, presenting three-dimensional characters rather than stereotypes.

Some sociologists have also studied and advocated for more (and better) representations of Asian Americans and Pacific Islanders in the media. Nancy Wang Yuen discusses her findings and accomplishments in the Sociologists in Action feature.

SOCIOLOGISTS IN ACTION
Nancy Wang Yuen

Reel Inequality: Using Sociology to Reveal and Increase the Representation of People of Color in Hollywood

As a sociologist, I want to make the world more just. This desire began in graduate school when I led the team that created the first policy report on Asian Americans and Pacific Islanders (AAPIs) on television, published in 2005. With a team of fellow Asian American graduate students and the support of a national civil rights organization, Asian Americans Advancing Justice (AAJC), we examined prime-time television shows using content analysis. We found that AAPIs were severely underrepresented on screen—just 2.7% of the total number of regular characters. Our research received national media coverage, and AAJC shared the results with television networks. In 2017, we published a 10-year follow-up report demonstrating how AAPIs, despite making significant numerical progress, remain tokens on the small screen.

When I wrote my book, *Reel Inequality: Hollywood Actors and Racism*, I wanted to document Hollywood's discriminatory casting practices and dispel the myths that perpetuate its racist system. Based on 100 in-depth interviews I conducted with working actors, *Reel Inequality* was one of the first books to compare the experiences of African American, Asian American, Latinx, and White actors. Since the book's publication in 2016, numerous Hollywood actors have shared with me how *Reel Inequality* gave voice to and clarified their experiences in the industry.

Sociology underpins my public writing and speaking. I appear regularly on radio networks like National Public Radio (NPR) and television networks like the British Broadcast Corporation (BBC) to speak on why Asian American representation in film and television matters. In 2018, I got invited to be a panelist on *Dr. Phil* to speak about racial privilege. In my public writing, I combine critical analysis with personal experience to explore topics like masculinity, cultural norms, and how I felt when seeing an Asian American woman in a romantic comedy for the first time.

I feel especially fulfilled when advocating for the increased representation of people of color in Hollywood. In 2018, I published a *HuffPost* article, "'Fresh Off the Boat' Expanded: What Family Looks Like. Don't Cancel It." I pointed out the significance of *Fresh Off the Boat* as one of the few multigenerational immigrant families on television, and the only family sitcom centered on Asian Americans on the air at the time. I also emphasized how, based on my 2017 study, the cancellation of *Fresh Off the Boat* could decrease the number of Asian American television regulars by 9%. The show was ultimately renewed. To my surprise, one of the show's writers e-mailed me to let me know that my article got circulated around the network and made a difference in saving the show. Words matter. Sociology matters.

Nancy Wang Yuen is associate professor of sociology at Biola University and the author of Reel Inequality: Hollywood Actors and Racism.

Discussion Question

Sociologists are called to notice patterns in society and to help change those that are unjust. Nancy Wang Yuen describes how she does just that with her sociological tools. What unjust social pattern(s) would you like to address? Why?

CONSIDER THIS

Why has the growing number of media outlets led to more Asian Americans appearing on legacy media? How can media portrayals of racially disadvantaged groups both help and hurt them?

There has also been an increase in shows with Asian American leads and costars, such as *Grey's Anatomy* (2005–present) with Sandra Oh (2005–2014), *The Big Bang Theory* (2007–2019) with Kunal Nayyar, *The Mindy Project* (2012–2017) with Mindy Kaling, *Elementary* (2012–2019) with Lucy Liu, *Quantico* (2015–2018) with Priyanka Chopra, *Dr. Ken* (2015–2017) with Ken Jeong, and *Andi Mack* (2017–2019) with Peyton Elizabeth Lee. Asian Americans can be seen on the silver screen in movies like *Crazy Rich Asians* (2018), *Searching* (2018), *The Farewell* (2019), and *Minari* (2021). Asian Americans are not only writing, producing, and starring in more nuanced depictions on YouTube, television, streaming services, and the silver screen, but they are also creating their own production companies (such as Henry Golding's Long House Productions), which means we may expect to see continued Asian American representation and nuanced portrayals in the future.

PHOTO 9.6 Director and cast members of *Crazy Rich Asians* at Kore Asian Media's 17th Annual Unforgettable Gala held at the Beverly Hilton in Beverly Hills, California, in December 2018.

Sthanlee B. Mirador/Sipa via AP Images

DOING SOCIOLOGY 9.4

Constance Wu's Reflections on Crazy Rich Asians

In this exercise, you will consider Constance Wu's thoughts on the groundbreaking film Crazy Rich Asians. *Wu, who starred as Rachel Chu in the film, was born in Virginia and is the child of Taiwanese immigrants.*

Write your answers to the following questions:

1. Two weeks before *Crazy Rich Asians* was released in 2018, Wu commented on the significance of the film on Twitter. In her post, she points out that *Crazy Rich Asians* "is the first Hollywood Studio film in over 25 years to center an Asian American's story." What is the difference between a film including an Asian American story and a film centering an Asian American story?

2. Wu explains that she never expected a role like this one: "Before CRA, I hadn't even done a tiny part in a studio film, I never dreamed I would get to *star* in one... because I had never seen that happen to someone who looks like me." Why is it important that people see actors who look like them starring in films? Why does this type of representation matter?

3. At the end of her post, Wu—addressing her Asian American fans—notes that "CRA won't represent every Asian American." Why do you think she includes this acknowledgment?

Check Your Understanding

1. How did the Internet contribute to Asian American community building?

2. How has Asian work on YouTube influenced media portrayals of Asian Americans?

CONCLUSION

This chapter highlighted Asian Americans' long history of immigration to the United States, activism, and cultural contributions. Though the pan-ethnic label *Asian American* unifies the varied Asian ethnic groups, there remain distinct immigration histories and contemporary experiences of Asians in America that cannot be overlooked. In the next chapter, we examine Hispanic and Latinx groups, another ethnic group with varied immigration histories and a pan-ethnic movement for self-determination.

CHAPTER REVIEW

9.1   What is the connection among early Asian immigration, anti-Asian immigration policies, and Asian activism?

Although U.S. businesses facilitated Asian immigration labor, anti-Asian fears became widespread, often resulting in threats and violence by White Americans. Policies that restricted Asian immigration followed. However, Asians in America engaged in collective action to fight for their rights—socially, politically, culturally, and economically.

9.2   What were key events that shaped an "Asian American" consciousness?

In 1968, when UC Berkeley students Yuji Ichioka and Emma Gee coined the term *Asian American* it signified a pan-ethnic Asian unification of traditionally separate groups of Asian students and challenged the derogatory term *Oriental*. It was a signal of "yellow power," a power for self-determination and a call against racism, imperialism, and inequality. The San Francisco State College strike (1968–1969), International Hotel protests (1968–1977), and Vincent Chin's murder (1982) shaped an Asian American consciousness.

9.3   What are the similarities and differences between the "Yellow Peril" and "model minority" stereotypes?

Both the Yellow Peril and model minority myth stereotypes emphasize Asian Americans' inherent difference from White Americans and immutable foreignness. The Yellow Peril stereotype portrayed Asian Americans as a foreign threat to the American way of life, whereas the model minority myth assumes Asian Americans have inherent cultural values around family, education, and hard work that enable them to assimilate into the United States whereas other racial and ethnic minority groups have not.

9.4   How does Asian American–created media challenge stereotypical portrayals of Asians in America?

Asian American–created media, such as blogs, YouTube channels, television shows, and movies, present a range of Asian American experiences with nuanced and three-dimensional characters. Rather than historic stereotypical portrayals of Asian Americans as a Yellow Peril, exotic, or model minorities, Asian American–created media normalize the presence of Asians in America.

KEY TERMS

Asian American (p. 184)

Bamboo ceiling (p. 191)

Chinese Exclusion Act (1882) (p. 179)

Executive Order 9066 (1942) (p. 182)

Hart-Celler Immigration and Nationality Act (1965) (p. 183)

Japanese internment (p. 182)

The Orient (p. 184)

Oriental (p. 184)

Picture brides (p. 180)

Yellow Peril (p. 179)

Yellow power (p. 185)

10 UNDERSTANDING LATINXS' PRESENCE IN THE UNITED STATES

Maria Isabel Ayala

LEARNING QUESTIONS

10.1 How do the Hispanic, Latino/a, and Latinx classifications differ?

10.2 How do Latinx groups vary demographically? Give examples that address fertility, population control efforts, and the residential distribution of Latinxs.

10.3 What is the relationship among income, occupation, education, and socioeconomic status among Latinxs?

10.4 How have Latinxs engaged in political mobilization seeking justice and racial equity?

One time I was in line . . . in the cafeteria and this girl, she was like, "Oh my god I love your . . . um . . . like the color of your skin . . . like you are dark, but you are not dark. . . . What are you? Like are you . . . you know . . . what country are you from?" "American," I said. American because I know what you mean, and I know what you are trying to ask me, and obviously I am not White, and I know what you are trying to get at. You know . . . sometimes . . . people just make assumptions about you because of the way you look. (22 years old, self-identified Latina)

Honestly, like . . . every time I meet someone, they do not get that I am Latina, they are always like, "I thought you were American or even French or like you know like something like that. I didn't think you were Latina, and I hear your accent, but I could not like place it to like a country." And they say that "the way you dress and the way like you look you know like you are super White. I would have never thought you were Mexican." It is somewhat weird because "Oh you are Mexican, oh it is cool because you are a different Mexican." (21 years old, self-identified Mexican and Latina)

Like my grandpa, my grandma, my aunts and uncles all speak Spanish, and I am the only one that really speaks English. . . . I never, ever thought that I was not Hispanic or Dominican, but I guess when it comes to identity it hit me when I came to [college] where people would ask me, "What are you? Are you Black? Or what?" and I would be like "I am Hispanic." And they would be like, "Where are you from?" and I would be like "Dominican Republic," and I guess that is where I kind of questioned my identity. . . . [Growing up in the Bronx] there was one girl at school in my class and people also made fun of her because they thought she was Caucasian, but she was actually Cuban, and she had lighter skin, and so growing up in that environment where everyone is Hispanic or from Puerto Rico or from Cuba we always knew we were Hispanic. (self-identified Hispanic American male) (Quotes from Ayala n.d.)

These stories help reveal the complexity of Latinx experiences in the United States. Recognizing the differences within the Latinx population helps us understand the various experiences of inequality and privilege among Latinx groups. It also reveals how larger social forces shape Latinxs' lives. In this chapter, we present an overview of the Latinx presence in the United States by highlighting its within-group diversity and how Latinx peoples have shaped and been shaped by the United States.

HOW I GOT ACTIVE IN SOCIOLOGY

María Isabel Ayala

When I was in college, I did not know what sociology was, yet I enrolled in Introduction to Sociology. Every time I would leave class, I would think and reflect on the material—specifically the discussions on migration and inequality. Being a first-generation Mexican immigrant in South Texas, the readings spoke of my experiences of marginalization but also of privilege. With time, I developed a sociological lens that drove me to question existing systems of stratification as well as the role of race and education in people's social mobility. Specifically, I became passionate about Latinxs' college attainment.

Today, I teach sociology and Chicano/Latino studies. I enjoy watching my students develop and grow their critical thinking and ability to apply their knowledge to real-life situations. I strive to help them recognize and value the complexity of people's life experiences and feel comfortable with their own voices—just as I have.

DEVELOPMENT OF HISPANIC, LATINO/A, AND LATINX CLASSIFICATIONS AND IDENTITIES

Latinx is a gender-neutral classification that refers to people who possess Latin American ancestry. Figure 10.1 shows the nations whose populations fall under the Latinx label. Latinx people make up the largest subordinate racialized group in the United States—59.9 million people comprising 18.3% of the U.S. population (U.S. Census Bureau 2019).

Hispanic, Latino/a, and Latinx are pan-ethnic categories, meaning they are umbrella terms consisting of various ethnic groups (e.g., Puerto Rican, Nicaraguan, Bolivian). Despite the diversity of people described by these categories—Hispanic, Latino/a, and Latinx—these groups often face stereotypes, or an oversimplified description of a group, image, or idea. For example, common stereotypes about Latinxs include (a) they all speak Spanish and (b) most Latinxs in the United States are undocumented immigrants. In this section, we discuss the development of the classification of people of Latin American ancestry in the United States and how these classifications shape Latinxs' identities.

The Social Construction of Hispanic, Latino/a, and Latinx

As discussed in Chapter 1, race is a social construction, without biological foundations, and the U.S. government has changed racial categories many times over its history. In the United States, the Office of Management and Budget (OMB) sets the standards by which government agencies racially classify groups. Today, the five racial categories are White, Black or African American, Asian, American Indian and Alaska Native, and Native Hawaiian and Other Pacific Islander. These racial categories influence society as well as individuals. For example, the OMB influences the information the U.S. census collects. With this data, the census helps determine the distribution of federal program dollars and the number of seats in Congress for each state. The data also influence corporations and organizations' hiring plans and investment strategies and allow the government to monitor conformity with civil rights laws.

Yet, as you may have noticed, even though racial classifications play a key role in our society, the OMB does not have a separate racial category for people of Latin American origin or Latinxs. This is because the OMB understands people of Hispanic, Latino, or Spanish (or Latinx) origin ancestry as an ethnic rather than a racial group—a group that shares a common Latin American ancestry, as seen in their nationality, language, and religion. However, even while the OMB constructs Latinx groups as ethnic groups whose members can be of any race, Latinxs experience racialization based on their Latinx attributes—their Spanish speech or accent and other parts of their cultural background signal that Latinxs, like other racialized peoples, are a different and subordinate group. These differences often act to justify their unequal treatment.

Yet U.S. government agencies adhere to standards issued by the OMB that stipulate that race and Hispanic origin (ethnicity) are two different concepts. As you can see in Figure 10.2, the OMB

FIGURE 10.1 ■ **Map of Latin America**

standards used in the census include two minimum categories for data on ethnicity: "Hispanic, Latino or Spanish Origin" and "Not Hispanic, Latino or Spanish Origin." People who self-identify as Hispanic, Latino, or Spanish origin can be of any race. Consequently, the second question focuses on race (i.e.. White, Black or African American, Asian, American Indian and Alaskan Native, and Native Hawaiian and Other Pacific Islander). We discuss racialization and the changing racial categories over time in the U.S. census more in Chapter 11.

FIGURE 10.2 ■ Overview of Hispanic Origin and Race Questions, 2020 Census

Person 1

5. Please provide information for each person living here. If there is someone living here who pays the rent or owns this residence, start by listing him or her as Person 1. If the owner or the person who pays the rent does not live here, start by listing any adult living here as Person 1.

What is Person 1's name? *Print name below.*

First Name   MI

Last Name(s)

6. **What is Person 1's sex?** *Mark* ☒ *ONE box.*

☐ Male ☐ Female

7. **What is Person 1's age and what is Person 1's date of birth?** *For babies less than 1 year old, do not write the age in months. Write 0 as the age.*

Print numbers in boxes.

Age on April 1, 2020   Month   Day   Year of birth

☐ years

→ NOTE: Please answer BOTH Question 8 about Hispanic origin and Question 9 about race. For this census, Hispanic origins are not races.

8. **Is Person 1 of Hispanic, Latino, or Spanish origin?**

☐ **No,** not of Hispanic, Latino, or Spanish origin
☐ Yes, Mexican, Mexican Am., Chicano
☐ Yes, Puerto Rican
☐ Yes, Cuban
☐ Yes, another Hispanic, Latino, or Spanish origin – *Print, for example, Salvadoran, Dominican, Colombian, Guatemalan, Spaniard, Ecuadorian, etc.* ↙

9. **What is Person 1's race?**
Mark ☒ *one or more boxes AND print origins.*

☐ White – *Print, for example, German, Irish, English, Italian, Lebanese, Egyptian, etc.* ↙

☐ Black or African Am. – *Print, for example, African American, Jamaican, Haitian, Nigerian, Ethiopian, Somali, etc.* ↙

☐ American Indian or Alaska Native – *Print name of enrolled or principal tribe(s), for example, Navajo Nation, Blackfeet Tribe, Mayan, Aztec, Native Village of Barrow Inupiat Traditional Government, Nome Eskimo Community, etc.* ↙

☐ Chinese   ☐ Vietnamese   ☐ Native Hawaiian
☐ Filipino   ☐ Korean   ☐ Samoan
☐ Asian Indian   ☐ Japanese   ☐ Chamorro
☐ Other Asian – *Print, for example, Pakistani, Cambodian, Hmong, etc.* ↙   ☐ Other Pacific Islander – *Print, for example, Tongan, Fijian, Marshallese, etc.* ↙

☐ Some other race – *Print race or origin.* ↙

→ If more people were counted in Question 1 on the front page, continue with Person 2 on the next page.

Source: U.S. Census Bureau. 2020.

Distinguishing Between Hispanic, Latino/a, and Latinx

Hispanic emerged from the U.S. government and media's desire to account for the growing U.S. population who have Latin American ancestry and, for the most part, includes people whose ancestors are from Spanish-speaking countries. As such, Hispanic is a pan-ethnic classification popular at the government level and remains a preferred classification among certain Latinx groups, specifically those that have origins in Spanish-speaking countries (e.g., Cuba, Spain). Thus, throughout the chapter, you will often see information on Hispanics rather than Latinx. Yet the association of the Hispanic classification with Spanish colonial power and its language exclusivity—which ignores non–Spanish speaking countries and neglects the internal diversity of the group—makes this classification somewhat problematic. Due to these limitations, the Latino/a classification emerged.

The "Latino/a" category originates from the word *Latinoamericano*, or a person from Latin America. Many people think *Latino/a*, also a pan-ethnic label, better captures Latinxs' "struggle for empowerment in the United States" (Oquendo 1995, 97). These struggles involve not only lower wages, higher poverty rates, and lower educational attainment than Whites and Asian Americans but also the subordinate status that Latinxs as a group experience. "Empowerment" because, even when experiencing a secondary status, *Latino* is a term that developed from the community, and in doing so, its adoption "could be regarded as part of a broader process of self-definition and self-assertion" (Oquendo 1995, 98). Supporters of this label also propose that *Latino/a* is more descriptive and inclusive than the Hispanic classification because it includes people of Latin American ancestry who do not speak Spanish (e.g., from Brazil or parts of the Caribbean).

Just as with the Hispanic classification, the Latino/a classification masks the diversity of people of Latin American ancestry in the United States. Moreover, the Latino/a classification reproduces understanding of gender as a dichotomy (man vs. woman) by its use of Latino (man with a Latin American ancestry) and Latina (woman with a Latin American ancestry). Hence, the term *Latinx* has gained momentum, especially among younger Latin American ancestry populations. *Latinx* is a gender-neutral nonbinary alternative to *Latino/a*. The Latinx classification remains controversial, however, because some people oppose the imposition of the English *x* onto a Spanish-based term. Nevertheless, because *Latinx* is the most inclusive term today, we use it in this chapter. However, often government and nongovernmental agencies and organizations refer to Latin American–origin people as Hispanic or Latino. As such, when presenting information from these sources, we switch and use the classification presented (e.g., Hispanic).

CONSIDER THIS

What are some of the challenges to understanding Latinxs' experiences in the United States when the group is classified in different ways (Hispanic, Latino/a, and Latinx)?

Hispanic, Latino/a, and Latinx classifications also relate to peoples' identities. Identities refer to how people define "what it means to be who they are as persons" (Burke 2004, 5). Identities reflect the group to which people belong as well as the boundaries that separate them from other groups. For example, being Latinx differs from being Black, and being Mexican differs from being Cuban, as each group has unique cultures and experiences. Moreover, while some people self-identify in a consistent way, others change their racial or ethnic identity at different times and places. For example, a person who identifies as Mexican at their church may choose to identify as Latina in their college application (Khanna 2011).

DOING SOCIOLOGY 10.1

Hispanic, Latino/A, and Latinx: Which Should the U.S. Census Use?

In this exercise, you will determine the pros and cons of categorizing ethnic groups; explain the different meanings of Hispanic, Latino/a, and Latinx; and explain why you think the census should use one of them over the other two.

Imagine the Office of Management and Budget (OMB) has asked you to explain the difference among the Hispanic, Latino/a, and Latinx categories and why they should use one instead of the other two. Write down answers to the following questions and be prepared to share them with the class. Then, with a classmate, share your answers, and answer the questions again, together.

1. What are the differences among the terms *Hispanic, Latino/a*, and *Latinx*?

2. If you could pick just one, which should the census use? Why?

3. What information do you need to make this decision? Why?

Colorism and Becoming White

How others perceive your race also has a major impact on your life. In the United States (and in other nations across the world), colorism provides people privileges or disadvantages based on skin color (Hunter 2016). Knowing this allows us to understand peoples' different experiences not only across racial and ethnic groups but also within them. For example, due to the higher status placed on Whiteness, light-skinned Latinxs who may pass as "White" tend to experience more privilege than darker-skinned Latinxs (Ayala and Chalupa 2016; Bonilla-Silva 2015).

In 2010, just over half (53%) of the Hispanic and Latino population racially identified as White on the U.S. census. Some may do so because as Pedro Noguera, Peter L. Agnew Professor of Education at New York University, states, this racial classification is "aspirational; they know that 'White' is considered the prestige box" (Valle 2014, 1). Others do so because they and others see and respond to them as White based on their appearance. For example, Cuban Americans (many of whom appear White) are the most likely (62%) of all Latinx groups to choose a "White" racial identity. Latinxs with darker skin, on the other hand, tend to be treated and to identify as Black.

As Figure 10.3 shows, among all cross-racial, opposite-sex, newly married couples, there are far more Hispanic–White marriages than any other combination—almost 3 times more than Black–White marriages. These data do not tell us the racial appearance of the Hispanic newlyweds, but it does indicate that White people tend to be much more accepting of Hispanics than Black people and thus more likely to marry a Hispanic who appears more White than Black. This—and the fact that most light-skinned Hispanics racially identify as White—points to the offspring of these couples appearing, identifying, and becoming White.

SOCIOLOGISTS IN ACTION

Angelica Ruvalcaba

Resilience in Institutions of Higher Education

My many identities have shaped my life in significant ways. I am a Tejana, Chicana, daughter of Mexican immigrants, first-generation college student, and doctoral student. As an undergraduate student, I faced financial hardships, unanswered requests for guidance from academic and financial aid advisors, and racially charged microaggressions at the hands of peers, faculty, and administrators. I constantly felt that the university was not a place for me or people like me.

As a sociology major during my undergraduate career at a primarily White institution (PWI) in Texas, I began to understand how systemic the inequalities I lived were. I began to organize with other students to address the ways the university further marginalized already vulnerable communities. My colleagues and I organized workshops to discuss race, racism, and the discrimination students of color faced on campus. Through this work, we became aware that many people believe the United States is in a postracial era and, therefore, have a colorblind perspective on society. I became aware that administrators and fellow college students did not recognize my experiences as a product of racism, nor did they see how they contributed to a racially hostile campus climate. By addressing the challenges of being a racial and ethnic minority, my friends and I helped uncover the complicated and sophisticated ways in which racial structures operate.

My friends and I also noticed the lack of resources, opportunities, information, and networks available to first-generation college students. We started informational sessions to provide students with knowledge and resources on how to navigate their undergraduate experience. We also established networks with professors across the university, shared opportunities for internships and research opportunities, and hosted graduate school informationals. Moreover, to address the systemic omission of Latinx history and contributions to society, we worked with students, faculty, and university administrators to establish a Latina/o and Mexican American studies (LMAS) minor. We faced resentment from colorblind students, faculty, and administrators who believed our push for LMAS was an act of reverse racism. However, we overcame this opposition, and students at that school can now take that minor.

I am now a PhD student in the Department of Sociology and the Chicano/Latino Studies Program at a PWI in the Midwest. Here, I see undergraduates struggle as I did. Consequently, my colleagues and I decided to create a workshop series for undergraduate Latinx migrant students on how to thrive in college and to prepare and apply to graduate school. My antiracism efforts here and at my undergraduate institution relate directly to sociology. My sociological education has allowed me to notice systemic racism in higher education, bring it to light, address it, and support other students in their efforts to persevere in a White-centered university.

Angelica Ruvalcaba is a doctoral student in the Department of Sociology and Chicano/Latino Studies Program at Michigan State University.

Discussion Question

How can Latinx students experience marginalization in predominantly White institutions of higher education?

FIGURE 10.3 ■ Intermarriages by Race, Ethnicity, and Gender

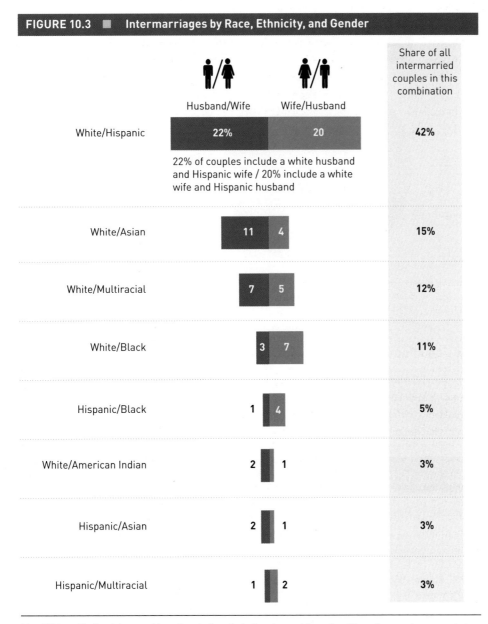

	Husband/Wife	Wife/Husband	Share of all intermarried couples in this combination
White/Hispanic	22%	20	42%

22% of couples include a white husband and Hispanic wife / 20% include a white wife and Hispanic husband

	Husband/Wife	Wife/Husband	Share
White/Asian	11	4	15%
White/Multiracial	7	5	12%
White/Black	3	7	11%
Hispanic/Black	1	4	5%
White/American Indian	2	1	3%
Hispanic/Asian	2	1	3%
Hispanic/Multiracial	1	2	3%

Note: Whites, blacks, Asians and American Indians include only non-Hispanics. Hispanics are of any race. Asians include pacific Islanders. Racial and ethnic combinations that add up to less than 2% are excluded. Totals are calculated prior to rounding.

Source: Pew Research Center. "Intermarriage in the U.S., 50 Years after *Loving v. Virginia*." https://www.pewsocialtrends.org/2017/05/18/1-trends-and-patterns-in-intermarriage/.

1. What percentage of the U.S. population is Latinx?

2. What is the difference among Hispanic, Latino/a, and Latinx classifications?

3. What role has colorism played in Latinxs' different experiences and self-classifications?

DEMOGRAPHIC PATTERNS

As noted earlier, Hispanics comprise 18% of the total U.S. population—about 60 million people. By 2060, demographers expect the Hispanic population will be 119 million (28.6% of the total population; U.S. Census Bureau 2017). This description, however, masks the diversity of Latinxs' demographic behavior. As such, it is important to look at the demographic composition of each Latinx group in the United States. Figure 10.4 shows the 2017 population of Hispanics in the United States.

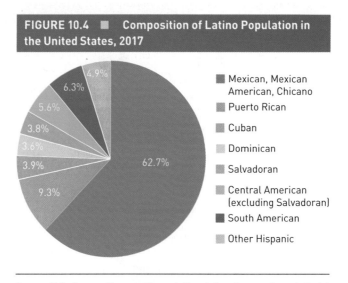

FIGURE 10.4 ■ Composition of Latino Population in the United States, 2017

- Mexican, Mexican American, Chicano
- Puerto Rican
- Cuban
- Dominican
- Salvadoran
- Central American (excluding Salvadoran)
- South American
- Other Hispanic

Source: U.S. Census Bureau, Current Population Survey, Annual Social and Economic Supplement, 2019. Data from https://www.census.gov/data/tables/2019/demo/hispanic-origin/2019-cps.html.

Fertility and Population Growth or Decline

Fertility—or the number of children women have—plays a key role in the size of any population. Societies with high fertility rates (e.g., Niger and Angola) experience population growth while populations in societies with low fertility rates (e.g., Singapore and Japan) decline (unless they bring in enough immigrants to counter the low birth rate).

DOING SOCIOLOGY 10.2

Controlling Population Growth

In this exercise, you will consider U.S.-imposed efforts to control population growth in Puerto Rico, including the sterilization of Puerto Rican women.

In 1937, Blanton Winship, the U.S. governor of Puerto Rico (1934–1939) signed Law 136, which instituted a mass sterilization policy effort to "fill the urgent need to avoid the menace of the ever-growing population." The surplus of workers was due, in large part, to U.S. officials and businessmen turning the island into a one-crop (sugar) economy after the United States gained control of it in 1898. Farmers across the island lost their livelihoods. Also, textile manufacturers began to see Puerto Rican women as a good source of cheap labor. Believing women without children were the most reliable workers, they encouraged their female employees to undergo sterilization. Some factories included their own family clinics where women were given free sterilization and others were encouraged to take experimental contraceptive drugs. Many were unaware that the sterilization procedures were irreversible. The procedure became so common that, from the 1930s to the 1970s, about a third of the women in Puerto Rico were sterilized (Andrews 2017).

1. Why might U.S. governors of Puerto Rico look at the Puerto Rican population as a threat?

2. Why might they deem it appropriate to promote the mass sterilization of Puerto Rican women to reduce the Puerto Rican population?

3. What are ethical ways governments can address high fertility rates and overpopulation?

4. Were you aware of this history before reading the chapter? Why?

Latinx women in the United States have higher fertility rates than Whites, Blacks, and Asians. However, this masks differences in fertility within racial and ethnic groups. Differences in income, educational attainment, and age at first birth play a role in people's fertility behavior. As such, there are differences not only across racial and ethnic groups but also within them. For example, Latinas who self-identify as Mexican or Central American have more children than women who self-identify as Cuban (Ayala 2017). However, the past few years have seen a decline in fertility across Hispanic groups (see Figures 10.5 and 10.6). The decline of Hispanics' fertility, in addition to the decline in immigration from Latin America, poses challenges to the United States' ability to replace its population. When a society has more older than younger people, its ability to produce goods and supply services declines, affecting the economic stability of the nation.

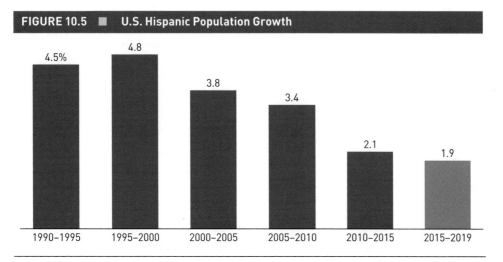

FIGURE 10.5 ■ U.S. Hispanic Population Growth

1990–1995	1995–2000	2000–2005	2005–2010	2010–2015	2015–2019
4.5%	4.8	3.8	3.4	2.1	1.9

Note: Based on annual population estimates as of July 1 for each year. Hispanics are of any race.

Source: Noe-Bustamante, Lopez, Krogstad. "U.S. Hispanic population surpassed 60 million in 2019, but growth has slowed."PewResourceCenter.2020.https://www.pewresearch.org/fact-tank/2020/07/07/u-s-hispanic-population-surpassed-60-million-in-2019-but-growth-has-slowed/.

New Residential Patterns

Traditionally, Latinx immigrants to the United States settled in specific regions—California, Texas, and Florida. However, differences in geographic location exist across Latinx subgroups. For example, whereas Puerto Ricans tended to move to New York City, Cubans are concentrated in Miami.

Figure 10.7 shows that, since 2008, Latinos have settled in many new areas across the United States—particularly in the South and Midwest. In these parts of the nation are many slaughterhouses and farms that need laborers for physically demanding, low-paying jobs that White people tend to refuse. For the past several decades, the populations of the towns where Latinx immigrants have recently put down roots have dwindled. New Latinx immigrants have helped revive these towns and led town leaders to construct more schools, hospitals, and housing to accommodate them.

FIGURE 10.6 ■ Hispanic Birth Rates

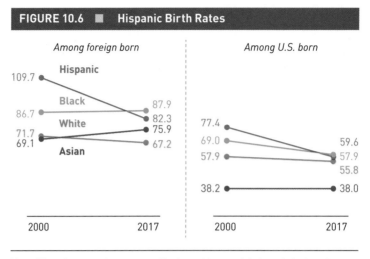

Among foreign born

Hispanic
109.7

Black
86.7 ● ● 87.9

White
● 82.3
● 75.9
71.7 ●
69.1 ● ● 67.2
Asian

Among U.S. born

77.4 ●
69.0 ● ● 59.6
57.9 ● ● 57.9
55.8

38.2 ● ● 38.0

2000   2017   2000   2017

Note: Hispanics are of any race. Blacks, whites and Asians include only non-Hispanisc. Asians include Pacific Islanders.

Source: Livingston. "Hispanic women no longer account for the majority of immigrant births in the U.S." Pew Research Center. https://www.pewresearch.org/fact-tank/2019/08/08/hispanic-women-no-longer-account-for-the-majority-of-immigrant-births-in-the-u-s/.

FIGURE 10.7 ■ Latino Population Growth

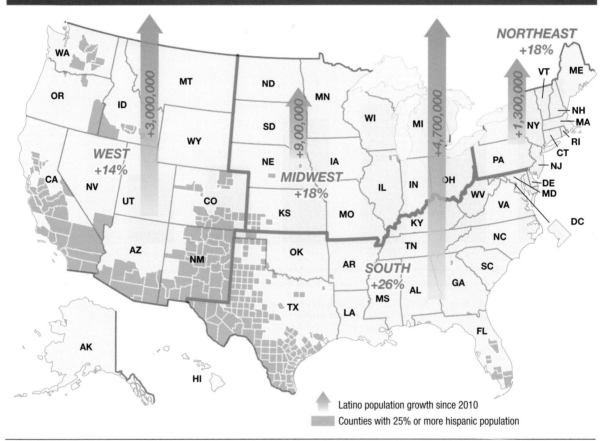

Latino population growth since 2010

Counties with 25% or more hispanic population

Source: Pew Research Center. 2020. "South has seen the nation's biggest Latino population growth since 2010" from "U.S. Hispanic population surpassed 60 million in 2019, but growth has slowed." (Noe-Bustamante, Lopez, Krogstad.) https://www.pewresearch.org/fact-tank/2020/07/07/u-s-hispanic-population-surpassed-60-million-in-2019-but-growth-has-slowed/.

CONSIDER THIS

Imagine you live in a southern town experiencing hypergrowth from Latinx people. What types of changes would you expect to see in your community?

Check Your Understanding

1. What role does Latinx fertility play in the United States' ability to replace its population?

2. What role does Latinx immigration play in the ability of the United States to replace its population?

3. What kind of work do immigrant Latinx people tend to do in the South and Midwest? Why?

LATINXS' SOCIOECONOMIC EXPERIENCES

Income, occupational prestige, and education shape Latinxs' socioeconomic status (SES). Figure 10.8 shows that, overall, Latinos in the United States have a lower income than Asians and Whites and a higher income than African Americans. Why?

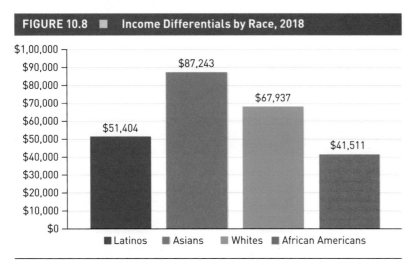

FIGURE 10.8 ■ Income Differentials by Race, 2018

Source: Guzman, Gloria. 2019. Household Income: 2018. American Community Survey Briefs ACSBR/18-01. https://www.census.gov/content/dam/Census/library/publications/2019/acs/acsbr18-01.pdf.

Jobs, Unemployment, and Education

Figure 10.8 reveals differences in incomes among Latinos, Asians, Whites, and African Americans in the United States. As Figure 10.9 reveals, more Hispanics or Latinos work in sales and service (47%) than in management and professional-related occupations (21%). This reflects the relatively low income for Latinx people in the United States.

As seen in Figure 10.10, income level relates to educational attainment. Fortunately, as Figure 10.11 shows, the high school dropout rate among Hispanics has fallen dramatically over the past 20 years, and college enrollment has also increased. In fact, the share of Hispanic college and university students increased from 8.0 percent (1996) to 19.1 percent (2016) (Bauman 2017).

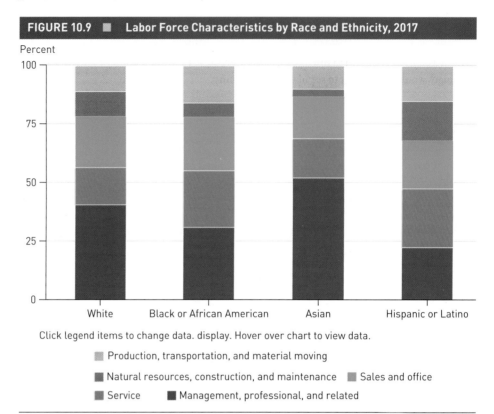

FIGURE 10.9 ■ Labor Force Characteristics by Race and Ethnicity, 2017

Click legend items to change data. display. Hover over chart to view data.

- Production, transportation, and material moving
- Natural resources, construction, and maintenance
- Sales and office
- Service
- Management, professional, and related

Source: "Labor force characteristics by race and ethnicity, 2018" https://www.bls.gov/opub/reports/race-and-ethnicity/ 2018/home.htm.

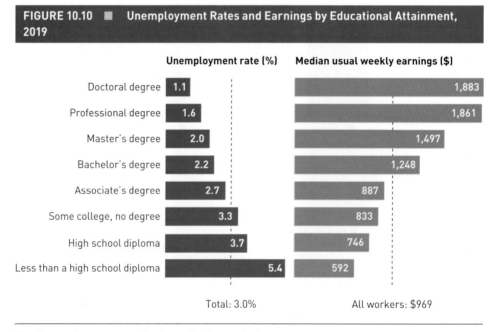

FIGURE 10.10 ■ Unemployment Rates and Earnings by Educational Attainment, 2019

	Unemployment rate (%)	Median usual weekly earnings ($)
Doctoral degree	1.1	1,883
Professional degree	1.6	1,861
Master's degree	2.0	1,497
Bachelor's degree	2.2	1,248
Associate's degree	2.7	887
Some college, no degree	3.3	833
High school diploma	3.7	746
Less than a high school diploma	5.4	592

Total: 3.0%   All workers: $969

Note: Data are for persons age 25 and over. Earnings are for full-time wage and salary workers.

Source: Bureau of Labor Statistics. 2019. https://www.bls.gov/emp/chart-unemployment-earnings-education.htm.

CONSIDER THIS

Why is it in the economic interest of California and other states to encourage Latinx students to attend and graduate college?

However, racial **discrimination** exists in higher education, as Angelica Ruvalcaba, the Sociologist in Action for this chapter, points out. She uses her sociological tools to improve the college experience for Latinx college students.

Unemployment also shows inequities across racial and ethnic lines. Figure 10.11 reveals that Hispanic women in management earn lower wages than White females in management. Furthermore, Asian males in sales earn more than Hispanic males in sales (Hegewisch, Phil, and Tesfaselassie 2019). According to the Bureau of Labor Statistics, in 2019, for example, Hispanics or Latinos (4.2%) had higher unemployment rates than Asians (2.8%) and Whites (3.4%) and lower rates than Blacks (5.6%).

PHOTO 10.1 Latinx college students attending an Afro-Latino festival.

Memorial Student Center Texas A&M University, CC BY 2.0 <https://creativecommons.org/licenses/by/2.0>, via Wikimedia Commons

The Latinx high school dropout rate has fallen dramatically (see Figure 10.11), and more Latinxs are enrolling in college than ever before. Latinxs' increasing presence in higher education institutions reflects not only their demographic growth but also their increased high school graduation rate and their higher college enrollment rate immediately after high school graduation (Ryan and Bauman 2016). California, with 40% of its population Latinos and Latinas, has led the way in reaching out to Latinx students and their parents by promoting college and assisting them in the application process (Krupnick 2019). However, many Latinx students face race, class, and cultural hurdles they must overcome in college, and Latinxs' college attainment remains lower than that of Asians, Whites, and Blacks (see Figure 10.12).

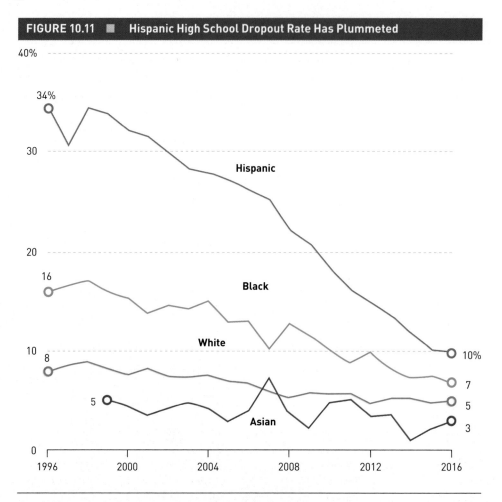

FIGURE 10.11 ■ Hispanic High School Dropout Rate Has Plummeted

Note: Civilian noninstitutionalized population. Blacks and Asians include the Hispanic portions of those groups. Whites include only non-Hispanics. Hispanics are of any race.

Source: Pew Research Center. https://www.pewresearch.org/fact-tank/2017/09/29/hispanic-dropout-rate-hits-new-low-college-enrollment-at-new-high/.

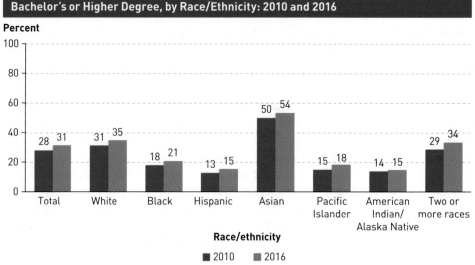

FIGURE 10.12 ■ Percentage of Adults Age 25 and Older Who Have Completed a Bachelor's or Higher Degree, by Race/Ethnicity: 2010 and 2016

Source: National Center for Educational Statistics from U.S. Department of Commerce, Census Bureau, American Community Survey, 2010 and 2016. https://nces.ed.gov/programs/raceindicators/indicator_RFA.asp.

DOING SOCIOLOGY 10.3

Improving College Graduation Rates

In this exercise you will compete to create the most effective policy proposal to improve the college graduation rate among Latinx people.

With a group, put together a policy to improve the college graduation rate among Latinx people. Then, write answers to the following questions.

1. What reasons might prevent Latinx from entering and graduating from college?

2. Write up a national policy that could effectively address the most important reasons you identified.

Check Your Understanding

1. How do Latinxs compare economically with other racial and racialized groups?

2. In what occupations are Latinxs concentrated?

3. What factors help explain Latinxs' concentration in relatively low-wage work?

4. What is the relationship between educational attainment and unemployment?

POLITICAL MOBILIZATION: FIGHTING FOR EQUITY AND JUSTICE

When you were in high school did you learn about the history of activism among Latinx? For example, when you read the words *Chicano movement* or *Prop 187*, what comes to mind? We now turn to some examples of how Latinx people have changed society for the better.

Social Mobilization and Activism

Latinx have a history of social mobilization and activism to resist their subordinate status in the United States. For more than a century, for example, farmworkers in California faced terrible labor conditions even though their work has been critical to the state's economy. Dolores Huerta and Cesar Chavez—organizers who established the United Farm Workers (UFW) in 1962—mobilized and fought to improve the working conditions of farmworkers through strikes and nationwide boycotts of the food they grew and picked. At a time when civil rights movements, including the Black Power movement, were gaining momentum, Chicano activists brought together community groups and churches, and developed interracial coalitions among Filipinos, Chicanos, Anglos, and Black workers to push for better living conditions.

The Eurocentric foundation of the United States shaped the construction of Mexican Americans as "other." The **Chicano movement** in the 1960s and 70s played a key role in the reconstruction of Mexican Americans' presence in the United States (Ayala and Ramirez 2019; Blackwell 2016). Through underscoring the cultural connection of American-born Mexican Americans with Aztlán, the Mexican homeland, and highlighting the contributions of Mexican Americans to the United States, the Chicano movement stimulated the empowerment of Mexican Americans. By addressing the negative perception of Latinxs, fighting for labor and voting rights for Spanish-speaking Latinxs, and establishing ethnic studies curricula that reflect the contribution of Latinxs in the United States, the Chicano movement showed the ability to gain and use power (Sáenz and Morales 2015).

PHOTO 10.2 Dolores Huerta speaking at the induction of the farm worker movement into the Labor Hall of Honor.

US Department of Labor, CC BY 2.0 <https://creativecommons.org/licenses/by/2.0>, via Wikimedia Commons

Since the 1970s, several policies affecting the Latinx population have reached the ballot box. For example, in 1994, California's Proposition 187 passed. It was designed to prohibit undocumented immigrants from accessing health care, public education, and other services. Whereas supporters of the law, including Republican governor Pete Wilson, argued it was driven by economic concerns, critics, including President Bill Clinton, argued that Proposition 187 discriminated against Hispanic and Asian immigrants. The courts agreed and deemed it unconstitutional. One key result of the proposition was the backlash proponents of it faced. The governor, Pete Wilson, who supported it enthusiastically, lost in the next election, along with many Republican legislators who backed Proposition 187. Today, Democrats control both houses of the legislature and the governorship of California.

Recently, Latinxs and allies have addressed immigration and deportation issues. Many Latinx families, particularly those with mixed legal status—citizens, undocumented migrants, and naturalized citizens—face the terror of ICE arresting and deporting them or a family member. Children go to school not knowing if their parents will come home from work. In 2019, millions of people took to the streets in what was one of the largest protests for immigrants' rights. They not only opposed the criminalization of undocumented status but also advocated for "legalization to regularize immigrants without legal residency, as well as their family members and friends" (Bloemraad and Voss 2019, 2). Deferred Action for Childhood Arrivals (DACA), for example, is an immigration policy announced by President Barack Obama in June 2012 that enables undocumented people to qualify for a renewable 2-year period of deferred action from deportation. To be considered for DACA, a person must have come to the United States before the age of 16 and not have any felonies or misdemeanors on their record. DACA, however, does not provide a path to citizenship. President Trump tried to end DACA, but the Supreme Court declared in June 2020 that he had not made a sufficient argument to end the program (Macaya, Wagner, and Hayes 2020).

Why Do Latinx Come to the United States?

According to the Pew Research Center, immigrants from Latin America make up 50.4% of the U.S. immigrant population (Radford and Noe-Bustamante 2019). People from each of the sending nations, however, have had different reasons for moving to the United States. We'll look at some examples next.

Mexicans

Mexican Americans differ from other people with Latin American heritage in that many Mexicans were forcibly incorporated into the United States after the Mexican-American War through the Treaty of Guadalupe Hidalgo in 1848. With the signing of the treaty, Mexico ceded about half its land to the United States. In doing so, Mexicans who grew up in one nation were separated overnight. Those in the United States became Mexican Americans (Alvarez 1973).

In addition to presence by conquest, Mexicans have migrated to the United States voluntarily. Lack of opportunities, socioeconomic mobility, family reunification, and educational attainment are some of the forces driving Mexican immigrants' movement. However, migration streams between Mexico and the United States have been complicated. In some historical periods, a need for Mexican labor has favored this movement as shown with the Bracero program (1942–1964). During World War II, the United States faced labor shortages, specifically in agriculture. The Bracero program allowed Mexicans to serve as contract labor to the United States for a certain amount of time.

During some periods, however, anti-immigrant sentiment drove a forced return migration. For example, during the Great Depression—as an attempt to prevent people of Mexican heritage competing for jobs—President Hoover created the Mexican Repatriation program whereby he and President Roosevelt deported Mexicans and Mexican Americans. Sixty percent of the deportees were U.S. citizens born in the United States (Balderama and Rodríguez 2006). Operation Wetback (*Wetback* is a derogatory name for Mexicans who enter the United States without documents) in 1954 was a similar program of apprehension and deportation of Mexicans and Mexican Americans.

While structural and cultural forces influence the migration or deportation of Mexicans to and from the United States, they also affect Mexicans' acculturation and incorporation into U.S. society. Just as in the case of Puerto Ricans and Cubans (discussed later), earlier Mexican immigrants were encouraged to assimilate and internalize U.S. values. Organizations such as the League of United Latin American Citizens (LULAC)—the oldest (established in 1929 in Corpus Christi, Texas) and largest Hispanic organization (132,000 members) in the United States—facilitate the incorporation and advancement of Hispanics in the United States. Through its volunteer and community-based programs, LULAC focuses on the educational attainment, civil rights, socioeconomic status, and political influence of the Hispanic population.

Puerto Ricans

Puerto Ricans' presence in the United States also stems from an unequal relationship. As discussed earlier, in 1898, through the Treaty of Paris that ended the Spanish-American War, Puerto Rico became a commonwealth of the United States. Puerto Ricans became U.S. citizens in 1917.

Regardless of possessing formal citizenship (with the exception of the right to vote in presidential elections), Puerto Ricans hold a secondary status in the United States. Symbolically and culturally, colonization led to a social construction of Puerto Ricans as non-American *others*. This helps explain why even though their status as U.S. citizens allows Puerto Ricans to move freely between Puerto Rico and the mainland of the United States, most Puerto Ricans, if given a choice, would remain on the island. The devastation caused from Hurricane Maria (2017), lack of assistance from the federal government, and corruption in the government of Puerto Rico, however, pushed many Puerto Ricans from the island to the mainland, especially to Florida and New Jersey.

Central Americans

Central America contains six countries—Costa Rica, Belize, El Salvador, Honduras, Guatemala. and Nicaragua. Many of these nations—El Salvador, Honduras, Guatemala, and Nicaragua—have a history of political repression, civil war, and economic turmoil (some encouraged by the United States) that continues to trigger migration from these nations to the United States. Except for the first wave of Cuban immigrants, who were mostly White and politically aligned with the United States, the United States government has not recognized many Central Americans as refugees, thus making their migration and incorporation experience more challenging.

Like in the case of other Latin American immigrants, civil groups formed to help Central American immigrants. Their efforts include organizing to suspend the deportation of Central American immigrants who have protected status. Through the Immigration Act of 1990, the United States Congress created temporary protected status (TPS). TPS provides people of specifically designated countries (e.g., those confronting armed conflict, environmental disaster, or extraordinary and temporary conditions) a work permit and stay of deportation.

Cubans

Historical, political, and economic forces also influenced the movement of Cubans to the United States. In the late 19th century, the United States and Cuba had a strong commercial and cultural relationship shaped, in part, by the cigar industry. However, a corrupt dictator ruled the island. In 1959, Fidel Castro toppled the dictator, and many Cubans were hopeful that the conditions in Cuba would improve. Castro's socialist policies, however, led many White or light-skinned Cuban professionals (e.g., doctors, lawyers, scientists) to flee to the United States.

The first wave of Cuban immigrants, considered political refugees by the U.S. government, entered the United States under the Cuban Adjustment Act (1966), which provided them access to Medicaid, food stamps, and English courses and scholarships that contributed to their acculturation and social mobility. As time went on, however, Cuba faced financial problems, and more people fled to the United States. These later waves tended to consist mainly of people who were poorer and darker-skinned than those in the first wave (Clark, Fowler, Loring, and Weigel 2016). These latter waves of immigrants faced discrimination even from fellow Cuban immigrants. Overall, however, the Cuban experience is seen as a "success story." Their initial immigrant refugee status, aid from the United States government, and organizations that promoted acculturation greatly helped them adjust to U.S. society. Together, they promoted a sense of *Cubanidad* that slowly redefined the image of Cubans, not as temporary immigrants but as permanent residents. Their high educational attainment and occupational status and lighter skin tone also facilitated the incorporation of early waves of Cuban immigrants.

As you can see, Latin Americans moved and continue to move to the United States for a variety of reasons (e.g., gang violence, failing governments, political persecution, domestic violence, and to reunite families and gain employment). The factors driving people's migration help to determine the characteristics of the migrant populations.

Lack of U.S. citizenship prevents most from gaining access to socioeconomic resources to improve their quality of life, including food stamps (Supplemental Nutrition Assistance Program), welfare (Temporary Assistance for Needy Families), SocialSecurity, and Medicare. Therefore, many Latin American immigrants are desperate to obtain United States citizenship.

In the past few decades, more Latin American immigrants have applied for naturalization—the process by which a person becomes a citizen of the United States. From 2005 to 2015, 7 of the 10 sending countries whose naturalization rates increased were Latin American (i.e., Ecuador, Peru, Dominican Republic, Colombia, Guatemala, El Salvador, and Mexico). Many, however, may not be able to apply for U.S. citizenship for a host of reasons, including fear of arrest, a lack of English proficiency, and the cost of the application (increased under President Trump) (Gonzalez-Barrera and Krogstad 2019).

PHOTO 10.3 A protestor holding a Defend DACA sign.

Charles Edward Miller, CC BY-SA 2.0 <https://creativecommons.org/licenses/by-sa/2.0/>, via Flickr

Politics and Political Engagement of Latinxs

The Latinx electorate has increased dramatically over the past two decades, particularly in highly contested states (Igielnik and Budiman 2020). Latinxs, like other Americans, turned out in record numbers during the 2020 presidential election. More and more young adults are voting, and Latinx are a major part of this newly energized portion of the electorate. Each year, for the next 20 years, approximately 1 million Latinx will turn 18—expanding the influence of the Hispanic vote (Acevedo 2020).

While there was not uniformity among Hispanic voters (e.g., a majority of Cuban Americans voted for Trump), about two out of every three Latinx voted for Joe Biden, playing a major role in his victory (Sonneland 2020). They also helped propel more Latinx into Congress than ever before. As of 2021, there were 39 representatives and 5 senators of Latinx descent in the U.S. Congress.

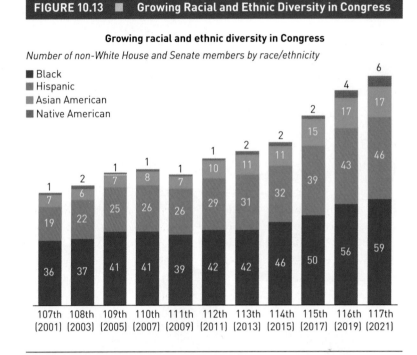

FIGURE 10.13 ■ **Growing Racial and Ethnic Diversity in Congress**

Growing racial and ethnic diversity in Congress

Number of non-White House and Senate members by race/ethnicity

■ Black
■ Hispanic
■ Asian American
■ Native American

Note: Nonvoting delegates and commissioners are excluded. Figures for the 117th Congress are as of Jan. 26, 2021. Asian Americans include Pacific Islanders, and Hispanics are of any race. Members who have more than one racial or ethnic identify for the above groups are counted in each applicable group.

Source: "Growing racial and ethnic diversity in Congress" 2021. https://www.pewresearch. org/fact-tank/2021/01/28/racial-ethnic-diversity-increases-yet-again-with-the-117th-congress/ft_21-01-25_raceethnicitycongress_1/.

CONSIDER THIS

How might an increase in the racial and ethnic diversity in Congress affect legislation?

Check Your Understanding

1. What did the Chicano movement accomplish?

2. Why do many Latinx come to the United States without documents?

3. How has Latinx political participation changed in the past 20 years?

DOING SOCIOLOGY 10.4

Fees to Apply for Citizenship

In this exercise, you will react to the Trump administration's increase of the application fee for citizenship.

The Trump administration attempted to raise the $640 application fee for citizenship to $1,170 (or $1,160 if online). The U.S. Citizenship and Immigration Services claimed that the proposed increase reflected an effort to address the rising costs of processing and vetting these applications.

Write your answers to the following questions:

1. Do you approve of the price hike? Why?

2. If you had to apply for citizenship right now, would you be able to afford to do so?

3. What do you think will be the repercussions of the price hike? (Who will it help? Who will it hurt? How will it effect the U.S. society?)

4. Do you want to change your answer to the first question now? Why or why not?

CONCLUSION

Latinx, members of the largest subordinate racialized group in the United States, face various issues today, including—for many—the threat of deportation; stereotypes, such as all Latinx are undocumented; a racial divide between darker-skinned and lighter-skinned Latinx; and more Latinx self-identifying as White (non-Hispanic) as the number of Latinx and White marriages climb. Fortunately, Latinx people have a history of effective organizing and activism. Many use those tools today as they fight for racial equity in immigrations policies. In the next chapter, we look at other racialized groups in the United States—Jewish, Arab, Middle Eastern, and Muslim Americans.

CHAPTER REVIEW

10.1 How do the Hispanic, Latino/a, and Latinx classifications differ?

Hispanic emerged from the interest by the U.S. government and media to account for the growing U.S. population who had Latin American ancestry. It includes people with ancestors from Spanish-speaking countries. The "Latino/a" category originates from the word *Latinoamericano*, or a person from Latin America. "Latinx" is a gender-neutral, nonbinary alternative to Latino/a.

10.2 How do Latinx groups vary demographically? Give examples that address fertility, population control efforts, and the residential distribution of Latinxs.

Latinx women have higher fertility than Whites, Blacks, and Asians. Specifically, we see that Latinas who self-identify as Mexican or Central American have more children than women who self-identify as Cuban. Simultaneously, Latinas who racially self-identify as White have fewer children that non-White Latinas. Attempts to limit population growth and alleviate "excess labor" on the island of Puerto Rico included a mass sterilization of women.

Overall, Latinxs have been residentially concentrated in specific regions of the United States—California, Texas, and Florida. However, since 2008, Latinx immigrants tend to go to states that traditionally have had few Latinxs, such as in the South and Midwest where many slaughterhouses and farms need to fill jobs so difficult and so low-paying most Whites refuse to do them.

10.3 What is the relationship among income, occupation, education, and socioeconomic status among Latinxs?

Latinxs' have a lower income than Asians and Whites and a higher income than African Americans. Latinxs are overconcentrated in sales and service jobs that have low status. However, even Latinxs that work in professional jobs have lower wages than Whites and Asians, pointing to the role of discrimination in this process. In terms of education, more Latinxs are enrolling in college than ever before, but their college graduation rate remains lower than that of Asians, Whites, and Blacks.

10.4 How have Latinxs engaged in political mobilization seeking justice and racial equity?

Organized Latinx have gained the extension of labor rights to farmworkers, realized the extension of voting rights to linguistic citizen minorities, and pushed for ethnic studies curricula that reflect the contributions of Latinxs in the United States. More recently, Latinxs have taken to the streets to address immigration issues such as deportation and to save the Deferred Action for Childhood Arrivals (DACA) policy. Also, over the past few years, more Latinxs are showing up to vote and gaining more elected offices.

KEY TERMS

Chicano movement (p. 213)

Colorism (p. 204)

Deferred Action for Childhood Arrivals (DACA) (p. 214)

Discrimination (p. 211)

Ethnic group (p. 200)

Identities (p. 203)

Income (p. 209)

Latinx (p. 200)

Naturalization (p. 216)

Office of Management and Budget (p. 200)

Pan-ethnic category (p. 200)

Stereotype (p. 200)

11 JEWISH, ARAB, AND MUSLIM AMERICANS: EXPERIENCING ETHNOCENTRISM AS RACISM

Bradley J. Zopf

LEARNING QUESTIONS

11.1 What characteristics distinguish the Jewish American, Arab American, and Muslim American populations in the United States?

11.2 What are antisemitism, Orientalism, and Islamophobia?

11.3 Why do we use racism as a framework for explaining the prejudice and discrimination experienced by Jews, Arabs, and Muslims?

11.4 What are the similarities and differences among Jewish, Arab, and Muslim Americans' struggles for racial justice?

When you think about race and racism, what comes to mind? Do you ever think about language, accent, national origin, religion, or other cultural characteristics? Ethnocentrism and racism are two related ways of separating people, ranking them as superior or inferior, and making sure more rewards go to the "superior" group. While ranking cultural and religious differences are examples of ethnocentrism, they also can be examples of racialization. Racialization occurs when the dominant group uses ethnicity, national origin, or religion to create an image of other people as different—and inferior—from them culturally to justify the unequal treatment of that group.

This chapter focuses on the historical and contemporary experiences of Jews, Arabs, and Muslims in the United States. You will examine how ethnicity, national origin, and religious differences become racialized and how legal Whiteness, especially for Jews and Arabs, does not protect them from racism.

HOW I GOT ACTIVE IN SOCIOLOGY

Bradley J. Zopf

My official foray into sociology began my freshmen year of college; however, the roots of my sociological journey began in high school unbeknownst to me at the time. When I was a senior in high school I was a member of the student newspaper. I had this idea for a story on the changing norms, values, and understandings around etiquette. I designed an awful survey that I distributed to every student in my school (approximately 500 at the time) during their homeroom class. I received about 150 responses that I tabulated in Excel and analyzed by making graphs and tables by gender and class position. At the time I knew nothing about random or probability sampling or statistical analysis; more importantly, I had never heard of cultural norms, collective consciousness, stereotypes, or other buzzworthy sociological concepts. Needless to say, that survey was not very scientific or even informative, but as I look back it represents a pivotal moment in my own realization that we are very much products of our social world. The funny thing is that I am a qualitative sociologist, so it represented my first, last, and only attempt at designing a survey to answer sociological questions.

JEWS, ARABS, AND MUSLIMS IN THE UNITED STATES

Jews, Arabs, and Muslims are distinct ethnic and religious groups in the United States. Within each group, people share unique characteristics that help them define themselves as a group. Jews use ethnic ancestry, Arabs draw on language and culture, and Muslims employ religion to distinguish their group from others.

Jewish Americans

As Figure 11.1 reveals, for the majority of the 5–7 million Jews currently living in the United States, ethnicity, ancestry, and culture are more important aspects of their Jewish identity than religion. For example, as shown in Figure 11.2, not only do religious Jewish Americans follow a variety of diverse Jewish religions, but 44% of Jewish Americans do not identify as religious at all. Also, while the vast majority of Jewish Americans racially identify as either White or simply as Jewish, Jews of color now represent 12% to 15% of the American Jewish population (Kelman, Tapper, Fonseca, and Saperstein 2019).

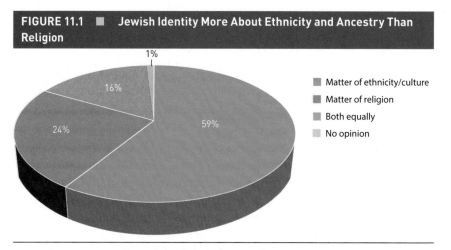

FIGURE 11.1 ■ Jewish Identity More About Ethnicity and Ancestry Than Religion

- Matter of ethnicity/culture
- Matter of religion
- Both equally
- No opinion

Source: Data from https://www.ajc.org/news/survey2019 ("AJC 2019 Survey of American Jewish Opinion"). Figure created by author. "Jewish Identity More About Ethnicity and Ancestry Than Religion."

Survey N = 1,001.

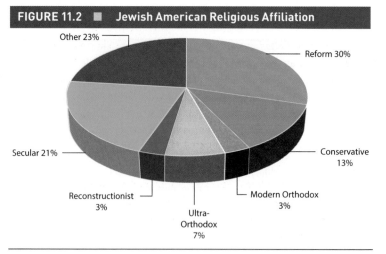

FIGURE 11.2 ■ Jewish American Religious Affiliation

Source: Data from https://www.ajc.org/news/survey2019 ("AJC 2019 Survey of American Jewish Opinion"). Figure created by author. "Jewish Identity More About Ethnicity and Ancestry Than Religion."

Survey N = 1,001.

History of Jewish Americans

In 1654, 23 Jewish refugees from a Dutch colony in Recife, Brazil, settled in New Amsterdam (now New York) as the first Jewish migrants to what became the United States. They faced hostility from then-governor Peter Stuyvesant who called them "the deceitful race" and "the hateful enemies and blasphemers of the name of Christ" (Wenger 2007, 2). That changed, however, beginning in the early 18th century when Sephardic Jews migrated from the Iberian Peninsula—Portugal and Spain—and established a presence in New York as merchants and shopkeepers. Because of their wealth and occupations, by the late 1700s, Jewish people in New York had assimilated into the small European Protestant middle- and upper-class communities, clubs, and organizations. For example, in 1742 Phila Franks, daughter of a prominent Jewish family, married Oliver DeLancy, a member of an upper-class Protestant family in New York City (Wenger 2007). Such unions among Christian and Jewish elites, while rare, were not surprising given the small proportion of educated and upper-class families in New York in the late 18th century (just 1 out of 20 New York residents).

> ### CONSIDER THIS
>
> Remember a time when you started something new: joined a sports team, moved to a new neighborhood, began college, or started a new job. What kinds of difficulties did you face? Now imagine moving to a new country with a different language, culture, and religion. What kinds of difficulties are you likely to encounter?

In the early half of the 19th century, Ashkenazi Jews from German-speaking regions of the Ottoman Empire, Prussia, Bohemia, and Bavaria began migrating to the United States seeking greater economic and religious freedoms. They, too, found success as both peddlers and entrepreneurial business owners. For example, Levi Strauss—founder of Levi Strauss & Co.—arrived in the United States in 1847 as a peddler (Wenger 2007). Though both Sephardic and Ashkenazi Jews initially faced prejudice, they were legally defined as White, providing them access to both citizenship and freedom from institutionalized racial barriers (Fox and Guglielmo 2012).

During the late 19th and early 20th century, more than 2 million Yiddish-speaking Jews escaping religious persecution, especially the pogroms—state-sanctioned violent attacks aimed at the extermination of particular ethnic or religious groups—in Russia, Poland, and Germany, came to the United States. Unlike previous Jewish immigrants, eastern European Jews were unskilled laborers and did not assimilate quickly. In fact, even established Jewish American communities distanced themselves from Yiddish Jews and did not want to be associated with them.

The most well-known Yiddish community established itself on New York City's Lower East Side. There, a robust cultural, economic, and religious enclave developed to cater to the needs of these new immigrants. Yiddish Jews established New York's largest garment industry and owned and operated the famous Triangle Shirtwaist Company, where 145 workers perished in a 1911 fire. The Lower East Side had a popular theater in which dramas, musicals, and operas performed in Yiddish dominated New York City's entertainment scene from 1910 to 1920 (Wenger 2007). As this brief history highlights, Jews in the United States not only built vibrant Jewish communities celebrating their ethnic and religious heritage, but they did so while integrating themselves into American culture.

PHOTO 11.1 Poster advertising Jewish play *Der Rabbi's Mischpocha* (circa 1900) at the Vibrant Jewish Theatre. The advertisement uses incorrect Yiddish, as well as English.

Buyenlarge/Getty Images

Arab Americans

While many people believe that Arabs, Middle Easterners, and Muslims are the same, not all Arabs are Muslim and not all Muslims are Arab. In fact, in the United States there are more Arab Christians than Muslims, and most American Muslims are South Asian. **Arab** is a linguistic and ethnic identity referring to individuals who speak Arabic and/or have family ancestry in Arab regions. **Muslim** is a religious identity referring to those who follow Islam and the Prophet Mohammed's teachings. The term **Middle East** refers to a geographic region including parts of western Asia and North Africa pictured in Figure 11.3.

FIGURE 11.3 ■ **The Middle East is an Ambiguously Defined Geographic Area that Extends from North Africa and Western Asia—morocco to Afghanistan.**

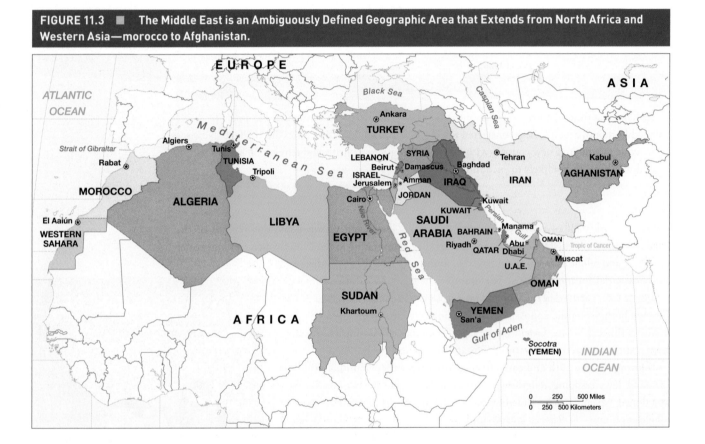

Official statistics indicate that approximately 2 million Arabs live in the United States, but unofficial estimates suggest there are more than 3.5 million (Arab American Institute 2018). This discrepancy between official and unofficial population counts relates to the classification of Middle Eastern, Arab, and North African people in the United States as White. While Arab Americans share a common language and culture, as you can see in Figure 11.4, Arab Americans are among the most ethnically and geographically diverse groups in the United States. Their collective racialization, however, makes it difficult to notice that diversity.

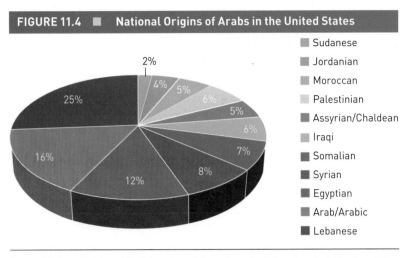

FIGURE 11.4 ■ National Origins of Arabs in the United States

Legend:
- Sudanese
- Jordanian
- Moroccan
- Palestinian
- Assyrian/Chaldean
- Iraqi
- Somalian
- Syrian
- Egyptian
- Arab/Arabic
- Lebanese

Source: "National Origins of Arab Americans" figure from Arab American Institute Foundation, 2018. https://censuscounts.org/wp-content/uploads/2019/03/National_Demographics_SubAncestries-2018.pdf

History of Arab Americans

From 1885 until World War I, approximately 110,000 Arab Christians from the Levant region (now Syria and Lebanon) migrated to the United States seeking both increased economic opportunities and escape from religious persecution in the Muslim-dominant Ottoman Empire (Orfalea 2006). Arab Christian migrants viewed themselves as "*al-Nizaleh*—travelers or guests" who would eventually return to their homelands (Suleiman 1994, 38). Like Jews during this time, Arab Christians became peddlers because it required limited initial resources.

The impact of World War I, alongside the restrictive Immigration Acts of 1921 and 1924, significantly reduced the flow of Arab immigrants. It also meant that Arabs in the United States were not free to leave and then return. They began forming distinctive communities and making the United States their new home.

Until the 1948 Arab-Israeli war and the establishment of Israel as an independent nation, most Arabs in the United States were Christian. The 1948 war drove millions of Palestinians—mostly Muslim—from their homeland into countries such as Syria, Lebanon, Jordan, and Iraq. Over 45,000 Palestinian Muslims sought asylum in the United States. Political and economic upheaval in the Middle East during the 1950s and 60s contributed to additional Arab Muslims leaving their countries of origin in hopes of better economic opportunities in the United States and Europe. For example, after the Immigration and Naturalization Act of 1965, more than 750,000 Arabs, mostly Muslims, came to the United States seeking political freedom and economic opportunity (Orfalea 2006). Unlike Jews who shared ethnic culture and religion, religious differences between first- (Christian) and second-wave immigrants (Muslim) made it difficult to create Arab American communities in the United States.

Muslim Americans

Did you know that 15% to 30% of the African slave population in North America were Muslims? While still only 1.1% of the U.S population (estimates of 3 to 6 million), Muslims are the fastest growing religious group in the United States (Mohammed, Smith, Cooperman, and Schiller 2017). Like Jews and Christians, Muslims belong to different branches—Sunni, Shia, and Sufism. As you can see in Figure 11.5, Muslims are among the most racially and ethnically diverse religious groups in the United States. They represent more than 75 countries, including White Muslims from Europe and White and Black American converts to Islam. Much like Jews and Arabs in the United States, White

FIGURE 11.5 ■ Racial Demographics of U.S. Muslims				

Four-in-ten Muslim American adults are white

	White	Black	Asian	Hispanic	Other/mixed
	%	%	%	%	%
All U.S. Muslims	41	20	28	8	3=100
Foreign born	45	11	41	1	1
U.S. born	35	32	10	17	5
Second generation	52	7	22	17	2
Third generation+	23	51	2	18	7
U.S. general public	64	12	6	16	2

Note: Results repercentaged to exclude nonresponse. Figures may not add to 100% due to rounding. White, black, Asian and other races include only those who are not Hispanic; Hispanics are of any race.

Source: "Four-in-ten Muslim American adults are white." Page 36 of "Findings from Pew Research Center's 2017 survey of U.S. Muslims." Mohammed et al. 2017. https://www.pewresearch.org/wp-content/uploads/sites/7/2017/07/U.S.-MUSLIMS-FULL-REPORT.pdf

Muslims are rarely viewed and treated as White. Instead, their Muslim religious identity often supersedes their race (Husain 2019). Rather than White, Black, or Asian, people view them primarily as Muslim.

Though media portrayals of Muslims in the United States may lead you to assume that most Muslims in the United States are Arab, the majority are South Asian. Muslims from India and Pakistan started immigrating to the United States after the 1965 Immigration and Naturalization Act ended racially restrictive quotas and gave preference to well-educated and highly skilled workers. Highly educated professionals from India and Pakistan came to the United States and tended to establish themselves in the fields of medicine, engineering, and technology. Starting in the 1970s, a group of working-class migrants from Bangladesh started immigrating to the United States as a result of political turmoil in the region (Kurien 2007).

Additionally, many Americans mistake Punjabi Sikhs, members of a monotheistic religion originating in the northern regions of India, for Muslim. This means that many Sikhs face anti-Muslim discrimination and violence. For example, four days after 9/11, a person full of hatred for Muslims shot and killed Balbir Singh Sodhi, a 49-year-old Sikh American, after mistaking him for a Muslim.

African Americans constitute about 20% of the American Muslim population. Perhaps the most well-known group of Black Muslims in the United States is the Nation of Islam (NOI)—a Black religious movement that focuses on Black liberation and self-determination. It describes itself as a Muslim organization but bases its beliefs on a mythology different from that of mainstream Muslim teachings, values, and practices. Using both anti-Christian and radical anti-White rhetoric that appealed to many working-class African Americans, the NOI grew the most during the 1950s and early 1960s when Malcom X, pictured speaking in Photo 11.2, was an active member (Curtis 2002; Tinaz 1996). Today, the Southern Poverty Law Center describes it as a hate group and points out that its current leader, Louis Farrakhan, blames Jewish people for all of the hardships African Americans have faced throughout the history of the United States (Southern Poverty Law Center n.d.).

As you can see, Muslims in the United States are extremely diverse. Despite this diversity, Islam remains a unifying factor for Muslims. In fact, most mosques are multiethnic and cater to the needs of Muslims from diverse national origins and ethnic backgrounds.

PHOTO 11.2 Malcom X speaking at a 1961 Nation of Islam convention in Chicago with then leader of the NOI Elijah Mohammed (center with hat) listening.

Frank Scherschel/The LIFE Picture Collection via Getty Images

---

DOING SOCIOLOGY 11.1

The Diversity of Jews, Arabs, and Muslims in the United States

This exercise requires you to consider the diversity of Jews, Arabs, and Muslims in the United States.

As noted in this section, the racialization of Arab Americans, for example, can make it difficult for some people to appreciate the diversity of people living in the United States who speak Arabic and/or have familial ancestry that traces back to the Arab regions. For each of the three groups discussed in this section—Jews, Arabs, and Muslims—challenge a widely held misconception about the identity with a fact that you learned in this textbook or elsewhere.

Check Your Understanding

1. What aspects do Jews find most important in defining Jewishness?

2. What characteristics do Arabs share?

3. What are the definitions of the following terms: Arab, Middle East, and Muslim?

4. What distinguishes the waves of Arab immigrants to the United States?

5. Why is the Nation of Islam not considered representative of mainstream Islam?

ANTISEMITISM, ORIENTALISM, AND ISLAMOPHOBIA

In Chapter 1 we explained that racism includes both prejudicial beliefs and discriminatory actions. In Chapters 2–5, we described the institutional and cultural supports for systemic racism. In this chapter, we explain why we use racism when examining the prejudice and discrimination experienced by Jews, Arabs, and Muslims.

Antisemitism

Antisemitism, the attitudes used to justify discrimination, exploitation, and exclusion of Jews or those perceived to be Jewish, has a long history characterized by religious persecution, political oppression, and social exclusion (Feldman 2018). Though the term came into use only in the 19th century, anti-semitism has long existed as

> *a persisting latent structure of hostile beliefs toward Jews as collectivity manifested in individuals as attitudes, and in cultures as myth, ideology, folklore, and imagery, and in actions—social or legal discrimination, political mobilization against Jews, and collective or state violence—which result in and/or is designed to distance, displace, or destroy Jews as Jews.* (Fein 1987, 67)

Antisemitism contains the same elements as racism. As you can see in Photo 11.3, antisemitism is a form of individual prejudice, collectively shared beliefs, and institutional practices targeting Jews as people, Judaism as a religion, and Jewish customs.

PHOTO 11.3 A storefront window in the Bronx, New York, in 1944 vandalized by antisemitic graffiti that reads "Please Jaffess vote for Dewey so Jews like you can be thrown out of America."

FPG/Hulton Archive/Getty Images

CONSIDER THIS

What are the first 10 words that come to mind when you think of the Middle East? Why do think you have these ideas about the Middle East?

Orientalism

Orientalism is the ethnocentric practice of seeing cultures in the East (Middle East, Asia, and northern Africa) as inferior to those in the West (Europe and the United States) (Said 1978). The U.S. media has long portrayed Arabs through stereotypes (Alsultany 2012; Shaheen 2008). In Photo 11.4, you can see an illustration of the "Streets in Cairo," exhibited during the 1893 Columbian Exposition in Chicago.

Booths with Syrian, Egyptian, Bedouin, and other Arab groups during this fair served as the earliest cultural representations of the Middle East for widespread consumption by the American public. Stereotypes of Arabs and the Middle East as exotic, uncivilized, barbaric, and sexualized yet oppressed continue to endure in modern-day television shows like *Homeland* and Hollywood films such as *The Dictator* (2012), *American Sniper* (2014), *American Assassin* (2018), and Disney's *Aladdin* (1992/2019) (Haider 2020).

PHOTO 11.4 An illustration of the "Streets in Cairo," an exhibition during the World's Fair in Chicago, Illinois, in 1893.

Museum of Science and Industry, Chicago/Getty Images

Islamophobia

Islamophobia, the irrational fear or prejudice used to justify discrimination, exploitation, and surveillance of Muslims or those perceived to be Muslim, has roots in the wars between Christians and Muslims in the 11th to 13th centuries, as well as the Spanish Inquisition in the 15th century (Rana 2007). Much like antisemitism, Islamophobia contains the same elements as systemic racism. It is a form of individual prejudice, collectively shared beliefs, stereotypes, and institutional practices targeting Muslims.

Antisemitism, Orientalism, and Islamophobia are all forms of prejudicial beliefs. We often use such beliefs to justify unequal treatment and discrimination of such groups. For example, as you learned in Chapter 4, when prejudice is institutionalized, political, economic, and social inequalities result. This makes it important to understand how antisemitism, Orientalism, and Islamophobia impact Jewish, Arab, and Muslim Americans.

PHOTO 11.5 Islamophobic poster stating "Every Real Muslim Is a Jihadist" held by a Trump supporter outside the Republican National Convention in July 2016 in Cleveland, Ohio.

Jim Watson/AFP via Getty Images

DOING SOCIOLOGY 11.2

Understanding Implicit Bias

This exercise requires you to examine implicit biases against Muslims.

In Barack Hussein Obama's 2004 Democratic National Convention speech that amplified his political career, he alluded to the prejudice and discrimination he has faced for simply having an Arabic, "Muslim-sounding" name. In his speech, he asserted "that in a tolerant America, your name is no barrier to success."

Reflect on and write responses to the following questions:

1. What social institutions (e.g., media, education, family) influence the development of implicit Islamophobia?

2. What are some of the Islamophobic ideas that these social institutions promote?

3. How does implicit Islamophobia harm Muslims? What barriers to success do Muslims face as a result of implicit Islamophobia?

4. What can people do to counteract their own implicit biases against Muslims?

Check Your Understanding

1. How do you define the following terms: antisemitism, Orientalism, and Islamophobia?

2. What elements of racism do antisemitism, Orientalism, and Islamophobia share?

3. Why do we need to examine the experiences of Jewish, Arab, and Muslim Americans as a form of racism?

NEGOTIATING RACE AND RACISM: JEWS, ARABS, AND MUSLIMS

Neither Jews, nor Arabs, nor Muslims are officially classified as racial groups. Instead, both Jews and Arabs are officially classified as White, while Muslims may identify as any race. Despite their official classification as White, neither Jews nor Arabs have experienced the full benefits of Whiteness in the United States. What kinds of prejudice and discrimination have Jewish, Arab, and Muslim Americans experienced? At various times in U.S. history, societies have viewed each of these groups as a threat. While Jews tend to be viewed as political and economic threats, Arabs and Muslims share a reputation as the preeminent national security threat (Zopf 2018).

Jews

As Whites, Jews were able to become citizens, own property, intermarry with Christians, and practice their faith relatively free from institutionalized racism. In 1657, four Jewish men were granted "burgher rights"—rights to own property and have political representation—in New Amsterdam. By the early 1700s, Jewish people had established synagogues in the cities of Philadelphia, Newport, Savannah, and Charleston, including Shearith Israel in New York, the first Jewish synagogue in the United States. Although Jews numbered only around 2,500 at the start of the American Revolution, they played a vital role in the revolution. The Continental Congress included Jewish synagogues in its request for prayers of peace months after fighting in Lexington and Concord began in 1775. Hayam Salomon, a prominent Jewish merchant and member of the Sons of Liberty, is often referred to as the "financier of the revolution" for his role in securing loans and other finances necessary for the revolution (American Jewish Historical Society 1999, 4). In 1787, Jonas Phillips of Philadelphia's "Mikveh Israel" (Hope of Israel) congregation successfully lobbied the Continental Congress to include religious freedom in the U.S. Constitution (Wenger 2007).

In 1843, Jewish people formed the oldest and largest Jewish fraternal order, B'nai B'rith (Sons of the Covenant), in New York City. It provided social services for many thousands of Jews and non-Jews. By 1851, the order had established 10 more lodges in other cities (American Jewish Historical Society 1999).

While most Jewish people in the early years of the United States had maintained their religious faith and ethnic heritage, many also adopted American social, political, and cultural practices and customs. American Reform Judaism—a liberal and progressive denomination defined by its willingness to change Orthodox customs, practices, and even beliefs, began in Charleston, South Carolina, in 1824 and Beth Elohim (1841) became the first permanent Reform synagogue in the United States. From the 1850s to the 1870s, Rabbi Isaac Mayer Wise, often referred to as the "architect of the Reform movement," helped establish Reform Judaism as the largest denomination of Judaism in the United States. By 1880, nearly 90% of the 200 Jewish congregations nationwide had some affiliation with the Reform movement (Wenger 2007).

The end of the 19th and beginning of the 20th century were tumultuous times in the United States. During this period, the largest influx of poor, unskilled laborers came to the United States from eastern Europe, China, and Japan. As part of the "broader pattern of late-nineteenth-century racism against all southern and eastern European immigrants," racial pseudoscience defined Blacks, along with incoming immigrants—including Irish, Italians, and Jews—as inferior to Whites (Brodkin 1994, 26). For example, Madison Grant's (1916) book *The Passing of the Great Race* defined Jews as non-White, rather than White. In the South, the Ku Klux Klan terrorized Jews alongside Blacks. The case of Leo Frank provides one example. In 1913, he was falsely accused and convicted of raping and killing a girl who worked in his factory. After the governor, who believed Frank was innocent, commuted his sentence from death to life in 1915, a group of prominent members of the community took him out of the prison and lynched him. This made Jews in the South realize that they, as well as Blacks, were targets for racism. The episode prompted the establishment of the Anti-Defamation League (ADL), the prominent Jewish civil rights group.

In the wake of the Bolshevik Revolution (1919), Jews faced accusations of being communists and portrayals as dangerous radicals and "seditious revolutionaries" (Wenger 2007, 201). In fact, Henry

Ford (founder of Ford Motor Co.) began to regularly publish antisemitic diatribes in the *Dearborn Independent* from 1919 to 1927 outlining his political fears of Jews. As scapegoats, persons or groups blamed for prevailing social, economic, and political problems, Jews endured prejudice and discrimination. For example, because Jews were disproportionately enrolled in America's top universities, many schools began instituting quotas for Jewish applicants. In 1922, Harvard University president A. Lawrence Lowell proposed a quota as an attempt to stem rising antisemitism on campus and protect the reputation of the university (Wenger 2007).

During the 1930s, perhaps the apex of antisemitism in the United States, Americans were reeling from the effects of the Great Depression. Although many held positions of social, economic, and political power, Jewish people as a community found themselves once again the center of blame. For example, President Franklin Delano Roosevelt had many Jews in his cabinet, including Henry Morgenthau Jr. who was secretary of treasury. As a result, "Jews became so closely associated with Roosevelt's program that antisemitic groups frequently attacked the New Deal as the 'Jew Deal'" (Wenger 2007, 213). Meanwhile, Father Coughlin, known as the "radio priest" in the 1930s, spouted vile antisemitic speeches to three out of four Americans (90 million people tuned in every week, out of a population of 123 million) (Wenger 2007).

Public opinion polls in 1938 and 1939 showed that Americans were not concerned about the fate of Jews facing violent discrimination in Europe. Indeed,

- more than half of Americans blamed European Jews for their own persecution,

- more than 75% did not want the United States to increase the quota of Jewish refugees, and

- nearly half of Americans thought Jews had too much power (Welch 2014).

Even as Hitler murdered 6 million Jewish people through his "final solution" (and more people from other marginalized groups), most Americans were not moved to open the nation to more Jewish people fleeing death. It was not until Secretary Morgenthau presented President Roosevelt with "The Report to the Secretary on the Acquiescence of This Government in the Murder of the Jews" at the beginning of 1944 that FDR established a War Refugee Board with the primary purpose of saving Jews from the Nazis (Wenger 2007, 215; see also Jewish Virtual Library n.d.).

Only after the war, when American public media started to spread word of the atrocities of the Holocaust, did attitudes toward Jews become more sympathetic. Public opinion polls of the 1950s demonstrated a sharp decrease in antisemitic attitudes, with only 2% of Americans saying they would not want Jewish neighbors (Wenger 2007). Also, unlike Black soldiers returning from WWII, Jewish GIs benefited from the Servicemen's Readjustment Act of 1944 (or GI Bill), which provided low-interest mortgages to White soldiers returning home.

Today Jewish Americans are among the most educated, socioeconomically mobile, and politically active ethnic communities in the United States. Eight Jewish Americans have become Supreme Court justices, most notably Louise Brandeis (the first in 1916), Ruth Bader Ginsburg (1993–2020), Stephen Breyer (1994–present), and Elena Kagan (2010–present). However, while Jewish Americans are fully integrated into mainstream American society, they continue to face prejudice and discrimination. FBI (2018) hate crime statistics show that only Black Americans face more hate crimes than Jewish Americans. The ADL notes that, in 2019, hate crimes against Jewish people were more numerous than at any time since they started counting them in 1979 (Walters 2020). Americans also have identified another social, cultural, religious, and political enemy: Arabs and Muslims.

Arabs

Arabs in the United States have an ambiguous and complicated relationship with race. While they are officially classified as White, they tend not to receive the same treatment as Whites. How did Arabs come to be officially classified as White? The earliest Arab immigrants were, often incorrectly, classified as Turkish, Greek, Armenian, Asian, or African (Hooglund 1987). Immigration and Naturalization

Services began classifying Arabs as White in 1943 (Cainkar 2018), and the Office of Management and Budget Directive 15 in 1977 led the census to define White as including Arabs, Middle Easterners, and North Africans.

During the early 1900s, in a series of naturalization cases, court cases that determine eligibility for U.S. citizenship, Syrians, Armenians, and other Arabs fought to be classified as White (Gualtieri 2001, 2009; Tehranian 2009). The most famous case involved Syrian George Dow. The courts twice denied Dow's request for naturalization, arguing that Arabs are not members of the "Caucasian race" and are thus not White. However, in Dow's third attempt, in 1915, the U.S. Court of Appeals (*Dow v. United States*) granted him the right to naturalize, establishing for the first time that Arabs could be racially classified as White.

Being classified as White, however, did not prevent Arab Americans from experiencing racism. In 1929, the *New York Evening World* reported the murder of N. G. Romey, a Syrian grocery store owner in Florida, using the headline "Mob in Florida Lynches White Man." Similar to Leo Frank's lynching mentioned earlier, Romey's killing "confirmed that the 'race crisis' was far from over for Syrians and that their status as [White] was suspect" (Gualtieri 2009, 112).

Many Americans started to view Arabs as enemies of the United States after the 1948 Arab-Israeli war that resulted in the creation of Israel as an independent Jewish nation. The one-sided support of Israel and Jewish Americans by the United States coincided with increasingly negative media coverage of Arabs as greedy, uncivilized, violent, and oppressive (Suleiman 1999). Such media coverage adversely affected the relationship between Arab American communities and the rest of the American population. As you can see in Figure 11.6, a majority of Americans continue to support Israelis over Palestinians.

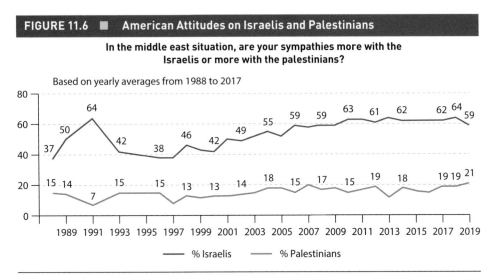

FIGURE 11.6 ■ American Attitudes on Israelis and Palestinians

In the middle east situation, are your sympathies more with the Israelis or more with the palestinians?

Based on yearly averages from 1988 to 2017

At first using the FBI's COINTELPRO program (1956–1971), designed to surveil, disrupt, and infiltrate political organizations such as the Black Panthers, Nation of Islam, and the Southern Christian Leadership Conference, the U.S. government began targeting Arab American organizations and identifying them as enemies of the United States. Immediately after COINTELPRO ended, the U.S. government created Operation Boulder (1972), the first terrorist prevention program. Operation Boulder acted as a screening program for Arabs traveling to the United States. Shortly thereafter, a series of international events solidified narratives depicting Arabs as enemies of the United States (Cainkar 2018). These included the decision by the Organization of Arab Petroleum Exporting Countries (OPEC) in 1973 to stop selling oil to countries supporting Israel (which caused gas shortages in the United States) and the 1979 Iranian hostage crisis, during which Iran held 52 Americans captive for 444 days.

The attack by Al-Qaeda, a Muslim extremist group, on 9/11 increased prejudice against Arabs and Muslims. For example, a Gallup poll taken a few days after 9/11 showed that nearly 50% of respondents felt Arabs in the United States should be required to carry special identification cards. It also indicated that most Americans favored profiling Arabs, especially in airports (Jones 2001). Similarly, in 2003, nearly 49% of Americans surveyed supported increased surveillance of Muslim Americans, and 41% supported detentions of Arabs or Muslims suspected of terrorist activity without any evidence (Jamal 2008). Even more troubling, FBI data show a doubling of anti-Arab hate crimes from 2015 to 2017, a period during the presidential campaign of 2016 and the early years of Donald Trump's presidency. In that time, Trump repeatedly and loudly associated Arab Muslims with terrorism and prohibited immigration from five predominantly Muslim nations (and Venezuela and North Korea). This history makes clear that Arab Americans do not have the privileges of Whiteness despite having a White racial classification.

Muslims

How can Muslims, a religious group composed of people from different races and ethnicities, experience racism? The U.S. government began to treat Muslims as potential terrorists prior to 9/11. For example, a Reagan administration policy allowed federal officers to arrest and detain legal migrants from Arab Muslim countries. However, the terrorist attacks of September 11, 2001, in which four planes hijacked by Al-Qaeda operatives, two of which destroyed the World Trade Center towers, ushered in an unending "war on terror." This war involved political, economic, and military policies, programs, and practices aimed at ending radical Islamic terrorism both at home and abroad. It first targeted Al-Qaeda, then the Taliban, and now ISIS (Independent Islamic State of Iraq and Syria).

Shortly after 9/11, President George W. Bush signed off on the USA PATRIOT Act (otherwise known as Uniting and Strengthening America by Providing Appropriate Tools Required to Intercept and Obstruct Terrorism). The PATRIOT Act expanded surveillance of Muslims in the United States by allowing law enforcement broader discretion to arrest and detain those suspected of potential terrorist activity. The U.S. government justified such policies, programs, and practices under the framework of national security. Within 7 days of 9/11, the FBI fielded 96,000 calls about potential terrorist activity, most of which involved suspicions related to Arab, South Asian, and/or Muslim citizens of the United States. After 9/11, more than 1,200 citizens and noncitizens of primarily Arab and South Asian ancestry were detained and interrogated (Cainkar 2018).

PHOTO 11.6 President Bush gives a 2004 speech in Hershey, Pennsylvania, trying to garner support to expand provisions of the USA PATRIOT Act.

Luke Frazza/AFP via Getty Images.

CONSIDER THIS

Think about the last time you visited an airport. What were some of the things you worried most about? What is the process of going through TSA checkpoints like for you?

Racial profiling of Muslims in airports by TSA has risen in the past decade such that phrases like "flying while Muslim" and "flying while brown" have become almost as common as "driving while Black" (Blackwood, Hopkins, and Reicher 2015). Heightened surveillance of Muslims has been described as "**terror profiling**," the selective targeting of Muslims for additional searches based on a combination of skin color, religious dress, Arabic name, and national origin (Chon and Arzt 2005). For example, numerous news stories have documented the experiences of Muslims (and those mistakenly assumed to be Muslim) being harassed, and even removed from planes, when trying to travel. For example, a flight attendant told passenger Mohamed Ahmed, "I'll be watching you" (Revesz 2016). More recently, Isam Abdallah and Abderraoof Alkhawaldeh found themselves questioned by the FBI and TSA after their initial flight was canceled because a flight attendant reported them as suspicious (Al Jazeera 2019).

As you can see in Figures 11.7 and 11.8, Muslim Americans experience all forms of discrimination, and such experiences are becoming more common. Eighty-two percent of people in the United States say that Muslim Americans face some or a lot of discrimination (Masci 2019). Fueled by vitriolic attacks in news and social media, including those of President Trump, the 3-year span from 2015 to 2017 saw a nearly 122% increase in anti-Muslim hate crimes compared to the 13-year average prior, including those years immediately after 9/11 (Council on American-Islamic Relations 2018).

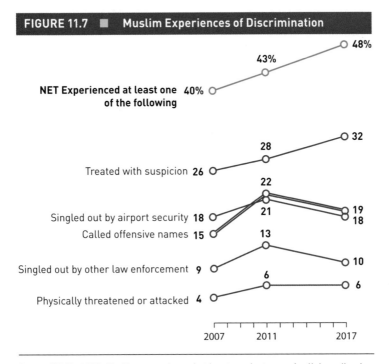

FIGURE 11.7 ■ Muslim Experiences of Discrimination

Source: "Half of U.S. Muslims experienced at least one instance of religious discrimination in the past year" from Pew Research Center survey conducted Jan. 23-May 2, 2017. From "U.S. Muslims Concerned About Their Place in Society, but Continue to Believe in the American Dream," 2017. https://www.pewforum.org/2017/07/26/findings-from-pew-research-centers-2017-survey-of-us-muslims/

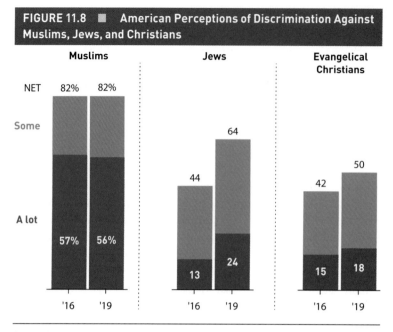

FIGURE 11.8 ■ American Perceptions of Discrimination Against Muslims, Jews, and Christians

Source: "Most Americans say Muslims subject to discrimination," Pew Research Center survey of U.S. adults conducted March 20-25, 2019. From "U.S. Muslims Concerned About Their Place in Society, but Continue to Believe in the American Dream," 2017. https://www.pewresearch.org/wp-content/uploads/sites/7/2017/07/U.S.-MUSLIMS-FULL-REPORT.pdf

So why do we use racism as a framework for explaining the prejudice and discrimination faced by Jews, Arabs, and Muslims in the United States? First, like Blacks, Latinx, Asians, and Native Americans, stereotypes portray Jews, Arabs, and Muslims as inferior biologically and culturally. Second, Jews, Arabs, and Muslims face prejudice and discrimination that has resulted in disadvantages and inequality for them. Racism, thus, best captures the consequences of historical and contemporary antisemitism, Orientalism, and Islamophobia.

DOING SOCIOLOGY 11.3

Perceived Discrimination Against Religious Groups

This exercise requires you to think about the results of a Pew Research Center poll that measured American perceptions of discrimination against Muslims, Jews, and evangelical Christians. (See Figure 11.8.)

Write your answers to the following questions and be prepared to discuss them with your peers:

1. As you learned in this chapter, there was nearly a 122% increase in anti-Muslim hate crimes from 2015 to 2017. Given this spike in anti-Muslim discrimination, why do you think the percentage of people who said that there is "some" or "a lot" of discrimination against Muslims did not increase as well?

2. Why do you think there was a 20% increase in Americans who said that Jews are subject to some or a lot of discrimination from 2016 to 2019?

3. Why do you think there was an 8% increase in Americans who said that evangelical Christians are subject to some or a lot of discrimination from 2016 to 2019?

4. Are you surprised by the results of this poll? Why or why not?

1. What types of prejudice and discrimination have Jewish, Arab, and Muslim Americans experienced?

2. Why were most Americans unsympathetic to Jewish people facing extermination during World War II?

3. When did Arab American communities first begin to experience governmental surveillance?

4. What is the USA PATRIOT Act, and how did it impact Arab and Muslim Americans?

FIGHTING FOR RACIAL JUSTICE

Jewish, Arab, and Muslim Americans have not been passive in the face of negative stereotyping, prejudicial attitudes, and various forms of discrimination. They have created organizations that continually fight for racial justice—both for themselves and others.

Jewish American Activism and Advocacy

As noted earlier, Jewish leaders established the Anti-Defamation League (ADL), the largest and most active Jewish American advocacy organization, in 1913 in response to the Leo Frank case. Since its founding, the ADL has fought tirelessly to improve the image and lives of Jewish people in the United States. For example, in addition to supporting the defense of Leo Frank, the ADL published "the Poison Pen: Further Revelations Concerning Anti-Semitic Propaganda in the United States" to counter Henry Ford's vitriol in the *Dearborn Independent*; it also campaigned to stop negative stereotyping of Jewish immigrants in New York City. Beyond struggling against antisemitism, the ADL has been at the forefront of racial justice efforts for other marginalized groups, such as Blacks during the civil rights movement. Its mission is "to stop the defamation of the Jewish people, and to secure justice and fair treatment for all" (ADL n.d.).

Jewish Americans have been at the forefront of social justice advocacy, combating all forms of discrimination and oppression. For example, the reform movement issued a "call to racial justice" in 1963, "imploring members to work for universal civil rights as part of their responsibilities as Jews" (Wenger 2007, 294). Jewish Americans, especially women, participated in the women's liberation movement in the 1960s and 1970s. Betty Friedan, author of the *Feminine Mystique*, referenced her Jewish heritage in several speeches during the movement (Wenger 2007). More recently, the Anti-Defamation League has publicly supported Black Lives Matter.

PHOTO 11.7 Rabbi Abraham Joshua Heschel marching alongside Reverend Martin Luther King Jr. on the first March to Montgomery in March 1965.

William Lovelace/Daily Express/Hulton Archive/Getty Images

Arab American Activism and Advocacy

Early activism by Arab Americans during the Jim Crow era focused on gaining access to the racial label of White. This enabled them to avoid some racial segregation and discrimination and become citizens (Love 2017). Perhaps because of this label, Arab Americans tended not to become politically or socially active until the latter half of the 20th century.

The creation of the first Arab American organization, the Association of Arab American Undergraduates (AAUG) in 1968 was a direct response to negative news coverage of Arabs during the second Arab-Israeli war in 1967 (Gualtieri 2018). The AAUG focused on American foreign policies and urged President Nixon to recognize the interests of Palestinians in both the United States and abroad. While the AAUG focused on foreign policy issues, the American-Arab Anti-Discrimination Committee (ADC), established in 1980, works on countering negative stereotypes and anti-Arab bias by promoting ethnic and cultural knowledge of Arabs. Today it is the largest Arab American grass-roots organization in the United States and has 24 chapters across 20 states. The ADC also provides legal advice, educational programming, and a variety of academic scholarships to Arab Americans. Meanwhile, the Arab American Institute (AAI), created in 1985, focuses on increasing Arab Americans' political and civic engagement and produces demographic, political, social, and economic information on Arabs in the United States.

Since the 1980s, the ADC and AAI have worked together advocating for a separate ethnic or racial classification for Arab Americans (Kayyali 2013). For example, immediately prior to the 2010 census the AAI launched a "Check It Right, You Ain't White" campaign directing Arab Americans to select the "other" racial category. In response, the U.S. Census Bureau successfully tested a Middle Eastern/North African (MENA) category. However, the census decided not to include the MENA category in the 2020 census, opting instead for more testing.

DOING SOCIOLOGY 11.4

U.S. Racial Classifications and Fighting Racism

This exercise requires you to evaluate the racial and ethnic categories on the United States census.

The 2020 U.S. census included six racial categories: American Indian or Alaska Native, Asian, Black or African American, Native Hawaiian or Other Pacific Islander, White, and Some Other Race. It also included two ethnic categories: Hispanic and Latino and Not Hispanic or Latino.
  Write answers to the following questions:

1. How do you racially identify? Which racial category or categories does this place you in? Do you feel that your racial identity and categorization are consistent? Why or why not?

2. Are these classifications consistent or inconsistent with the experiences of Jews, Muslims, and Arabs in the United States? Why might Arab Americans want their own racial category? Should all racialized groups have racial categories? Why or why not?

3. How do racial and ethnic categories in the U.S. census relate to racial justice?

4. What changes, if any, would you suggest for the current racial categories on the U.S. census—and why?

Muslim American Activism and Advocacy

Organizations such as the Islamic Society of North America, the Council on American-Islamic Relations, and South Asian Americans Leading Together have become integral in countering Islamophobia. Today, the Council on American-Islamic Relations (CAIR) is the largest Muslim American advocacy organization in the United States. CAIR counters negative stereotyping in the media; provides educational programming about Islam and Muslims; promotes youth development through internships; tracks hate crimes and incidents of Islamophobia targeting Muslims; and actively lobbies local, state, and federal governments on behalf of Muslim American rights.

South Asian Americans Leading Together (SAALT), formed in 2000, is a "national, nonpartisan, nonprofit organization that fights for racial justice and advocates for civil rights of all South Asians in the United States" (SAALT n.d.). Though not specifically Muslim, South Asians often face Islamophobia. SAALT's racial justice programs include raising awareness about Islamophobia and racial profiling targeting Muslims, South Asians, Arabs, and Sikhs alike.

As mentioned earlier, both Muslim and African American communities experience heightened surveillance and policing of their communities. Today, in addition to fighting Islamophobia, Muslim Americans fight alongside African Americans against police violence. For example, after the police shooting of Michael Brown in Ferguson, Missouri, in 2014, Linda Sarsour, a Palestinian Muslim, founded Muslims for Ferguson in solidarity with Black Lives Matter. CAIR also publicly supports the Black Lives Matter movement (CAIR 2020). In 2020, local organizations, such as the Arab American Action Network in Chicago, participated in the protests following the killing of George Floyd by a Minneapolis police officer. Our Sociologist in Action, Maheen Haider, recognizes the importance of building interracial, interethnic, and interreligious movements.

SOCIOLOGISTS IN ACTION
Maheen Haider

How Being a Brown, Pakistani, Muslim, Academic and Immigrant Woman Influences My Work

I was born in a region notoriously known by Westerners as the breeding ground of terrorism, yet I recall it as the most peaceful place in the world: Pakistan. Pakistan is my home, my country of origin, and the place where I first learned the virtues of self-reflection and tolerance. Today, Pakistan is simultaneously fighting an internal war against terrorism and an external war against the politically and socially constructed image of itself as the breeding ground of terror. Little did I know as a child that my identity as a Pakistani and the intersection of my identities today as a Brown, Pakistani, Muslim, academic, and immigrant woman would raise questions and concerns for me both personally and professionally in my country of destination, my new home, the United States.

My contributions to the ideals of ethno-racial and cultural diversity and inclusion stem from my multifaceted identity and my sociological work. My racial, ethnic, gender, and professional identities allow me to view society through multiple, intersecting lenses. I use them in everything I do. Regarding research, I conduct in-depth interviews

PHOTO 11.8

© Maheen Haider

to examine the complex construction of non-White, high-skilled, and Muslim immigrant identity in the United States, and the first-generation experience of transitioning from short- to long-term migrant status. I also examine the construction of the Muslim identity in visual media, specifically the post-9/11 representations of Muslims and Arabs in high-grossing Hollywood films.

My sociological work and my own experiences enable me to comprehend the struggles of underrepresented populations. They both have taught me how to understand the processes of inclusion and exclusion. They also impact my perceptions of diversity that I inculcate both in my teaching pedagogy and analytical research.

I draw from the sociological insights of my personal experiences and bring them into my class to ensure that all my students feel included—regardless of their identities. I work passionately with my students to create an environment of inclusivity so they can share their viewpoints and engage respectfully with each other while acknowledging their differences. I foster an environment of reconciliation and engaged scholarship because I firmly believe that diverse thoughts are pro-foundly important for intellectual advancement.

Maheen Haider is an advanced graduate student in the Sociology Department at Boston College.

Discussion Question

What do you think Haider means when she says "diverse thoughts are profoundly important for intellectual advancement"? Do you agree? Why or why not?

Check Your Understanding

1. How have Jewish Americans advocated for themselves and other marginalized groups against stereotypes and discrimination?

2. How has Arab American activism changed since the Jim Crow era?

3. How have Muslims mobilized across racial and ethnic boundaries to form solidarity movements for racial justice?

CONCLUSION

By examining how national origin, ethnicity, and religion are racialized, you can understand how Jews, Arabs, and Muslims share experiences of prejudice, discrimination, and racism similar to that of the racial groups you examined in Chapters 6–10. While both Jews and Arabs are officially White, they often do not experience their Whiteness as a form of privilege. Unlike Jews and Arabs, Muslims are neither a racial nor ethnic group but rather experience a collective racialization as anti-American terrorists. Looking ahead, Chapter 12 focuses on how interracial marriage and multiracial identification further challenge conceptualizations of race in the United States.

CHAPTER REVIEW

11.1 What characteristics distinguish the Jewish American, Arab American, and Muslim American populations in the United States?

*   The U.S. census classifies Jewish people as White. Jewish Americans use ethnic ancestry, culture, and religion to define their Jewishness. Among the 5 to 7 million Jews in the United States, most racially identify as White, though 12% to 15% identify as Jews of color. Jewish Americans identify across several branches of Judaism, including Reform, Orthodox, Ultra Orthodox, and Reconstructionist.

*   The U.S. census defines White as any of the original peoples of Europe, the Middle East, or North Africa. It defines Arab Americans as White. Among the 2 to 4 million Arabs in the United States, the majority share a common language and ancestry they use to identify themselves. Arabs in the United States use national origin, ethnicity, and especially religion to distinguish between themselves.

*   Muslims share a religious identity but are racially, ethnically, and religiously diverse. They are the fastest growing religious group in the United States. Among the 3 to 6 million Muslims in the United States, most are South Asian, followed by Arab and Black.

11.2 What are antisemitism, Orientalism, and Islamophobia?

*   *Antisemitism* is the set of attitudes used to justify practices resulting in discrimination, exploitation, and/or exclusion of Jews or those perceived to be Jewish. Historical examples include excluding Jews from public office and blaming Jews for political and/or economic

problems. Contemporary examples include hate crimes against Jews and stereotypes portraying Jews as greedy and untrustworthy.

- *Orientalism* is a set of ideologies and practices that produce distorted images and knowledge about Arab peoples and culture, Middle Eastern geography, and Islam as a religion. Historic examples include movies such as Disney's *Aladdin* that employ stereotypes of Arabs as exotic, barbaric, or uncivilized. Contemporary examples include movies such as *American Sniper* that depict Arab women as oppressed and the Middle East as backward and uncivilized (i.e., a place of sand, tents, and camels). Orientalism includes governmental programs, such as COINTELPRO and Operation Boulder, that target Arabs as potential terrorists.

- *Islamophobia* is the irrational fear or prejudice against Islam as a religion and Muslims as people. Islamophobia justifies negative stereotyping of Muslims, as well as institutional policies and practices designed to surveil and police Muslims and those perceived to be Muslim. Historical examples of Islamophobia include the Crusades and Spanish Inquisition. Contemporary forms of Islamophobia include President Trump's travel ban, policies enacted under the USA PATRIOT Act, and terror profiling of Muslims at airports.

11.3 Why do we use racism as a framework for explaining the prejudice and discrimination experienced by Jews, Arabs, and Muslims?

We use racism as a framework for understanding the experiences of Jews, Arabs, and Muslims in the United States because it signifies the historical and contemporary similarities in experiences of prejudice and discrimination experienced by Jews, Arabs, and Muslims and Blacks, Hispanics/Latinx, Asians, and Native Americans. First, we use racism because it best captures how stereotypes portray Jews, Arabs, and Muslims as biologically and culturally inferior. Second, we use racism because Jews, Arabs, and Muslims faced, and continue to experience, prejudice and discrimination that limits their opportunities and creates inequalities. Finally, racism best captures the consequences of historical and contemporary antisemitism, Orientalism, and Islamophobia.

11.4 What are the similarities and differences among Jewish, Arab, and Muslim Americans' struggles for racial justice?

Jewish, Arab, and Muslim Americans fight for racial justice in a variety of ways. Each group has both its own history of activism and unique strategies to achieve justice. Jewish Americans have challenged antisemitism through political and media campaigns. Jewish Americans also fought alongside Blacks and women in their struggles for equality. Arab Americans have addressed Orientalism through educational awareness programs. They also worked to attain a White racial classification so that they could become naturalized citizens. For the past couple of decades, many Arabs have advocated (without success) for a separate racial or ethnic MENA category on the U.S. census. Muslims have fought Islamophobia through media, political, and grassroots organizing and, recently, have joined interethnic and interracial solidarity movements (e.g., with Black Lives Matter).

KEY TERMS

Antisemitism (p. 230)

Arab (p. 226)

COINTELPRO (p. 235)

Islamophobia (p. 231)

Middle East (p. 226)

Muslim (p. 226)

Nation of Islam (p. 228)

Naturalization cases (p. 235)

Operation Boulder (p. 235)

Orientalism (p. 230)

Pogroms (p. 225)

Racialization (p. 223)

Reform Judaism (p. 233)

Scapegoats (p. 234)

Terror profiling (p. 237)

USA PATRIOT Act (p. 236)

War on terror (p. 236)

CHALLENGING AND CHANGING RACIAL CATEGORIES? INTERRACIAL MARRIAGE AND MULTIRACIAL AMERICANS

Naliyah Kaya

LEARNING QUESTIONS

12.1 Why have interracial relationships between Whites and people of color been viewed as a problem in the United States?

12.2 How has racial discrimination affected interracial families and bi/multiracial people in the United States?

12.3 How has the media shaped our views about interracial relationships, multiracial families, and bi/multiracial people?

12.4 How has the multiracial movement used organized power and social science to change attitudes, laws, policies, and practices?

12.5 Why does multiraciality fail to solve institutional racism?

Getting married is an exciting time in many of our lives. Imagine booking your wedding venue, beginning wedding preparations, and suddenly being told, without an explanation, that you can no longer get married there. That is exactly what happened to a couple living in Mississippi.

After hearing this news, the groom-to-be's sister immediately contacted the owner of the event hall. The owner explained the cancellation was due to her religious beliefs, saying, "First of all, we don't do gay weddings or mixed race . . . because of our Christian race, I mean, our Christian belief" (Chiu 2019). It is likely that the venue owner discovered the couple is **interracial** (of different races) from looking at the bride-to-be's Facebook page. The event hall owner apologized online, after millions of people saw a video of the conversation on social media. The responses online were overwhelmingly negative. Many labeled the event hall owner a racist and advocated for shutting down the venue. The venue owner attempted to explain herself saying that "as a child growing up in Mississippi" it was an unspoken rule that you stay "with your own race" (Chiu 2019).

HOW I GOT ACTIVE IN SOCIOLOGY

Naliyah Kaya

I've always had a passion for reading. Drawn to biographies and autobiographies, I was intrigued by how peoples' environments and experiences shaped their lives. My mom once found library books about gang members in my room and confronted me, thinking I wanted to join a gang. The truth was that she had a budding sociologist on her hands who wanted to understand why people joined gangs. The more I learned about how social structures created a role for gangs, the more I wanted to find avenues to address social problems such as poverty, racism, and mass incarceration. One of the ways I felt this could be done was through the power of storytelling.

In college I began getting involved in spoken-word poetry and volunteered at a local men's prison. I facilitated poetry classes for the Black Prisoner's Caucus and shared their stories at my college to raise awareness about the social structures that led to many of the men being incarcerated. Now as a "poetic" public sociologist, I continue to use the power of storytelling in my spoken word and sociology courses and remain involved in the arts and educational initiatives for currently and formerly incarcerated and justice-impacted students.

HISTORICAL OVERVIEW OF MULTIRACIAL PEOPLE IN AMERICA

As you were reading the opening story, you may have initially thought it was a historical case of discrimination that took place before or during the U.S. civil rights era (1940s–1960s) until the references about social media and the owner receiving backlash for her racist views. Sadly, this situation happened in 2019. It provides an example of the fact that racist ideas about interracial marriages persist. Sexual, romantic, and abusive interracial relationships and biracial (descended from two races) and multiracial (descended from several or many races) offspring have existed throughout history as people came into contact with one another through war, trading routes, religion, labor, and colonization. Some of the first well-documented intimate interracial relationships and bi/multiracial offspring, in what is now the United States, appeared after European settler colonizers arrived. One of the most well-known examples of racial mixing is that of Matoaka, famously known by her nickname Pocahontas, and John Rolfe.

PHOTO 12.1 Painting of Matoaka (Pocahontas) by W. Langdon Kihn.

Interfoto / GRANGER.

Their marriage likely occurred as a way of forging an alliance between the English and the Powhatan. Englishman John Rolfe was under pressure to make the Virginia colony of Jamestown profitable for England. He realized that by marrying Pocahontas, he would gain access to the sacred practice of curing tobacco from the Powhatan, which was not shared with outsiders. After learning how the Powhatan processed tobacco, Rolfe began using their techniques. His tobacco became sought after in England, and the profits saved Jamestown (Schilling 2017). In such relationships, women tended to have little—if any—choice. Moreover, with the power differential between White men and women of color, it is difficult to describe interracial relationships between them during this time as consensual. This is particularly true of interracial contact between enslaved Africans and White Americans.

Such relationships posed a problem for the institution of slavery. Colonists soon created **antimiscegenation** laws prohibiting marriage, sexual relations, and cohabitation between people of different races. Many of these laws lasted through most of the civil rights era as a way of protecting the "purity" of the White race from "inferior races." For White women and Black/African men, breaking antimiscegenation laws resulted in severe punishment for those involved. For example, An Act Concerning Negroes & other Slaves (1664) in Maryland punished White women who married enslaved Black men with enslavement. Both the women and their children became the property of the husband's master. However, White slave holders could rape the people they enslaved, viewed as property, without fear of repercussion. This created quite the conundrum. How could White racial purity be preserved if White slave holders were producing mixed-race children?

Race, Multiracial People, and Slavery

To maintain White purity *and* allow for the rape of enslaved women, the offspring created from these assaults were deemed non-White and the property of their fathers. As noted, race and racism developed out of the need for cheap labor and as a way wealthy, White landowners could rationalize their use of an enslaved workforce. To protect the White race from contamination by the offspring of male owners and enslaved women, southern states created legislation that became known as the "one-drop rule." This worked to ensure that anyone who had even one ancestor of sub-Saharan African ancestry would be considered and treated as non-White.

Because the original antimiscegenation laws focused on White–Black relationships, as immigrants from other countries considered racially inferior to Whites arrived (as new sources of inexpensive labor) states expanded their antimiscegenation laws to include them as well. For example, in 1865, Arizona expanded its antimiscegenation laws to ban and nullify marriages and any other kind of sexual relationship between White residents and " negroes, mulattoes, indians, or mongolians" (Hoyt 1877, 317). People who violated the law were subject to fines and up to 10 years in prison.

Some Whites felt that antimiscegenation laws were not widespread enough. Because state rules and punishments for interracial marriage varied by location, with some states never adopting them, there was the potential for legal interracial relationships to occur in some parts of the United States. This led to multiple efforts to amend the Constitution to ban interracial marriage between Whites and people of color on a federal level. Had they succeeded in amending the Constitution, the few states without antimiscegenation laws would have been required to adopt them.

Race and Class: Maintaining the Social Hierarchy

As briefly discussed at the beginning of the chapter, White **eugenicists** (people who strove to "improve" the genetics of the human population by eliminating so-called negative or inferior traits) saw non-Whites as a threat to the purity and continuance of the White race. They also saw people of color as a threat to their superior position in society—particularly if they should eventually outnumber Whites. Rather than acknowledging the racial discrimination designed to hurt people of color and benefit Whites, eugenicists argued that the lower socioeconomic status of non-Whites proved their biological inferiority. In fact, eugenicists and some social workers argued that sterilizing women of color was helpful to them. They believed that by taking away their ability to have children they were saving these women from a lifetime of poverty.

Sterilization of women of color was also a way to prevent the birth of interracial children. White people heard warnings that having children with non-Whites would be disastrous. For example, in *The Passing of The Great Race*, Madison Grant (1936, 18) argued that the "crossing" of a White person with a non-White person (e.g., Native American, Asian, Black, Hindu, Jewish—he viewed these latter religious designations as non-White racial categories) would result in the creation of a "lower type," thus polluting and ending the White race.

The designation of children of mixed racial ancestry to the subordinate (lower) racial category within a society is known as **hypodescent**. In some states, health officials acted as "racial police" making sure people did not list children with non-White ancestry as White. During the Jim Crow era in Virginia, the state defined a White person as one with "no trace whatsoever of any blood other than Caucasian" with the exception of "persons who have one-sixteenth or less of the blood of the American Indian and have no other non-Caucasic blood" (Plecker 1924, 4). This exception, informally called the "Pocahontas clause/exception," allowed elite families of Virginia, who proudly claimed to be the descendants of Thomas Rolfe—Pocahontas and John Rolfe's son, to remain White despite asserting Native American ancestry (Wolfe 2015).

CONSIDER THIS

How does the "Pocahontas clause" reveal that racial groupings are socially constructed?

DOING SOCIOLOGY 12.1

Race as a Social Construct

In this exercise you will explore how you racially identify people, particularly when you are unsure of a person's racial identity.

Write answers to the following questions:

1. If someone's racial identity is not immediately apparent to you, how do you attempt to determine it? Do you use the one-drop rule or stereotypes to help you place them in a racial category or categories? If so, why?

2. Is this phenomenon of not being able to immediately place people in a racial category or categories new? Why or why not?

3. Is your own racial category or categories clear to others, or do people have difficulty racially identifying you? How does this affect your life?

Asian Immigration: Xenophobia

With immigration laws closing the door on Chinese and Japanese immigrants in the late 1800s and early 1900s, U.S. employers turned to Filipinos for a source of low-cost labor. After the United States took possession of the Philippines following the Spanish–American War in 1898, Filipino agricultural laborers began to settle in Hawaii and California. They, like Chinese and Japanese immigrants, were met with anti-Asian sentiment and discrimination.

The United States greatly valued Filipinos as a source of cheap labor, but their existence was conditional. Filipino immigrants were expected to assimilate but refrain from personal interactions with Whites. If they abided by these conditions they were tolerated. If not, their lives were at risk.

In 1930, shortly after the start of the Great Depression, Watsonville, California, erupted in violent mobs. For 5 days, young, mostly White men attacked, robbed, and ran Filipinos out of their homes. One victim, Fermin Tobera, was shot while hiding in a closet. His killer was never indicted. Of the hundreds of White men who participated in the anti-Filipino terrorism, only eight were arrested and convicted (Showalter 1989). The economic downturn and interracial relationships were the primary sparks behind the attacks. In an interview in the local paper Judge Rohrback summed up much of the anti-Filipino sentiment Whites held:

> With the arrival of every boat-load of Filipinos . . . a boatload of [White] American men and women are thrown out of the labor markets to lives of crime, indolence and poverty because, for a wage that a white man can not exist on, the Filipinos will take the job and, through the clannish, low standard mode of housing and feeding, practiced among them, will soon be well clothed, and . . . strutting about like a peacock and endeavoring to attract the eyes of the young American and Mexican girls. (Resolution Flaying 1930, p. 1)

He further warned that White and Filipino marriages would become common and predicted the following:

> If the present state of affairs continues . . . there will be 40,000 half-breeds in the State of California before ten years have passed . . . the union of east and west will produce a group that will in all measures be a detriment to the attainment of a higher standard of man and woman-hood. The Filipino, through his unsanitary living habits . . . is a disease carrier. He spreads meningitis germs among the products he handles and innocent persons suffer through their consumption. (Resolution Flaying 1930, p. 1)

Judge Rohrback was certainly not alone in his beliefs about the inferiority of people of color and immigrants during that time. Even today we continue to see similar attitudes displayed—blaming immigrants for "stealing jobs" and accusing them of seeking out American marriage partners for money and/or access to citizenship—as shown in the popular shows *90 Day Fiancé* and *90 Day Fiancé: The Other Way*. The next section further explores the impacts of prejudice and discrimination on immigrants and people of color participating in interracial relationships in the United States.

Check Your Understanding

1. Why have some people viewed interracial relationships between Whites and people of color as a problem in the United States?

2. What is the connection between eugenics and racism?

3. What are the "one-drop rule" and hypodescent?

4. What purpose did antimiscegenation laws serve?

5. What two things sparked the Watsonville riots?

IMPACTS OF DISCRIMINATION

Marysville, Michigan, city council candidate Jean Cramer made headlines in 2019 when she said that she wanted to keep her city as White as possible and that interracial couples shouldn't get married (Smith 2019). To this day, interracial couples face stares and discrimination. When traveling through some parts of the United States or when deciding where to live, they have to consider their safety. In essence, they face sanctions for personal decisions read by society as political statements.

CONSIDER THIS

See Figure 12.1. As someone who is in an interracial relationship, part of a multiracial family, or a bi/multiracial person, which cities or states would you feel most safe to live and work in in the United States? Why? Where do you think you would feel least safe? Why?

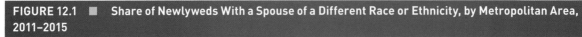

FIGURE 12.1 ■ Share of Newlyweds With a Spouse of a Different Race or Ethnicity, by Metropolitan Area, 2011–2015

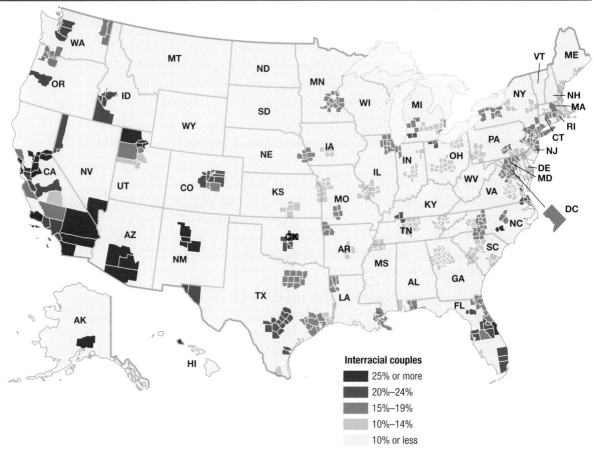

Source: "Intermarriage across the U.S. by metro area" 2017. https://www.pewsocialtrends.org/interactives/intermarriage-across-the-u-s-by-metro-area/

Sanctioning of Personal Decisions

Bi/multiracial people were historically, and in some areas continue to be, considered and treated as deviants. They have faced labels often used to describe animals, such as half-breed, crossbreed, mutt, mixed breed, mongrel, and mixed blood. These terms came out of a culture where belonging to a singular (**monoracial**) racial group and marrying within it was viewed as the norm. When a person dates or marries interracially, many people see it as a public rejection of their own race and culture. Japanese "war brides" and their U.S. soldier husbands dealt with such reactions in Japan and the United States during and after World War II.

War Brides

Military occupations have always brought people from different countries and cultures together, sometimes resulting in interracial marriage. These marriages do not necessarily have fairytale endings. Historically, foreign women, particularly women of color, who came to the United States with their American husbands found themselves caught between home countries—where some viewed them as traitors—and a new home where, in addition to language and cultural differences, they encountered prejudice, racism, and xenophobia. Japanese war bride daughters Lucy Craft, Karen Kasmauski, and Kathryn Tolbert describe such experiences in the 2015 film *Fall Seven Times, Get Up Eight: The Japanese War Brides.* They state that in Japan, even today, the term *war bride* invokes thoughts of stigmatized women—bar girls and prostitutes who married the enemy.

Hiroko Tolbert recalls her trip to America in 1951 after marrying a White G.I. (U.S. soldier) in Japan. Trying to make a good first impression on her in-laws, particularly after hearing that New York had beautiful homes and fashion, she put on her favorite kimono to greet them. Seeing her in traditional Japanese clothing made the family very upset. They asked her to change into Western clothes and renamed her "Susie." Already contending with a new way of dressing and being called by a different name, Hiroko was shocked by her new living conditions. In Japan she was used to living in a clean home where people removed their shoes prior to entering. In New York she found herself on a chicken farm, with lots of manure and no practice of removing shoes before entering a home (Barford 2015).

In addition to the difficulties she faced in America, Hiroko had to deal with knowing that her own family was unhappy about her decision to marry an American G.I. However, with the destruction in Japan from the U.S. bombing, she felt she had little choice but to leave her home country. Over time, Hiroko found a supportive community in New York that helped her adjust to her new life. She eventually divorced her husband and remarried. Japanese women who married White G.I.s living in small cities and towns tended to have the hardest time. Historian Paul Spickard explains that Japanese women who married Black Americans were able to settle into the United States more easily because "Black families knew what it was like to be on the losing side. They [Japanese war brides] were welcomed by a sisterhood of black women. But in small white communities [like Hiroko's] . . . their isolation was often extreme" (Barford 2015).

PHOTO 12.2 Japanese war brides with their American husbands who served in WWII. Seattle, Washington, 1951.
GRANGER.

Persistence of the One-Drop Rule

Actress and TV personality Tamera Mowry-Housley, whose mother is Black and father is White, has also experienced ostracism due to her choice of a marriage partner. In an interview she recalls her mom's advice when she began seeing her now husband Adam Housley:

> When my mom found out that I was dating a white man, she said, "Listen, I went through a lot and I want to make sure you love this man, because it's not easy. You'll face scrutiny. So make

sure that you guys are in this together and make sure you understand what you will face." I said, "Mom, what are you talking about? It's 2005. People aren't going to care!" But she was right. (Juneau 2017)

In an interview with her sister on the Oprah Winfrey Network (2017), Tamera broke down in tears recalling the hateful comments she received because of her marriage to Adam, saying,

People choose to look past the love and spew hate. That's what hurts me because I've never experienced so much hate ever in my life. . . . I get called "White man's whore." The new one was . . . back in the day you cost three hundred dollars [as a slave], but now you're givin' it [sex] to him for free. . . . They say, "Oh, Tia's [her twin sister] a *true* Black woman because she married a Black man."

PHOTO 12.3 Tamera Mowry-Housley with her husband Adam and their two children Aden and Ariah.

AXELLE WOUSSEN/Bauergriffin/Newscom

Tia responded by saying that she has received the opposite reaction to her marriage to a Black man, with some saying that Tamera got it right by marrying a White man.

This is an example of how the one-drop rule persists and how the personal decisions of bi/multiracial people become politicized.

Despite their having a White father, most people look at Tamera and Tia's physical features and see Black women. Some African Americans view Tia's marriage as an **intraracial** (same race) one that validates her authenticity as a Black woman but view Tamera as a race traitor because she married a White man. Bi/multiracial people commonly find that people view the partner they choose as a declaration of either rejecting or embracing each of their racial communities. Seeing interracial couples, particularly Black women and White men, can also act as a trigger and reminder of the horrific history of slavery and sexual abuse in America.

Conversely, some African Americans think Tamera "got it right" by marrying a White man. This view has ties to a strategy, used by some people of color, of marrying or just having children with a White person or someone with a lighter skin tone. Some think that offspring with a lighter or even "White passing" complexion will gain protection from prejudice and racism.

Passing

Historically in the United States, racial passing refers to someone with some non-White ancestry (usually someone of Black/African American ancestry) identifying as White to avoid racial discrimination. This is exactly what White Americans feared when they created the 1924 Racial Integrity Act in Virginia. If a person of mixed racial ancestry could pass as White, they could also intermingle undetected with Whites. Sometimes families have "passed" as White for so long that their descendants are unaware they have Black ancestry. Less than 40 years ago, this happened to a woman in Louisiana—and the results put a spotlight on the one-drop rule.

Upon ordering a copy of her birth certificate in preparation for ordering a passport to go on a vacation abroad, a White woman named Susie Guillory Phipps discovered her birth certificate classified her as Black. Refusing to accept a Black racial identity, Susie and her wealthy White husband spent much time and money on legal fees in unsuccessful efforts to get the state of Louisiana to change the racial classification on her birth certificate to White (*Jane DOE v. STATE of Louisiana* 1985; Jaynes 1982). The *New York Times* summed up what some referred to as Phipps's almost obsessive attempts to change her birth certificate, writing, "The story, a story as old as the country, has elements of anthropology and sociology special to this region, and its message, here in 1982 America, is that it is still far better to be white than black" (Jaynes 1982).

Some people were aware of their mixed racial ancestry and worked hard to conceal it at all costs. However, racial passing, even when feasible, is not an easy solution to racism. It usually meant moving away from and denying your family, marrying a White person, living in fear of being found out, and having to come up with explanations for a child having "non-White" features.

In some cases, White parents have raised their bi/multiracial children to believe they have only White ancestors. In the 2015 film *Little White Lie*, Lacey Schwartz shares her own story of finding out why she had darker skin and curlier hair than her siblings. Throughout her life, her mother had told Schwartz that she gained her appearance from her father's Sicilian grandpa. Really, however, it came from the African American man with whom her mother had an affair.

In *White Like Her* Gail Lukasik (2017) details the discovery of her mother's racial ancestry. She describes her mother's strange habits and explanations for avoiding the sun, wearing makeup to bed, refusing to visit her family in New Orleans, and the absence of family photographs. While searching the Louisiana census, Gail discovered that her maternal grandfather's entire family is listed as Black. When confronted with this information, her mother begged Lukasik not to tell anyone before she dies. Lukasik kept her mother's secret until her death 17 years later. She describes how her mother's "White privilege" came at a high cost. Passing prevented her from acknowledging her family or allowing her children to get to know them. She had to keep this secret even from her husband and children. Lukasik imagines that all of this must have been particularly painful because her dad and his family openly expressed racial prejudices in front of her mother.

DOING SOCIOLOGY 12.2

Understanding the Impact of Passing

In this exercise you will consider the pros and cons of passing as White during the one-drop era.

Consider what you have learned about passing and imagine you are living in the early 20th century. Then write answers to the following questions:

1. If you knew that your child would be treated better, be safer, and given advantages if they passed for White, would you encourage them to do so? Why or why not? Would the pros outweigh the cons?

2. If you were passing as White and confronted with the decision of continuing to pass or attend a family member's major life event such as a wedding, birth, or funeral and publicly exposing yourself as non-White, what would you do? How would your decision affect your life?

Colorism

Colorism exists within racial groups and globally, particularly in places that experienced European colonization. In the United States a well-known children's rhyme summarizes the concept: "If you're black, stay back; if you're brown, stick around; if you're yellow, you're mellow; if you're white, you're all right" (Kareem Nittle 2019). Colorism, like racism, can have real impacts. Numerous studies have examined the effects of skin tone, particularly among Black, Hispanic, and Latinx people. They show that the darker your skin tone the more likely you are to experience negative outcomes, including those related to economics, perceived attractiveness, trustworthiness, and criminality (Kareem Nittle 2019). Colorism is apparent within the film industry, which has the power to shape our views and standards of beauty. Sande Alessi Casting, originally responsible for finding actresses for the movie *Straight Outta Compton*, posted a casting call ranking the roles for actresses in the film from A to D by race, skin tone, and other physical features such as hair texture:

> A GIRLS: These are the hottest of the hottest. Models. MUST have real hair—no extensions, very classy looking, great bodies. You can be black, white, asian, hispanic, mid eastern, or mixed race too. Age 18–30. . . . B GIRLS: These are fine girls, long natural hair, really nice bodies. Small waists, nice hips. You should be light-skinned. Beyonce is a prototype here. Age 18–30. . . . C GIRLS: These are African American girls, medium to light skinned with a weave. Age 18–30. . . . D GIRLS: These are African American girls. Poor, not in good shape. Medium to dark skin tone. Character types. Age 18–30. (Cadet 2014)

Aware of colorism and how it might affect them, some people have gone to great lengths to lighten or prevent the darkening of their skin through the use of harmful skin bleaching creams (some known to cause illnesses such as mercury poisoning and kidney, liver, and nerve damage) and avoiding the sun. You can see more evidence of colorism by searching the hashtags #teamlightskin and #teamdarkskin on social media. You will find posts, tweets, videos, and commentary that feed into skin tone–based stereotypes and prejudices. In fact, some argue that it was President Obama's biracial background and relatively light complexion that made him seem to many as an acceptable Black president.

Check Your Understanding

1. How have racial prejudice and discrimination affected interracial families and bi/multiracial people in the United States?

2. What have been the pros and cons of White racial passing in the United States?

3. What is the historical connection between interracial relationships and colorism?

RACE AND MEDIA

As discussed in Chapter 5, media is a powerful socializing agent and tool for propagating antimiscegenation agendas. In this section, we look at the relationship between race and media in the United States.

Cultural Hegemony and Racism

Before television, news stories, posters, and pamphlets stirred up emotions about the "dangers" of interracial relationships. Images of White women with Black men or other men of color warned of impending danger. These were early images of a culture that supported racism.

PHOTO 12.4 Anti-Japanese propaganda poster from World War II portraying Japanese men as a threat to White women. Full credit: Pictures from History / Granger, NYC -- All rights reserved.

Cultural hegemony refers to the way that **cultural texts** (e.g., TV, music, film, magazines, books) get us to see particular views and beliefs as "normal" in our culture. For example, if the majority of TV shows, movies, magazines, and advertisements show same-race couples, we are likely to see intraracial dating and marriage as the norm. When we watch media where there are few interracial couples, we tend to view them as going against the norms of society and be less likely to engage in such relationships.

CONSIDER THIS

Even if you were somehow able to avoid looking at or listening to media, it would still influence you. Why?

DOING SOCIOLOGY 12.3

Exploring Cultural Hegemony in Media

In this exercise you will consider depictions of biracial or multiracial individuals, interracial relationships, and multiracial families in advertisements.

Write answers to the following questions:

1. Consider advertisements you see regularly. How often do they depict biracial or multiracial individuals, interracial couples, or multiracial families? When biracial or multiracial individuals, interracial couples, or multiracial families are shown, what do they tend to look like?

2. If you were in charge of creating a television ad or TV series that challenged stereotypes about biracial or multiracial individuals, interracial couples, or multiracial families, who would you include (e.g., a middle-class Middle Eastern woman with a dark skin tone who is married to a wealthy Native American woman)? Why would you choose these characters? How do they challenge stereotypes? What would be your plot? How would it challenge stereotypes?

3. Do you believe the commercials and advertisements are helpful, harmful, or both helpful and harmful for interracial couples and multiracial families? Why?

Race and Media Representation Today

Compared to 50 years ago, there are many more depictions of interracial relationships, multiracial families, and bi/multiracial people in film, TV, and advertisements. Series such as *Mixed-ish, The Walking Dead, Scandal, Jane the Virgin, The Unbreakable Kimmy Schmidt, Master of None*, and *Dear White People* and ads for Cheerios, Tide, Swiffer, Old Navy, Macy's, and McDonald's provide proof of this. While some see this as an indication of a more inclusive and representative society, others argue that many of these portrayals continue to be problematic due to a lack of dual-person-of-color representation, colorism, and a failure to fully explore the complexity of identities and experiences present in interracial relationships, families, and the lives of bi/multiracial individuals.

PHOTO 12.5 The cast of *Mixed-ish*, a television series set in the 1980s that portrays the experiences of a mixed-race family who moves from a hippie commune to the suburbs.

Admedia, Inc/Billy Bennight/AdMedia/Sipa USA/Newscom

Overrepresentation of Black–White Couples

When you were completing the Doing Sociology 12.3 exercise you likely found numerous ads featuring Black–White and White–person of color relationships. Why does an overrepresentation of Black–White interracial couples exist in the media? Why are we more likely to see interracial relationships where one partner is White? The answer is that being bi/multiracial in many ways has been synonymous with being "part" White and the product of a Black–White relationship. Therefore, many of our depictions of bi/multiracial people exclude those who come from dual-person-of-color backgrounds (e.g., Black and Asian). This way of defining interracial and bi/multiraciality results from America's historical fixation on preventing interracial relationships between Whites and people of color—specifically African Americans. Because U.S. policies were less concerned with interracial relationships among people of color our media representations, research, literature, and art also reflect this bias.

Frequently showing White people as the love interests of people of color in the media also contributes to the idea that proximity to Whiteness is the ultimate goal and desire of people of color—that being in such a relationship means they have ascended the racial hierarchy, even if only symbolically (Kini 2017). Stories where an upper-class White person falls in love with a lower-class person of color and attempts to "save" them from their dreary life perpetuate this idea. For example, in the movie *Maid in Manhattan* wealthy White senatorial candidate Christopher Marshall (Ralph Fiennes) falls in love with a Latina maid (Jennifer Lopez) after mistaking her for a guest. These types of portrayals also contribute to the erasure of intraracial and non-White interracial relationships. If a Latino, Asian, Black, Native American, Middle Eastern, or bi/multiracial actor played the character of Christopher Marshall it would be a different film.

Sexual stereotypes and curiosities can also take center stage in media portrayals between interracial couples—film director Spike Lee calls this "jungle fever." The White characters in these movies feel drawn to a person of color (usually Black) based on stereotypes rather that a true connection (Ebert 1991). In such portrayals of romantic relationships, White love interests often find their partner's features (e.g., hair texture, skin color) and culture intriguing and exotic.

Breaking Out of the Black–White Binary

Some forms of media that deal with race break out of the Black–White binary by featuring and highlighting the experiences of interracial couples and bi/multiracial people who are not part White. For example, the book *Red & Yellow Black & Brown: Decentering Whiteness in Mixed Race Studies* (Rondilla, Guevarra, and Spickard 2017) is a collection of stories that center on the social, psychological, and political situations of mixed-race individuals who identify as two or more non-White races. Films such as *Mississippi Masala*, featuring an interracial Indian and African American couple, and *A Weekend with the Family*, in which a biracial (Black and Asian) woman introduces her Black boyfriend to her family serve as counternarratives to the majority of films featuring people of color with White partners. Popular TV series including *Grey's Anatomy*, where Dr. Preston Burke (who is Black) and Dr. Christina Yang (who is Asian) are romantically involved, and *Scrubs*, in which nurse Carla Espinosa (who is Dominican) and Dr. Christopher Turk (who is Black and Japanese) also seek to break stereotypical images of interracial partnering patterns. However, it is not enough just to have visual diversity, writers and producers should also strive to show nuanced depictions of bi/multiracial individuals, interracial relationships, and multiracial families.

PHOTO 12.6 Actor Wesley Snipes out with his wife Nakyung "Nikki" Park, a South Korean painter and artist, and their children in New York in 2008.

Splash News/Newscom

Check Your Understanding

1. How does the media shape our views about interracial relationships, multiracial families, and bi/multiracial people?

2. What are two explanations for the overrepresentation of Black–White and White–person of color depictions in the media?

3. What are some examples of movies and shows that break out of the Black–White binary?

ABOLISHING ANTIMISCEGENATION LEGISLATION AND THE MULTIRACIAL MOVEMENT

The media representations of interracial couples described earlier would not exist without the organized efforts to ban antimiscegenation laws in the United States. The Supreme Court abolished such laws in 1967 with its *Loving v. Virginia* decision. The fight against them, however, started much earlier.

Fighting Antimiscegenation Laws

Efforts to prevent, go around, and repeal antimiscegenation laws appear throughout the history of the United States. For example, activists in Washington State were able to block antimiscegenation bills in 1935 and 1937 by working together across racial lines (Cayton 1935a, 1935b; Johnson 2005). African Americans, Filipinos, communists, and organized labor communities led the efforts to prevent the laws, with Chinese and Japanese communities contributing as well (Johnson 2005). They all understood the power that came from working together.

Interracial couples living in states with antimiscegenation laws used various strategies to skirt the law. The sensational story of "White Romeo," a White man living in Georgia in the mid-1930s, provides one vivid example. "Romeo" was determined to marry his sweetheart, an African American woman, despite the Georgia law that prohibited such interracial marriages. He underwent a blood transfusion that injected a pint of "African American" blood into his vein and declared that, since he now had Black blood running through his body, he was free to marry an African American woman. The authorities agreed and allowed the couple to marry despite the antimiscegenation law in Georgia at the time (White Romeo 1935).

A lesser known interracial love story involves a White Mexican American woman and an African American man who were denied a marriage license in California in the 1940s. They decided to fight the antimiscegenation law through the California Supreme Court, claiming that it was unconstitutional because it prevented them from fully participating in their Catholic religion (*Perez v. Sharp* 1948). In a close decision, the California Supreme Court agreed and declared that antimiscegenation laws violated the U.S. Constitution.

Some interracial couples living in states that maintained antimiscegenation laws tried to circumvent them by marrying in a state that had repealed or never enacted such laws. That is exactly what Richard Loving (a White man) and Mildred Jeter (a Black and Native American woman) decided to do in 1958 when the Racial Integrity Act of Virginia prevented them from getting married. They drove to Washington, DC, got married, and returned home. However, it was not that simple. Virginia did not allow residents to marry interracially out of state and return to live as husband and wife. Asleep in their Virginia home, police ripped the Lovings out of their bed in the middle of the night and then arrested and jailed them.

The Lovings' sentences were suspended, but they were ordered to leave the state, the only home they had known. They moved to Washington, DC, but Mildred was extremely unhappy there. When they went back to Virginia the police arrested them once again. Eventually their fight to live as a married couple in Virginia reached the Supreme Court. In 1967, in the *Loving v. Virginia* decision, the Court found antimiscegenation laws unconstitutional, legalizing interracial marriages across the United States. As seen in Figure 12.2, the number of such marriages has steadily increased since then. The number of offspring of interracial relationships has also increased dramatically since the *Loving* decision and sparked major changes in how we view and count race and races.

CONSIDER THIS

Do you think the Lovings would have won their case and overturned antimiscegenation laws if Mildred was White and Richard was Black? Why?

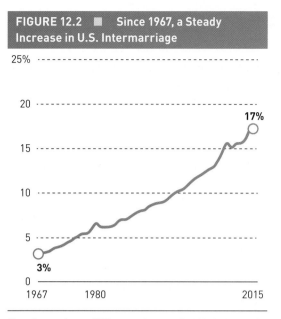

FIGURE 12.2 ■ Since 1967, a Steady Increase in U.S. Intermarriage

Note: Data prior to 1980 are estimates. See Methodology for more details.

Source: "Since 1967, a steady increase in U.S. intermarriage," 2017. From "Intermarriage in the U.S. 50 years after Loving v. Virginia." "https://www.pewsocialtrends.org/2017/05/18/intermarriage-in-the-u-s-50-years-after-loving-v-virginia/pst_2017-05-15-intermarriage-00-05/

Multiracial Movements and the U.S. Census

As more people with parents of different races entered the U.S. population, they began to organize themselves and demand recognition as multiracial people. Many were those with one Black parent who rejected the "one-drop rule" that viewed them as (only) Black. They have done much to change the way people in the United States view race and interracial relationships.

Multiracial organizations have influenced both attitudes and policies affecting bi/multiracial individuals and families. Many of them were instrumental in changing the 2000 U.S. census to allow bi/multiracial individuals to check all racial categories with which they identify (rather than just one). This change to the census shined a spotlight on monoracial norms (monoracism) that exclude bi/multiracial people, preventing them from fully acknowledging and reporting their racial identities. It also led colleges, employers, researchers, and other people who collect racial data to likewise update their demographic forms.

While indicators of progress, these changes have not been without hiccups. Some multiracial people report that organizations have reclassified them into singular racial categories. Also, bi/multiracial individuals who identify solely as bi/multiracial still do not have a racial category with which they identify. Proponents of adding a multiracial category to the census contend that it would provide protections for bi/multiracial people when dealing with race-based discrimination. They argue that the discrimination faced by bi/multiracial people is rooted in their identification as a separate distinct racial category not yet officially recognized by the U.S. government.

On the other hand, some people believe that a multiracial category deracializes mixed-race people and takes power away from monoracial people of color (Phillips 2017). For example, a multiracial category would make it harder to track data about specific racial groups. Moreover, it will appear that some races have decreased in size, which affects funding and resources for government programs serving specific racial and ethnic groups.

DOING SOCIOLOGY 12.4

A Separate Multiracial Category on the U.S. Census

In this exercise you will consider the pros and cons of adding a separate category for bi/multiracial people on the U.S. census.

Write answers to the following questions:

1. Consider the arguments for and against adding a separate category for bi/multiracial people on the U.S. census. Do these arguments make sense? Why or why not?

2. Can you think of additional arguments for and against adding a separate category for bi/multiracial people on the U.S. census? If so, what additional points should be considered?

3. Which stance do you find more convincing? Why? If you are unsure, what additional questions do you have about the implications of adding a separate multiracial category for bi/multiracial people on the U.S. census?

Debunking Identity Myths

Multiracial organizations and social scientists have also worked to refute and dispel deficit-based perspectives about bi/multiracial people. Research studies have combated the long-held belief that children of interracial couples are confused, are maladjusted, and experience higher rates of low self-esteem and identity crises. Through recognizing and discussing monoracism, social scientists have exposed the ways that social structures and societal norms create difficulties for bi/multiracial people. They argue that confusion surrounding the racial identification of bi/multiracial people and their contingent acceptance in society is not an internal trouble for individual mixed-race people but a social issue.

Society creates situations that result in exclusion or isolation (e.g., a multiracial person told they have to choose one racial identity or that they are not Black, Native, or Asian enough), exotification and objectification (e.g., mixed-race people are so pretty; being asked "What are you?"), assumptions of monoracial identities (e.g., assuming a multiracial person's family member is their nanny), and pathologizing of multiracial identities and experiences (e.g., mixed-race people are confused; they don't know what they are) (Franco and O'Brien 2018; Johnston and Nadal 2010). Multiracial psychologist Maria P. Root is well known for her work with multiple multiracial organizations and research on multiracial families and individuals. Her Bill of Rights for People of Mixed Heritage is somewhat of an anthem for mixed-race individuals:

I HAVE THE RIGHT . . .
Not to justify my existence in this world.
Not to keep the races separate within me.
Not to justify my ethnic legitimacy.
Not to be responsible for people's discomfort with my physical or ethnic ambiguity.

I HAVE THE RIGHT . . .
To identify myself differently than strangers expect me to identify.
To identify myself differently than how my parents identify me.
To identify myself differently than my brothers and sisters.
To identify myself differently in different situations.

I HAVE THE RIGHT . . .
To create a vocabulary to communicate about being multiracial or multiethnic.
To change my identity over my lifetime—and more than once.
To have loyalties and identification with more than one group of people.
To freely choose whom I befriend and love. (Root 2003, 32)

These statements are significant as they address the fluidity of bi/multiracial identities across time and place and acknowledge that there is no universal terminology embraced by all bi/multiracial people. Bi/multiracial people identify in various ways, sometimes *monoracially*; as *multiple monoracial categories*; and as *mixed or bi/multiracial*, without specifying particular racial background. Some reject racial categorization altogether—although this does not mean members of society see them as "raceless" (Renn 2008; Tran, Miyake, Martinez-Morales, and Csizmadia 2016). When we say that identity is fluid, we mean that an individual might identify differently in different spaces or various stages of their life.

The creation of identity models and language for talking about the bi/multiracial experience has been particularly important for monoracial parents of bi/multiracial children. Multiracial organizations have served an important function for multiracial families by creating spaces where they can build community and discuss topics unique to interracial couples and raising bi/multiracial and transracially and/or transnationally adopted children. A perfect example of this is the MAVIN Foundation's *Multiracial Child Resource Book* (Root 2003) created to assist parents, teachers, and professionals in raising happy, healthy mixed-race youth within a monoracially structured society. Multiracial organizations and social scientists have also created space for and recognition of bi/multiracial people on college campuses and in academia, the arts/media, and health care.

Carving Out Space: Multiracial Organizations

The MAVIN Foundation, started in 1998 by Matt Kelley—a 19-year-old at Wesleyan University in Connecticut—is perhaps the organization that has come closest to addressing all the aforementioned topics. MAVIN was groundbreaking in its variety of accomplishments. It produced a series of magazines featuring articles, artwork, and narratives about mixed-race experiences; hosted bone marrow drives and fundraising efforts; sponsored social and support groups for mixed-heritage people and families; and put together the largest national conference focused on the mixed-race experience at that time (in 2003). MAVIN also created a national resource center and launched the Generation MIX National Awareness tour—during which five mixed-heritage young adults went across the United States raising awareness about the multiracial experience through speaking engagements and a documentary about the experience. Unfortunately, the foundation is no longer active, but numerous organizations continue to advance the work it began.

The Critical Mixed Race Studies (CMRS) Association (2019), started in 2010 at DePaul University in Chicago, is a collective of scholars, artists, community activists, clinicians, and students who work to undo local and global systemic injustice rooted in systems of racism and White supremacy through scholarship, teaching, advocacy, the arts, activism, and other forms of social justice work. Its conferences bring together hundreds of individuals from around the world. MidWest Mixed (2019) is a similar organization that hosts a conference and seeks "to expand our understanding of race and identity through courageous conversations, arts engagement, educational outreach, and a biennial conference." Running an organization is difficult work. To avoid burnout and increase their power, many of these organizations work collectively.

Mixed Roots Stories (2019), an arts organization that creates space for diverse mixed communities, advocates for racial justice by promoting "public awareness of the stories and storytellers that contribute to Arts, Culture, Education, Media, and Politics of the Mixed experience," works closely with CMRS on its arts programming at conferences. Members of CMRS and Mixed Roots Stories also support the Mixed Remixed Festival (2019), hosted in Los Angeles, California, another space dedicated to "celebrating stories of mixed-race and multiracial families and individuals through films, books and performance."

Mixed Marrow (2019) collaborates with numerous organizations, colleges, and communities to educate the public about the difficulty people of multiethnic/racial descent have finding bone marrow and blood cell donors. It hosts drives to register donors as a community recruitment partner for Be the Match, the national registry in the United States. Ultimately, the key goal of all multiracial organizations is to dismantle White supremacy and racism. This effort begins with addressing anti-Blackness. During the 2020 Black Lives Matter protests, the Critical Mixed Race Studies Association took a strong stance on anti-Blackness in its "In Solidarity with BLM" statement that commits them to both short- and long-term racial justice actions.

1. Which Supreme Court case repealed antimiscegenation laws at the federal level?

2. What are the arguments for and against a legal multiracial category?

3. How has the multiracial movement used organized power and social science to change attitudes, laws, policies, and practices?

REVISING OR CURBING RACISM?

While bi/multiracial populations grow and the United States is on its way to becoming a country where people of color outnumber Whites, racism still exists throughout the nation. Having a Black biracial president and seeing unions such as that of Prince Harry and Meghan Markle may seem like indications of progress, but if we do not dismantle the systems that reproduce racial inequity, we will continue to experience the same problems. Even those in interracial relationships and their family members can experience and perpetuate prejudice and racism.

Monoracism and Multiracial Families

CONSIDER THIS

If you saw a Black woman with Asian children, what's the first thought that would come to mind explaining their relationship? Why? If you saw a White woman with Asian children, what's the first thought that would come to mind explaining their relationship? Why?

Parents of bi/multiracial children and parents of mixed ancestry themselves who do not look like their children often face assumptions and questions about their relationship with their children. Aware of this reality, some parents of bi/multiracial children keep documents such as copies of birth certificates and travel permission letters readily available in case they are detained or questioned (Cooper 2019).

DOING SOCIOLOGY 12.5

When Multiracial Becomes Monoracial: Encounters with Law Enforcement

In this exercise, consider how members of multiracial families handle encounters with the police.

Write answers to the following questions. Be prepared to share your responses with the rest of the class.

1. If you had (or perhaps you have) a bi/multiracial child of color, when and how would you talk to them about racial profiling and police interactions? Why?

2. If you had (or perhaps you have) a bi/multiracial (or transracially adopted) child who did/does not look like you, what sort of safety precautions might you take to ensure that if stopped by the police or other officials you could prove your child belongs with you?

3. How did answering these questions make you feel? Why?

Working for Racial Justice Means Confronting Anti-Black and -Brown Prejudice and Discrimination

Champion golfer Tiger Woods famously came up with the term *Cablinasian* to describe his multiracial heritage. However, when he was arrested in 2017 for driving under the influence, the racial category listed on the incident report was not White, American Indian or Alaskan Native (government classification for Native Americans/Indigenous people of the Americas), Asian, or multiracial—it was Black (Moskovitz 2017; Oprah Winfrey Show 1997/2018).

PHOTO 12.7 Tiger Woods at a press conference in Japan after winning the Zozo Championship in 2019.

Kyodo/Newscom

Likewise, former quarterback Colin Kaepernick's Black identity came to the forefront after he began kneeling during the national anthem in 2016 to protest racial inequality and police brutality. While Kaepernick is a biracial person with lighter skin, his alignment with his Blackness and stance against racism and police brutality led the NFL to freeze him out and prevent him from getting a contract. His position was a direct threat to White supremacy in a society built to support it. The experiences of Woods and Kaepernick remind us that we cannot look at bi/multiracial issues apart from the anti-Black and -Brown sentiment that continues to permeate America. If we wish to dismantle a racist system, we must actively work to eradicate racism through antiracist practices. The Sociologist in Action for this chapter, Dr. Rashawn Ray, has done just that.

SOCIOLOGISTS IN ACTION
Rashawn Ray

Improving Policing in America

My research examines the social psychological factors that create, maintain, and reduce racism. Over the past several years, I have conducted research on policing. Being a police officer is a difficult job. I know because my great-uncle, Walter Gooch, was the first Black police chief of my hometown of Murfreesboro, Tennessee. My wife's grandfather, Jimmy Davis, was the first Black captain over the detectives. Despite being from a police family, I have been stopped by police nearly 40 times (this is one time for basically every year of my life). I should not have to say it, but I do not have a criminal record and have a PhD. My experience, however, is not uncommon.

Relative to Whites, Blacks are more likely to be profiled and stopped by police. Blacks are 3.5 times more likely to be killed by police when they are not attacking nor have a weapon. My research center, the Lab for Applied Social Science Research (LASSR), has developed a virtual reality decision-making program for officers. This innovative program immerses officers in a 360-degree virtual environment to interact in different settings with people who vary by race and gender. We capture officers' physiological outcomes including heart rate, stress level, eye movement,

PHOTO 12.8

Courtesy of Rashawn Ray

and reaction time. Rather than aiming to highlight "bad apples," our program focuses on factors that lead to the positive policing outcomes that everyone desires. I have presented my research on policing on Capitol Hill and conducted dozens of trainings with law enforcement including the Department of Homeland Security. LASSR regularly conducts police–community forums to bridge the divide between law enforcement and local residents.

Studies show that most Americans are tired of dealing with racism. Well, we can individually and collectively work to dismantle it. First, we can be a "racial equity learner" by understanding the inequitable ways that racism impacts our lives. Second, we can be a "racial equity ally" by speaking up when we hear or see racism, particularly with family and friends. Third, we can be a "racial equity advocate" by advocating for fair and restorative policies at our workplaces and in our neighborhoods.

I have published over 50 books, articles, and book chapters, and nearly 20 op-eds in outlets including the New York Times and NBC News. I have appeared on C-SPAN, MSNBC, and NPR, and had my research cited by the Associated Press, CNN, and ESPN's *The Undisputed*. Beyond all of this, one thing I know is that conversations matter. The more we have candid conversations with people similar to *and* different from us, the better we will be and the better that society will be.

Dr. Rashawn Ray is a David M. Rubenstein fellow in governance studies at the Brookings Institution; an associate professor of sociology and executive director of the Lab for Applied Social Science Research (LASSR) at the University of Maryland, College Park; and a coeditor of Contexts Magazine: Sociology for the Public.

Discussion Question

How do you define a "racial equity learner," "racial equity ally," and "racial equity advocate"? How will you become a racial equity ally and advocate to reduce racial inequality?

1. Why does multiracialism fail to solve institutional racism?

2. How does monoracism impact multiracial families?

3. Why does working for the rights of multiracial people mean combating anti-Black and -Brown prejudice and discrimination?

CONCLUSION

Throughout this chapter we examined the contexts in which interracial relationships have existed throughout U.S. history. We also looked at racism and discrimination against people in interracial relationships and bi/multiracial people—and how to combat them. The increasing number of bi/multiracial Americans alone will not solve racism, but antiracist practices can. In the next chapter we discuss how racism hurts everyone and how antiracism can eradicate it and benefit everyone.

CHAPTER REVIEW

12.1 Why have interracial relationships between Whites and people of color been viewed as a problem in the United States?

Many Whites sought to protect the purity and perceived superiority of their race. They believed that people of color—Black Americans in particular—were socially, culturally, and biologically inferior and racial mixing would bring about the destruction of the White race. Some Whites also feared that if Whites and people of color saw each other as equals it would threaten the economic and social systems that advantaged the wealthiest Whites.

12.2 How has racial discrimination affected interracial families and bi/multiracial people in the United States?

Interracial families and bi/multiracial people have faced discrimination on both institutional (antimiscegenation laws) and interpersonal levels (social rejection). People in interracial relationships do not have the luxury of having their relationships viewed as a personal choice. Many people view selection of an out-group partner as a public rejection of one's own racial background(s). Strategies of marrying lighter and racial passing often require people to deny or reject parts of themselves and their families, which can result in psychological trauma. These strategies can also perpetuate colorism and its harmful effects on individuals with darker skin tones and create divisiveness within the multiracial community.

12.3 How has the media shaped our views about interracial relationships, multiracial families, and bi/multiracial people?

Through cultural hegemony the media has socialized us to see intraracial relationships as the norm. The interracial relationships that are shown tend to be Black–White and White–other-person-of-color partnerships, which can feed into stereotypes and the exotification of bi/multiracial people. Dual-person-of-color couples and bi/multiracial people with darker complexions remain rarely seen in the media.

12.4 How has the multiracial movement used organized power and social science to change attitudes, laws, policies, and practices?

Multiracial organizations and social scientists have created space for and recognition of bi/multiracial people on the census, on college campuses, in academia, in the media, and in health care through scholarship, teaching, advocacy, the arts, activism, and other forms of racial justice work.

12.5 Why does multiraciality fail to solve institutional racism?

Institutionalized racism must be addressed through antiracist practices. Becoming a majority-person-of-color nation, with a growing bi/multiracial population, can increase representation of various identities and perspectives, but it cannot solve racial inequity. To reduce racial inequity, we must dismantle the ideologies, policies, laws, and practices that perpetuate it.

KEY TERMS

Antimiscegenation (p. 247)

Biracial (p. 246)

Cultural texts (p. 255)

Eugenicists (p. 247)

Hypodescent (p. 248)

Interracial (p. 245)

Intraracial (p. 252)

Monoracial (p. 250)

Monoracism (p. 259)

Multiracial (p. 246)

13 HOW RACISM HURTS AND ANTIRACISM HELPS EVERYONE

David J. Luke

LEARNING QUESTIONS

13.1 How does racism hurt everyone, including White people?

13.2 Why is it hard to talk about racism—and why have we done so, anyway, in recent years?

13.3 What is White fragility?

13.4 How can interest convergence help show that antiracism benefits everyone?

When you think of racism do you tend to think about its negative impacts on people of color? Do you ever think about how it hurts everyone—including White people? If no, why not? Who benefits from this lack of knowledge, and what are its repercussions on society? How can understanding the ways that racism and racial hierarchy hurt everyone help mobilize a multiracial antiracist coalition to fight racism? This chapter answers these questions.

HOW I GOT ACTIVE IN SOCIOLOGY

David J. Luke

Growing up as a multiracial person who presents as racially ambiguous, and in a household where our religious beliefs were deeply connected to issues of justice and equity, I found myself often asking questions about race and inequality and striving for a deeper understanding of these issues.

When I attended Grand Valley State University, I took several sociology courses as part of the general education requirements and fell in love with the discipline. It gave me the language and tools to better articulate and structure some of the thoughts in my mind, and better understand social phenomena. So while I attended college with the thought that I needed to get a job (which led me to a brief stint in the public accounting world before earning my PhD at the University of Kentucky), I ultimately knew I wanted to work in higher education and have the opportunity to facilitate the process I was part of in my undergraduate courses as a student. Further, I wanted to apply that sociological lens to work related to student programming and structural change in institutions, focused on justice and equity. I am fortunate to work in all of these areas now, thanks to sociology.

HOW DOES RACISM HURT EVERYONE, INCLUDING WHITE PEOPLE?

Racism is usually framed as a positive for White people and a negative for people of color. However, this narrow framing of racism clouds our understanding of a complex issue. We can map some of the ways racism materially advantages White people relative to people of color rather easily, but the system also has real drawbacks for White people. When we begin to think more broadly about the consequences of racism in the United States, the magnitude and breadth of the damage it does becomes clearer.

Examples of How Racism Hurts Everyone

We go into greater depth about this later in this chapter, but we can think about what we know about contemporary racial inequality in the United States to understand ways that racism hurts everyone. For example, in the United States, people generally support the idea of meritocracy, that is, that those with merit reap rewards proportionate to that merit. While there is vast evidence to suggest that a meritocracy does not exist in the United States, many people hold onto the notion. We tend to like the idea that you are rewarded for your work. So, when research indicates that job applicants with White-sounding names are more likely to receive a callback after applying for a job (Bertrand and Mullainathan 2004; Quillian et al., 2019), or that White job applicants with a criminal record are more likely to get called back than Black applicants with no record (Pager 2007), it suggests that merit is not the only thing employers consider.

This racial discrimination also means that the people getting interviews and hired for these jobs may not be as good or deserving as those overlooked by virtue of their race. Imagine heading into surgery knowing that your hospital only hires people of a particular race. How would you feel? Frequently, critiques of affirmative action use this line of argument against people of color, suggesting they are likely to get jobs they don't deserve. However, research indicates just the opposite. Among equally qualified applicants, Whites are more likely to attain employment (e.g., Quillian et al., 2019).

Also, think of the policies and practices that held people of color back and functioned as affirmative action for White Americans (Katznelson 2005). They were systemic violations of meritocracy in the United States. The government essentially created a White middle class by creating White suburban neighborhoods and urban ghettos where people of color, especially African Americans, were relegated to living. Today, critics of affirmative action programs argue that they violate the ideals of a meritocracy. They also say affirmative action hurts its beneficiaries and puts a label of "undeserving" on them. Such a stigma, however, applies more to White Americans—whose history is that of undeserving beneficiaries. In fact, it is partially this privilege and unearned advantage that contribute to the guilt some White Americans feel during conversations about race.

White transparency, the idea that Whiteness often goes unnamed and unnoticed, can also hurt White people (Haney-Lopez 1996). Programs and places not identified with a particular race tend to be White-centered. For example, in the United States, we have historically Black colleges and universities (HBCUs), but other institutions of higher education are simply considered colleges or universities without a racial label. Those institutions not identified as historically Black, however, are largely historically White, but White transparency means that many people, especially White people, identify them as race neutral. This transparency, not seeing White-centered institutions, practices, and policies as racialized, allows many White Americans to conclude that anti-White bias is a bigger problem than anti-Black bias (Norton and Sommers 2011). In this way, White Americans look at racism with a blind eye, which can frustrate people of color and be a major obstacle to close cross-racial relationships.

The idea of transparency holds for other identities as well. If a man and woman get married, they have a marriage, but if a man marries another man often it's rarely simply called a marriage, and almost always includes some qualifiers (e.g., "same sex" or "gay"). People resist things like LGBTQ+ pride marches, asking why there is not a "straight pride" march, not noticing that most marches and events center on heterosexual, cisgender people. This transparency helps maintain the privilege of the dominant group, but this privilege is innately a violation of meritocracy. If we believe in the principles of fairness and meritocracy, violations of these principles hurt everyone.

Finally, think of our educational system. Students given the opportunity may go on to help find cures for diseases, solve social problems, invent new technologies that change our lives, and generally accomplish great things. Systemic racism in education that leaves White students with better teachers and facilities than students of color robs society of many potential contributions and, in the process, harms everyone.

Systemic racism in education shows up in numerous ways, including through bias in standardized testing metrics, public school funding, and tracking. In U.S. schools, White and Asian students tend to be "tracked" into gifted programs much more than Black, Latinx, and American Indian students who receive less academic attention and encouragement (Yaluma and Tyner 2018). One of the most famous examples of this comes from Malcolm X, who describes in his autobiography how his high school counselor attempted to dissuade him from his aspirations to practice law and suggested he work with his hands (X and Haley 1965).

While pushing Black people to work in manual labor jobs is itself problematic, there's an additional problem. In some skilled trades, social networks keep opportunities away from people of color. Apprenticeship opportunities and word-of-mouth referrals often travel within racially segregated groups—preventing, once again, the "best available candidate" from getting the job.

DOING SOCIOLOGY 13.1

Recognizing Collateral Consequences

In this exercise, you will consider collateral consequences of criminal convictions and explore what function these have for society as a whole, and the harm they cause to all.

1. Spend some time thinking about the impacts of sending people to prison that extend beyond those incarcerated. Consider the families of prisoners, their communities, local organizations like their workplaces or schools, and their participation in the economic and political spheres. What impacts can you identify?

2. The Collateral Consequences Resource Center website states that "collateral consequences are the legal restrictions and discrimination that burden people with a criminal record long after their criminal case is closed." What collateral consequences of conviction can you identify? Which collateral consequence do you think is most problematic? What can you do to push for reform in that area?

Durkheim's External and Internal Inequality

Emile Durkheim, one of sociology's founders, differentiates two types of inequality: internal and external (Durkheim 1933/1997). In doing so, he creates a powerful argument against the social construction of race and racial classifications. According to Durkheim, these divisions and resulting inequalities are counterproductive to the well-being of a society.

Internal inequality stems from the personal characteristics of individuals. Durkheim argues that this type of inequality contributes to society, because it ensures that the most capable and productive people receive more rewards than the less capable and productive. This reward system encourages people to work hard and contribute to society in Durkheim's view.

Durkheim uses the term *external inequality* to describe a different type of inequality; external inequality is based on ascribed statuses that individuals cannot control (like race) (Durkheim 1933/1997). This type of inequality prevents some people from fully participating and contributing to society. It harms society because it deprives it from what some of its members could contribute, if given the chance. Essentially, external inequality is problematic because this type of inequality based on ascribed status is undeserved.

CONSIDER THIS

How might the racial makeup of colleges be different if we had an admission system based on internal inequality?

Check Your Understanding

1. Why does racism prevent decisions based on merit?

2. What is White transparency?

3. What are internal and external inequality, and why does external inequality hurt society?

WHY IS IT HARD TO TALK ABOUT RACISM—AND WHEN DO WE?

Why is it hard to talk about racism? As we work toward answering that question, let's start with a few more questions for you to reflect on. Do you often engage in conversations about race and racism with your friends? Your family? People in your religious communities? Coworkers? Do you find these conversations to be easy or difficult? Comfortable or uncomfortable?

CONSIDER THIS

Are you comfortable talking about racial issues with people who share your racial identity? What about those of a different race? Why?

Many White people often find it difficult to have healthy, productive conversations about race and racism. Research has consistently indicated that people of color tend to talk about race more than White Americans. While African American parents tend to start talking to their children about race at age 3, White parents do not do so with their children until about age 13, when their children start learning about racism in school. In fact, as Figure 13.1 indicates, White parents are much less likely than parents of color to *ever* discuss race with their children.

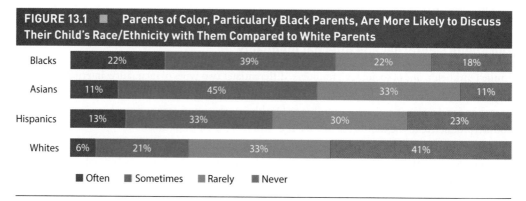

FIGURE 13.1   ■   Parents of Color, Particularly Black Parents, Are More Likely to Discuss Their Child's Race/Ethnicity with Them Compared to White Parents

	Often	Sometimes	Rarely	Never
Blacks	22%	39%	22%	18%
Asians	11%	45%	33%	11%
Hispanics	13%	33%	30%	23%
Whites	6%	21%	33%	41%

Source: © 2019 Sesame Workshop. Kotler, J.A, Haider, T.Z. & Levine, M.H. (2019). Identity matters: Parents' and educators' perceptions of children's social identity development. New York: Sesame Workshop.

Further, White American mothers tend to prefer *colorblind* approaches to racial discussions or to simply avoid conversations about race altogether (Van Ausdale and Feagin 2001; Vittrup 2018). Why? Most African American parents seek to prepare their children for living in a racist society whereas White people tend not to want to talk about (or even notice) the advantages race and racism give them. To address the systems that reproduce racial inequality, however, we must recognize and talk about them. Unfortunately, that is something many people resist, especially those in positions of power and privilege.

Normalization of Racism and the Racial Hierarchy

Rather than admitting that racism is real and a natural (and intended) by-product of racial classifications, many Whites normalize racial inequality. This is easy for most White people to do if they avoid

PHOTO 13.1 African American parents and children tend to begin conversations about race at earlier ages than White American parents and children.

FatCamera

conversations about race. Such avoidance is usually not difficult as their social networks tend to be so racially homogeneous that they avoid interracial interactions. This denial of racism works to preserve the systemic racism in the "normal" operation of society. For example, the consequences of believing (or convincing yourself) that the criminal justice system operates fairly is to dismiss the racially disparate outcomes as normal.

Believing the criminal justice system is fair also means there's no collective social responsibility to change it. It makes it possible to believe that the racial inequities in the system result from the way

PHOTO 13.2 People's perceptions of the criminal justice system vary by race; not everyone believes justice is blind.

GeorgePeters

different racial groups behave. Further, it allows White Americans who benefit from an unjust system that privileges them to wash their hands of any responsibility to remedy the injustice. If the system is just and working properly, a White person does not need to feel badly that Black people are disproportionately likely to be arrested, convicted, and sentenced. Ultimately, this supports negative stereotypes and unconscious biases aimed at disadvantaged subordinate racial groups. Sometimes, however, the injustice of racism can become too obvious for most people to ignore. The picture of young Emmett Till's disfigured body brought the brutality of racist lynchings into the average American's living room in the 1950s. In recent years, we have seen videos of police murders of Black men and women on our screens again and again and again.

Recognizing and Talking About Racism in the Criminal Justice System

The murder of George Floyd on Memorial Day in 2020 and the police killings of other Black men and women publicized through social media in recent years brought systemic racism into the mainstream public discourse. Protesters—of all races—demanded change. Suddenly many White Americans used their sociological imaginations and saw police killings of unarmed Black people as a systemic issue. Just a few years earlier, most saw such killings as isolated instances, as Figure 13.2 indicates. During and after the 2016 presidential election, as racism became more open and publicly discussed, it became harder and harder to ignore—even for White people.

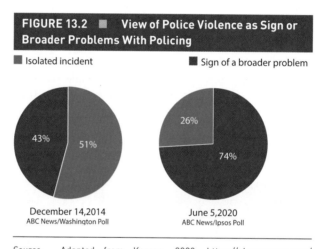

FIGURE 13.2 ■ View of Police Violence as Sign or Broader Problems With Policing

■ Isolated incident   ■ Sign of a broader problem

43%   51%

26%   74%

December 14, 2014
ABC News/Washington Poll

June 5, 2020
ABC News/Ipsos Poll

Source: Adapted from Karson, 2020, https://abcnews.go.com/Politics/74-americans-view-george-floyds-death-underlying-racial/story?id=71074422

The majority of respondents to this ABC News/*Washington Post* poll viewed the death of George Floyd as a sign of broader problems, as opposed to when the same question was asked about Michael Brown's killing in Ferguson, Missouri, in 2014.

With many people working less due to the COVID-19 pandemic, they had more time to focus on Floyd's murder than previous police killings of Black people and discuss why such deaths keep happening. They were able to make the connection between the graphic and gruesome murder of George Floyd and the broader trend of racial inequality imbedded within the structures of the United States. Functioning like public sociologists, protestors took to the streets, calling for the reallocation of police funding to social service and job creation programs that would be more effective in lowering crime rates. As they did so, they also demanded an end to the root of systemic racism—the racial hierarchy in the United States.

Racism's Reliance on Hierarchy

For racism to persist, a racial hierarchy must exist. For any group to be systemically advantaged and another systemically disadvantaged by virtue of race, there needs to be a formal or informal ranking that legitimates the advantaging and disadvantaging. In this way, racism relies on hierarchy, without which racial difference would have no relationship with inequality.

Impacts of the Racial Hierarchy in the United States

The impacts of the racial hierarchy, however, are multifaceted. It does not only benefit those on top and harm those lower on the hierarchy. That is an oversimplified view. Earlier in the book, we discussed how the creation of racial categories worked to bring together Whites of all classes and to divide the working and lower classes (including enslaved people) based on race. Today, the dominance of the racial divide continues to obscure what the working and lower classes—across racial groups—have in common.

Through promoting an "upstairs/downstairs" view of society, the wealthiest, most powerful (and almost entirely White) people in the United States work to divide people by race by assuring White people "downstairs" that their safety depends on their trusting those "upstairs" to protect them from their numerous internal and external enemies. This story helps the upstairs people to keep those downstairs focused on fighting among themselves rather than overthrowing the unfair system that allows a few people to be upstairs but consigns many more people (of all races) to the downstairs. Among the internal enemies in this security story are people of color and immigrants—racial outsiders (Derber and Magrass 2019).

The racial hierarchy can also generate resentment throughout the hierarchy. While members of more esteemed groups may look to racial outsiders as enemies, people at the lower levels of the hierarchy often feel resentment as well. People of color can be suspicious of or mistrust those White Americans who sit atop the hierarchy. Further, among people of color, there is often resentment toward higher-ranking non-White populations like Asian Americans, who are often considered the "model minority" (Luke 2014). These divisions create material advantages for a select few White Americans (who occupy the upstairs) but generally lessen social cohesion as a whole, which hurts everyone.

DOING SOCIOLOGY 13.2

Talking Across Racial Lines

In this exercise, you will think about how often you talk across racial lines and the challenges involved in having conversations about racism.

Consider and write answers to the following questions. Please explain your answers and be ready to share them with the class.

1. How do you identify racially? Why?

2. How often do you talk to people of a different race about issues related to race and racism? Why?

3. What do you think the effect on the racial hierarchy would be if most people talked about race and racism across racial lines less than you do? What if most people talked about race across racial lines more than you do?

Check Your Understanding

1. Why do White families talk to their children about race later than Black families?

2. What is the normalization of racism, and how does it help support the racial hierarchy?

3. What are some of the reasons behind the mass antiracism protests after the murder of George Floyd?

4. How do the wealthiest, most powerful (and almost entirely White) people in the United States promote an upstairs/downstairs view of society that helps divide people by race?

WHITE FRAGILITY

White Americans are the most segregated racial group in the United States. Because Whiteness is normative, transparent, and treated as default, we rarely look at the effects of racial segregation on Whites. This segregation, however, impacts White people in many ways, from increasing in-group cohesion to less awareness and understanding of those in different groups. What develops from this is *White habitus*, "a racialized, uninterrupted socialization process that *conditions* and *creates* Whites' racial tastes, perceptions, feelings, and emotions and their views on racial matters" (Bonilla-Silva 2018, 121).

Racial segregation leads Whites to interact disproportionately with each other and limits interaction with people outside of their race. This limited cross-racial interaction can harm White people in many ways, including leading them to try to avoid working with people of color or feeling uncomfortable if they cannot avoid doing so. Diverse teams, if they work well together, perform better and more effectively than homogeneous ones (Page 2017). In being segregated, White Americans miss out on productive and efficient teamwork, and society in general misses out on what they could accomplish—leaving problems unsolved and other positive benefits of diversity forfeited. These lost benefits include many potential relationships (social, collegial, romantic, or otherwise) that White people forfeit by virtue of segregation.

This segregation affects the architecture of our brains, as well. Our minds use shortcuts to make sense of a complicated world in which we are constantly bombarded by information. These shortcuts connect images and concepts with ideas and values, and manifest in what psychologists refer to as implicit (or unconscious) bias. Our minds are constantly making these connections and using the information we have available to us to do so. When a group is segregated, like White Americans are, they have limited information about people of other races. Moreover, what information they have is not gleaned from direct personal experience but from other sources (e.g., television, movies, word of mouth).

Unfortunately, as discussed in Chapter 5, media portrayals of people of color tend to be oversimplified and one-dimensional, and often reflect and reinforce existing stereotypes. For example, if a person is watching a crime drama, they're likely to see a disproportionate number of Black or Latino actors portraying a criminal. Consciously, they may not believe that people of color are usually criminals, but in their unconscious, they make a connection between a concept (criminality) and a physical appearance (brown skin). Being socially isolated increases the likelihood that these negative stereotypes take root in the minds of many White Americans, consciously or unconsciously.

Some losses related to racial segregation are more detrimental to White Americans than to people of color. Most people of color, especially those who are upwardly mobile, have some experience interacting or engaging with White folks. The media has also shown them a diverse (and overwhelmingly positive) representation of White people. They do not have the opportunity to live the same sort of racially segregated life as White Americans can. The evidence on implicit bias bears this out.

One of the most popular methods for exploring one's own implicit biases is the implicit associations test (IAT). The results of the race IAT show that the majority of people of all races indicate some level of preference for European Americans over African Americans, except for Black respondents (only half of Black respondents show such a preference). The fact that half of Black respondents show preference for European Americans relative to African Americans also indicates how pervasive anti-Blackness and positive perceptions of Whiteness are.

This is a problem for White Americans because these unconscious biases often run contrary to what people consciously believe and can manifest in behaviors antithetical to our conscious orientations. For Whites, unconscious bias could cause them to behave in ways that are subtly racist, make assumptions based on stereotypes, or other problems. Being racially segregated increases the likelihood of these challenges.

CONSIDER THIS

Why do you think most people ignore the negative impact of racism for White Americans?

The biggest fear, for many White people, is the fear of being labeled a racist. In her book *White Fragility: Why It's So Hard for White People to Talk About Racism*, Robin DiAngelo (2018) discusses this in depth and breaks down how and why many Whites are resistant to conversations about race through her conception of White fragility. Dictionary.com defines the term as "the tendency among members of the dominant White cultural group to have a defensive, wounded, angry, or dismissive response to evidence of racism." This fear of being labeled racist prevents many conversations from occurring. It also works in opposition to the widely held conscious wish for a society that celebrates diversity and encourages intergroup community and solidarity.

It helps to think of racism as an adverb (acting racist) rather than a noun (you are a racist) (Kendi 2019). Racism describes actions or consequences of actions (e.g., racist laws or policies) rather than people. Here lies one of the strengths of understanding racism sociologically. It allows us to move away from the idea of racism as rooted in individuals' mind-set or as a disease to be cured. We no longer look for symptoms to identify the sick "racist." Instead, we focus on systemic reform that emphasizes the importance of addressing real, material inequities on a broad scale, as we discuss in the next chapter.

SOCIOLOGISTS IN ACTION

Robin DiAngelo

Recognizing White Fragility

I grew up in poverty, in a family in which no one was expected to go to college. Thus, I came late to academia, graduating with a BA in sociology at age 34. Unsure what I could do with my degree, I went to my college's career center for help. A counselor told me that a job announcement had just arrived for a "diversity trainer," and she thought I would be a good fit. The state's Department of Social and Health Services (DSHS—the "welfare" department) had been sued for racial discrimination and had lost the suit. The federal government had determined that the department was out of compliance regarding serving all clients equally across races and, as part of the settlement, mandated that every employee in the state (over 5,000 people) receive 16 hours (2 full workdays) of diversity training.

As the years went by and I was involved in hundreds of discussions on race, clear and consistent patterns, or racial "scripts," emerged among White participants. There is a foundational sociological question that has never failed me in my efforts to uncover how our institutions continue to reproduce racial inequality. This question is not whether a narrative is true or false or right or wrong, but *how does it function*? As I looked at my findings with my sociological tools, I gained more clarity about why White people expressed so much resistance about discussing race and how that resistance functioned—whether it was conveyed explicitly through angry outbursts or implicitly through silence, apathy, and superficiality.

In 2011, I wrote an academic article titled "White Fragility," describing the patterns White people demonstrate when challenged racially and offering a theory on how these patterns functioned to protect systemic racism and White advantage. The article went viral and circulated worldwide. In 2018 I turned the article into an accessible nonacademic book titled *White Fragility: Why It's So Hard for White People to Talk About Racism*. The book debuted on the *New York Times'* bestseller list, and the concept has influenced the international dialogue on racism.

One of the most common critiques I receive from White readers is that I am generalizing about White people. My response is, "I am a sociologist, and social life is patterned and predictable in ways that can be described and analyzed." My hope is that having the language to speak to these patterns makes it harder for White people to engage in them without accountability. In that way, we may create a more racially just environment for Black, Indigenous, and all peoples of color.

Robin DiAngelo is a racial and social justice trainer, consultant, and professor who is most famous for her concept of White fragility, the topic of her bestselling book and a primary focus of her training and consultation activities.

Discussion Question

How does "the tendency among members of the dominant White cultural group to have a defensive, wounded, angry, or dismissive response to evidence of racism" protect systemic racism and White advantage?

DOING SOCIOLOGY 13.3

Explaining White Fragility

In this exercise, you will think about what White fragility means and how it manifests.

Consider and write answers to the following questions:

1. What does White fragility mean, in your own words?

2. What are ways you have witnessed White fragility in yourself or in others?

3. In her book, Robin DiAngelo suggests a path forward for her White target audience that includes embracing the discomfort of taking constructive feedback from people of color regarding racial missteps and taking this as a sign of faith in the relationship. What do you think about this feedback? What other suggestions do you have for dealing with or overcoming White fragility?

Check Your Understanding

1. Why do we rarely look at the effects of racial segregation on Whites?

2. What is "White habitus"?

3. What is unconscious bias?

4. What is White fragility?

HOW CAN ANTIRACISM BENEFIT EVERYONE?

We have discussed some of the ways in which racism hurts everyone, including people whom we wouldn't expect it to hurt. The converse is also true. Antiracism can benefit everyone, but we first need to understand what antiracism is and some of the forms it can take.

What Is Antiracism?

In *How to be an Antiracist*, Ibram X. Kendi (2019) says that the actions of both individuals and institutions are either "racist" or "antiracist." No action is "nonracist." Actions that do not work against racism are racist. So, every policy in every institution either supports racial equity or inequity, according to Kendi. Right now, our social institutions sustain racial inequity. Thus, anything antiracist must challenge the way society operates. Antiracism is, by definition, revolutionary action that works against racism.

Many people view racism as based on ignorance and misinformation and that education, then, is the solution. And while biases (conscious and unconscious) are sometimes related to ignorance or lack of information, systemic racism is not attributable to ignorance. Policymakers tend to know the effects of their policies (Kendi 2019). So, while helpful, education is not enough to eradicate systemic racism.

CONSIDER THIS

What is your reaction to the fact that education, alone, will not curb racism?

Antiracist work must take place on multiple levels. On the individual level, challenging racial prejudice and unconscious bias through education is helpful. At the institutional level, we need to look at the institutions in which we are members—where we work and where we hold positions of authority—critically and challenge their support for the racist status quo.

What about the school you attend? If you are studying at a historically White college or university (HWCU), use your sociological eye to see if it operates in a way that centers White people and marginalizes people of color. Frequently, institutional leaders at these schools make use of policies and procedures, symbols, or ideas that privilege Whiteness and make it more difficult for students of color to succeed. These institutions were designed with White students in mind and have not changed much, despite (in some cases) now having a more racially diverse student body. This tends to contribute to lower retention and graduation rates among students of color (Bonilla-Silva 2012; Luke 2018).

Finally, on the structural level, we need to recognize and address how our institutions interact with one another to reinforce racial inequality. For example, in the criminal justice system, why are returning citizens in some states prohibited from voting after completing their sentence? Why is there a school to prison pipeline for Black, Latinx, and American Indian students? Why is it still harder for Black people than White people to buy a home in an area with well-funded schools? We need to see these connections among institutions, recognize how they support racial inequality, and help them perform in antiracist, rather than racist, ways.

White Antiracist Activism

As we have noted throughout this book, White people consciously created systemic racism in the United States, and most still support it (consciously or unconsciously). Therefore, White people are especially obliged to challenge our racist system and actively work against it. It's important to remember, however, that White people need to let those disadvantaged the most by racism lead antiracist efforts.

White antiracist writers and activists JLove Calderon and Tim Wise created a "Code of Ethics for Antiracist White Allies" that lists suggestions for how White Americans can become antiracist activists.

1. Acknowledge our racial privilege.

2. Develop interpersonal connections and structures to help maintain antiracist accountability.

3. Be prepared to alter our methods and practices when and if people of color give feedback or offer criticism about our current methods and practices.

4. Listen to constructive feedback from other White people, too.

5. If we speak out about White privilege, racism, and/or White supremacy, whether in a public forum or in private discussions with friends, family, or colleagues, we should acknowledge that people of color have been talking about these subjects for a long time and yet have been routinely ignored in the process.

6. Share access and resources with people of color whenever possible.

7. If you get paid to speak out about White privilege, racism, and/or White supremacy or in some capacity make your living from challenging racism, donate a portion of your income to organizations led principally by people of color.

8. Get involved in a specific, people of color–led struggle for racial justice.

9. Stay connected to White folks, too.

10. Connect antiracism understanding to current political struggles and provide suggestions for avenues for White people to get involved (Calderon and Wise 2012).

Interest Convergence

One way to work toward gaining support for antiracist measures is to present them through the perspective of **interest convergence**. The idea behind interest convergence is that Whites will support antiracist policies when they see that they will meet their interests, as well as those of people of color (Bell 1980). Diversity and inclusion professionals often leverage interest convergence. For example, when affirmative action policies in higher education were challenged at the Supreme Court, many businesses submitted amicus briefs that explained how their businesses will suffer if there are not enough college graduates of color. Pointing out that they need a racially diverse group of college-educated employees to be successful, these corporate leaders made a business (financial) case for the importance of diversity as opposed to simply relying on the moral case.

PHOTO 13.3 Affirmative action supporters make their voices heard.

David Butow/Corbis via Getty Images.

For many passionate about social justice and moved by moral arguments for antiracism, interest convergence doesn't feel good because it involves centering the interests of those in power—White people. But interest convergence is a pragmatic approach in a system that privileges Whiteness. If we discuss antiracism's benefits to White people more, providing evidence against the widely held belief that the gains of people of color come at the expense of White folks, then White Americans are more likely to support antiracism.

Let's look at student loan debt. The rapid increase in this kind of debt over the past few decades has widened the racial wealth gap. However, student loan debt is a problem for many White people, as well as people of color. So, a policy to forgive student loan debt would likely gain the support of White folks as well as people of color. The result? Benefits to both groups and less racial inequality (Seamster and Charron-Chénier 2017).

In some ways, interest convergence is the focus of this chapter. Racism hurts everyone, and antiracism helps everyone—including White people. When the interests of White Americans and people of color converge, antiracist efforts have a much greater chance of succeeding and benefiting us all in the process.

DOING SOCIOLOGY 13.4

Interest Convergence and Antiracism

In this exercise, you will examine the pros and cons of leveraging interest convergence for antiracism efforts.

Interest convergence seems to be a way of treating the symptoms (e.g., advocating for policies to remedy racial inequality) rather than the cause (racial prejudice and systemic racism). Consider and write answers to the following questions:

1. Is focusing most on the needs of and benefits for White Americans as opposed to people of color problematic?

2. What other tactics would appeal to you more and be as or more effective?

Check Your Understanding

1. What is antiracism?

2. Why are White people especially obliged to challenge our racist system and actively work against it?

3. What is interest convergence?

4. Why does antiracism benefit everyone?

CONCLUSION

This chapter discussed some of the ways that racism harms and antiracism benefits everyone. The next chapter focuses on how to dismantle systemic racism and gives more concrete recommendations for how each of us can be antiracists working to dismantle the systemic racism that hurts us all.

CHAPTER REVIEW

13.1 How does racism hurt everyone, including White people?

Racism hurts everyone, including White people, in numerous ways. It robs society of our best potential doctors, lawyers, researchers, and politicians through external discrimination. Racism limits the social networks and relationships of Whites. It also produces White fragility, which makes it difficult for Whites to talk about and connect across race, and, in general, hampers racial progress. Racism does not function as a zero-sum game, where one group's gain is a loss for the other; instead, racism harms all of society.

13.2 Why is it hard to talk about racism—and why have we done so, anyway, in recent years?

Talking about racism is difficult for several reasons, including the fact that many people have limited practice doing so. Further, many White Americans get defensive and fear being labeled a racist. This is, at least partly, due to an individualized understanding of racism. Robin DiAngelo's work on White fragility illustrates some of the obstacles facing productive conversations about racism among Whites, who tend to be most resistant to such conversations. The politically charged 2016 and 2020 elections, the Black Lives Matter movement, and the police killings of Black men and women publicized through social media in recent years brought systemic racism into the mainstream public discourse.

13.3   What is White fragility?

White fragility is "the tendency among members of the dominant White cultural group to have a defensive, wounded, angry, or dismissive response to evidence of racism" (Dictionary. com). Navigating the resistance that many White people have toward conversations about race can be difficult. Understanding White fragility can help you navigate those conversations to ultimately get to the point of actively combatting racism.

13.4   How can interest convergence help show that antiracism benefits everyone?

Antiracism benefits everyone because racism hurts everyone. Derrick Bell's idea of interest convergence can be leveraged to advance antiracist causes, in part, because our collective interests converge so frequently. There are numerous rationales for antiracism, including economic, academic, moral, and social justice. While we might feel more personally aligned with one or the other antiracist tactic, leveraging the various ways that antiracism can benefit society and using interest convergence can help lead to antiracist progress that will benefit everyone.

Leveraging interest convergence might get even people who are skeptical about the persistence of racism to support policies that will ultimately reduce racial inequity. For instance, there is evidence that student loan debt increases the racial wealth gap. So a student loan debt forgiveness policy that would clearly benefit everyone (regardless of race) with student loans would work to reduce the racial wealth gap—and have a good chance of gaining the support of White people as well as folks of color.

KEY TERMS

Antiracism (p. 278)

Interest convergence (p. 280)

White fragility (p. 277)

White transparency (p. 270)

14 DISMANTLING SYSTEMIC RACISM

Michael L. Rosino

LEARNING QUESTIONS
14.1 How do agency, sociological knowledge, and social norms relate to social change to dismantle systemic racism?
14.2 What are racial justice practices? What are three types of practices that can dismantle systemic racism?
14.3 What are racial justice policies? What are four types of policies that can dismantle systemic racism?

What do you do now? How will you use your sociological understanding of systemic racism? After all, what matters most is not whether we understand how society works or even how it makes us feel but what we do with this understanding. Now that you understand systemic racism, this chapter focuses on what you can do to help dismantle it.

HOW I GOT ACTIVE IN SOCIOLOGY

Michael L. Rosino

I grew up in a predominantly White, upper-middle-class neighborhood in a rural suburb in northern Ohio. However, many of my friends were working-class or impoverished, and some lived in trailer parks. As I made my way through the local public school, I became highly engaged in academics and labeled as a gifted student. I received an opportunity to attend a private high school with an advanced curriculum. Entering this new school afforded me access to a new social world. A majority of the students came from intergenerational wealth. At the same time, many of my classmates were second-generation immigrants of various ethnic backgrounds.

Contrasting these two worlds, marked by cultural difference and class status, had awoken in me a more profound curiosity about how people's social backgrounds and access to resources and opportunities influence their lived experiences. Over time, my appreciation for understanding social group differences grew into a passion for social equity and a critical awareness of systems of oppression. I have continued to explore these questions—first as a student and now as an assistant professor of sociology, a researcher, and an educator—while working with organizations and communities to advance racial justice and civic engagement.

SYSTEMIC RACISM, AGENCY, AND SOCIAL CHANGE

In earlier chapters, we defined systemic racism. Before we talk about how to change the system, here's a quick two-point refresher on systemic racism.

1. *Systemic racism takes place through and across institutions.* People deal with institutions (such as education, religion, families, the economy, or the state) throughout their lives. Just today, you may have read the news (mass media) or completed assignments and attended class (education). What you learn in school might impact how you interpret events in the news and vice versa. Understanding systemic racism helps us understand that racism exists within and influences us through institutions.

2. *Whites' economic and social domination of other racial groups drives racial inequality* (Feagin 2006). Sociologists use the term *racism* to describe the activities and arrangements that work to maintain that domination. Another name for this relationship between Whites and people of color is **oppression**—an ongoing social process whereby one group dominates another and uses power to maintain that unequal relationship.

Systemic racism will not diminish just because time passes and society changes. For example, since the first measure of it in the early 1960s, the wide disparity in wealth between Whites and Blacks remains (Oliver and Shapiro 2019). And while our sociological tools are crucial for social change, as noted in Chapter 13, it is not enough to simply gain sociological knowledge about racial oppression. Racial progress requires that we use our **agency**, our innate ability to identify opportunities, make choices, and act, to try to change systems so that they promote racial equality.

How Change Happens: Practices, Social Norms, and Policies

What does social change look like? Consider the dramatic changes in Americans' attitudes about race and ethnicity depicted in Figure 14.1. Many more Americans than in the past explain racial inequality as a product of discrimination and think the country needs to continue making changes to produce racial equality. However, to achieve racial justice, we need to do more than change our attitudes. For instance, reflect on the story told in Figure 14.2. Researchers found no decline in hiring discrimination against Blacks over 25 years (Quillian, Pager, Hexel, and Midtbøen 2017). While attitudes are essential, dismantling systemic racism requires fundamental changes in what people and institutions actually do.

Throughout this book, we identify aspects and examples of systemic racism. All of these provide starting points. Understanding problems is a crucial first step in creating solutions. However, it is not enough to simply "undo" or "destroy" the problems we identify. We also need to build alternatives. We need to engage in *new* social patterns and develop new institutions.

In other words, we need to establish and enact antiracist practices and policies that produce racial justice. **Practices** are actions people take on a regular basis. Changing the ways we think, talk, and interact with others can help build new social norms. **Social norms** are rules for behavior that we take for granted as "normal" in everyday life. Shifts in social norms can change the structure of society (Green 2016). When something no longer seems normal, people feel free to think, do, and say other things (Sunstein 2019). **Policies** are laws, rules, and regulations on how organizations and societies should operate. They reflect, reinforce, and sometimes alter social norms and the structure of society.

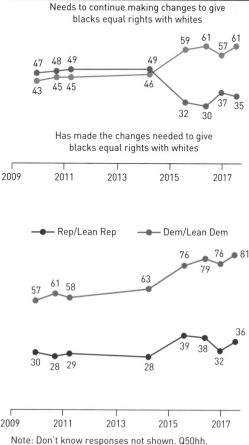

FIGURE 14.1 ■ Majority Says Country Needs to Continue Making Changes for Racial Equality

Needs to continue making changes to give blacks equal rights with whites

Has made the changes needed to give blacks equal rights with whites

—●— Rep/Lean Rep   —●— Dem/Lean Dem

Note: Don't know responses not shown. Q50hh.

Source: "Majority says country needs to continue making changes for racial equality" 2017. Pew Research Center survey conducted June 8-18 and June 27-July 9, 2017. https://www.pewresearch.org/politics/2017/10/05/4-race-immigration-and-discrimination/4_1-10/

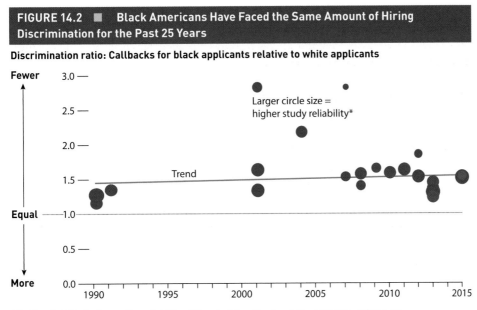

FIGURE 14.2 ■ **Black Americans Have Faced the Same Amount of Hiring Discrimination for the Past 25 Years**

Discrimination ratio: Callbacks for black applicants relative to white applicants

*Study reliability indicates the reliability of the study's estimate of discrimination relative to other studies, influenced by the number of applications a study sends out, among other factors.

Source: Quillian, Pager, Midtbøen, Hexel. "Hiring Discrimination Against Black Americans Hasn't Declined in 25 Years". Harvard Business Review 2017. https://hbr.org/2017/10/hiring-discrimination-against-black-americans-hasnt-declined-in-25-years.

CONSIDER THIS

What are some recent policies that have changed society? Your campus?

DOING SOCIOLOGY 14.1

Using Your Sociological Tool Kit

In this exercise, you will consider the sociological tools you can use to address racism. Sociology provides us with important tools. Thinking about all that you have learned throughout this book, answer the following questions:

1. Choose an issue or problem discussed in the book that you are most passionate about or find the most troubling. Why does that issue or problem matter to you?

2. What are three sociological tools you can use to address that problem?

3. For each of these tools, what are two things you could do to put that sociological tool into action for social change?

Check Your Understanding

1. What are the two major aspects of systemic racism?

2. What is agency, and how does it enable social change?

3. What is the difference between practices and policies? How might they influence one another?

RACIAL JUSTICE PRACTICES

"Practice makes perfect" is a common saying. It means that you need to choose to invest time and energy, learn, and exert effort if you want to see progress and achieve your goals. Yet our social practices, the repeated actions we take in social life, are often unconscious habits. We tend to be in this autopilot-like state as we engage with the racially unequal structure of society (Glaude 2017). Like all habits, our racial habits can provide us with a sense of comfort and familiarity (Giddens 1991; Glaude 2017). However, practicing racial justice requires that we reflect deeply on the things we do and cultivate new routines. Toward that end, here are three practices you can use to promote racial justice.

Building Racial Consciousness and Literacy

Before we can take part in racial justice practices, we must first become aware of the relationship among racial oppression, ourselves, and the rest of society. In other words, it requires a particular type of consciousness or awareness. **Racial consciousness** is the ability to understand situations, problems, issues, and experiences in ways that focus on social relations, power imbalances, and the impacts of racist social arrangements (Twine 2010). No matter your racial background, after reading the earlier chapters, you should have that now.

Differences in racial consciousness help shape how we act and interact. Ignorance of systemic racism and its influence on people's lives can lead Whites, regardless of their intentions, to engage in racist practices. In a broad sense, when it comes to whether we promote or help dismantle systemic racism, ignorance can be as harmful as cruelty. People are not born with racial consciousness—they gain it.

One way of working to dismantle systemic racism is through consciousness-raising—working with other people to increase your and their awareness of institutional racism. For instance, groups of Black feminist activists, scholars, and writers such as the Combahee River Collective (1986) engaged in consciousness-raising in the 1970s and 80s to better understand the forms of oppression they experienced as Black women and develop new visions and strategies for liberation. From those consciousness-raising sessions, new ideas and practices emerged that continue to highlight the power of solidarity in the face of oppression and to shape activism, cultural expression, and politics more than four decades later (Taylor 2017).

Simply taking the time to learn, talk, and reflect with others is crucial. To pass on racial consciousness to others, you need to develop **racial literacy**—the ability to communicate and apply racial consciousness to new situations (Twine 2010). The more we engage in conversations and work with others to understand issues of racial injustice and inequality, the more our tool kit for dismantling systemic racism expands.

For White people, engaging in racial justice practices also requires breaking with White solidarity (DiAngelo 2018). Solidarity is a feeling of agreement and shared interest. If you are White, you likely feel pressure at times to conform to the expectations of friends and family to either avoid racial topics all together or to simply "go along" with racist speech and acts (Picca and Feagin 2007). If you are a person of color, you face risks for addressing racism, such as being labeled as aggressive or problematic (Essed 1991; Evans and Moore 2015; Meghji 2019). You can also become emotionally exhausted if you lack social support. Working to dismantle systemic racism takes bravery and willingness to take risks and be uncomfortable. Dismantling systemic racism means confronting potentially difficult truths and realities.

Humanization, Storytelling, and Representation

It is incredibly difficult to justify systemic racism if you see those being harmed as human beings with the same experiences and needs as yourself. As discussed in earlier chapters, alongside racial oppression, there is always dehumanization. When we dehumanize people, we see them as less than fully human—as fundamentally alien and inferior.

Understanding the support beams that uphold systemic racism, such as dehumanization, helps us identify strategies for dismantling them. The stories that we tell and how we represent people in those stories can humanize or dehumanize them. Dehumanization can take on extreme and deadly forms. In the days of legal slavery, books and images depicted enslaved Black people as docile and naturally suited to hold inferior positions in society—helping to normalize the idea that slavery was morally justifiable (Collins 1990). Cultures of dehumanization enable people to deny the basic human dignity of the targeted group and rationalize their oppression.

Dehumanizing representations of people of color have remained a widespread problem in many institutions and contexts, especially with the use of social media. A recent investigation found that "hundreds of active-duty and retired law enforcement officers from across the United States are members of Confederate, anti-Islam, misogynistic or anti-government militia groups on Facebook" (Carless and Corey 2019). The mob that attacked the Capitol on January 6, 2021, responded to President Trump's invitation via Twitter and organized themselves online. They included some off-duty police officers and many people related to the military. Twenty percent of those arrested for the attack on the Capitol were active or former members of the U.S. armed forces (Dreisbach and Anderson 2021; Griffith 2021). Police officers and the military are not the only groups with cultures of dehumanization. They persist across many occupations, social groups, and networks. Given all this, what can you do?

You can engage in humanization. **Humanization** occurs when we recognize dehumanized people as full human beings deserving of the same rights, freedoms, and quality of life as everyone else. For example, the grassroots organization We Charge Genocide (WCG) formed in 2014 to address the Chicago Police Department's use of violence and torture against African American and Latinx youth. It focused on reporting and spreading the word about incidences of police brutality in Chicago. WCG even presented a shadow report to the United Nations to suggest that the UN Committee Against Torture "recognize the life-threatening struggles that young people of color in Chicago are enduring at the hands of the CPD and to support their organizing efforts to end police violence" (WCG 2014, 13). These activists relied on many tactics, including storytelling and humanization (Rosino 2018).

PHOTO 14.1 While testifying at the United Nations Committee against Torture, activists in We Charge Genocide used storytelling to humanize friends, family members, and neighbors—including 23-year-old Dominique "Damo" Franklin, Jr.—who were victims of police violence in Chicago.

DENIS BALIBOUSE/REUTERS/Newscom

WCG and many other racial justice advocates meet dehumanization with humanization. The U.S. Department of Justice (2017, 147) report on the Chicago Police Department demonstrates pervasive dehumanization—"a recurring portrayal by some CPD officers of the residents of challenged neighborhoods—who are mostly black—as animals or subhuman." WCG countered these images by telling the stories and experiences of friends and family members destroyed by police violence. In the process, it showed that the violence of racism affects fully human people with hopes, dreams, stories, and families. For example, in the UN and other public venues, WCG activists relayed the story of 19-year-old Roshad McIntosh, a young man who hoped to attend veterinary school, whose last words were "Please don't shoot, please don't kill me, I don't have a gun" (Berlatsky 2014). Awareness of McIntosh's story led to a criminal investigation into the officer who shot him that led to his firing (Hinkel 2020) and a CNN three-part documentary called *Beneath the Skin* that highlights his mother's struggle for answers about the killing of her slain son.

Statistics can be useful to demonstrate the scope of a problem like racial discrimination or police brutality. But when it comes to our ability to fight the impacts of dehumanization, stories can have a much richer and deeper impact. The humanizing work of WCG and other groups of activists led to a Department of Justice investigation into the Chicago Police Department (Horwitz, Nakashima, and Lowery 2015) and groundbreaking legislation that provided reparations to the victims of police torture in Chicago (Gwynne 2015).

DOING SOCIOLOGY 14.2

The Power of Stories

In this exercise, think about the stories that you regularly hear and see about race—and their effects. Stories can help us better understand each other and work for justice. However, they can also create or contribute to social division and promote inequality. Identify at least two stories that you regularly see and hear in the media or among your family and friends. Take notes about these stories, be prepared to share with others, and answer the following questions in writing.

1. How do these stories influence how you view people of other races? How do they make you feel about your own race(s)? Why?

2. If you were hired by a major media outlet to ensure that it did not deliver dehumanizing stories about racial groups, what policies would you suggest?

3. What are some things that you can do, in your own life, to avoid or correct dehumanizing stories?

Movement and Coalition Formation

It's no secret that movements are more powerful than individuals in producing social change. When people work together, they get more done. So, how can you participate in collective action that can tap into the resources, energy, and wisdom of a large group of people? One way is through checking out organizations near you. Just having more social contact with other people in your community can also help.

Organizations and groups often hold public events, meetings, and community dialogues where people get together to talk about issues with which they are concerned. For instance, in Hartford, Connecticut, there is an annual Stand Against Racism day organized by the YWCA and Everyday Democracy. For the 2019 event, community members, employees of nonprofit organizations, academics, and college students got together to hold a discussion about immigration and racial justice, meet new people, and develop an action plan for addressing these issues (Ramos 2019). Through talking to people, you can learn more about our common interests and who might want to work with you to address racism.

Social capital, the helpful social relationships that we form with others, provides an important resource for social change. However, a major step in movement building involves doing your homework to ensure you make strategic connections. In other words, you must research organizations, individuals, opportunities, and movements in your community. This process is known as asset mapping. It allows you to find the people, materials, and opportunities that can help you make an impact. Social capital and asset mapping will also help you form coalitions—relationships and cooperative efforts among different organizations. Just as groups are more powerful than individuals, coalitions of organizations can be stronger than one lone organization. One quick search can make you see that you don't have to work for change as just one person. It simply takes some digging and the courage to make new connections.

For example, a coalition among law enforcement officers, community members, activists, national organizations, experts, and policymakers worked together recently to push for racial justice reforms in the criminal justice system in North Carolina. One of those experts was Felicia Arriaga, the Sociologist in Action featured in this chapter.

SOCIOLOGISTS IN ACTION
Felicia Arriaga

Local Opportunities to Get Involved

My parents were farmworkers, migrating between Florida and North Carolina until my mom decided to leave her extended family to stay in Hendersonville, North Carolina, to raise my siblings and me. There, I had to navigate a K–12 school system as one of few Latinx students. These experiences led me into an academic career focusing on how Latinx interact with law and immigration enforcement—parts of the prison industrial complex. For example, while I was completing my PhD at Duke University, I used my sociological skills in these ways:

1. As a lobbying intern for the Adelante Education Coalition, working on an in-state tuition equity fight for undocumented students.
2. Creating a teaching and learning guide for *Sociology Compass* that helps students ask questions about local immigration enforcement in their own backyards (see Arriaga 2016).
3. Serving as a representative on the City of Durham's Human Relations Commission.
4. Cofounding Durham Beyond Policing, a coalition fighting for divestment from policing and prisons and investing in resources to support the health of Black and Brown communities and benefit all residents of Durham, North Carolina.
5. Participating in the Latino Migration Project at UNC–Chapel Hill, conducting oral histories, and taking students to Mexico to learn about migration.
    These were ways I worked with others to challenge systemic racism.
    These opportunities also strengthened my qualitative data collection skills and allowed me to work alongside community members to find answers to questions such as these:

PHOTO 14.2
© FELICIA ARRIAGA

- What does a sheriff's office that is accountable to its community look like?
- How many people do county jails deport? Who funds these deportations? What can local law enforcement do to end this practice? How does this practice affect our local public safety budgets?
- What keeps us safe? How does the definition of safety differ by one's social identity?
    I'm excited to bring other scholars into more community-engaged research—research that comes from impacted people who can take it directly to policymakers—to advocate for alternatives to current policies and procedures that support systemic racism.

Dr. Felicia Arriaga is assistant professor of sociology in the criminology concentration at Appalachian State University. She is an activist-scholar especially interested in how policies and procedures of crimmigration, the intersection of criminal and immigration law, relate to broader issues of criminal justice accountability, transparency, and reform.

Discussion Question

How can community-based research help bridge the gap between the experiences and issues of community members and the decisions made by policymakers?

Bringing people together for a shared cause requires focusing on what they can do together rather than their differences. In North Carolina, activists emphasized the moral importance of policy reforms and the harms of racist policies. The sheriffs in the coalition cared most about legal and public accountability, and Black and Latinx community members were interested primarily in challenging racial profiling, harsh conditions, and the mistreatment of people of color (Graham 2019). Together, this coalition put aside their differences to change policies that caused racial discrimination and inequality in their communities.

The task of forming large coalitions can seem daunting, but it is often the result of simple but disruptive and effective acts of resistance and solidarity. Consider just how many individual people are involved and invested in institutions that maintain racial oppression and how many individual daily choices contribute to harmful systems like the prison industrial complex. As grassroots organizer Sarah Freeman-Woolpert (2020) points out,

> Systems of power . . . are upheld by the tacit acceptance and cooperation of millions of people, from the dockworkers who receive shipments of weapons to the school boards who sign contracts that bring police into schools. By attracting people from pillars like the business sector, education system and religious institutions to . . . join with the movement, activists can tip the scales of power in their favor.

We can build coalitions by using our own opportunities and resources to support movements against systemic racism and empowering others from a range of different regions, occupations, and backgrounds to do the same.

CONSIDER THIS

What are some organizations, groups, or resources on campus or in your community that you could connect with to help dismantle systemic racism?

Check Your Understanding

1. What is the difference between racial consciousness and racial literacy?

2. Why does dismantling systemic racism demand courage from different groups?

3. How did the organization WCG use humanization as a strategy for social change?

4. Why does storytelling matter in terms of dismantling systemic racism?

5. What is asset mapping, and how does it help us build movements and coalitions against racism?

RACIAL JUSTICE POLICIES

One of the best ways to change society is to change the rules of society. Imagine you are playing a game with a friend. The rules of the game dictate that your friend gets more opportunities and resources and that you face more barriers and difficulties. Regardless of how talented, skilled, or hardworking you are, you just can't win. So, the solution is to create new rules. By changing the rules of the game, you can make the game fairer, more enjoyable, and less frustrating. Similarly, policies are sets of rules that shape social outcomes by setting guidelines for how institutions and organizations should operate. Previous chapters have shown how systemic racism is upheld by the policies of various institutions including the laws set forth by our government. Racial justice policies rewrite the rules of society to dismantle systemic racism. We take a look at four racial justice policies.

Destroying the Material Base

As relayed in earlier chapters, the unequal distribution and control of private property, material resources, and financial assets is central to racial oppression (Feagin 2006). For instance, the racial wealth gap, the differences in wealth ownership between racial groups, plays a central role in systemic racism. Racial justice policies, then, must address the institutional and structural causes and consequences of the wealth gap to ensure a more equal and just society. A large-scale redistribution of the wealth in our society can be difficult to imagine. However, wealth is redistributed all the time—but mostly in ways that maintain or exacerbate the massive wealth advantage held by Whites over other racial groups. So, the key is to think about how we can turn the tide.

Many people think an individual's wealth (or lack thereof) relates only to their decisions and behaviors. So how is this a policy issue? Well, as a research report points out,

Blacks cannot close the racial wealth gap by changing their individual behavior—i.e. by assuming more "personal responsibility" or acquiring the portfolio management insights associated with "financially literacy"—if the structural sources of racial inequality remain unchanged. . . . For the gap to be closed, America must undergo a vast social transformation produced by the adoption of bold national policies, policies that will forge a way forward by addressing, finally, the long-standing consequences of slavery, the Jim Crow years that followed, and ongoing racism and discrimination that exist in our society today. (Darity et al. 2018, 4–5)

In other words, because the racial wealth gap was produced by policies, it needs to be solved by policies. So, what are some policies that could close the racial wealth gap and dismantle the material base of systemic racism?

One such policy proposal is baby bonds (Hamilton and Darity 2010). If enacted, the U.S. government would give, at birth, *every* U.S. child "a bond between $500 and $50,000 . . . adjusted for their family's wealth [that] would remain locked until the child turned 18, when the funds would become available to pay for college, buy a home, or start a business" (Oliver and Shapiro 2019, 19). The baby bonds proposal represents a daring policy that would have major payoffs. According to a recent study and illustrated in Figure 14.3, if baby bonds were implemented one generation ago, it would have eliminated the racial wealth gap for people aged 18 to 34 (Annie E. Casey Foundation 2016). Other research suggests that baby bonds could reduce the overall racial wealth gap by half by 2060 (Weller, Maxwell, and Solomon 2019).

A federal jobs guarantee policy could help dismantle race-based income inequality. It would alleviate involuntary unemployment and ensure that the minimum wage is high enough to keep a family of four above the poverty line (Oliver and Shapiro 2019). This proposed policy has the potential to cut down on poverty and reduce the impacts of income inequality on the wealth gap. Moreover, some versions of the policy would also provide benefits including "health insurance, paid sick leave, maternity/paternity leave, paid vacation time, and retirement plans [that] protect wealth while building it (Oliver and Shapiro 2019, 21).

The material base of systemic racism is not just built on wealth inequality but also debt inequality. We can think of debt as negative wealth. Many people need to get out of debt before they can even start to build wealth. Student loans are a particularly strong driver of debt with which you are likely familiar. Not only is debt racially unequal, it has different functions for different racial groups. Due to financial rules and programs, Whites, in general, are better able to use debt as a temporary way to invest and build wealth. In contrast, debt tends to extract resources from Black families and communities (Seamster 2019). For example, as noted in earlier chapters, because of racial discrimination in lending, Blacks tend to have student and home loans with relatively high interest rates. These loans saddle the loan recipients with debt they often cannot afford to pay.

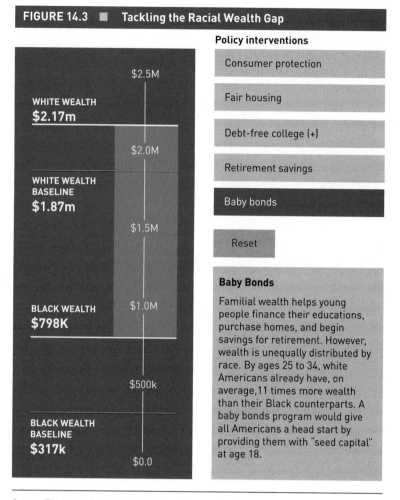

FIGURE 14.3 ■ Tackling the Racial Wealth Gap

Source: This material "Simulating How Progressive Proposals Affect the Racial Wealth Gap" by Christian E. Weller, Connor Maxwell, and Danyelle Solomon was published by the Center for American Progress. (https://www.americanprogress.org/issues/race/reports/2019/08/07/473117/simulating-progressive-proposals-affect-racial-wealth-gap/)

Let's take the example of student loan debt. Forgiving student loan debt of those with incomes of less than $50,000 would reduce the racial wealth gap between Whites and Blacks by almost 37%. Forgiving the student loan debt of those with incomes of less than $25,000 would decrease the gap by over 50% (Huelsman et al. 2015).

Advancing Democracy and Political Equality

As described in Chapter 4, racial discrimination in the distribution of political power—such as suppression of the votes of people of color—remains a problem. These issues are a matter of democracy. Racial inequality prevents us from tapping into the wisdom, interests, and experiences of people of color and achieving the best possible society for all people (Du Bois 1945/2004). So how can we remedy political inequality and achieve greater democracy?

One effective solution is to support policies based on active inclusion. **Active inclusion** is the idea that we can only achieve justice if everyone impacted by a policy or decision is included in the deliberations and political processes that determine it (Young 1999). This means that we need to develop policies that identify and reduce the impact of all forms of exclusion on the political process. Even in the absence of *active exclusion*—i.e., explicit policies barring people from participation because of their racial background—*passive exclusion* still results in political inequality. As mentioned in Chapter 4, Black and Latinx people face more barriers to spaces where voting or other forms of political engagement take place due to policies, decisions, and arrangements that, while appearing race "neutral" on the surface, negatively affect them more than Whites.

Several proposed policies would address political inequality and help us dismantle racialized barriers to participation in civic life and democracy. Here are only a few examples. One solution to disenfranchisement is automatic voter registration, a policy that would ensure that "when a state's public agencies and/or systems already have the information to know if a person is eligible to vote, the state's elections officials will add that person to the voter rolls unless the individual declines to be registered" (Kennedy, Daly, and Wright 2015, 21).

Another area ripe for policy reform is redistricting. In many states, elected officials draw electoral district lines in ways that reduce the influence of certain communities and populations. Politicians and political parties that rely heavily on the White vote use this practice to reduce the political influence of communities of color (Anderson 2018). This strategy is also known as racial gerrymandering. Policies to move toward fairer and more nonpartisan means of drawing political lines include increased input from independent commissions or the public, bipartisan approaches, and greater transparency about the criteria and processes used to draw these boundaries (FairVote 2019).

Finally, we need to stop the racial barriers to democracy enacted since the Supreme Court struck down the enforceability clause of the Voting Rights Act in 2013 (Anderson 2018). As described in Chapter 4, this decision means that state and local governments covered under the clause no longer have to demonstrate that new restrictions they place on voting are not racially discriminatory. So, perhaps most importantly, we need a new voting rights act to ensure a more racially inclusive and just democracy.

DOING SOCIOLOGY 14.3

Practicing Active Inclusion

In this exercise you will practice active inclusion.

Individually or with a group, begin by identifying a social problem related to race and ethnicity. Work through the following steps to consider how you could practice active inclusion while trying to solve a social problem through policymaking.

1. Start with some brainstorming. Take your time and make a list of all the groups of people impacted by the issue you want to address.

2. Which of the groups that you listed may be marginalized or often not included in deliberations and initiatives around this issue?

3. Identify the specific barriers to inclusion. What might prevent individuals from these groups from being active participants in events, dialogues, and action planning? For each, is this a passive or an active barrier?

4. Work on developing policies. For each barrier to inclusion, identify at least one policy that you could make to actively counter it and ensure inclusion of that social group. What resources, rules, or relationships would help you in this policymaking practice?

Working for Decarceration and Legal Justice

The disproportionate and harmful impact of the court systems, policing practices, and prison and jail systems are another major dimension of systemic racism. Many of these issues have already been covered in earlier chapters. Here we suggest some policy changes that could help transform how we achieve justice to push us closer to racial equality. The overall goal of these policies is decarceration, or reducing and reversing the scope and impact of racialized mass incarceration on society.

After decades of growth and expansion since the late 1970s, the U.S. prison population is now beginning to decline. However, while this reversal is a positive sign, these reductions in the prison population have been relatively small and slow. Figure 14.4, developed by the Sentencing Project, predicts future imprisonment rates based on current trends. At this pace, without major policy reforms, it would take 75 years just to cut the prison population in half (Ghandnoosh 2019). Moreover, decarceration is not simply about getting people out of prisons. It is a more holistic effort aimed at "healing trauma, restoring civil rights, and ending the suffering this system has imposed on American families and communities" (Drucker 2016).

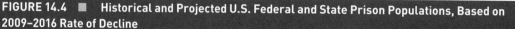

FIGURE 14.4 ■ Historical and Projected U.S. Federal and State Prison Populations, Based on 2009–2016 Rate of Decline

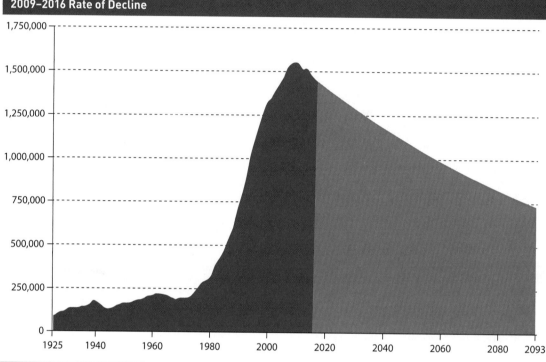

Source: "Figure 1: Historical and projected U.S. federal and state prison populations, based on 2009-2016 rate of decline." Source of historical figures: Bureau of Justice Statistics (1982) "Prisoners 1925-81"; Bureau of Justice Statistics Corrections Statistical Analysis Tool. From "Can We Wait 75 Years to Cut the Prison Population in Half?" Nazgol Ghandnoosh, Ph.D., 2018. https://www.sentencingproject.org/publications/can-wait-75-years-cut-prison-population-half/

Drug prohibition laws in the United States have played a huge role in increasing racially targeted and aggressive policing in Black and Latinx communities and mass incarceration (Cooper 2015; Rosino and Hughey 2018). While the eventual full legalization of cannabis across the United States seems more and more likely, we also need to fix the immense damage that the war on drugs did to communities. This requires policies that take a racial equity approach to assigning permits for sellers of recreational cannabis and that use the increased tax revenue on communities most negatively impacted by the drug war. For instance, in San Francisco, the city's Cannabis Equity Program offers incentives and waives permit fees for potential sellers "who meet equity eligibility criteria based on residency, income, criminal justice involvement and housing insecurity" (San Francisco Office of Cannabis 2019).

Decarceration policies reduce the use of incarceration as a form of punishment and reform the bail system so that fewer people overall, and particularly the disproportionately Black and Latinx prison population, are in prisons and jails across the country (Drucker 2017). There is already a strong decarceration movement. Seventy-one percent of Americans, across the ideological spectrum, support reductions to the prison population (ACLU 2017), and many states have already begun this process. On November 4, 2019, advocates and community members celebrated the news that the Oklahoma Pardon and Parole Board granted commutation to 527 inmates, with 462 released in one day in the largest mass commutation in U.S. history (Hoberock 2019). In states such as Connecticut, Michigan,

Mississippi, Rhode Island, and South Carolina, "data-driven policy reforms that pursued bipartisan consensus" reduced the prison population by focusing on "risk and needs assessment, community supervision, alternatives to incarceration, sentencing and sanctions, prison release mechanisms, prisoner reentry and community reintegration" (Schrantz, DeBor, and Mauer 2018, 5).

PHOTO 14.3 Community members and criminal justice reform advocates celebrate the release of over 500 inmates who had their sentences commuted on a single day in Oklahoma. Commutation is an important tool for reducing the prison population.

Sarah Phipps/The Oklahoman via AP

We also need to enact policies and build institutions that deal with problems like violence, victimization, and injustice in more fundamental and humane ways (Drucker 2017). Policies that bolster people's access to education, health care, and economic stability empower communities to solve problems. Using restorative justice, reparation, and rehabilitation rather than punishment would do a lot to help dismantle systemic racism.

We should also create policies that alter the function and role of policing. Many problems related to racial injustice and policing stem from the socialization police officers receive. Police training in the United States varies wildly by department. Many departments across the United States offer training focused on tactical skills and use of force that encourages the mentality of police seeing themselves as combatants or warriors in the community. However, others focus on reducing racial discrimination, encouraging officers to reduce and deescalate conflict and tension, and fostering greater communication and relationships with communities (MacLean et al. 2019). Mandating such trainings on a national scale would ensure that those who work in the interest of public safety are less likely to use violence and arrests as a means of dealing with conflict or regard racialized communities as inherently suspicious or threatening.

These reforms connect to efforts to humanize those impacted by the legal system, encourage transparency and accountability, and bolster decarceration. A sociological study had 130 volunteers take notes in everyday courtroom settings in Cook County, one of the United States' largest and most racially unequal prison systems. The study found patterns of racial discrimination, bias, and even wrongful convictions (Gonzalez Van Cleve 2016). Many of us don't realize the public has the right to observe courtroom trials. Instead, we often rely on sensationalized media accounts. To truly understand racialized mass incarceration, one immediate action you can take is to observe the processes that produce it as "a way to lend a conscience to an otherwise unaccountable system" (Gonzalez Van Cleve 2016, 189).

In the wake of mounting cases of anti-Black oppression and violence at the hands of police officers in the spring and summer of 2020, a wave of protests and consciousness-raising strengthened ongoing decarceration efforts and produced concrete policy reforms. For example, in the aftermath of the brutal police killing of George Floyd and in response to issues of systemic racism and anti-Black violence endemic to the Minneapolis Police Department, the Minneapolis City Council announced that it would disband the department and shift to new practices and policies for community safety. The alternate ways to protect their security and human rights include "community fire brigades, a people's ambulance, a transit support system, food banks and hot meal bars, and community safety and defense teams" (Shim 2020). Meanwhile, other cities outlawed chokeholds and neck restraints like the one used against George Floyd (and many others). New York State rescinded a policy that kept disciplinary procedures against police hidden from the public. At the same time, many U.S. schools removed police from their buildings and focused more on guidance and counseling (Kamenetz 2020).

Redefining Racial Discrimination

This increased awareness of systemic racism is vitally important. The protests in 2020 have awakened many Americans, particularly Whites, to the institutional actions and policies that maintain racial inequality. Recognizing their impact helps us understand the causes and consequences of racial inequality.

Consider the following. A city is planning to tear down a local housing complex whose residents are predominantly people of color. A community member who grew up in that complex attends a city meeting on the demolition. At the meeting, city officials report on the required assessment of the environmental impact of the demolition. They determine that the environmental impact is neutral so the plan can move forward. As she sits through the meeting, the community member begins to wonder why the city isn't required to report on the impact that this change would have on the building's residents. Bringing to light the impacts of policies and public decision-making on racial and ethnic groups is a vital step toward racial justice.

How can you know new policies won't strengthen systemic racism rather than dismantle it? As noted previously, new policies and development projects routinely undergo a fiscal and environmental impact before they are advanced. These allow us all to see the possible monetary and environmental consequences and weigh them against the potential benefits. Racial and ethnic impact assessments that bring to light the impacts of policies and public decision-making on racial and ethnic groups, in a similar way, is a vital step toward racial justice. Requiring such assessments can provide the information needed to dismantle systemic racism in approval processes.

We do not need to work from scratch to advance these policies. For example, the Drug Policy Alliance, an organization concerned with the racial justice impacts of drug law enforcement, is one organization among many advocating for racial and ethnic impact statements. It points out that

> A Racial and Ethnic Impact Statement (REIS) requires policymakers proposing new legislation or changes to existing legislation to assess the potential impact on racial disparities. Such statements are similar to fiscal or environmental impact statements, which are routinely required before new programs or developments can be implemented and are now widely considered responsible mechanisms of government. (Drug Policy Alliance 2015)

These efforts are already taking shape on the local level. In 2018, the state of Connecticut passed Senate Bill No. 256 Public Act No. 18-78, which requires racial and ethnic impact statements "with respect to certain bills and amendments" that could, if passed, increase or decrease the pretrial or sentenced population of the correctional facilities in the state. There is already evidence that these requirements yield positive results. A study in Iowa, the first state to pass a similar act, in 2008, found that "only six out of 26 bills' REIS statements described as having a disproportionate effect on minorities passed both chambers and became law . . . [whereas] bills that were rated as having no effect or a positive effect on minority incarceration rates were nearly twice as likely to pass" (Foley 2015). Using racial and ethnic impact reporting, we could better recognize and dismantle systemic racism.

CONSIDER THIS

What policies can you think of that would help dismantle systemic racism?

Check Your Understanding

1. What is decarceration? How might a decarcerated society deal with issues of violence and victimization?

2. What are some policies that would reduce economic inequalities between racial groups?

3. What is the difference between active and passive forms of exclusion? How do active inclusion policies reduce political inequality?

4. What are the shortcomings of our current legal approach to discrimination? What are racial and ethnic impact assessments? How did these assessments shape the likelihood that bills will pass in Iowa?

CONCLUSION

Dismantling systemic racism requires that we not only change the current system but also build a new one in its place that produces more racial equality. Like all forms of dismantling and building, this requires a toolset. Fortunately, you already have many of the tools you need. You can start by identifying the resources, skills, and networks you already have. With a little research and effort, you can also seek out more. Then, you simply need to muster up the courage to put your knowledge, agency, and social connections into action. People at all levels of society—including activists, academics, political leaders, students, and artists—are already working to dismantle systemic racism. They are just waiting for you to join them.

CHAPTER REVIEW

14.1 How do agency, sociological knowledge, and social norms relate to social change to dismantle systemic racism?

Sociological knowledge, our understanding of how society operates, is a major tool we can apply in work for racial justice. If we understand how social problems such as racism, discrimination, and inequality operate, we are that much closer to coming up with solutions. Moreover, we can make choices based on our knowledge so we can support practices and policies to dismantle systemic racism.

14.2 What are racial justice practices? What are three types of practices that can dismantle systemic racism?

Racial justice practices are daily activities we engage in, whether we do so intentionally or habitually, that help reduce racial inequality in society. *Racial consciousness*—growing, using, and spreading our awareness about racial oppression; *humanization*—recognizing the full humanity of people of color in storytelling and representation; and *movements and coalitions* are three practices we can use when working with other people, organizations, and communities in collective efforts at social change.

14.3 What are racial justice policies? What are four types of policies that can dismantle systemic racism?

Racial justice policies are rules and ways of organizing institutions that ultimately produce greater racial equality. The *material base*—closing the massive gap in wealth, income, and debt between racial groups; *political equality*—reducing the numerous barriers that prevent marginalized groups from participating in the democratic process; *legal justice*—finding less oppressive alternatives to the legal, policing, and criminal justice systems; and *impact assessments*—measuring the consequences that laws and large-scale decisions have on racial and ethnic groups so we can make more mindful policy choices, are four types that can dismantle systemic racism.

KEY TERMS

Active inclusion (p. 294)

Agency (p. 286)

Asset mapping (p. 290)

Baby bonds (p. 293)

Coalitions (p. 290)

Decarceration (p. 295)

Humanization (p. 289)

Oppression (p. 286)

Policies (p. 286)

Practices (p. 286)

Racial and ethnic impact assessments (p. 298)

Racial consciousness (p. 288)

Racial literacy (p. 288)

Social norms (p. 286)

GLOSSARY

2nd Treaty of Fort Laramie (1868). A treaty by which the U.S. government established the Great Sioux Reservation, which included the Black Hills—a sacred place for the Sioux in what are now South Dakota and Wyoming. As part of this treaty, the U.S. government declared that it would never allow White people to settle in the Black Hills.

Active inclusion. The idea that we can only achieve justice if everyone who is impacted by a policy or decision is included in the deliberations and political processes that determine it.

Advocacy. Use of resources to empower communities.

Agency. Our innate ability to identify opportunities, make choices, and act.

Alaska's Anti-Discrimination Act of 1945. An act that prohibited open discrimination of Alaska Natives, such as signs in stores that said "No Dogs or Natives Allowed."

Antihaitianismo. The dislike and opposition to Haiti and Haitians.

Antimiscegenation. Opposing or prohibiting marriage, sexual relations, and cohabitation between people of different races or racial categories.

Antiracism. Acting in opposition to the racist operation of society on the individual, institutional, or societal level.

Antisemitism. Attitudes used to justify practices resulting in discrimination, exploitation, and/or exclusion of Jews or those perceived to be Jewish.

Apartheid. A regime of legal segregation in South Africa.

Arab. An ethnic and/or linguistic identity claimed by individuals who speak Arabic and/or whose family heritage is traced to one of the 22 countries of the Arab League of Nations.

Articles of Confederation. The first Constitution of the United States.

Asian American. A pan-ethnic label created in 1968 to unite Asian ethnic groups for collective action and challenge the derogatory term *Oriental*.

Asset mapping. Researching the organizations, individuals, opportunities, and movements in your community so that you can make strategic connections with them.

Assimilation. The process of taking on another group's culture.

Audit study. Research method used to identify patterns of racism on average. It involves the creation of fake auditors who are identical in all aspects, except for the category of focus (e.g., race). Auditors are then distributed to subjects in the real world and the researcher determines if any group is favored on average.

Baby bonds. A policy proposal that would reduce the racial wealth gap wherein children receive a bond at birth that is higher or lower inversely based on the wealth of their family and becomes available when they turn 18 to invest in education, homeownership, or other opportunities.

Bamboo ceiling. Refers to the specific obstacles that Asian Americans face in attaining senior leadership positions.

Battle of Little Bighorn (1876). Battle during the Black Hills War where George Armstrong Custer and almost all his men died.

Biracial. Composed of, combining, representing, relating to, or descended from two races.

Black Hills War of 1876. Prompted by the U.S. government's takeover of the Black Hills after Lieutenant Colonel George Armstrong Custer discovered gold in the Black Hills and allowed White people to occupy the area. This was the last of the big wars on the Great Plains.

Black Is Beautiful. Slogan that became popular during the 1960s and counteracted the negative prevailing perception of Black people's bodies in the United States.

Black Lives Matter movement (BLM). Founded in 2014 to protest the continual racial injustices within the criminal justice system, it initially focused on police brutality and police shootings of Black women and men. This movement has expanded to address all injustices facing Black people.

Black migration. A large amount of the Black Southern population leaving the harsh conditions of the South to find work and better opportunities initially in the North but also in the West during the 20th century.

Black Power movement. Popularized by Stokely Carmichael (Kwame Ture) to encourage Black people to come together as a political force to meet the needs of Black people not being addressed by the government.

Blackbirding. The coercion and entrapment of Pacific Islanders for slave labor.

Blackface. A phenomenon in which White men blackened their faces, donned wigs, and painted their lips to appear wide and bright white in an effort to mock African Americans; blackface was popular in minstrel shows and early American film.

Boarding schools. Usually located far from Indian reservations, Indian boarding schools focused more on assimilation than education. At the schools, American Indian boys and girls were forced to cut their hair, wear clothes worn by White people, speak English, and embrace Christianity rather than the religion of their people. The teachers beat those who violated the rules, and many boys and girls faced sexual assault from teachers and administrators. The students graduated estranged from their families and still not accepted by White people.

Boundaries. The dividing lines between social groups.

Chattel. Personal property that owners can do with as they wish. Enslaved people in colonial and U.S. society were seen as chattel.

Chicano movement. Civil rights movement responsible for the extension of labor rights to farmworkers, the extension of voting rights to linguistic citizen minorities (e.g., Spanish-speaking Latinxs), and engaging in cultural and community projects throughout the U.S. Southwest.

Chinese Exclusion Act (1882). Legislation that created a moratorium on Chinese labor immigration, effectively banning all Chinese immigration; unique in that it engaged in class and race-based immigration discrimination.

Civil Rights Act of 1964. Outlawed discrimination based on race, color, religion, sex, or national origin.

Civilizing mission. The justification for colonizing people due to what was considered an inferior culture, religion, and intellect.

Coalitions. Relationships and cooperative efforts among different organizations.

COINTELPRO. A set of FBI programs designed to surveil, disrupt, and infiltrate civil rights and other political organizations such as the Black Panthers, Nation of Islam, and Southern Christian Leadership Council.

Colonialism. Expanding one nation into another geographic area through violent social control practices.

Colonialism. The practice of exerting political, social, and economic control over another territory and its inhabitants.

Color line. Concept used in Du Bois's *The Souls of Black Folk* that refers to race and racism and their effects on opportunities for African Americans.

Colorblind ideology. A type of racism that refers to the belief that racism will disappear if people ignore race and racial differences.

Colorblind racism. A dominant racial ideology that operates discreetly, with social actors who frequently mention "not seeing color" while advocating for maintaining White supremacist ideals in the form of structural inequalities such as mass incarceration, housing discrimination, and wealth inequality.

Colorblindness. Pretending not to see racial differences.

Colorism. A system of power that provides people privileges or disadvantages based on their skin color.

Colorism. The prejudicial discrimination or bias against people with darker skin.

Controlling images. Term popularized by Patricia Hill Collins to refer to stereotypes and negative images that provide ideological justification for race, class, and gender inequality.

Convict leasing. The selling or renting of Black inmates, usually arrested for frivolous reasons, to a White person or the government for forced labor. A tool used after the end of slavery to control the Black population in a way similar to slavery.

Cultural ideology. Refers to the ideals, principles, and shared set of beliefs held by a given society or culture.

Cultural racism. A form of racism that depicts groups as naturally or biologically inferior because of their cultural or religious practices.

Cultural texts. Actions, behaviors, objects, and symbols that communicate or reveal cultural meanings.

Cumulative disadvantage. Inequities and negative consequences that continue and combine to hurt us more and more throughout our lives.

Decarceration. Reducing and reversing the scope and impact of racialized mass incarceration on society and finding alternative ways to solve problems like violence, victimization, and injustice.

Deferred Action for Childhood Arrivals (DACA). A policy that enables people who came to the United States before age 16 to apply for "deferred action" and a work permit.

Deindividuation. A social psychological term that refers to when people lose their sense of self, thus creating a feeling of anonymity.

Direct racism. Form of racism that is direct, obvious, and intentional. Found often in racist laws and policies.

Discrimination. Refers to the unequal treatment of people based on their race, ethnicity, and/or gender.

Discrimination. Treating people differently due to prejudicial beliefs about their race, ethnicity, sex, class, age, sexuality, ability, religion, belief system, or other aspect of their status.

Dominant group. The group within a social hierarchy that maintains control of economic, political, social, and cultural power.

Double consciousness. Concept used by Du Bois in *The Souls of Black Folk* that describes an individual whose identity is split in two.

Economic institution. The wide range of activities that provide us with the means to create and distribute goods and services.

Environmental racism. When environmental hazards are disproportionally borne by racial and ethnic minority groups.

Ethnic group. Refers to a group of people who share social or cultural characteristics such as nationality, language, or religion.

Ethnicity. Shared cultural heritage including, but not limited to, a person's birthplace or country of origin, familial ties and lineage, religion, language, and other social practices.

Ethnocentrism. Believing one's own ethnic group is superior to others and assessing other groups' language, cultural practices, and other ethnic distinctions as inferior to yours.

Eugenicists. People who study, advocate for, or participate in the practice of "improving" the qualities of humans through the reduction or elimination of undesirable genetic traits.

Executive Order 9066 (1942). A legislative response to the Japanese attack on Pearl Harbor that authorized the internment of American citizens of Japanese descent and resident aliens of Japan.

Explicit bias. Bias that is overt and blatant.

Fair Housing Act. Civil rights legislation from 1968 that protects people from racial discrimination in housing. Outlawed the racist real estate practices that produce racialized suburbanization and concentrated home equity among Whites.

Federal Housing Administration. Government agency created in 1934 with the task of designing mortgage rules and insuring loans for home construction and purchase.

General Allotment Act of 1887. An attempt to turn Indians into individual farmers—like White people—by breaking up reservation land, assigning a plot to each Indian household, and giving the remaining land to White people.

Genocide. According to the International Criminal Court (ICC),genocide consists of "any of the following acts committed with intent to destroy, in whole or in part, a national, ethnical, racial or religious group: killing members of the group; causing serious bodily or mental harm to members of the group; deliberately inflicting on the group conditions of life calculated to bring about its physical destruction in whole or in part; imposing measures intended to prevent births within the group; forcibly transferring children of the group to another group"(ICC 2019).

Ghost Dance. A dance created by a Paiute holy person who claimed that the dance would bring back loved ones and the buffalo from the dead and return the dancers to a time before Europeans arrived. It spread from reservation to reservation because it gave defeated Indians hope that they could go back to a better time.

Harlem Renaissance. The explosion of Black social, intellectual, and artistic expression centered in Harlem during the 1920s and 1930s.

Hart-Celler Immigration and Nationality Act (1965). Reversed the national origins quota system of immigration that had governed U.S. immigration policy since the 1920s; prioritized family reunification, focused on employment-based or skills-based immigration, and welcomed refugees.

Hayes-Tilden Compromise of 1877. A secret negotiation between Republican presidential candidate Rutherford Hayes and Southern Democrats. Hayes agreed to remove the remaining federal troops from the South so he could secure their vote and win the election. This compromise officially ended Reconstruction.

Historical trauma. Trauma experienced by our mothers and earlier generations of mothers can change the structure of our genes and make us react in negative ways to stresses we face today.

Humanization. A process whereby we recognize dehumanized people as full human beings deserving of the same rights, freedoms, and quality of life as everyone else.

Hypodescent. The automatic assignment of biracial or multiracial people, by the dominant cultural group, to the singular racial category of a subordinate group in their ancestry.

Identities. Refers to understandings of self or the meaning people hold for themselves that defines what it means to be who they are as persons.

Imperialism. The ideology of wanting to seek control and power over other nations, groups, or territories.

Implicit bias. Bias that is hidden—even from the person who holds it; this type of bias occurs at the subconscious level and without conscious awareness.

Income. Money brought into a household from various sources during a given period.

Indian Removal Policy of 1830. This policy gave President Andrew Jackson permission to exchange land west of the Mississippi for the land of Indian nations east of the Mississippi. It also stated that the United States would never take the "Indian land" in the West away from Indian nations.

Indian Reorganization Act (IRA). An act signed by President Franklin Delano Roosevelt in 1934 that stopped the allotment process, gave reservations some additional land, and encouraged nations to create their own governments with limited autonomy.

Indian Self-Determination and Education Assistance Act of 1975. This act allows tribes to control their own education and teach through their cultural lens. It also lets them run programs formerly led by federal agencies.

Indirect racism. Form of racism that results in unequal outcomes but is only indirectly related to anything racial. Often seen through the legacy of previous direct racism.

Individual racism. Racism in which one person discriminates against another person based on race or ethnicity.

Institutional racism. Discriminatory laws, policies, and practices carried out by institutions that result in racial inequity.

Institutional racism. Policies, laws, and institutions that produce and reproduce racial inequities.

Interest convergence. Coined by Derrick Bell, interest convergence suggests that Whites will support an antiracist policy that directly benefits them, a policy in which their interests converge with the intended beneficiaries.

Interracial. Involving or between different races.

Intersectionality. A practice and concept that lets us see how social categories we belong to—such as class, gender, and race—are interconnected and work together to reinforce people's advantages or disadvantages in society.

Intersectionality. Interconnectedness between social categories. We occupy racial categories simultaneously with gender, age, nationality, and social class.

Intraracial. Within or between people of the same race, of the same racial classification.

Iroquois League. A federation created in what is now New York state sometime between 1100 and 1400 of Mohawks, Oneidas, Onondagas, Cayugas, and Senecas (the Tuscaro joined in 1722); also known as the Great League of Peace. The Iroquois were the dominant American Indians in the region.

Islamophobia. Irrational fear or prejudice against Islam as a religion and/or Muslims as people.

Islamophobia. The hate, fear, or discrimination of Muslims or those that appear Muslim.

Japanese internment. The forced removal, relocation, and incarceration of Japanese Americans and Japanese nationals in the United States.

Jim Crow laws. State and local laws that legalized and enforced racial segregation and discrimination.

Johnson-Reed Immigration Act. 1924 immigration act intended to end immigration from southern and eastern European sources.

King Philip. One of Massasoit's sons, King Philip gathered other tribes together and attacked the Separatists. After a bloody war, the tribes lost, and the Separatists put King Philip's head on a pike for 20 years.

Latinx. Gender-neutral classification that refers to people who possess Latin American ancestry.

Legacy. This typically refers to a child or grandchild of an alumnus of a particular college or university; legacy programs give preference to legacy students in college or university admissions.

Living while Black. Regular and varied injustices that occur to Black people in the United States because they are Black.

Managed migration. The attempt by European countries and the European Union (EU) to restrict migration into and within the EU.

Manifest destiny. The belief that the United States has a God-given obligation and inevitable destiny to expand and take over territories occupied by inferior peoples (e.g., Mexicans and American Indians).

Massasoit. The leader of the Wampanoag when the Separatists arrived. Having just lost almost all his people to disease, Massasoit made an alliance with the Separatists.

Media. Refers to the various channels of mass communication in a society; some examples include film, television, books, Internet, music and music videos, newspapers, magazines, advertising, and product and sports logos.

Meritocracy. An ideology that posits that merit explains success in a given society; for example, the belief that America is a meritocracy means that one believes that hard work and perseverance lead to success.

Mexican–American War. The 1846–1848 war between Mexico and the United States instigated by the United States to fulfill its "manifest destiny." It resulted in Mexico ceding 55% of its land (and the people on it) to the United States.

Middle East. A contested and ambiguous geographic area including regions of North Africa and western Asia.

Milliken v. Bradley. The 1974 Supreme Court 5–4 decision that ruled against a statewide desegregation plan in favor or predominantly White suburban districts arguing that, since they had not intended to racially segregate the Detroit schools, they should not have to do anything to desegregate them.

Minstrel shows. On-stage productions popular in the 19th and early 20th centuries in which White actors donned blackface to imitate and mock how they believed enslaved Blacks looked and acted on Southern plantations.

Monoracial. Composed of, representing, relating to, or descended from a single racial category.

Monoracism. The privileging and use of monoracial norms in society, at both the individual and institutional level, that do not include or acknowledge multiraciality.

Multiracial. Composed of, combining, representing, relating to, or descended from several or many races.

Muslim. A religious identity referring to a follower of Islam.

Nation of Islam. An African American and Black religious movement focused on Black liberation and self-determination influenced by Islamic teachings, practices, and values.

National Association for the Advancement of Colored People (NAACP). Founded in 1909, an organization of women and men, Black and White, that promotes racial equality and fights to stop violence and injustice toward Black Americans.

Naturalization cases. Court cases determining the eligibility of immigrants to become U.S. citizens.

Naturalization. Process by which a person becomes a citizen of the United States.

Naturalization. The process through which an immigrant gains citizenship.

Office of Management and Budget. Sets the standards by which government agencies racially classify groups.

Operation Boulder. A screening program, primarily targeting Arabs, implemented after the 1972 Olympic bombings in Munich, Germany, designed to keep terrorists out of the United States.

Oppression. An ongoing social process whereby one group dominates another and uses power to maintain that unequal relationship.

Oriental. A pejorative label applied to people from Asia emphasizing their inferiority to and difference from people from Western nations.

Orientalism. The ideologies and practices that produce distorted images and knowledge about Arab peoples and culture, Middle Eastern geography, and Islam as a religion.

Pogroms. State-sanctioned violent attacks aimed at the extermination of particular ethnic or religious groups.

Pan-ethnic category. An umbrella term that encompasses several subgroups.

Partus sequitur ventrem. Latin for "that which is brought forth follows the womb." Law passed in the colony of Virginia in 1662 that made it clear that a child would be enslaved or free based on the condition of the mother.

Past-in-present discrimination. When discrimination in the past affects people in the present.

Permanent Fund. A fund based on contributions of one-quarter of profits from oil and mineral earnings that the state of Alaska invests and uses to provide every Alaskan a guaranteed dividend each year.

Picture brides. Women who were promised in marriage via matchmakers in their home countries who made recommendations based on the exchange of pictures between the potential bride and groom.

Policies. Rules for how institutions are organized and run that reflect and reinforce social norms and the structure of society.

Power. The possession of authority over individuals, groups, or systems.

Practices. Actions that people take on a regular basis.

Prejudice. The belief or feeling that one group is superior to another.

Race. A system of organizing human beings into groups *perceived* to be distinct because of physical appearance (not genetic makeup).

Racial and ethnic impact assessments. Policies that require identifying the impacts of policies and public decision-making on racial and ethnic groups to provide the information needed to dismantle systemic racism in approval processes.

Racial consciousness. The ability to understand situations, problems, issues, and experiences in ways that focus on social relations, power imbalances, and the impacts of racist social arrangements.

Racial literacy. The ability to communicate and apply racial consciousness to new situations.

Racial microaggressions. Harmful interpersonal statements or behaviors (usually by White people toward people of color), often unnoticeable to individuals not negatively impacted by them.

Racial slavery. A system of lifelong forced servitude based on race and racial categories as a means of seeing and organizing human beings into groups.

Racialization. The process of ascribing racial characteristics to a group of people.

Racialization. When the dominant group uses ethnicity, national origin, and/or religion to create an image of other people as different—and inferior—from them physically and culturally to justify the unequal treatment of that group.

Racism. Historical, cultural, institutional, and interpersonal dynamics that create and maintain a racial hierarchy that advantages Whites and hurts people of color.

Racism. Prejudicial beliefs and/or discriminatory actions causing widespread harm for a specific racial group because members of the prejudiced/discriminatory group are disproportionately in positions of power. In an era of colorblindness, racism can also exist without overt prejudice.

Reconstruction. The decade after the Civil War when newly freed Black people gained citizenship rights, land, and political representation. It lasted from 1865 to 1877.

Reform Judaism. A liberal and progressive denomination defined by its willingness to change Orthodox customs, practices, and even beliefs.

Scapegoats. Persons or groups blamed for prevailing social, economic, or political problems.

Scientific racism. The use of science or pseudoscience to prove innate racial inferiority of some groups to justify the racial superiority of other racial groups.

Separatists. Now known as Pilgrims, the Separatists landed in Massachusetts in 1620. They were seeking a place where they could start a new life guided by strict religious rules and beliefs. Separatists gained their name because they had separated themselves from the Church of England, which they viewed as corrupt.

Settler colonies. Territories where large populations from metropoles—the controlling states—migrated to dominate the Indigenous populations and take over all aspects of life (social, cultural, political, and economic).

Side-effect racial discrimination. Racial discrimination in one institution (or area of an institution) that leads to inequality in other institutions or areas.

Social construction. The process through which social realities are created by society itself, rather than being natural, biological, or God-given.

Social institutions. Ways of acting encoded in laws, policies, and common practices.

Social norm. Patterns of behavior established by a culture and regarded as normal or expected.

Social norms. Rules for behavior that we take for granted as "normal" in everyday life.

Social policy. The implementation of a course of action through a formal program or law and advocacy; refers to the employment of resources to empower communities.

Socially constructed. Refers to ideas created by human beings in their interactions with one another.

Sociological imagination. The ability to see and understand the connections among individual lives and larger historical, political, social, and economic forces.

Stereotype. Oversimplified description of a group, image, or idea.

Structural mechanisms. Large-scale factors and practices typically constructed by White people in positions of power. No particular person has control over them—they are built into institutions and legal systems.

Structural racism. Interactions across institutions that produce and reproduce racial inequities.

Symbolic ethnicity. Nostalgic and superficial connections to one's ethnic origin commonly practiced by White Americans.

Systemic racism. Racism that exists at individual, institutional, and structural levels.

Takeover of Alcatraz. For 19 months, from 1969 to 1970, people from at least 12 tribes participated in the occupation of the island and former prison off the coast of San Francisco. They called themselves "Indians of all tribes."

Termination Act of 1953 and Relocation Act of 1956. Acts signed by President Dwight Eisenhower. The Termination Act stopped payments promised to American Indian nations. The Relocation Act provided moving expenses to American Indians willing to move off a reservation to an urban area. The goal was to cease government expenditures for people on reservations, force them to move to poor neighborhoods in cities, and break the connection between individual Indians and their tribal culture (Dunbar-Ortiz 2014).

Terror profiling. Selectively targeting individuals, or groups, for increased surveillance and searches based on a combination of skin color, religious dress, Arabic name, and/or national origin in an attempt to prevent terrorist attacks.

The Alaska Native Claims Settlement Act (ANSCA) of 1971. Through ANSCA, Alaskan Natives agreed to give up their claims on most of the land in Alaska in exchange for $962.5 million and one-ninth of the state's land. They also agreed to create 200 Alaska Native village corporations and 12 Alaska Native land-owning, for-profit, regional corporations (a 13th was created for those living outside of Alaska but is not active now).

The Orient. A historic Eurocentric term used to describe the "Far East" implying that people, commodities, and cultures from Asia were exotic and subordinate to "the West."

The Trail of Tears. Poorly planned and executed forced march of Cherokees from Georgia to "Indian land" in Oklahoma in the 1830s. Between one-quarter and one-half died along the way from hunger, disease, cold, exhaustion, and heartache.

Tracking. Refers to the placement of students into different educational programs or levels (such as in gifted, remedial, and honors programs).

Trump effect. The apparent connection between former president Trump's controversial racial rhetoric and the commission of hate crimes documented in social research.

Universalism. The philosophical tradition that states that France is one and indivisible, and that everyone is the same, regardless of race.

USA PATRIOT Act. A collection of laws and policies designed to strengthen national security by allowing federal law enforcement agencies broader powers to monitor, arrest, and detain individuals suspected of terrorism (or potential terrorism).

Voting Rights Act of 1965. Prohibited voter suppression and discrimination.

Wages of Whiteness. The social status provided to poor Whites simply because they are White and not Black. The identification of Whiteness is the wage.

War on terror. Political, economic, and military policies and programs aimed at ending terrorism both home and abroad.

White fragility. Coined by Robin DiAngelo, refers to the racial stress and defensive responses triggered when White people engage in conversations about race and privilege.

White privilege. Taken-for-granted ways in which society advantages Whites.

White transparency. The idea that Whiteness often goes unnamed and unnoticed and in this way maintains power.

Wild West shows. Traveling stage shows in the 19th century; they were rodeo performances that presented American Indians as wild savages that needed to be tamed.

Worcester v. Georgia. The 1832 Supreme Court decision ruling that the state of Georgia had no power over the Cherokee because the Cherokee were a sovereign nation, and only the federal government had authority over them. President Jackson ignored the ruling.

Wounded Knee. The scene of the 1890 massacre of Big Foot and most of his followers by U.S. troops.

Xenophobia. The fear, dislike, or hatred of people from other countries.

Yellow Peril. A stereotype introduced in the 1870s to describe the threats of Asian immigration.

Yellow power. A power for self-determination and a call against racism, imperialism, and inequality.

REFERENCES

CHAPTER 1

Allen, T. W. (2012). *The invention of the white race: Racial oppression and social control* (Vol. 1). Verso.

Anderson, N., & Svrluga, S. (2020, July). Trump administration backs off plan requiring international students to take face-to-face classes. *Washington Post.* https://www.washingtonpost.com/local/education/ice-rule-harvard-international-students-rescinded/2020/07/14/319fdae0-c607-11ea-a99f-3bbdffb1af38_story.html

Appiah, K. A. (2020, June 18). *The case for capitalizing the B in black. The Atlantic.* https://www.theatlantic.com/ideas/archive/2020/06/time-to-capitalize-Blackand-White/613159/

Becker, S., & Paul, C. (2015). "It didn't seem like race mattered": Exploring the implications of service-learning Pedagogy for reproducing or challenging color-blind racism. *Teaching Sociology, 43*(3), 184–200.

Berkowitz, D., Windsor, E., & Winter Han, C. (Forthcoming). *Male femininities.* NYU Press.

Bertrand, M., & Mullainathan, S. (2004). Are emily and greg more employable than Lakisha and Jamal? A field experiment on labor market discrimination. *American Economic review, 94*(4), 991–1013.

Bonilla-Silva, E. (2010). *Racism without racists: Color-blind racism & racial inequality in contemporary america* (3rd ed.). Rowman & Littlefield.

Bonilla-Silva, E. (2018). *Racism without racists: Color-blind racism and the persistence of racial inequality in America.* Rowman & Littlefield.

Buchanan, L., Bui, Q., & Patel, J. K. (2020, July 3). Black lives matter may be the largest movement in U.S. history. *New York Times.* https://www.nytimes.com/interactive/2020/07/03/us/george-floyd-protests-crowd-size.html

Combahee River Collective. (1979). The combahee river collective: A black feminist statement. *Women's Studies Quarterly, 42*(3–4), 271–280.

Crenshaw, K.. (1991). Mapping the margins: Intersectionality, identity politics, and violence against women of color. *Stanford Law Review, 43*(6), 1241–1299.

Davenport, F. G. (1917). *European treaties bearing on the history of the United States and its dependencies to 1648.* Carnegie Institution. https://www.papalencyclicals.net/nichol05/romanus-pontifex.htmhttps://www.papalencyclicals.net/nichol05/romanus-pontifex.htm

De la Fuente, H., & Sterling, W. (2020). *Redskins: Washington team says it will change name and logo.* CNN. https://www.cnn.com/2020/07/13/us/washington-redskins-nickname-change-spt/index.html

DiAngelo, R. (2018). *White fragility: Why it's so hard for white people to talk about racism.* Beacon Press.

Frayssinet, F. (2015). Rural women in Latin America define their own kind of feminism. *Inter Press Service News Agency.* http://www.ipsnews.net/2015/04/rural-women-in-latin-america-try-to-define-their-own-kind-of-feminism/

Guiliano, J. (2013). *The fascination and frustration with native American mascots.* Society Pages. https://thesocietypages.org/specials/mascots/

Kang, S. K., DeCelles, K. A., Tilcsik, A., & Jun, S. (2016). Whitened resumes: Race and self-presentation in the labor market. *Administrative Science Quarterly, 61*(3), 469–502.

Lopez, W. D., Novak, N. L., Harner, M., Martinez, R., & Seng, J. S. (2018). The traumatogenic potential of law enforcement home raids: An exploratory report. *Traumatology, 24*(3), 193–199.

Marx, K., & Engels, F. (1932). *The german ideology.* Marx-Engels Institute.

Massey, D. S., & Denton, N. A. (1993). *American apartheid: Segregation and the making of the underclass.* Harvard University Press.

McIntosh, P. (2009). *White people facing race: Uncovering the myths that keep racism in place.* The Saint Paul Foundation.

Mitchell, T. D., & Donahue, D. M. (2009). "I do more service in this class than I ever do at my site": Paying attention to the reflections of students of color in service-learning. In J. R. Strait & M. Lima (Eds.), *The future of service-learning: New solutions for sustaining and improving practice* (pp. 172–190). Stylus.

O'Brien, E. (2008). *The racial middle: Latinos and Asian Americans living beyond the racial divide.* NYU Press.

Parker, K., Horowitz, J. M., Morin, R., & Hugo Lopez, M. (2015). Race and multiracial Americans in the U.S. Census. In *Multiracial in America.* Pew Research Center. https://www.pewsocialtrends.org/2015/06/11/chapter-1-race-and-multiracial-americans-in-the-u-s-census/

Picca, L. H., & Feagin, J. R. (2007). *Two-faced racism: Whites in the backstage and frontstage.* Routledge.

Ritchie, B. (2017). *Invisible no more: Police violence against black women and women of color.* Beacon Press.

Roediger, D. R. (2007). *The wages of whiteness: Race and the making of the American working class.* Verso.

Russell, G., & Karlin, S. (2020). *Coronavirus Disparity in Louisiana: About 70% of the Victims Are Black, buy why?* https://www.nola.com/news/coronavirus/article_d804d410-7852-11ea-ac6d-470ebb61c694.html

Simko-Bednarski, E., Snyder, A., & Ly, L. (2020, July 18,). Lawsuit claims Breonna Taylor lived for "5 to 6 minutes" after being shot. *CNN.* https://www.cnn.com/2020/07/18/us/breonna-taylor-lawsuit/index.html

Smedley, A. (2011). *Race in North America: Origin and evolution of a worldview* (4th ed.). Westview Press.

Tatum, B. D. (2017). *Why are all the black kids sitting together in the cafeteria? And other conversations about race*. Basic Books.

VanAusdale, D., & Feagin, J. R. (2001). *The first R: How children learn about race and racism*. Rowman & Littlefield.

Wells, I. B. (1893). *Lynch law*. http://www.historyisaweapon.com/defcon1/wellslynchlaw.html

Whitaker, T. R. (2016). Parenting while powerless: Consequences of "the talk. *Journal of Human Behavior in the Social Environment, 26*(3–4), 303–309.

CHAPTER 2

Applestein, D. (2013). *The three-fifths compromise: Rationalizing the irrational*. Constitution Daily: The National Constitution Center. https://constitutioncenter.org/blog/the-three-fifths-compromise-rationalizing-the-irrational/

The Aspen Institute. (2016). *11 terms you should know to better understand structural racism*. https://www.aspeninstitute.org/blog-posts/structural-racism-definition/

Blakemore, E. (2018). *The brutal history of anti- discrimination in America*. https://www.history.com/news/the-brutal-history-of-anti-latino-discrimination-in-america

Du Bois, W. E. B. (1903/1997). *The souls of black folk*. Bedford Books.

Elshabazz-Palmer, A. (2017). Scientific racism: The exploitation of African Americans. *Intertext, 25*(1), 23–27.

Feagin, J. (2006). *Systemic racism: A theory of oppression*. Routledge.

Feagin, J. (2012). *White party, white government: Race, class, and U.S. politics*. Routledge.

Ford, T. N., Sarah, R., & Reeves, R. V. (2020, June 16). *Race gaps in Covid-19 deaths are even bigger than they appear*. Brookings. https://www.brookings.edu/blog/up-front/2020/06/16/race-gaps-in-covid-19-deaths-are-even-bigger-than-they-appear/

Groark, V. (2002, May 5). Slave policies. *New York Times*, 14.

Johns Hopkins Medicine. (2019). *Honoring henrietta: The legacy of henrietta lacks*. https://www.hopkinsmedicine.org/henriettalacks/

Jones, J. (1993). *Bad blood: The Tuskegee syphilis experiment* (New and expanded ed.). The Free Press.

Kendi, I. (2016). *Stamped from the beginning: The definitive history of racist ideas in America*. Bold Type Books.

Kendi, I. (2019). *How to be an antiracist*. Bodley Head.

Mills, C. W. (1959/2000). *The sociological imagination* (40th Anniversary ed.). Oxford University Press.

Morris, A. (2015). *The scholar Denied: W. E. B. Du Bois and the birth of modern sociology*. University of California Press.

National Science Foundation, National Center for Science and Engineering Statistics. (2018). *Doctorate recipients from U.S. Universities: 2018. Special report NSF 19-301*. https://ncses.nsf.gov/pubs/nsf19301/

Nittle, N. K. (2019). *The U.S. government's role in sterilizing women of color*. ThoughtCo. https://www.thoughtco.com/u-s-governments-role-in-sterilizing-women-of-color-2834600

Romero, M. (2019, August 11). *Sociology: Engaging with social justice*. Presented at the Annual Meeting of the American Sociological Association, New York, NY. https://www.asanet.org/news-events/meetings/asa-annual-meeting-video-archive

Skloot, R. (2011). *The immortal life of Henrietta lacks*. Broadway Books.

Wilder, C. S. (2013). *Ebony & Ivy: Race, slavery, and the troubled history of America's Universities*. Bloomsbury Press.

CHAPTER 3

Abdelgadir, A., & Fouka, V. (2019). How will Austria's new headscarf ban affect Muslims? *Washington Post*. https://www.washingtonpost.com/politics/2019/06/03/how-will-austrias-new-headscarf-ban-affect-muslims/

Al Jazeera. (2017). *"Islamophobia to blame" for cape town mosque attacks*. https://www.aljazeera.com/news/2017/01/cape-town-mosque-attacks-islamophobia-170112105620599.html

Americans for Democracy & Human Rights in Bahrain. (2019). *UAE migrant and domestic workers abuse*. https://www.adhrb.org/2019/05/uae-migrant-and-domestic-workers-abuse/

Amnesty International. (2019). *Myanmar: Two years since Rohingya exodus, impunity reigns supreme for military*. https://www.amnesty.org/en/latest/news/2019/08/myanmar-two-years-since-rohingya-crisis/

Attiah, K. (2017). Macron blames "civilization" for Africa's problems. France should acknowledge its own responsibility. *Washington Post*. https://www.washingtonpost.com/news/global-opinions/wp/2017/07/14/macron-blames-civilization-for-africas-problems-france-should-acknowledge-its-own-responsibility/

Australian Institute of Health and Welfare. (2017). *Australia's welfare 2017: In brief*. https://www.aihw.gov.au/reports/australias-welfare/australias-welfare-2017-in-brief/contents/Indigenous-australians

Bancel, N., Blanchard, P., & Lemaire, S. (2000, August). Ces Zoos Humains de la République Coloniale. *Le Monde Diplomatique*.

Baker, A. (2019, May 2). What South Africa can teach us as worldwide inequality grows. *Time*. https://time.com/longform/south-africa-unequal-country/.

Banerji, R. (2016). In the dark: What is behind India's obsession with skin whitening? *New Statesman America*. https://www.newstatesman.com/politics/feminism/2016/01/dark-what-behind-india-s-obsession-skin-Whitening

BBC. (2018). *Windrush: "Home office ignored warnings"*. https://www.bbc.com/news/education-46445109

BBC. (2019). *South Africa's xenophobic attacks: Why migrants won't be deterred.* . https://www.bbc.com/news/uk-wales-49797720

Bennhold, K. (2019). A political murder and far-right terrorism: Germany's new hateful reality. *New York Times*. https://www.nytimes.com/2019/07/07/world/europe/germany-murder-far-right-neo-nazi-luebcke.html

Berteaux, JA. (2017). Black France, black America: Engaging historical narratives. *Cosmopolitan Civil Societies: An Interdisciplinary Journal, 9*(2), 57–71.

Black Building Workers Act. *Parliament of South Africa, Act No. 27 of 1951.*

Bourcier, N. (2012, October 23). Brazil comes to terms with its slave trading past. *The Guardian.* https://www.theguardian.com/world/2012/oct/23/brazil-struggle-ethnic-racial-identity

Butterly, L. (2019). *Black vests: Who are the gilets noirs and what do they want?* https://www.aljazeera.com/indepth/features/Black-vests-gilets-noirs-190813084140464.html

Clark, K. B., & Clark, M. K. (1940). Skin color as a factor in racial identification of negro preschool children. *Journal of Social Psychology, 11*, 159–169.

Committee on the Elimination of Racial Discrimination. (2012). *Consideration of reports submitted by states parties under article 9 of the convention. United Nations.* https://www.refworld.org/publisher,CERD,,ISR,506189622,0.html

Coloured Persons Education Act. Parliament of South Africa, Act No. 47 of 1963.

Défenseur des Droits. (2017). *Enquête sur l'accès aux droits. Vol. 1. Relations police/population: le cas des contrôles d'identité.* https://www.defenseurdesdroits.fr/sites/default/files/atoms/files/rapport-enquete_relations_police_population-20170111_1.pdf

Dugard, J. (2019). *Why aren't Europeans calling Israel an apartheid state? Al Jazeera.* . https://www.aljazeera.com/indepth/opinion/aren-europeans-calling-israel-apartheid-state-190410081102849.html

Eltis, D., & David Richardson, D. (2010). *Atlas of the transatlantic slave trade.* Yale University Press.

European Commission Directorate-General for Justice and Consumers. (2019). *Data collection in the field of ethnicity. Analysis and comparative review of equality data collection practices in the European Union.* Publications Office of the European Union.

Falk, R. (2014). *Report of the special rapporteur on the situation of human rights in the Palestinian territories occupied since 1967, Richard Falk. United Nations, Human Rights Council. A/HRC/25/67.*

Flint, J. E. (1974). *Cecil Rhodes.* Little Brown.

Gigler, BS. (2015). *Poverty, inequality, and human development of indigenous peoples in Bolivia. Development as freedom in a digital age: Experiences from the rural poor in Bolivia.* https://doi.org/10.1596/978-1-4648-0420-5_ch3

Groupe antiracist d'accompagnement et de defense des étrangers et migrants. (2018). *Coûts et blessures. Rapport sur les operations des forces de l'ordre menées dans le nord du Maroc entre juillet et septembre 2018. Eléments factuels et analyse.*

Hall, S. (2017). *Antihaitianismo: Systemic xenophobia and racism in the Dominican republic. Council on hemispheric Affairs.* http://www.coha.org/antihaitianismo-systemic-xenophobia-and-racism-in-the-dominican-republic/#_edn1

Hall, S. (1992). The west and the rest: Discourse and power. In S. Hall & B. Gieben (Eds.), *Formations of modernity* (pp. 184–227). Polity Press.

Hall, S. (1997). The spectacle of the other. In S. Hall, J. Evans, & S. Nixon (Eds.), *Representation: Cultural representations and signifying practices* (pp. 223–290). : Sage.

Higginbotham, W. (2017). Blackbirding: Australia's history of luring, tricking and kidnapping pacific islanders. *ABC News.* https://www.abc.net.au/news/2017-09-17/Blackbirding-australias-history-of-kidnapping-pacific-islanders/8860754

Hochschild, A. (1998). *King leopold's ghost.* Houghton Mifflin.

Human Rights Watch. (2014). *"I already bought you": Abuse and exploitation of female migrant domestic workers in the United Arab Emirates.* https://www.hrw.org/report/2014/10/22/i-already-bought-you/abuse-and-exploitation-female-migrant-domestic-workers-united

Immorality Amendment Act, Parliament of South Africa, Act No. 21 of 1950.

Kastner, B. (2019). In a changing Germany, taboo of racism is broken. *World Crunch.* https://www.worldcrunch.com/world-affairs/in-a-changing-germany-taboo-of-racism-is-broken

Kendi, I. X. (2019). The day "Shithole" entered the presidential lexicon. *The Atlantic.* https://www.theatlantic.com/politics/archive/2019/01/shithole-countries/580054/

Lang, J. (2019). Tear down the fortress: Europe and the refugee crisis. *Harvard Political Review.* https://harvardpolitics.com/columns-old/tear-down-the-fortress/

Lebsack, L. (2019). *Skin bleaching is poisoning women—but business is booming.* https://www.refinery29.com/en-us/2019/05/233409/skin-bleaching-lightening-products-safety-controversy

Lukaku, R. (2018). I've got some things to say. *The Players Tribune.* https://www.theplayerstribune.com/global/articles/romelu-lukaku-ive-got-some-things-to-say

Markwick, A., Ansari, Z., Clinch, D., & McNeil, J. (2019). Experiences of racism among aboriginal and Torres Strait islander adults living in the Australian state of victoria: A cross-sectional population-based study. *BMC Public Health, 19*, 309. https://doi.org/doi:10.1186/s12889-019-6614-7

Mahmud, T. (1999). Colonialism and modern constructions of race: A preliminary inquiry. *Law Review, 53*, 1219–1246. http://digitalcommons.law.seattleu.edu/faculty/501

Marx, C. (2017). *Settler colonies.* http://ieg-ego.eu/en/threads/europe-and-the-world/european-overseas-rule/christoph-marx-settler-colonies

Mezzofiore, G. (2019). Romelu Lukaku: Italian soccer pundit fired for racist on-air comments about inter Milan striker. *CNN.* https://edition.cnn.com/2019/09/16/football/romelo-lukaku-racist-remarks-juventus-ultras-trnd-spt-intl/index.html

Mohdin, A. (2019). Statistically speaking, black people in Germany don't exist. *Quartz.* https://qz.com/1078032/can-germany-combat-inequality-when-it-has-no-data-on-race/

Muzenda, M. (2018). Blac Chyna came to nigeria to launch a skin-lightening cream at $250 a Jar. *NPR.* https://www.npr.org/sections/goatsandsoda/2018/11/30/671879261/blac-chyna-came-to-nigeria-to-launch-a-skin-lightening-cream-at-250-a-jar.

National Agreement on Closing the Gap. (2020). https://www.closingthegap.gov.au/national-agreement-closing-gap-glance

National Collaborating Centre for Aboriginal Health. (2014). *Aboriginal experiences with racism and its impacts.* . https://www.nccih.ca/docs/determinants/FS-AboriginalExperiencesRacismImpacts-Loppie-Reading-deLeeuw-EN.pdf

Office of the Historian. (2019). *Decolonization of Asia and Africa, 1945–1960.* https://history.state.gov/milestones/1945-1952/asia-and-africa

Office of the High Commissioner for Human Rights, United Nations. (2020). *Disproportionate impact of COVID-19 on racial and ethnic minorities needs to be urgently addressed.* https://www.ohchr.org/EN/NewsEvents/Pages/DisplayNews.aspx?NewsID=25916&LangID=E

Open Society Foundations. (2019). *Why Roma political participation matters.* https://www.opensocietyfoundations.org/explainers/why-roma-political-participation-matters

Organization for the Security and Cooperation in Europe (OSCE) Office for Democratic Institutions and Human Rights (ODIHR). (n.d.). *Germany.* http://hatecrime.osce.org/germany

Panja, T. (2019, September 4). In Italy, racist abuse of Romelu Lukaku is dismissed as part of the game. *New York Times.* https://www.nytimes.com/2019/09/04/sports/romelu-lukaku-inter-milan-racist-chants.html

Population Registration Act, Parliament of South Africa, Act No. 30 of 1950.

Prohibition of Mixed Marriages Act, Parliament of South Africa, Act No 55 of 1949. .

Reuters. (2019). *UK miscounted EU, other immigrants before Brexit vote.* https://www.cnbc.com/2019/08/21/uk-miscounted-eu-other-immigrants-before-brexit-vote.html

Salmi, K. (2011). "Race does not exist here." Applying critical race theory to the french republican context. In K. Hylton, A. Pilkington, P. Warmington, & S. Housee (Eds.), Atlantic crossings: International dialogues on critical race theory (pp. 177–196). CSAP/Higher Education Academy.

Schifrin, N., & Sagalyn, D. (2019). China calls it re-education, but Uighur Muslims say it's "Unbearable Brutality". *PBS News Hour.* https://www.pbs.org/newshour/show/china-calls-it-re-education-but-uyghur-muslims-say-its-unbearable-brutality

Secorun, L. (2018, August 6). The perils of housecleaning abroad. *New York Times.* https://www.nytimes.com/2018/08/06/opinion/international-world/domestic-workers-middle-east.html

Skin Lightening Products Market Is Expected to Reach a Valuation of over US$ 24 Bn by the End of 2027. (2018). *Market watch.* https://www.marketwatch.com/press-release/skin-lightening-products-market-is-expected-to-reach-a-valuation-of-over-us-24-bn-by-the-end-of-2027-2018-08-30

South Africa: Overcoming Apartheid, Building Democracy. (2019). *"Forced removals" African studies center of Michigan State University.* . http://overcomingapartheid.msu.edu/multimedia.php?id=65-259-6

Stone, J. (2018). The EU has built 1,000 km of border walls since fall of berlin wall. *Independent.* https://www.independent.co.uk/news/world/europe/eu-border-wall-berlin-migration-human-rights-immigration-borders-a8624706.html

Sudworth, J. (2019). Searching for truth in China's Uighur "Re-education" camps. *BBC News.* https://www.bbc.com/news/blogs-china-blog-48700786

Tazamal, M. (2019). *Chinese Islamophobia was made in the west.* al Jazeera. . https://www.aljazeera.com/indepth/opinion/chinese-islamophobia-west-190121131831245.html

Telles, E., & Bailey, S. (2013). Understanding Latin American beliefs about racial inequality. *American Journal of Sociology, 118*(6), 1159–1195.

Tévanian, P., & Bouamama, S. (2017). *Can we speak of a postcolonial racism?* http://lmsi.net/Can-We-Speak-of-A-Postcolonial

UNESCO. (1969). *Four statements on the race question.* http://refugeestudies.org/UNHCR/UNHCR.%20Four%20Statements%20on%20the%20Race%20Question.pdf

UN Habitat. (n.d). *Slum upgrading.* https://new.unhabitat.org/topic/slum-upgrading

Wade, P. (2010). *Race and ethnicity in Latin America* (2nd ed.). Pluto Press.

Wade, P. (2017). Racism and race Mixture in Latin America. *Latin American Research Review.* https://larrlasa.org/articles/10.25222/larr.124/

Williams, K. (2016). *Where were South Africa's enslaved people from? Media diversified.* . https://mediadiversified.org/2016/05/18/where-were-south-africas-slaves-from/

World Bank. (2018). *Afro-descendants in Latin America: Toward a framework of inclusion.* https://openknowledge.worldbank.org/handle/10986/30201

Wylie, L., & McConkey, S. (2019). Insiders' insight: Discrimination against indigenous peoples through the eyes of health care professionals. *Journal of Racial and Ethnic Health Disparities, 6*(1), 37–45.

CHAPTER 4

Ajunwa, I., & Onwuachi-Willig, A. (2018). *Combating discrimination against the formerly incarcerated in the labor market, 112 Nw. U. L. Rev. 1385.* . https://scholarlycommons.law.northwestern.edu/nulr/vol112/iss6/6

Ansolabehere, S., & Hersh, E. D. (2017). ADGN: An algorithm for record linkage using address, date of birth, gender, and name. *Statistics and Public Policy, 4*(1), 1–10. https://doi.org/10.1080/2330443X.2017.1389620

Budiman, A., Cilluffo, A., & Ruiz, N. G. (2019, May 22). Key facts about Asian groups in the United States. *Pew Research Center.* https://www.pewresearch.org/fact-tank/2019/05/22/key-facts-about-asian-origin-groups-in-the-u-s/

Bullard, R. D. (1990). *Dumping in Dixie: Race, class, and environmental quality* (Vol. 3). Westview Press.

Bullard, R. D. (1993). *Confronting environmental racism: Voices from the grassroots.* South End Press.

Bureau of Indian Education. (2019). *Bureau of Indian education reorganization.* https://www.bie.edu/BFRI/index.htm

Campbell, C. (2017, April 21). 508 ineligible voters cast ballots in 2016, According to NC elections agency report. *The News & Observer.* https://www.newsobserver.com/news/politics-government/state-politics/article145971264.html

Domonoske, C. (2016, October 19). Interactive redlining map zooms in on America's history of discrimination. *NPR.* https://www.npr.org/sections/thetwo-way/2016/10/19/498536077/interactive-redlining-map-zooms-in-on-americas-history-of-discrimination

Dwyer, J. (2019, May 30). The true story of how a city in fear brutalized the central park five. *New York Times*. https://www.nytimes.co m/2019/05/30/arts/television/when-they-see-us-real-story.html

EdBuild. (2019). *NonWhite school districts get $23 billion less than white districts despite serving the same number of students*. https://edbuild.org/content/23-billion

EPA. (2019). *Health and environmental effects of particulate matter (PM)*. https://www.epa.gov/pm-pollution/health-and-environmental-effects-particulate-matter-pm

Fadulu, L. (2019, August 5). Trump proposal would raise bar for proving housing discrimination. *New York Times*. https://www.nytimes.com/2019/08/02/us/politics/trump-housing-discrimination.html

Gee, B., & Peck, D. (2018, May 31). Asian Americans are the least likely group in the U.S. to be promoted to management. *Harvard Business Review*. https://hbr.org/2018/05/asian-americans-are-the-least-likely-group-in-the-u-s-to-be-promoted-to-management

Glantz, A., & Martinez, E. (2019, August 5). Can algorithms be racist? Trump's housing department says no. *Reveal*. http://revealnews.org/article/can-algorithms-be-racist-trumps-housing-department-says-no/

Gramlich, J. (2019, April 30). The gap between the number of blacks and whites in prison is shrinking. *Pew Research Center*. https://www.pewresearch.org/fact-tank/2019/04/30/shrinking-gap-between-number-of-Blacks-and-Whites-in-prison/

Hud.gov. (2019). *History of fair housing*. https://www.hud.gov/program_offices/fair_housing_equal_opp/aboutfheo/history

Jones, R. P., Cox, D., Griffin, R., Fisch-Friedman, M., & Vandermaas-Peeler, A. (2018). American democracy in crisis: The challenges of voter knowledge, participation, and polarization. *PRRI*. https://www.prri.org/research/American-democracy-in-crisis-voters-midterms-trump-election-2018

Kauffman, J. (2018, October 22). 6 takeaways from Georgia's "use it or lose it" voter purge investigation. *NPR*. https://www.npr.org/2018/10/22/659591998/6-takeaways-from-georgias-use-it-or-lose-it-voter-purge-investigation

Kendi, I. X. (2019). *How to be an antiracist*. One World.

Korver-Glenn, E. (2018). Compounding inequalities: How racial stereotypes and discrimination accumulate across the stages of housing exchange. *American Sociological Review*, *83*(4), 627–656. https://doi.org/10.1177/0003122418781774

Krogstad, J. M., Flores, A., & Lopez, M. H. (2018, November 8). Key takeaways about Latino voters in the 2018 midterm elections. *Pew Research Center*. https://www.pewresearch.org/fact-tank/2018/11/09/how-latinos-voted-in-2018-midterms/

LDF. (2018). *School to prison pipeline*. https://www.naacpldf.org/case-issue/school-prison-pipeline/

Liptak, A. (2003, June 25). Supreme court invalidates key part of voting rights act. *New York Times*.

Lockhart, P. R. (2019, May 30). The lawsuit challenging Georgia's entire elections system, explained. *Vox*. https://www.vox.com/policy-and-politics/2018/11/30/18118264/georgia-election-lawsuit-voter-suppression-abrams-kemp-race

Looney, A., & Turner, N. (2018). Work and opportunity before and after incarceration. *The Brookings Institution*. https://www.brookings.edu/wp-content/uploads/2018/03/es_20180314_looneyincarceration_final.pdf

Marley, P. (2018, April 13). Attorney general brad Schimel suggests Donald trump won Wisconsin because of the state's voter ID law. *Journal Sentinel*. https://www.jsonline.com/story/news/politics/2018/04/13/attorney-general-brad-schimel-suggests-donald-trump-won-wisconsin-because-states-voter-id-law/514628002/

Meckler, L., & Barrett, D. (2021, January 5). Trump administration seeks to undo decades-long rules on discrimination. *Washington Post*. https://www.washingtonpost.com/education/civil-rights-act-disparate-impact-discrimination/2021/01/05/4f57001a-4fc1-11eb-bda4-615aaefd0555_story.html

Mikati, I., Benson, A. F., Luben, TJ., Sacks, J. D., & Richmond-Bryant, J. (2018). Disparities in distribution of particulate matter emission sources by race and poverty status. *American Journal of Public Health*, *108*(4), 480–485. https://doi.org/10.2105/AJPH.2017.304297

Milman, O. (2018, March 6). Environmental racism case: EPA rejects Alabama town's claim over toxic landfill. *The Guardian*. https://www.theguardian.com/us-news/2018/mar/06/environmental-racism-alabama-landfill-civil-rights

Milman, O. (2019, April 15). "We're not a dump"—Poor Alabama towns struggle under the stench of toxic landfills. *The Guardian*. https://www.theguardian.com/us-news/2019/apr/15/were-not-a-dump-poor-alabama-towns-struggle-under-the-stench-of-toxic-landfills

Nadworny, E., & Turner, C. (2019, July 25). This supreme court made school districts a tool for segregation. *NPR*. https://www.npr.org/2019/07/25/739493839/this-supreme-court-case-made-school-district-lines-a-tool-for-segregation

National Center for Education Statistics. (2019). *The condition of education*. https://nces.ed.gov/programs/coe/indicator_coi.asp

National Center for Education Statistics, Integrated Postsecondary Education Data System. (Winter 2016–17). Graduation rates component. *See Digest of Education Statistics 2017, table 326.10*. https://nces.ed.gov/programs/raceindicators/indicator_red.asp

NPR, Robert Woods Foundation, and Harvard T. H. Chan School of Public Health. (2017). https://www.npr.org/assets/news/2017/12/discriminationpoll-APIA-americans.pdf

Panetta, G., & Lee, S. (2019, January 12). This graphic shows how much more diverse the house of representatives is getting. *Business Insider*. https://www.businessinsider.com/changes-in-gender-racial-diversity-between-the-115th-and-116th-house-2018-12

Pierson, E., Simoiu, C., Overgoor, J., Corbett-Davies, S., Jenson, D., & Shoemaker, A. (2019). *A large-scale analysis of racial disparities in police stops across the United States. Stanford computational study lab*. https://5harad.com/papers/100M-stops.pdf?utm_source=The+Appeal&utm_campaign=3a050d7014-EMAIL_CAMPAIGN_2018_08_09_04_14_COPY_01&utm_medium=email&utm_term=0_72df992d84-3a050d7014-58394763

Pillion, D. (2018, April 20). Sewage problems still plague Uniontown after $4.8 million in repairs. *AL.com*. https://www.al.com/news/2018/04/uniontown_sewage_problems.html

Pillion, D. (2019, January 30). EPA closes civil rights complaints over Alabama landfill. *AL.com*. https://www.al.com/news/2018/03/epa_closes_civil_rights_compla.html

Presser, L. (2019, July 15). Their family bought land one generation after slavery. The reels brothers spent eight years in Jail for refusing to leave it. *ProPublica*. https://features.propublica.org/Black-land-loss/heirs-property-rights-why-Black-families-lose-land-south/

Quillian, L., Pager, D., Hexel, O., & Midtbøen, A. H. (2017, September). The persistence of racial discrimination in hiring. *Proceedings of the National Academy of Sciences*. https://doi.org/10.1073/pnas.1706255114

Reed, J., & McGregor, T. (2019, May 16). , Match volume in conversation with Selden award winners Aaron Glantz and Emmanuel Martinez & the US Census Bureau's James T. Christy. *USC Annenbug Media*. http://www.uscannenbergmedia.com/2019/05/16/match-volume-in-conversation-with-selden-award-winners-aaron-glantz-and-emmanuel-martinez-the-us-census-bureaus-james-t-christy/

Reilly, K. (2018, November 7). A new North Dakota law threatened native American votes. They responded by turning out in historic numbers. *Time*. https://time.com/5446971/north-dakota-native-american-turnout/

Rothstein, R. (2017). *The color of law: A forgotten history of how our government segregated America*. Liveright.

The State Energy & Environmental Impact Center, NYU School of Law. (2019). *Climate & health showdown in the courts*. https://www.law.nyu.edu/sites/default/files/climate-and-health-showdown-in-the-courts.pdf

Tran, V. C., Lee, J., & Huang, T. J. (2019). Revisiting the APIA second-generation advantage. *Ethnic and Racial Studies*, *42*(13), 2248–2269. https://doi.org/10.1080/01419870.2019.1579920

Underhill, M. (2019, January 17). Voter identification requirements | voter ID laws. *National Conference of State Legislatures*. http://www.ncsl.org/research/elections-and-campaigns/voter-id.aspx

U.S. Commission on Civil Rights. (2016). *Environmental justice: Examining the environmental protection agency's compliance and enforcement of title VI and executive order 12,898*. https://www.usccr.gov/pubs/2016/Statutory_Enforcement_Report2016.pdf

U.S. Sentencing Commission. (2017). *Demographic differences in sentencing: An update to the 2012 booker report*. https://www.ussc.gov/sites/default/files/pdf/research-and-publications/research-publications/2017/20171114_Demographics.pdf

West, D. M. (2020, June 22). How does vote-by-mail work and does it increase election fraud? *Brookings*. https://www.brookings.edu/policy2020/votervital/how-does-vote-by-mail-work-and-does-it-increase-election-fraud/

CHAPTER 5

Aswad, J. (2019, March 25). Dr. Dre boasts about daughter getting into USC "All on her own," then remembers $70 million donation. *Variety*.

Barrett, K. (2018, July 24). When school dress codes discriminate. *NEA Today*. https://www.nea.org/advocating-for-change/new-from-nea/when-school-dress-codes-discriminate

Battaglio, S. (2018, October 24). Megyn Kelly apologizes for blackface comments amid talks for a new role at NBC. *Los Angeles Times*.

Bendix, A. (2017, March 23). Boston puts a better map in the classroom. *The Atlantic*.

Blad, E., & Harwin, A. (2017, January 24). Black students are more likely to be arrested at school. *Education Week*.

Bonilla-Silva, E. (2010). *Racism without racists: Color-Blind racism & racial inequality in contemporary America* (3rd ed.). Rowman & Littlefield.

Branigin, A. (2018, January 25). We need to talk about how schools handle racist harassment against students. *The Root*.

Bryant, K. (2019, March 12). "Operation varsity blues" is the one scam to rule them all. *Vanity Fair*.

Chavez, S. M. (2018, February 1). American slavery isn't taught well in schools in Texas or across the U.S., Report says. *Kera News*. https://www.keranews.org/post/american-slavery-isnt-taught-well-schools-texas-or-across-us-report-says

Cherng, H.-Y. S., & Liu, J. L. (2017). Academic social support and student expectations: The case of second-generation Asian Americans. *Asian American Journal of Psychology*, *8*(1), 16.

Cummings, M. (2019, July 4). Racists are big mad that a black girl is playing Ariel in "The little mermaid". *BET*.

Cutler, D. (2017, November 15). Teaching kids about thanksgiving or Columbus? They deserve the real story. *PBS News Hour*.

Depenbrock, J. (2017, August 13). Ethnic studies: A movement born of a ban. *NPR*.

Desmond-Harris, J. (2015, March 26). NYC media coverage of black suspects is way out of proportion with black arrest rates. *Vox*.

Dwyer, L. (2017, August 17). 80% of America's teachers are white. *Good Education*. https://www.good.is/education/wake-up-call-teacher-diversity

Epstein, K. (2019, June 4). Racial posts from police officers' social media accounts trigger a wave of investigations. *Washington Post*.

Garber, M. (2017, June 30). The perils of meritocracy. *The Atlantic*.

Gershenson, S., Holt, S. B., & Papageorge, N. (2016). Who believes in me? The effect of student-teacher demographic match on teacher expectations. *Economics of Education Review*, *52*(June), 209–224.

Ghandnoosh, N. (2014). Race and punishment: Racial perceptions of crime and support for punitive policies. *The Sentencing Project*. https://www.sentencingproject.org/publications/race-and-punishment-racial-perceptions-of-crime-and-support-for-punitive-policies/

Glamour. (2020, July 3). *The crown act: Every state that's passed legislature banning hair discrimination*.

Gold, H. (2019, April 26). Houston high school under fire for instituting dress code? For parents. *The Cut*. https://www.thecut.com/2019/04/houston-high-school-implements-racist-dress-code-for-parents.html

Gordon, N. (2018). Disproportionality in student discipline: Connecting policy to research. *Brookings*. https://www.brookings.edu/research/disproportionality-in-student-discipline-connecting-policy-to-research/

Green, E. L., & Waldman, A. (2018, December 28). "I feel invisible": Native students languish in public schools. *New York Times*.

Greenberg, J. (2015, February 23). 7 reasons why "Colorblindness" contributes to racism instead of solves it. *Everyday Feminism*.

Greenwald, R., & Jones, V. (2016, June 16). What do you call white rioters? Anything but thugs. *The Huffington Post*.

Grissom, J. A., & Redding, C. (2016, January 19). Discretion and Disproportionality: Explaining the underrepresentation of High-Achieving students of color in gifted programs. *American Education Research Association*.

Grochowski, S. (2016, December 7). Fourth grade textbook saying slaves were like "Family" pulled from Connecticut school district. *New York Daily News*.

Hughes, E. (2019, April 12). Frustrated parents say the Greendale school district isn't doing enough to confront racism. *Milwaukee Journal Sentinel*.

Joseph, N. M., Viesca, K. M., & Bianco, M. (2016). Black female adolescents and racism in schools: Experiences in a colorblind society. *The High School Journal*, *100*(1), 4–25.

Joyner, A. (2019, July 4). Fans praise halle bailey playing Ariel in "The little mermaid": 'Black girls can have fairytales too. *Newsweek*.

Keegan, R. (2017, January 23). Oscar nominations: How will the newest members affect the results? *Vanity Fair*.

Klein, R. (2013, June 25). Ohio school apologizes after attempting to ban "Afro-puffs" and "Twisted braids.". *The Huffington Post*.

Klein, R. (2018, February 23). Schools see major uptick in racial harassment, New data suggests. *The Huffington Post*.

Larkin, M., & Aina, M. (2018, November 4). Legacy admissions offer an advantage? And not just at schools like Harvard. *NPR*.

Lattimore, K. (2017, July 17). When black hair violates the dress code. *NPR*.

Lazar, K. (2017, May 11). Black Malden charter students punished for braided hair extensions. *Boston Globe*.

Lockhart, P. R. (2018, August 1). Living while black and the criminalization of blackness. *Vox*.

Mahnken, K. (2017, April 12). Boston schools have vowed to combat "Racist" maps. Experts want a better geography curriculum. *The 74*. https://www.the74million.org/article/boston-schools-have-vowed-to-combat-racist-maps-experts-want-a-better-geography-curriculum/

Mazama, A. (2015, April 10). Racism in schools is pushing more black families to homeschool their children. *Washington Post*.

Meara, P. (2019, September 22). Six-year-old girl handcuffed and arrested in Florida for throwing a tantrum. *BET*.

Menon, R. (2019, April 2). American meritocracy is a Myth. *The Nation*.

Monmouth University Poll. (2020). https://www.monmouth.edu/polling-institute/documents/monmouthpoll_us_060220.pdf/

Nittle, N. K. (2019, January 15). How racism affects minority students in public schools. *Thought Co*. https://www.thoughtco.com/how-racism-affects-public-school-minorities-4025361

PBS News Hour. (2018, April 22). Black families increasingly choose to homeschool kids. .

Pirtle, W. (2019, April 23). The other segregation. *The Atlantic*.

Quinn, D. (2016, August 4). Kentucky high school lifts hairstyle ban after furious parents and students call policy racist. *People*.

Reese, A. (2018, April 25). Racist and sexist dress codes make school hell for black girls. *Jezebel*.

Rose, D. (2019, March 25). ACLU files complaint against Greendale school district, Accusing It of unhealthy racist culture. *WISN/ABC News*.

Safehome.org. (2017). *Hate on social media: A look at hate groups and their twitter presence*. https://www.safehome.org/resources/hate-on-social-media/

Shapiro, A. (2019, June 22). Dr. Marijuana Pepsi Won't change her name "To make other people happy:. *NPR*.

Shapiro, E. (2019, March 12). After racist video surfaces, Private school students protest with overnight Lock-In. *New York Times*.

Shiff, B. (2017, October 6). Blackface "Jazz singer" still influencing modern cinema 90 years after release. *ABC News*.

Simons, M. (2016, January 28). 100 times a white actor played someone who wasn't white. *Washington Post*.

Slater, D. (2016, September/October). The uncomfortable truth about children's books. *Mother Jones*.

Southeast Asia Resource Action Center. (2020). *Southeast Asian American journeys, A national snapshot of our communities*. https://www.searac.org/wp-content/uploads/2020/02/SEARAC_NationalSnapshot_PrinterFriendly.pdf

Spiegel, A. (2012, September 17). Teacher's expectations can influence how students perform. *NPR*.

Steinberg, S. (1989). *The ethnic myth: Race, Ethnicity, and class in America*. Beacon Press.

Sun, E. (2018, August 29). The dangerous racialization of crime in US News Media. *American Progress.org*.

Swaak, T. (2018, February 23). Racism in schools: Harassment claims rise as education department scales back civil rights investigations. *Newsweek*.

Tatum, B. D. (2017). *Why are all the black kids sitting together in the Cafeteria: And other conversations about race*. Basic Books.

Turner, C. (2016, September 28). Bias Isn't just a police problem, it's a preschool problem. *NPR*.

Welch, B. F. (2016). The pervasive whiteness of children's literature: Collective harms and consumer obligations. *Social Theory and Practice*, *42*(2), 367–388.

Willon, P., & Diaz, A. (2019, July 3). California becomes first state to ban discrimination based on one's natural hair. *Los Angeles Times*.

Wilson, J. (2016, July 29). Kentucky high school's dress code "Stinks of Racism," Bans dreadlocks, Cornrows and braids. *Essence*.

Wong, A. (2015, October 21). History class and the fictions about race in America. *The Atlantic*.

Young, B. (2015, June 11). Why I won't wear war paint and feathers in a movie again. *Time*.

CHAPTER 6

Alaska Department of Revenue, Permanent Fund Division. (2020). *2020 PFD amount*. https://pfd.alaska.gov/

Alaska Permanent Fund Corporation. (2019). *History of the Alaska permanent fund*. https://apfc.org/who-we-are/history-of-the-alaska-permanent-fund/

Alaska State Archives. (2019). *Boarding schools in Alaska*. https://archives.alaska.gov/education/boarding.html

Alcohol.org. (2019). *Alcohol abuse treatment for Native Americans*. https://www.alcohol.org/alcoholism-and-race/native-americans/

Bear, C. (2008, May 12). American Indian boarding schools haunt many. *NPR Morning Edition*. https://www.npr.org/templates/story/story.php?storyId=16516865#16627573#16627573B

Beitsch, R. (2020, June 17). Judge orders Mnuchin to give Native American tribes full stimulus funding. *The Hill*. https://thehill.com/policy/energy-environment/503175-judge-orders-mnuchin-to-give-tribes-full-stimulus-funding

Blue Cloud, P. (1972). *Alcatraz is not an island*. Wingbow Press.

Calloway, C. G. (2008). *First peoples: A documentary survey of American Indian history*. Bedford/St. Martin's.

Carlisle Indian School Digital Resource Center. (n.d). *Kill the Indian and save the man: Capt. Richard A. Pratt on the education of Native Americans*. .

Centre Communications. (1988). *Eyanopopi: The heart of the Sioux*.

Cooper, L. (2016). *Native American activism: 1960s to present*. https://www.zinnedproject.org/materials/native-american-activism-1960s-to-present/

Dunbar-Ortiz, R. (2014). *An indigenous people's history of the United States*. Beacon Press.

Edwards, M. (2016, February 26). Northern Arapaho seek healing for historic boarding school traumas. *Wyoming Public Media*. https://www.wyomingpublicmedia.org/post/northern-arapaho-seek-healing-historic-boarding-school-traumas#stream/0

Gilio-Whitaker, D. (2019). *As long as grass grows: The indigenous fight for environmental justice, from colonization to standing rock*. Beacon Press.

Harring, S. (1990). Crazy snake and the creek struggle for sovereignty: The Native American legal culture and American Law. *American Journal of Legal History*, *34*(4), 365–380. https://doi.org/10.2307/845827

Havard, G., & Vidal, C. (2003). *Histoire de l'Amérique française*. Flammarion.

Hietala, T. R.. (2003). *Manifest design: American exceptionalism and empire* (Rev. ed.). Cornell University Press.

Hill, K. (2019, August 1). *Lakota leaders urge a public hearing on DAPL expansion*. Indian Law Resource Center. https://www.lakotalaw.org/news/2019-08-01/public-hearing-on-dapl-expansion

Iggiagruk Hensley, W. L. (2017, March 29). Why Russia gave up Alaska, America's gateway to the arctic. *The Conversation*. https://theconversation.com/why-russia-gave-up-alaska-americas-gateway-to-the-arctic-74675

Indian Law Resource Center. (n.d). *Ending violence against native women*. https://indianlaw.org/issue/ending-violence-against-native-women

Indian Removal. (1999). *Africans in America: Judgment day*. WGBH Educational Foundation.

International Criminal Court. (2019). *How the court works*. https://www.icc-cpi.int/about/how-the-court-works

Jolivette, A. (2019). *American Indian and indigenous education: A survey text for the 21st century*. Cognella.

Kidd, T. S. (2019). *America's religious history: Faith, politics, and the shaping of a nation*. Harper Collins.

Koch, A., Brierly, C., Maslin, M., & Lewis, S. (2019, January 31). European colonization of the Americas killed 10 percent of world population and caused global cooling. *The Conversation*. https://theconversation.com/european-colonisation-of-the-americas-killed-10-of-world-population-and-caused-global-cooling-110549

Lakota People's Law Project. (2019, November 5). Native American leaders: Keystone spill highlights the need to oppose Dakota access expansion, KXL. *Common Dreams*. https://www.commondreams.org/newswire/2019/11/05/native-american-leaders-keystone-spill-highlights-need-oppose-dakota-access

LaPier, R. R. (2017, February 17). Dakota pipeline: What makes a place "sacred" for Native Americans? *LiveScience*. https://www.livescience.com/57929-dakota-pipeline-what-makes-a-place-sacred.html

Lasley, S. (2019, February 22). An Alaska native claims primer for miners. *North of 60 Mining News*. https://www.miningnewsnorth.com/story/2019/02/01/in-depth/an-alaska-native-claims-primer-for-miners/5582.html?m=false

Lawrence, J. (2000). The Indian health service and the sterilization of Native American women. *American Indian Quarterly*, *24*(3), 400–419. https://www.jstor.org/stable/1185911?mag=the-little-known-history-of-the-forced-sterilization-of-native-american-women&seq=11#metadata_info_tab_contents

Mann, C. C. (2005). Native intelligence. *Smithsonian*. https://www.smithsonianmag.com/history/native-intelligence-109314481/

Mathews, A. W., & Weaver, C. (2019, December 10). Six CEOs and no operating room: The impossible job of fixing the Indian health service. *Wall Street Journal*. https://www.wsj.com/articles/six-ceos-and-no-operating-room-the-impossible-job-of-fixing-the-indian-health-service-11575993216

McGirt v. Oklahoma, 140 S. Ct. 2452, 2459. (2020). https://www.supremecourt.gov/opinions/19pdf/18-9526_9okb.pdf

National Conference of American Indians. (2019). *Tribal governance*. http://www.ncai.org/policy-issues/tribal-governance

NativeAmericanNetroots. (2010). *American Indian relocation*. http://nativeamericannetroots.net/diary/496

New England Historical Society. (2018). *Exactly how New England's Indian population was decimated*. http://www.newenglandhistoricalsociety.com/exactly-new-englands-indian-population-decimated/

Northern Plains Reservation Aid. (n.d). *Indian self determination and education assistance act—1975*. http://www.nativepartnership.org/site/PageServer?pagename=airc_hist_selfdeterminationact.

Pember, M. A. (2017, October 3). *Trauma may be woven into DNA of Native Americans*. Indian Country Today. https://newsmaven.io/indiancountrytoday/archive/trauma-may-be-woven-into-dna-of-native-americans-CbiAxpzar0WkMALhjrcGVQ

Shamo, L., & Ball, A. (2019, March 26). *How 3 Native American tribes are fighting to protect sacred land from logging, oil pipelines, and a billion-dollar telescope.* Business Insider. https://www.businessinsider.com/native-americans-fight-for-environment-and-their-culture-2019-9

Siddons, A. (2018). The never-ending crisis at the Indian health service. *Roll Call.* https://www.rollcall.com/news/policy/never-ending-crisis-indian-health-service

Simpson, B. (1972, November 29). Native Americans take over bureau of Indian Affairs: 1972. *The Montgomery Spark.* https://washingtonareaspark.com/2013/03/26/native-americans-take-over-bureau-of-indian-affairs-1972/

Stricker, J. (2017, October 17). Alaska Native regional corporation 2017 review. *Alaska Business.* https://www.akbizmag.com/industry/alaska-native/alaska-native-regional-corporation-2017-review/

Strommer, G. D., & Osborne, S. D. (2014). The history, status, and future of tribal self-governance under the Indian self determination and education assistance act. *American Indian Law Review, 39*(1). http://digitalcommons.law.ou.edu/ailr/vol39/iss1/

Sunrise House. (2019). *Addiction among Native Americans.* https://sunrisehouse.com/addiction-demographics/native-americans/

Thorbecke, C. (2016, November 3). Why a previously proposed route for the Dakota access pipeline was rejected. *ABC News.* https://abcnews.go.com/US/previously-proposed-route-dakota-access-pipeline-rejected/story?id=43274356

Treuer, D. (2019, November 20). How a Native American resistance held Alcatraz for 18 months. *New York Times.* https://www.nytimes.com/2019/11/20/us/native-american-occupation-alcatraz.html?nl=todaysheadlines&emc=edit_th_191129?campaign_id=2&instance_id=14107&segment_id=19180&user_id=3123fbcd77f27d0c683c8971336fd60e&regi_id=295377531129

University of Alaska. (2019). *Alaska Native facts.* https://www.uaa.alaska.edu/alaska-natives/aknativefacts.cshtml

U.S. Census Bureau. (2018). *QuickFacts: Alaska.* https://www.census.gov/quickfacts/AK

Wamsley, L. (2020, July 9). Supreme court rules that about half of Oklahoma is Native American land. *NPR.* https://www.npr.org/2020/07/09/889562040/supreme-court-rules-that-about-half-of-oklahoma-is-indian-land

Zotigh, D. (2018, October 30). The 1868 treaty of fort Laramie, Never honored by the United States, Goes on public view. *Smithsonian National Museum of the American Indian.* https://www.smithsonianmag.com/blogs/national-museum-american-indian/2018/10/31/treaty-fort-laramie/

CHAPTER 7

Anti-Defamation League. (2019). *White supremacist propaganda and events soared in 2018.* ADL. https://www.adl.org/news/press-releases/White-supremacist-propaganda-and-events-soared-in-2018.

Arab American Institute. (2015). *Adding a MENA category to the U.S. census.* Arab American Institute. http://www.aaiusa.org/2020census

Baker, P., & Shear, M. D. (2019). El Paso shooting suspect's manifesto echoes trump's language. *New York Times.* https://www.nytimes.com/2019/08/04/us/politics/trump-mass-shootings.html

Beirich, H. (2019). Race against change: White supremacy flourishes amid fears of immigration and nation's shifting demographics. *Intelligence Report: Published by the Southern Poverty Law Center, 166,* 35–42.

Benedict, R. (1959). In M. Margaret (Ed.), *An anthropologist at work: Writings of ruth benedict.* Houghton Mifflin.

Bertrand, M., & Mullainathan, S. (2004). Are Emily and Greg more employable than Lakisha and Jamal? A field experiment on labor market discrimination. *American Economic Review, 94*(4), 991–1013.

Bonilla-Silva, E., & Glover, K. S. (2004). "We are all americans": The latin Americanization of race relations in the United States. In K. Maria & A. E. Lewis (Eds.), *The changing terrain of race and ethnicity* (pp. 144–183). Russell Sage Foundation.

Brodkin, K. (1998). *How Jews became white folks and what that says about race in America.* Rutgers University Press.

Cherelus, G. (2018). Anti-Semitic hate crimes spiked 37 percent in 2017: FBI. *Reuters.* https://www.reuters.com/article/us-usa-hate-crimes-report/u-s-anti-semitic-hate-crimes-spiked-37-percent-in-2017-fbi-idUSKCN1NI2H6

Coaston, J. (2019). Trump's new defense of his Charlottesville comments is incredibly false. *Vox.* https://www.vox.com/2019/4/26/18517980/trump-unite-the-right-racism-defense-charlottesville

Colby, S. L., & Ortman, J. M. (2015). *Projections of the size and composition of the U.S. population: 2014 to 2060. U.S. Census: Current population reports.* . https://www.census.gov/content/dam/Census/library/publications/2015/demo/p25-1143.pdf

Conley, D. (1999). *Being black and living in the red: Race, wealth, and social policy in America.* University of California Press.

Coolidge, C. (1921). Whose country is this? *Good Housekeeping, 72*(2), 13–14. http://hearth.library.cornell.edu/cgi/t/text/pageviewer-idx?c=hearth;:rgn=full%20text;: idno=6417403_1366_002;: view=image;: seq=15;: cc=hearth;: page=root;: size=s;: frm=frameset

Davidson Buck, P. (2001). Constructing race, creating white privilege. In P. S. Rothenberg & K. S. Mayhew (Eds.), *Race, class, and gender in the United States* (pp. 33–38). Worth.

Dunn, C., & Shames, M. (2019). *Stop-and-frisk in the de Blasio Era. New York Civil Liberties Union.* https://www.nyclu.org/sites/default/files/field_documents/20190314_nyclu_stopfrisk_singles.pdf

Feinberg, A., Branton, R., & Martinez-Ebers, V. (2019). Counties that hosted a 2016 trump rally saw a 226 percent increase in hate crimes. *Washington Post.* https://www.washingtonpost.com/politics/2019/03/22/trumps-rhetoric-does-inspire-more-hate-crimes/?noredirect=on&utm_term=.7adbdf94e19b

Franklin, B. (1751). *Observations concerning the increase of mankind.* https://founders.archives.gov/documents/Franklin/01-04-02-0080

Gaddis, S. M. (2014). Discrimination in the credential society: An audit study of race and college selectivity in the labor market. *Social Forces, 94*(4), 1451–1579.

Gans, H. (1979). Symbolic ethnicity: The future of ethnic groups and cultures in America. *Ethnic and Racial Studies, 2*(1), 1–20.

Gell-Redman, N. V., Crabtree, C., & Fariss, C. J. (2018). It's all about race: How state legislators respond to immigrant constituents. *Political Research Quarterly, 71*(3), 517–531.

Glantz, A., & Martinez, E. (2018, February 17). Modern-day redlining: How banks block people of color from homeownership. *Chicago Tribune*. https://www.chicagotribune.com/business/ct-biz-modern-day-redlining-20180215-story.html.

Gossett, T. F. (1963). *Race: The history of an idea in America*. Oxford University Press.

Huhta, A. (2014). Debating visibility: Race and visibility in the Finnish-American press in 1908. *Nordic Journal of Migration Research*, 4(4), 168–175.

Ignatiev, N. (1995). *How the Irish became white*. Routledge.

Jones, S. G. (2018). *The rise of far-right extremism in the United States*. Center for Strategic and International Studies. https://www.csis.org/analysis/rise-far-right-extremism-united-states.

Klein, C. (2019). *How St. Patrick's day was made in America*. History.com. https://www.history.com/news/st-patricks-day-origins-america

Klein, R. (2018). Trump said "Blame on both sides" in Charlottesville, now anniversary puts him on the spot. *ABC News*. https://abcnews.go.com/Politics/trump-blame-sides-charlottesville-now-anniversary-puts-spot/story?id=57141612

Kugelmass, H. (2016, July 8). "Sorry, I'm not accepting new patients": An audit study of access to mental health care. *Journal of Health and Social Behavior*, 57(2), 168–183.

Lee, M. Y. H. (2015). Donald Trump's false comments connecting Mexican immigrants and crime. *Washington Post*. https://www.washingtonpost.com/news/fact-checker/wp/2015/07/08/donald-trumps-false-comments-connecting-mexican-immigrants-and-crime/

Marte, J. (2017, May 16). Wells Fargo steered blacks and Latinos toward costlier mortgages, Philadelphia lawsuit alleges. *Los Angeles Times*. https://www.latimes.com/business/la-fi-wells-fargo-philadelphia-20170516-story.html

Massey, D. S., & Denton, N. A. (1993). *American apartheid: Segregation and the making of the underclass*. Harvard University Press.

McEldowneyM 2018What charlottesville changed*Politico*https://www.politico.com/magazine/story/2018/08/12/charlottesville-anniversary-supremacists-protests-dc-virginia-219353August12

McIntosh, P. (1988). White privilege and male privilege: A personal account of coming to see correspondences through work in women's studies. In M. L. Anderson & P. H. Collins (Eds.), *Race, class, and gender: An anthology* (pp. 76–87). Wadsworth.

McPhillips, D. (2020). Deaths from police harm disproportionately affect people of color. *U.S. News & World Report*. https://www.usnews.com/news/articles/2020-06-03/data-show-deaths-from-police-violence-disproportionately-affect-people-of-color

Mujcic, R., & Frijters, P. (2013). *Still not allowed on the bus: It matters if you're black or white!* SSRN. https://papers.ssrn.com/sol3/papers.cfm?abstract_id=2245970

Muller, K., & Schwarz, C. (2018). *Making America hate again? Twitter and hate crime under trump*. SSRN. https://papers.ssrn.com/sol3/papers.cfm?abstract_id=3149103

O'Brien, C. (2019). Kaine: Trump's rhetoric "Emboldens" white nationalists. *Politico*. https://www.politico.com/story/2019/03/17/kaine-trump-White-nationalists-klobuchar-1224199

Oliver, M. L., & Shapiro, T. M. (2006). *Black wealth/white wealth: A new perspective on racial inequality*. Routledge.

Ozawa v. United States, 260 U.S. 178 (1922).

Pager, D. (2003). The mark of a criminal record. *American Journal of Sociology*, 108(5), 937–975.

Pager, D., Bonikowski, B., & Western, B. (2009). Discrimination in a low-wage labor market: A field experiment. *American Sociological Review*, 74(5), 777–799.

Pittman, C. (2017). "Shopping while Black": Black consumers' management of racial stigma and racial profiling in retail settings. *Journal of Consumer Culture*. https://doi.org/10.1177/1469540517717777

Reilly, K. (2019). Trump says he doesn't see white nationalism as a rising global threat after New Zealand shooting. *Time*. http://time.com/5552850/donald-trump-White-nationalism-global-threat-new-zealand/

Rice, L., & Schwartz Jr, E. (2018). Discrimination when buying a car: How the color of your skin can affect your car-Shopping experience. *National Fair Housing Alliance* https://nationalfairhousing.org/wp-content/uploads/2018/01/Discrimination-When-Buying-a-Car-FINAL-1-11-2018.pdf

Russell Hochschild, A. (2018). *Strangers in their own land: Anger and mourning on the American right*. The New Press.

Russell Hochschild, A. (2019). The American right: Its deep story. *Global Dialogue: Magazine of the International Sociological Association*. http://globaldialogue.isa-sociology.org/the-american-right-its-deep-story/

Sherman, Amy. (2019). Donald Trump doesn't think white nationalism is on the rise. Date show otherwise. *Politifact*. https://www.politifact.com/truth-o-meter/article/2019/mar/20/donald-trump-doesnt-think-White-nationalism-rise-d/

Shin, R. Q., Smith, L. C., Welch, J. C., & Ezeofor, I. (2016). Is Allison more likely than Lakisha to receive a callback from counseling professionals? A racism audit study. *The Counseling Psychologist*, 44(8), 1187–1211.

Simon, M., & Sidner, S. (2018). *Trump says he's not a racist. That's not how white nationalists see it. CNN Politics*. https://www.cnn.com/2018/11/12/politics/White-supremacists-cheer-midterms-trump/index.html

Skocpol, T., & Williamson, V. (2016). *The tea party and the remaking of republican conservatism*. Oxford University Press.

Smith, S. L., Choueiti, M., Pieper, K., Case, A., & Choi, A. (2018). *Inequality in 1,100 popular films: Examining portrayals of gender, race/ethnicity, LGBT & disability from 2007 to 2017*. Annenberg Foundation.

Tessler, H., Choi, M., & Kao, G. (2020). The anxiety of being Asian American: Hate crimes and negative biases during the COVID-19 pandemic. *American Journal of Criminal Justice*, 45, 636–646. https://doi.org/10.1007/s12103-020-09541-5

United States v. Bhagat Singh Thind, 261 U.S. 204 (1923).

Waters, M. C. (1990). *Ethnic options: Choosing identities in America*. University of California Press.

White, A. R., Nathan, N. L., & Faller, J. K. (2015). What do i need tov? Bureaucratic discretion and discrimination by local election officials. *American Political Science Review*, 109(1), 129–142.

Wright, B. R. E., Wallace, M., Wisnesky, A. S., Donnelly, C. M., Missari, S., & Zozula, C. (2015). Religion, race, and discrimination: A field experiment of how American churches welcome newcomers. *Journal for the Scientific Study of Religion, 54*(2), 185–204.

Younkin, P. (2018). The colorblind crowd? Founder race and performance in crowdfunding. *Management Science, 64*(7), 2973–3468.

CHAPTER 8

Alexander, M. (2012). *The new Jim crow: Mass incarceration in the age of colorblindness*. New Press.

Anderson, C. (2017). *White rage: The unspoken truth of our racial divide*. Bloomsbury.

Anderson, M., & López, G. (2018). Key facts about black immigrants in the US. *Pew Research Center FactTank*. https://www.pewresearch.org/fact-tank/2018/01/24/key-facts-about-Black-immigrants-in-the-u-s/

Bloom, J., & Martin, E. W., Jr. (2013). *Black against empire: The history and politics of the black panther party*. University of California Press.

Collins, P. H. (1999/2008). . In *Black feminist thought: Knowledge, consciousness, and the politics of empowerment*. Routledge.

Collins, P. H. (2005). . In *Black sexual politics: African Americans, gender, and the new racism*. Routledge.

Du Bois, W. E. B. (1935/1998). *Black reconstruction in America 1860–1880*. Free Press.

Du Bois, W. E. B. (1940/2007). *Dusk of dawn*. Oxford University Press.

Foer, F. (2018, September). How trump radicalized ICE. *The Atlantic*. https://www.theatlantic.com/magazine/archive/2018/09/trump-ice/565772/

Foner, E. (2019). *The second founding: How the civil war and reconstruction remade the constitution*. W. W. Norton.

Gates, H. L., Jr., & Yacovone, D. (2016). *The African Americans: Many rivers to cross*. Smiley Books.

Grant, C. (2010). *Negro with a hat: The rise and fall of Marcus Garvey*. Oxford University Press.

Hirsch, J. S. (2002). *Riot and remembrance: The Tulsa race war and its legacy*. Houghton Mifflin Harcourt.

Horowitz, P., Bond, J., & Theoharis, J. (2021). *Julian Bond's time to teach: A history of the Southern civil rights movement*. Beacon Press.

Jeffries, H. K. (Eds.). (2019). (Ed.), *Understanding and teaching the civil rights movement*. University of Wisconsin Press.

Jones, E. E. (Ed.). (1998). (Ed.), *The black panther party (Reconsidered)*. Black Classic Press.

Lim, A. (2018). African immigrants are more educated than most?Including people born in US. *LA Times Online*. https://www.latimes.com/world/africa/la-fg-global-african-immigrants-explainer-20180112-story.html

Lincoln, C. E., & Mamiya, L. H. (1990). *The black church in the African American experience*. Duke University Press.

Lineberry, C. (2017). *Be free or die: The amazing story of Robert smalls' escape from slavery to union hero*. St. Martin's Press.

Miller, R. M., & Smith, J. D. (Eds.). (1997). Gradual abolition. In (Ed.), *Dictionary of Afro-American slavery*. Praeger.

Morgan, E. S. (2003). *American slavery, American freedom*. W. W. Norton.

Reinhard, B. (2017, May 12). Attorney general sessions revives policy of tougher sentences for drug offenders. *Wall Street Journal*. https://www.wsj.com/articles/attorney-general-sessions-revives-policy-of-tougher-sentences-for-drug-offenders-1494583202.

Rodriguez, J. P. (Ed.). (2006). Encyclopedia of slave resistance and rebellion. In (Ed.), *Greenwood milestones in African American history series*. Greenwood.

Sherman, E. (2016, March). Nixon's drug war, An excuse to lock up blacks and protestors. *Forbes*. https://www.forbes.com/sites/eriksherman/2016/03/23/nixons-drug-war-an-excuse-to-lock-up-Blacks-and-protesters-continues/#641483b342c8

Stevenson, B. (2015). Slavery to mass incarceration. In *Equal justice initiative*. YouTube video.

Waters, M. C. (2001). *Black identities: West Indian immigrant dreams and American realities*. Harvard University Press.

Williams, D., & Greenshaw, W. (2007). *The thunder of angels: The Montgomery bus boycott and the people who broke the back of Jim Crow*. Lawrence Hill Books.

Yellin, J. F. (2005). *Harriet jacobs: A life*. Civitas Book.

Zong, J., & Batalova, J. (2017, May). *Sub-Saharan African immigrants in the United States. Migration Policy Institute*. https://www.migrationpolicy.org/article/sub-saharan-african-immigrants-united-states#English_Proficiency

CHAPTER 9

AAPI Data. (2018). *Affirmative action: Favor or oppose?* https://aapidata.com/infographic-2018-affirmative-action-favor/

Alliance for Board Diversity. (2018). *Alliance for board diversity report*. https://www.leap.org/alliance-for-board-diversity-report

Angry Asian Man. (2014). *Angry reader of the week: Jenn Fang*. http://blog.angryasianman.com/2014/05/angry-reader-of-week-jenn-fang.html

Angry Asian Man. (n.d). *About*. http://blog.angryasianman.com/p/about.html

Asia Society. (2017). *35 years after Vincent Chin's murder, how has America changed?* https://asiasociety.org/blog/asia/35-years-after-vincent-chins-murder-how-has-america-changed

Center for Asian American Media. (n.d). *About CAAM: Mission statement*. https://caamedia.org/about-caam/

Chua, A. (2011). *Battle hymn of the tiger mother*. Penguin Books.

Considine, A. (2011, July 29). For Asian-American stars, many web fans. *New York Times*. https://www.nytimes.com/2011/07/31/fashion/for-asian-stars-many-web-fans.html

Daniels, R. (1993). *Prisoners without trial: Japanese Americans in World War II*. Hill and Wang.

Downes, L. (2010, December 29). No-No boy. *New York Times*. http://www.nytimes.com/2010/12/29/opinion/29wed4.html

First Days Project. (n.d). *My name is Roshan Sharma*. https://www.firstdaysproject.org/story/roshan-sharma

Franko, K. (2007, August). I-Hotel, 30 years later? Manilatown legacy honored. *SFGATE*. https://www.sfgate.com/bayarea/article/I-Hotel-30-years-later-Manilatown-legacy-3416119.php

Frayling, C. (2014). *The yellow peril: Dr Fu Manchu and the rise of Chinaphobia*. Thames & Hudson.

House, History & Archives, United States House of Representatives. (n.d). *The Philippines, 1898–1946*. https://history.house.gov/Exhibitions-and-Publications/APA/Historical-Essays/Exclusion-and-Empire/The-Philippines/

How to Tell Japs from the Chinese. (1941, December 22). *Life*, 81–82.

How to Tell Your Friends from the Japs. (1941, December 22). *Time*.

Hyun, J. (2006). *Breaking the bamboo ceiling: Career strategies for Asians*. Harper Collins.

Lanyon, C. (2018, November 20). The YouTubers who were making Asian-American films long before crazy rich Asians. *South China Morning Post*. https://www.scmp.com/lifestyle/article/2173873/youtubers-who-were-making-asian-american-films-long-crazy-rich-asians

Lee, E. (2015). *The making of Asian America: A history*. Simon & Schuster.

Lee, J. J. (2018, February). The forgotten Zine of 1960s Asian-American radicals. *Topic Magazine*. https://www.topic.com/the-forgotten-zine-of-1960s-asian-american-radicals

Nittle, N. K. (2020, August 27). Japanese-American no-no boys explained. *ThoughtCo*. thoughtco.com/the-japanese-american-no-no-boys-stood-up-for-justice-2834891

Office of Management and Budget. (1997). *Revisions to the standards for the classification of federal data on race and ethnicity*. https://www.whitehouse.gov/wp-content/uploads/2017/11/Revisions-to-the-Standards-for-the-Classification-of-Federal-Data-on-Race-and-Ethnicity-October30-1997.pdf

Schmitt, R. C. (1968). *Demographic statistics of Hawaii: 1778–1965*. University of Hawaii Press.

Simmons, A. M. (2018, April 6). *American Samoans aren't actually U.S. Citizens. Does that violate the constitution? Los Angeles Times*. https://www.latimes.com/nation/la-na-american-samoan-citizenship-explainer-20180406-story.html

Sorensen, E. (1998, March 3). *Asian groups attack MSNBC headline referring to Kwan?News web site apologizes for controversial wording. Seattle Times*. http://community.seattletimes.nwsource.com/archive/?date=19980303&slug=2737594

Underwood, J. H. (1973). Population history of Guam: Context of microevolution. *Micronesica, 9*(1), 11–44.

VanDeGraph. (2016, October 21). The top YouTubers throughout history. *Medium.com*. https://medium.com/@vandegraph/the-top-youtubers-throughout-history-9f22ac4bee45

Wang, F. K.-H. (2010, June 20). *Remembering vincent Chin 28 years later. Ann Arbor News*. http://www.annarbor.com/passions-pursuits/remember-vincent-chin-28-years-later/

Whitson, H. (1969). *Crises at SF state*. http://www.foundsf.org/index.php?title=STRIKE!..._Concerning_the_1968-69_Strike_at_San_Francisco_State_College

Yam, K. (2019, May 1). Phil Yu of "Angry Asian man": "Don't let anyone else tell your story". *Huffington Post*. https://www.huffpost.com/entry/angry-asian-man-phil-yu_n_5cc5ea8be4b0fd8e35bdd07c

CHAPTER 10

Acevedo, N. (2020, November 27). Young latinos mobilized, voted and were pivotal in 2020. Organizers want to keep it going. *NBC News*. https://www.nbcnews.com/news/latino/young-latinos-mobilized-voted-were-pivotal-2020-organizers-want-keep-n1246853

Allen, C. H. (1901). *First annual report of Charles H. Allen, Governor of Porto Rico*. U.S. Government Printing Office.

Alvarez, R. (1973). The psycho-historical and socioeconomic development of the Chicano Community in the United States. *Social Science Quarterly, 53*, 920–942.

Ayala, M. I. (2017). Intra-Latina fertility behavior. *Women, Gender, and Families of Color, 5*(2), 129–152.

Ayala, M. I. (n.d). *Identity and inclusivity: Assessing the role of racial/ethnic identity empowerment on Latino students' academic attainment*. Michigan State University.

Ayala, M. I., & Chalupa, D. (2016). Beyond the Latino essentialist experience: Racial and ethnic self identification and college attainment. *Hispanic Journal of Behavioral Sciences, 38*(3), 378–394.

Ayala, M. I., & Ramirez, C. (2019). Coloniality and Latinx college students' experiences. *Equity & Excellence in Education, 52*(1), 129–144.

Baca Zinn, M., & Wells, B. (2000). Diversity within Latino families: New lessons for family social science. In D. H. Demo, K. R. Allen, & M. A. Fine (Eds.), *Handbook of family diversity* (pp. 252–273). Oxford University Press.

Balderama, F. E., & Rodríguez, R. (2006). *Decade of betrayal: Mexican repatriation in the 1930s*. University of New Mexico Press.

Bauman, K. (2017). *School enrollment of the Hispanic population: Two decades of growth*. United States Census. https://census.gov/newsroom/blogs/randoms-amplings/2017/08/school_enrollmentof.html

Blackwell, M. (2016). *Contested histories of feminism in the Chicano movement*. University of Texas Press.

BloemraadIVossK 2019Movement or moment? Lessons from the pro-immigrant movement in the United States and contemporary challenges*Journal of Ethnic and Migration Studies*https://doi.org/10.1080/1369183X.2018.1556447

Bureau of Labor Statistics. (2019). *Labor force statistics from the current population survey: Unemployment rates by age, sex, race, and Hispanic or Latino ethnicity*. https://www.bls.gov/web/empsit/cpsee_e16.htm

Bonilla-Silva, E. (2015). The structure of racism in color-blind, "post-racial" America. *American Behavioral Scientists, 59*(11), 1358–1376. https://doi.org/10.1177/0002764215586826

Burke, P. J. (2004). Identities and social structure: The 2003 Cooley-Mead award address. *Social Psychology Quarterly, 67*(1), 5–15.

Clark, L., Fowler, A., Loring, G., & Weigel, A. (2016). The creation of Cuban minority status in America. In *The creation of Cuban minority status in America* (pp. 1–33). http://purl.flvc.org/fsu/fd/FSU_libsu bv1_scholarship_submission_1461432750

Gonzalez-Barrera, A., & Krogstad, J. (2019). Most of the United States' 20 largest immigrant groups experienced increases in naturalization rates between 2005 and 2015. *Pew Research Center.* https://www.pewresearch.org/wp-content/uploads/2018/01/FT_ 18.01.17_naturalizations_all.png?w=416

Hegewisch, A., Phil, M., & Tesfaselassie, A. (2019). *The gender wage gap by occupation 2018.* Institute for Women's Policy Research. https://iwpr.org/publications/gender-wage-gap-occu pation-2018/

Hunter, M. (2016). Colorism in the classroom: How skin tone stratifies African American and Latina/o students. *Theory Into Practice, 55*(1), 54–61.

Igielnik, R., & Budiman, A. (2020, September 23). The changing racial and ethnic composition of the U.S. Electorate. *Pew Research Center.* https://www.pewresearch.org/2020/09/23/the-changing-racial-and-ethnic-composition-of-the-u-s-electorate/

Khanna, N. (2011). *Biracial in America: Forming and performing racial identity.* Lexington Books.

Krupnick, M. (2019). High school graduation rates for one important group are starting to get better. *The Hechinger Report.* https://hechingerreport.org/high-school-graduation-rates-for-one-imp ortant-group-are-starting-to-get-better/

Macaya, M., Wagner, M., & Hayes, M. (2020). Supreme court blocks Trump's attempt to end DACA. *CNN.* https://www.cnn.com/politic s/live-news/scotus-daca-decision-06-18-20/index.html

Oquendo, A. R. (1995). Re-imagining the Latino/a race. *Harvard BlackLetter Law Journal, 12,* 93–108.

Radford, J., & Noe-Bustamante, L. (2019). *Facts on U.S. immigrants, 2017. Statistical portrait of the foreign-born population in the United States.* https://www.pewresearch.org/hispanic/2019/06/03 /facts-on-u-s-immigrants/

Ryan, C., & Bauman, K. (2016). *Educational attainment in the United States 2015. Population characteristics. Current population reports.* U.S. Department of Commerce, Economics and Statistics Administration. https://www.census.gov/content/dam/Census/li brary/publications/2016/demo/p20-578.pdf

Sáenz, R., & Morales, M. C. (2015). *Latinos in the United States: Diversity and change.* Polity Press.

Sonneland, H. K. (2020). *Chart: How U.S. Latinos voted in the 2020 presidential election.* AS/COA. as-coa.org/articles/chart-how-us-l atinos-voted-2020-presidential-election

U.S. Census Bureau. (2017). *Facts for features: Hispanic heritage month 2017.* https://www.census.gov/newsroom/facts-for-feature s/2017/hispanic-heritage.html

U.S. Census Bureau. (2019). *Hispanic heritage month 2019.* https://www.census.gov/newsroom/facts-for-features/2019/hispanic-h eritage-month.html

Valle, M. (2014). Afro-Latinos seek recognition, and accurate census count. *NBC News.* https://www.nbcnews.com/storyline/hispa nic-heritage-month/afro-latinos-seek-recognition-accurate-cen sus-count-n207426

CHAPTER 11

Al Jazeera. (2019). *Muslim men seek inquiry after "racially profiled" on US flight.* https://www.aljazeera.com/news/2019/09/muslim-m en-seek-probe-racially-profiled-flight-190920053406942.html

Alsultany, E. (2012). *Arabs and Muslims in the media: Race and representation after 9/11.* New York University Press.

American Jewish Committee. (2019). *AJC 2019 survey of American Jewish opinion.* https://www.ajc.org/news/survey2019

American Jewish Historical Society. (1999). *American Jewish desk reference: The ultimate one-volume reference to the Jewish experience in America.* Random House.

Anti-Defamation League. (n.d). https://www.adl.org/

Arab American Institute. (2018). *Demographics.* https://assets.na tionbuilder.com/aai/pages/9843/attachments/original/155119864 2/National_Demographics_SubAncestries_2018.pdf?1551198642

Blackwood, L., Hopkins, N., & Reicher, S. (2015). "Flying while Muslim": Citizenship and misrecognition in the airport. *Journal of Social and Political Psychology, 32*(2), 148–170.

Brodkin, K. (1994). *How Jews became white folks: And what that says about race in America.* Rutgers University Press.

Cainkar, L. (2018). Fluid terror threat: A genealogy of the racialization of Arab, Muslim, and South Asian Americans. *Amerasia Journal, 44*(1), 27–59.

Chon, M., & Arzt, D. (2005). Walking while Muslim. *Law and Contemporary Problems, 68*(2), 215–254.

Council on American-Islamic Relations. (2018). *Targeted: 2018 civil rights report.* http://www.islamophobia.org/reports/224-2018-civ il-rights-report-targeted.html

Council on Arab-Islamic Relations. (2020). *CAIR-Chicago stands in solidarity with black lives matter.* https://www.cairchicago.org/soli darity

Curtis, E. (2002). *Islam in Black America: Identity, liberation, and difference in African-American Islamic thought.* State University of New York Press.

Federal Bureau of Investigation. (2018). *Hate crime statistics: Table 1.* https://ucr.fbi.gov/hate-crime/2018/tables/table-1.xls

Fein, H. (1987). *The persisting question. Sociological perspectives and social contexts of modern Antisemitism.* De Gruyter.

Feldman, D. (2018). Toward a history of the term "anti-semitism.". *The American Historical Review, 123*(4), 1139–1150. https://doi.org/1 0.1093/ahr/rhy029

Fox, C., & Guglielmo, T. (2012). Defining America's racial boundaries: Blacks, Mexicans, and European immigrants, 1890–1945. *American Journal of Sociology, 118*(2), 1890–1945.

Grant, M. (1916). *The passing of the great race.* Scribner.

Gualtieri, S. (2001). Becoming "white": Race, religion and the foundations of Syrian/Lebanese ethnicity in the United States. *Journal of American Ethnic History, 20*(4), 29–58.

Gualtieri, S. (2009). *Between Arab and White: Race and ethnicity in the early Syrian American diaspora.* University of California Press.

Gualtieri, S. (2018). Edward said, the AAUG, and Arab American archival methods. *Comparative Studies of South Asia, Africa, and the Middle East, 38*(1), 21–29.

Haider, M. (2020). Racialization of the Muslim body and space in Hollywood. *Sociology of Race and Ethnicity*, 6(3).

Hooglund, E. J. (1987). Introduction. In E. Hooglund (Ed.), *Crossing the waters: Arabic speaking immigrants to the United States before 1940* (pp. 1–16). Smithsonian Institution Press.

Husain, A. (2019). Moving beyond (and back to) the Black–White binary: A study of black and White Muslims' racial positioning in the United States. *Ethnic and Racial Studies*, 42(4), 589–606.

Jamal, A. (2008). Civil liberties and the otherization of Arab and Muslim Americans. In A. Jamal & N. Naber (Eds.), *Race and Arab Americans before and after 9/11: From visible citizens to visible subjects* (pp. 114–130). Syracuse University Press.

Jewish Virtual Library. (n.d). *Report on the acquiescence of FDR government in the murder of the Jews.* https://www.jewishvirtualli brary.org/report-on-the-acquiescence-of-fdr-government-in-th e-murder-of-the-jews-january-1944

Jones, J. (2001). The impact of the attacks on America. *Gallup.* ht tps://news.gallup.com/poll/4894/impact-attacks-america.aspx? version=print

Kayyali, R. (2013). US census classifications and Arab Americans: Contestations and definitions of identity markers. *Journal of Ethnic and Migration Studies*, 39(8), 1299–1318.

Kelman, A., Tapper, A. H., Fonseca, I., & Saperstein, A. (2019). *Counting inconsistencies: An analysis of American Jewish population studies, with a focus on Jews of color.* Swig Program in Jewish Studies and Social Justice at the University of San Francisco. https://jewsofcolorfieldbuilding.org/wp-content/uploads/2019/05/Cou nting-Inconsistencies-052119.pdf

Kurien, P. (2007). *A place at the mulitcultural table: The development of American Hinduism.* Rutgers University Press.

Love, E. (2017). *Islamophobia and racism in America.* New York University Press.

Masci, D. (2019). Many Americans see religious discrimination in U.S.?Especially against Muslims. *Pew Research Center.* https://w ww.pewresearch.org/fact-tank/2019/05/17/many-americans-se e-religious-discrimination-in-u-s-especially-against-muslims/

Mohammed, B., Smith, G., Cooperman, A., & Schiller, A. (2017). U.S. Muslims concerned about their place in society, but continue to believe in the American dream. *Pew Research Center.* https://w ww.pewforum.org/2017/07/26/findings-from-pew-research-cent ers-2017-survey-of-us-muslims/

Orfalea, G. (2006). *The Arab Americans: A history.* Olive Branch Press.

Rana, J. (2007). The story of Islamophobia. *Souls*, 9(2), 148–161.

Revesz, R. (2016). *Muslim passenger kicked off American airlines flight after attendant announces: "I'll be watching you.".* http://www .independent.co.uk/news/world/americas/muslim-kicked-off-pl ane-american-airlines-racial-discrimination-cair-uncomfortabl e-a7147311.html

Said, E. (1978). *Orientalism.* Vintage Books.

Shaheen, J. (2008). *Guilty: Hollywood's verdict on Arabs after 9/11.* Olive Branch Press.

South Asian Americans Leading Together. (n.d). *About.* www. salt.org

Southern Poverty Law Center. (n.d). https://www.splcenter.org/fi ghting-hate/extremist-files/individual/louis-farrakhan

Suleiman, M. (1994). Arab-Americans and the political process. In E. McCarus (Ed.), *The development of Arab-American identity* (pp. 37–60). University of Michigan Press.

Suleiman, M. (1999). Introduction: The Arab immigrant experience. In M. Suleiman (Ed.), *Arabs in America: Building a new future* (pp. 1–21). Temple University Press.

Tehranian, J. (2009). *Whitewashed: America's invisible middle eastern minority.* New York University Press.

Tinaz, N. (1996). The Nation of Islam: Historical evolution and transformation of the movement. *Journal of Muslim Minority Affairs*, 16(2), 193–209.

Walters, Q. (2020). Anti-semitic crime in the U.S. reaches record levels. *WBUR.* https://www.wbur.org/news/2020/05/12/antisemiti c-crime-record-level

Welch, S. (2014). American opinion toward Jews during the Nazi era: Results from quota sample polling during the 1930s and 1940s. *Social Science Quarterly*, 95(3), 615–635.

Wenger, B. (2007). *The Jewish Americans: Three centuries of Jewish voices in America.* Doubleday.

Zopf, B. (2018). A different kind of brown: Arabs and middle easterners as Anti-American Muslims. *Sociology of Race and Ethnicity*, 42(2), 178–191.

CHAPTER 12

An Act Concerning Negroes & other Slaves, 1 Maryland Archives 533-534. (1664). https://msa.maryland.gov/msa/speccol/sc5600/ sc5604/html/september.html

Barford, V. (2015, August 16). The Japanese women who married the enemy. *BBC.* https://www.bbc.com/news/magazine-33857059

Cadet, D. (2014, July 17). The "Straight outta Compton" casting call is so offensive it will make your jaw drop. *HuffPost.* https://w ww.huffpost.com/entry/straight-out-of-compton-casting-call_n _5597010

Cayton, R. (1935a, February 15). Anti-intermarriage Bill Is Attempt to Smash Unity. *Voice of Action*, p. p. 3.

Cayton, R. (1935b, March 29). Defeat of Todd Bill victory of unity between white workers, Negro people. *Northwest Enterprise*, p. 1, 4.

Chiu, A. (2019, September 3). A Mississippi wedding venue rejected an interracial couple, citing "Christian belief." Facing a backlash, the owner apologized. *Washington Post.* https://www.washingtonp ost.com/nation/2019/09/03/mississippi-wedding-venue-rejects-i nterracial-couple-christian-belief-apologized/

Cooper, J. J. (2019, February 13). Strangers' suspicions Rankle parents of mixed-race children. *Associated Press.* https://apnews .com/9e73ee4106c74188b643f91c7ed59157.

Critical Mixed Race Studies. (2019). *About.* https://criticalmixedrac estudies.com/about-cmrs/

Ebert, R. (1991, June 7). Jungle fever. *RogerEbert.com.* https://ww w.rogerebert.com/reviews/jungle-fever-1991

Franco, M. G., & O'Brien, K. M. (2018). Racial identity invalidation with multiracial individuals: An instrument development study. *Cultural Diversity and Ethnic Minority Psychology*, 24(1), 112–125.

Grant, M. (1936). *The passing of the great race* (4th ed.). Charles Scribner's Sons.

Hoyt, J. P. (1877). *The compiled laws of the territory of Arizona*. Richmond, Backus & Co., Printers.

Jane DOE v. STATE of Louisiana (479 So. 2d 369 [1985]).

Jaynes, G. (1982, September 30). Suit on race recalls lines drawn under slavery. *New York Times*. https://www.nytimes.com/1982/09/30/us/suit-on-race-recalls-lines-drawn-under-slavery.html.

Johnson, S. (2005). *Blocking racial intermarriage laws in 1935 and 1937*. Seattle Civil Rights & Labor History Project. https://depts.washington.edu/civilr/antimiscegenation.htm

Johnston, M. P., & Nadal, K. L. (2010). Multiracial microaggressions: Exposing Monoracism in everyday life and clinical practice. In D. W. Sue (Ed.), *Microaggressions and marginality: Manifestation, dynamics and impact* (pp. 123–144). Wiley & Sons.

Juneau, J. (2017, May 22). Tamera Mowry-Housley says criticism over her interracial marriage and family with Adam Housley "is even worse now.". *Essence*. https://www.essence.com/celebrity/tamera-mowry-housley-interracial-marriage-family-criticism/

Kareem Nittle, N. (2019, August 15). The roots of colorism, or skin tone discrimination. *ThoughtCo*. https://www.thoughtco.com/what-is-colorism-2834952

Kini, A. N. (2017, July 6). I'm tired of watching brown men fall in love with white women onscreen. *Jezebel*. https://themuse.jezebel.com/i-m-tired-of-watching-brown-men-fall-in-love-with-white-1796522590

Little White Lie. (2015). *[film] Directed by L. Schwartz*. OTB Production.

Loving v. Virginia, 388 U.S. 1 (1967). https://supreme.justia.com/cases/federal/us/388/1/#tab-opinion-1946731

Lukasik, G. (2017, October 29). My mother passed as white?even to me. *The Daily Beast*. https://www.thedailybeast.com/my-mother-passed-as-whiteeven-to-me?ref=scroll

MidWest Mixed. (2019). *About*. https://www.midwestmixed.com/about

Mixed Marrow2019*About us*http://mixedmarrow.org/aboutus/sample-page

Mixed Remixed Festival. (2019). *About*. http://www.mixedremixed.org/about-mixed-remixed/

Mixed Roots Stories. (2019). *About*. https://mixedrootsstories.com/about/

Moskovitz, D. (2017, May 30). Here are the full police reports from tiger Woods's DUI arrest. *Deadspin*. https://deadspin.com/here-are-the-full-police-reports-from-tiger-woodss-dui-1795665976

Oprah Winfrey Network. (2017). *Tamera Mowry on critics of her interracial marriage | where are they now*. https://www.youtube.com/watch?v=ngwvHYqYGS0

Oprah Winfrey Show. (1997/2018). *Tiger Woods interview with Oprah Winfrey after 1997 masters victory (Full)*. https://www.youtube.com/watch?time_continue=12&v=z36FCcr9j2w&feature=emb_logo

Perez v. Sharp, 32 Cal. 2d 711 (1948). https://scocal.stanford.edu/opinion/perez-v-sharp-26107

Phillips, A. (2017). The multiracial option: A step in the white direction. *California Law Review*, *105*, 1853–1878. https://doi.org/10.15779/Z38H98ZD1S

Plecker, W. A. (1924). The new Virginia law to preserve racial integrity. *Virginia Health Bulletin*, *XVI*(2). https://lva.omeka.net/items/show/62

Renn, K. (2008). Research on biracial and multiracial identity development: Overview and synthesis. *New Directions for Student Services*, *123*, 13–21.

Resolution Flaying Filipinos Drawn by Judge D. W. Rohrback. (1930, January 10). *Evening Pajaronian*, 1.

Rondilla, JL., Guevarra, RP., Jr., & Spickard, P. (Eds.). (2017). *Red & yellow black & brown: Decentering whiteness in mixed race studies*. Rutgers University Press.

Root, M. (2003). Bill of rights for racially mixed people. In M. P. P. Root & M. Kelley (Eds.), *Multiracial child resource book: Living complex identities* (p. 32). MAVIN Foundation.

Schilling, V. (2017, September 8). The true story of Pocahontas: Historical myths versus sad reality. *Indian Country Today*. https://newsmaven.io/indiancountrytoday/archive/the-true-story-of-pocahontas-historical-myths-versus-sad-reality-WRzmVMu47E6Guz0LudQ3QQ/

Showalter, M. P. (1989). The Watsonville Anti-Filipino riot of 1930: A reconsideration of Fermin Tobera's murder. *Southern California Quarterly*, *71*(4), 341–348.

Smith, J. (2019, August 24). Doubling down on racist comments, council candidate says she opposes interracial marriage. *USA Today*. https://www.usatoday.com/story/news/nation/2019/08/24/marysville-council-candidate-jean-cramer-makes-racist-comments-again/2109750001/

Tran, A. G., Miyake, E. R., Martinez-Morales, V., & Csizmadia, A. (2016). "What are you?" Multiracial individuals' responses to racial identification inquiries. *Cultural Diversity and Ethnic Minority Psychology*, *22*(1), 26–37. https://doi.org/10.1037/cdp0000031

White Romeo Injected Negro Blood to Beat Marriage Law. (1935, March 14). *Northwest Enterprise*, p. 1.

Wolfe, B. (2015). Racial integrity laws (1924–1930). *Encyclopedia Virginia*. https://www.encyclopediavirginia.org/Racial_Integrity_Laws_of_the_1920s#start_entry

CHAPTER 13

Bell, D. A. (1980). Brown v. board of education and the interest-convergence Dilemma. *Harvard Law Review*, *93*(3), 518–533.

Bertrand, M., & Mullainathan, S. (2004). Are Emily and Greg more employable than Lakisha and Jamal? A field experiment on labor market discrimination. *American Economic Review*, *94*(4), 991–1013.

Bonilla-Silva, E. (2012). The invisible weight of whiteness: The racial grammar of everyday life in contemporary America. *Ethnic and Racial Studies*, *35*(2), 173–194.

Bonilla-Silva, E. (2018). *Racism without racists: Color-blind racism and the persistence of racial inequality in America* (5th ed.). Rowman & Littlefield.

Calderon, J. L., & Wise, T. (2012). Code of ethics for antiracist white allies. In J. Love Calderon (Ed.), *Occupying privilege: Conversations on love, race, and liberation*. Love-N-Liberation Press.

Derber, C., & Magrass, Y. R. (2019). *Moving beyond fear: Upending the security tales in capitalism, fascism, and democracy*. Routledge.

DiAngelo, R. (2018). *White fragility: Why it's so hard for white people to talk about racism*. Beacon Press.

Durkheim, E. (1933/1997). *The division of labor in society*. The Free Press.

Haney-Lopez, I. (1996). *White by law: The legal construction of race*. University Press.

Katznelson, I. (2005). *When affirmative action was white: An untold history of racial inequality in twentieth-century America*. W.W. Norton.

Kendi, I. X. (2019). *How to be an antiracist*. Penguin Random House.

Luke, D. J. (2014). Model minority stereotype. In L. H. . Cousins (Ed.), *Sage encyclopedia of human services and diversity* (pp. 878–879). Sage.

Luke, D. J. (2018). Increasing inclusion: The pursuit of racial diversity in three historically white universities in Kentucky, Michigan, and Ontario from 2000 to 2012. *Theses and Dissertations?Sociology, 36*. https://uknowledge.uky.edu/sociology_etds/36

Norton, M. I., & Sommers, S. R. (2011). Whites see racism as a zero-sum game that they are now losing. *Perspectives on Psychological Science, 6*(3), 215–218.

Page, S. (2017). *The diversity bonus: How great teams pay off in the knowledge economy*. Princeton University Press.

Pager, D. (2007). *Marked: Race, crime, and finding work in an Era of mass incarceration*. University of Chicago Press.

Quillian, L., Heath, A., Pager, D., Midtbøen, A. H., Fleischmann, F., & Hexel, O. (2019). Do some countries discriminate more than others? Evidence from 97 field experiments of racial discrimination in hiring. *Sociological Science, 6*, 467–496.

Seamster, L., & Charron-Chénier, R. (2017). Predatory inclusion and education debt: Rethinking the racial wealth gap. *Social Currents, 4*(3), 199–207.

Van Ausdale, D., & Feagin, J. R. (2001). *The first R: How children learn race and racism*. Rowman & Littlefield.

Vittrup, B. (2018). Color blind or color conscious? White American mothers' approaches to racial socialization. *Journal of Family Issues, 39*(3), 668–692.

X, M., & Haley, A. (1965). *The autobiography of Malcolm X*. Grove Press.

Yaluma, C., & Tyner, A. (2018). *Is there a gifted gap? Gifted education in high-poverty schools*. Thomas B. Fordham Institute. https://edexcellence.net/publications/is-there-a-gifted-gap

CHAPTER 14

ACLU. (2017). *ACLU campaign for smart justice national survey*. https://www.aclu.org/sites/default/files/field_document/aclu_campaign_for_smart_justice_poll_results.pdf

Anderson, C. (2018). *One person, no vote: How voter suppression is destroying our democracy*. Bloomsbury.

Annie E. Casey Foundation. (2016). *Investing in tomorrow: Helping families build savings and assets*. Federal Policy Brief. http://www.aecf.org/m/resourcedoc/aecf-investingintomorrow-2016.pdf

Arriaga, F. (2016). Teaching and learning guide for "understanding crimmigration: implications for racial and ethnic minorities within the United States.". *Sociology Compass, 10*(11), 1072–1076.

Berlatsky, N. (2014, November 17). At the United Nations, Chicago activists protest police brutality. *The Atlantic*. https://www.theatlantic.com/national/archive/2014/11/we-charge-genocide-movement-chicago-un/382843/.

Carless, W., & Michael, C. (2019, June 14). To protect and slur: Inside hate groups on Facebook, police officers trade racist memes, conspiracy theories and islamophobia. *Reveal*. http://www.revealnews.org/article/inside-hate-groups-on-facebook-police-officers-trade-racist-memes-conspiracy-theories-and-islamophobia/

Collins, P. H. (1990). *Black feminist thought: Knowledge, consciousness, and the politics of empowerment*. Routledge.

Combahee River Collective. (1986). *The Combahee river collective statement: black feminist organizing in the seventies and eighties*. Kitchen Table: Women of Color Press.

Cooper, H. L. F. (2015). War on drugs policing and police brutality. *Substance Use & Misuse, 50*(8–9), 1188–1194.

Darity, W., Jr., Darrick, H., Mark, P., Alan, A., Anne, P., Antonio, M., & Caterina, C. (2018, April). *What we get wrong about closing the racial wealth gap. Samuel DuBois cook center on social equity*. https://socialequity.duke.edu/sites/socialequity.duke.edu/files/site-images/FINAL%20COMPLETE%20REPORT_.pdf

DiAngelo, R. (2018). *White fragility: Why it's so hard for white people to talk about racis*. Beacon Press.

Dreisbach, T., & Meg, A. (2021, January 21). *Nearly 1 in 5 defendants in capitol riot cases served in the military. NPR*. https://www.npr.org/2021/01/21/958915267/nearly-one-in-five-defendants-in-capitol-riot-cases-served-in-the-military.

Drucker, E. (2016, September 20). What is decarceration? *Medium*. https://medium.com/@Decarceration/what-is-decarceration-e761feb6275f

Drucker, E. (2017). A public health approach to decarceration: Strategies to reduce the prison and jail population and support reentry. In M. Epperson & C. Pettus Davis (Eds.), *Smart decarceration: Achieving criminal justice transformation in the 21st Century* (pp. 179–192). Oxford University Press.

Drug Policy Alliance. (2015). *Racial and ethnic impact statements*. http://www.drugpolicy.org/sites/default/files/DPA_FactSheet_Racial_and_Ethnic_Impact_Statements_July2015.pdf.

Du Bois, W. E. B. (1945/2004). Human rights for all minorities. In P. Zuckerman (Ed.), *The social theory of W. E. B. Du Bois* (pp. 135–140). Pine Forge.

Essed, P. (1991). *Understanding everyday racism: An interdisciplinary theory*. Sage Publications.

Evans, L., & Moore, L. M. (2015). Impossible burdens: White institutions, emotional labor, and micro-resistance. *Social Problems, 62*(3), 439–454. https://doi.org/10.1093/socpro/spv009

FairVote. (2019). *Redistricting*. https://www.fairvote.org/redistricting

Feagin, J. R. (2006, January 21). Systemic racism: A theory of oppression. *Routledge*.

Foley, R. J. (2015). Racial-impact law has modest effect in Iowa. *Des Moines Register*. https://www.desmoin, esregister.com/story/news/politics/2015/01/21/racial-impact-law-effect-iowa-legislature/22138465/

Freeman-Woolpert, S. (2020, June 16). By targeting the pillars that uphold police violence, black lives matter is shifting power to the people. *Waging Nonviolence*. https://wagingnonviolence.org/2020/06/pillars-of-support-police-violence-black-lives-matter/.

Ghandnoosh, N. (2019). *Policy brief: Can We wait 75 years to cut the prison population in half?* The Sentencing Project.

Giddens, A. (1991). *Modernity and self-identity: Self and Society in the late modern age*. Stanford University Press.

Glaude, E. S., Jr. (2017). *Democracy in black*. Crown.

Gonzalez Van Cleve, N. (2016). *Crook County: Racism and injustice in America's largest criminal court*. Stanford Law Books.

Graham, D. A. (2019, July 3). Garry McFadden: The new sheriff in town. *The Atlantic*. https://www.theatlantic.com/ideas/archive/2019/07/new-sheriff-town/593116/.

Green, D. (2016). *How change happens*. Oxford University Press.

Griffith, J. (2021, January 21). Off-duty police were part of capitol mob. Some police unions feel they can't back them. *NBC News*. https://www.nbcnews.com/news/us-news/duty-police-were-part-capitol-mob-some-police-unions-feel-n1255061.

Gwynne, K. (2015, May 6). *Chicago to pay $5.5 million in reparations for police torture victims. Rolling Stone*. http://www.rollingstone.com/politics/news/chicago-to-pay-5-5-million-in-reparations-for-police-torture-victims-20150506.

Hamilton, D., & William, D., Jr. (2010). Can "Baby Bonds" eliminate the racial wealth gap in putative post-racial America? *The Review of Black Political Economy*, *37*, 207–216.

Hinkel, D. (2020, February 12). Chicago cop should be fired after video shows he lied about fatal shooting of 19-year-old, investigators say. *Chicago Tribune*. https://www.chicagotribune.com/investigations/ct-met-roshad-mcintosh-shooting-police-officer-lying-20200212-u2htz5p4dzfgxees6wxkacnxyq-story.html

Hoberock, B. (2019, November 2). Pardon and parole board approves record number of commutations. *Tulsa World*. https://tulsaworld.com/news/pardon-and-parole-board-approves-record-number-of-commutations/article_8e019a12-eea0-559f-908a-cce27236234f.html

Horwitz, S., Ellen, N., & Wesley, L. (2015, December 6). Justice department will investigate practices of Chicago police. *Washington Post*. https://www.washingtonpost.com/news/post-nation/wp/2015/12/06/justice-department-will-launch-investigation-into-practices-of-chicago-police/

Huelsman, M., Tamara, D., Tatjana, M., Lars, D., Thomas, S., & Laura, S. (2015). *Less debt, more equity: lowering student debt while closing the black-white wealth gap*. Demos.

Kamenetz, A. (2020, June 23). Why there's a push to get police out of schools. *NPR*. https://www.npr.org/2020/06/23/881608999/why-theres-a-push-to-get-police-out-of-schools.

Kennedy, L., Lew, D., & Brenda, W. (2015). Automatic voter registration: finding America's missing voters. *Demos*.

MacLean, K., Wolfe, S. E., Jeff, R., Alpert, G. P., & Smith, M. R. (2019). Police officers as warriors or guardians: Empirical reality or intriguing rhetoric? *Justice Quarterly*. https://doi.org/10.1080/07418825.2018.1533031

Meghji, A. (2019). Activating controlling images in the racialized interaction order: Black middle-class interactions and the creativity of racist action. *Symbolic Interaction*, *42*, 229–249. https://doi.org/10.1002/symb.398

Oliver, M. L., & Shapiro, T. M. (2019). Disrupting the racial wealth gap. *Contexts*, *18*(1), 16–21.

Picca, L. H., & Feagin, J. R. (2007). *Two-faced racism: Whites in the backstage and frontstage*. Routledge Press.

Quillian, L., Devah, P., Ole, H., & Midtbøen, A. H. (2017). Meta-analysis of field experiments shows no change in racial discrimination in hiring over time. *PNAS*, *114*(41), 10870–10875.

Ramos, V. (2019, May 15). Stand against racism?take action. *Everyday Democracy*. https://www.everyday-democracy.org/news/stand-against-racism-take-action.

Rosino, M. L. (2018). "A problem of humanity": The human rights framework and the struggle for racial justice. *Sociology of Race and Ethnicity*, *4*(3), 338–352.

Rosino, M. L., & Hughey, M. W. (2018). The war on drugs, racial meanings, and structural racism: A holistic and reproductive approach. *American Journal of Economics and Sociology*, *77*(3–4), 849–892.

San Francisco Office of Cannabis. (2019). *Equity program*. https://officeofcannabis.sfgov.org/equity.

Schrantz, D., DeBor, S. T., & Marc, M. (2018). *Decarceration strategies: How 5 states achieved substantial prison population reductions*. The Sentencing Project.

Seamster, L. (2019). Black debt, white debt. *Contexts*, *18*(1), 30–35.

Shim, J. H. (2020, June 12). *Minneapolis organizers are already building the tools for safety without police. Truthout*. https://truthout.org/articles/minneapolis-organizers-are-already-building-the-tools-for-safety-without-police/

State of Connecticut. (2018). Senate bill no. 256, public act no. 18-78 an act concerning racial and ethnic impact statements. .

Sunstein, C. R. (2019). *How change happens*. MIT Press.

Taylor, K. Y. (2017). *How we get free: Black feminism and the combahee river collective*. Haymarket Books.

Twine, F. W. (2010). *A white side of black Britain: Interracial intimacy and racial literacy*. Duke University Press.

U.S. Department of Justice. (2017). *Investigation of the Chicago police department*. https://www.justice.gov/opa/file/925846/download

We Charge Genocide. (2014, September). *Police violence against Chicago's youth of color: A report prepared for the United Nations committee against torture on the occasion of its review of the United States of America's third periodic report to the committee against torture*. Author.

Weller, C. E., Connor, M., & Danyell, S. (2019, August 7). *Simulating how progressive proposals affect the racial wealth gap. Center for American Progress*. https://www.americanprogress.org/issues/race/reports/2019/08/07/473117/simulating-progressive-proposals-affect-racial-wealth-gap/.

Young, I. M. (1999). Justice, inclusion and deliberative democracy. In S. Macedo (Ed.), *Deliberative politics: Essays on democracy and disagreement* (pp. 151–158). Oxford University Press.

INDEX